Global Politics and the Responsibility to Protect

This book provides an in-depth introduction to, and analysis of, the issues relating to the implementation of the Responsibility to Protect principle in international relations.

The Responsibility to Protect (RtoP) has come a long way in a short space of time. It was endorsed by the General Assembly of the UN in 2005, and unanimously reaffirmed by the Security Council in 2006 (Resolution 1674) and 2009 (Resolution 1894). UN Secretary-General Ban Ki-moon has identified the challenge of implementing RtoP as one of the cornerstones of his Secretary-Generalship. The principle has also become part of the working language of international engagement with humanitarian crises and has been debated in relation to almost every recent international crisis – including Sudan, Sri Lanka, Myanmar, Georgia, the Democratic Republic of Congo, Darfur and Somalia.

Concentrating mainly on implementation challenges including the prevention of genocide and mass atrocities, strengthening the UN's capacity to respond, and the role of regional organizations, this book introduces readers to contemporary debates on RtoP and provides the first book-length analysis of the implementation agenda.

The book will be of great interest to students of the responsibility to protect, humanitarian intervention, human rights, foreign policy, security studies and IR and politics in general.

Alex J. Bellamy is Professor of International Security at the Griffith Asia Institute/Centre for Governance and Public Policy, Griffith University, Australia. From 2007 to 2010 he was Executive Director of the Asia-Pacific Centre for the Responsibility to Protect.

Global Politics and the Responsibility to Protect

Series Editors: Alex J. Bellamy, *Griffith University*, Sara E. Davies
Griffith University and Monica Serrano, *The City University New York*

The aim of this book series is to gather the best new thinking about the Responsibility to Protect into a core set of volumes that provides a definitive account of the principle, its implementation, and role in crises, that reflects a plurality of views and regional perspectives.

Global Politics and the Responsibility to Protect
From words to deeds
Alex J. Bellamy

The Responsibility to Protect
Norms, laws and the use of force in international politics
Ramesh Thakur

Global Politics and the Responsibility to Protect

From words to deeds

Alex J. Bellamy

Routledge
Taylor & Francis Group

LONDON AND NEW YORK

First published 2011
by Routledge
2 Park Square, Milton Park, Abingdon, Oxon OX14 4RN

Simultaneously published in the USA and Canada
by Routledge
711 Third Avenue, New York, NY 10017

Routledge is an imprint of the Taylor & Francis Group, an informa business

© 2011 Alex J. Bellamy

The right of Alex J. Bellamy to be identified as author of this work
has been asserted by him in accordance with sections 77 and 78 of the
Copyright, Designs and Patents Act 1988.

Typeset in Bembo by
Florence Production Ltd, Stoodleigh, Devon

British Library Cataloguing in Publication Data
A catalogue record for this book is available from the British Library

Library of Congress Cataloging-in-Publication Data
Bellamy, Alex J., 1975–
    Global politics and the responsibilty to protect: from words to deeds/
    Alex J. Bellamy.
        p. cm.
    1. United Nations.   2. Humanitarian intervention.   3. Peacekeeping
    forces.   4. Peace-building.   5. Democratization.   6. Security,
    International.   I. Title.
    JZ4971.B45 2010
    341.5′84–dc22   2010022535

ISBN13: 978–0–415–56735–0 (hbk)
ISBN13: 978–0–415–56736–7 (pbk)
ISBN13: 978–0–203–83716–0 (ebk)

For Isaac

Contents

Illustrations

Figures

Tables

Acknowledgements

This book is the culmination of many years work on the Responsibility to Protect, some of it with extremely able collaborators. My wife, colleague, and best friend Sara Davies helped write Chapter 7 on regional arrangements and has played a pivotal part in everything I've done on this topic. In addition to co-writing a chapter in this book, she read the entire manuscript and offered sage advice. She also played the leading role in establishing the journal *Global Responsibility to Protect* and the book series of which this volume is a part. She is a talented scholar, wonderful wife and the best mum that our little boy Isaac could hope for. She has my unlimited and unending love and gratitude.

For more than a decade now, I've also benefited from the wisdom of my dear friend and colleague, Paul Williams, whose scholarship I admire and friendship I treasure. This book draws on a lot of the research and ideas that we have developed together in the past few years, especially relating to peace operations, the protection of civilians, and the question of moral hazard. Paul's influence can be seen on every page.

While all errors of fact and judgment are of course my own, the ideas in this book have benefited immensely from road-testing and the wise insights and advice of a number of people. Thanks here to Mely Caballero-Anthony, Sapna Chhatpar, Gareth Evans, Paul Evans, Brian Job, Herman Kraft, Edward Luck, Monica Serrano, Rizal Sukma, Ramesh Thakur, Thomas Weiss, Nicholas Wheeler, and Lawrence Woocher.

Finally, I owe a debt of gratitude to my former colleagues at the Asia-Pacific Centre for the Responsibility to Protect and to the students that I have worked with on all things 'RtoP', especially Noel Morada, Sarah Teitt, Stephen Mcloughlin, Luke Glanville, Jess Gifkins, Catherine Drummond, Deborah Mayersen and Annie Pohlman and the indefatigable and always helpful Marie Hobman.

This book is dedicated to my son, Isaac, in the hope that small steps can be taken to make a better world for him to grow up into.

Introduction

Since the nineteenth century at least, the commission of genocide and mass atrocities has provoked calls for international action to save the victims.[1] From the 1820s to the 1870s, for example, groups of activists collectively known as 'atrocitarians' agitated for armed intervention to protect Christians in Greece, Syria and Bulgaria. At the century's end, the US invaded Cuba partly in response to calls from former President Theodore Roosevelt that it should act to put an end to Spanish atrocities there.[2] In the twentieth century, the Armenian genocide, Holocaust, and more recent genocides in Bosnia and Rwanda all generated public agitation aimed at pushing governments to act to stop the slaughter. The present century is no different. Many activists in various parts of the world maintain that those with the power to have done so should have intervened in Darfur to protect civilians from their tormentors. This sort of activism is not surprising, because there is an overlapping and global moral consensus which holds that it is wrong to deliberately kill civilians in war or in peacetime pogroms and genocides.[3] Although this consensus became manifest in the laws of war only after the Second World War, non-combatant immunity is a deeply held moral principle with a long history, shared by most of the world's major ethical traditions.[4] Since then, the international community has made non-combatant immunity a customary principle of international law and its violation a universal crime.

Yet the international community's actual record of preventing and halting the mass killing of civilians is staggeringly poor. In the twentieth century Angola, Algeria, Burundi, Cambodia, China, El Salvador, Ethiopia, Guatemala, Indonesia, Iran, Iraq, Sudan, Uganda and Rwanda − among others − experienced mass atrocities and the victims saw little, if anything, in the way of international action to stop the killing. Even in the post-Cold War era, with its putative commitment to human rights and the emergence of doctrines of humanitarian intervention, sovereignty as responsibility, and the protection of civilians, state-perpetrators of mass murder have a less than 50–50 chance of being stopped in their tracks, and are as likely to succeed outright as fail when they turn to mass murder. In the cases where they are stopped in their tracks, more often than not it is by local opponents or external actors intervening for self-interested purposes − be it the RPF ending the Rwandan genocide (1994), Angola ending the killing of civilians by both parties in the short Congo-Brazzaville civil war (1999), and LURD forces defeating Charles Taylor's murderous regime in Liberia (2002–3). Non-state perpetrators are more likely to be stopped but most often by the government they are fighting, which are themselves only occasionally assisted by external actors (such as by the UK in the case of Sierra Leone in 2000). Therefore, despite all the talk about, and angst over, decisive international activism to prevent and halt mass atrocities – which some fear amounts to a new form of imperialism that threatens to destroy world order and others worry will encourage all sorts of criminally minded and politically deluded individuals to take up arms against their government in the hope of attracting foreign intervention[5] – in reality, such activism remains the exception, honoured most often in the breach.

Little wonder, then, that studies of why groups commit mass atrocities have found a stunningly simple, yet frequently recurring, explanation: political leaders select mass atrocities as a rational strategy for pursuing their objectives, such as countering a serious existential threat, when there are either no viable alternatives or when the costs of alternative strategies are prohibitively high.[6] In other words, actors commit mass atrocities because it helps them get what they want. When their back is against the wall, governments especially know that they are as likely to succeed as fail if they resort to mass atrocities – an attractive proposition if they think there are few viable alternatives.

Why, when there is so much agreement that mass killing is wrong, is our track record in actually stopping it so bad? Three reasons spring to mind. First, contemporary international community privileges sovereigns' rights over peoples' rights, making it difficult to build international consensus about preventive and responsive measures that might trample on a state's right to exclusive jurisdiction within its domain when it abuses its own population. Second, despite public proclamations to the contrary, national governments are reluctant to prioritize the prevention and halting of mass killing and commit resources to this goal. Third, even if new norms were crafted and political priorities amended, there would remain difficult prudential considerations concerning how we know when mass killing is likely to erupt, what sorts of policies might remedy that threat, and what the most effective and efficient responses might be. Let us consider each of these points in a little more detail.

Rules of international community

Questions about international activism to prevent and halt mass atrocities tend to be framed around an enduring struggle between sovereignty and human rights. In this context, sovereignty refers to the rights that states enjoy to territorial integrity, political independence and non-intervention. Where sovereign states are either unwilling or unable to protect the fundamental freedoms of their population, sovereignty and human rights come into conflict. This tension is evident in the UN Charter. While calling for cooperation to reaffirm faith in fundamental human rights (Article 1 (3)), the Charter (Article 2(4)) outlaws war as an instrument of policy with only two exceptions (each state's inherent right to self-defence (Article 51) and collective measures authorized by the UN Security Council (Chapter VII)) and affirms the principle of non-interference (Article 2(7)) by prohibiting the UN from interfering 'in matters essentially within the domestic jurisdiction of states'. These legal rights constitute a powerful barrier to international activism, especially when states murder their own population and use non-interference to shield themselves. Because many states remain committed to the principle of non-interference, seeing it as an essential legal right that protects them from the arbitrary power of strong states and allows them to determine their own political fate, it has proven very difficult to build sufficient international consensus in the UN Security Council to persuade that body to authorize coercive measures against states that perpetrate genocide or mass atrocities. Be it Yugoslavia over Bosnia or Kosovo, Sudan in relation to Darfur, Rwanda, Bangladesh or Cambodia, the Security Council has repeatedly privileged the non-interference rights of states over the rights of individuals not to be arbitrarily killed. In 1979, the Council even admonished Vietnam for invading Cambodia, even though Vietnamese intervention put an end to a genocide that killed 1.5 million people in three and a half years and would have killed many more if left unabated. China described Vietnam's act as a 'great mockery of and insult to the United Nations and its member states' and sponsored a resolution condemning Vietnam's 'aggression'. The US agreed. It argued that the world could not allow Vietnam's violation of Cambodian sovereignty to 'pass in silence' as this 'will only encourage Governments in other parts of the world to conclude that there are no norms, no standards, no restraints'.[7] France argued that 'the notion that because a regime is detestable foreign intervention is justified and forcible overthrow is legitimate is extremely dangerous. That could ultimately jeopardize the very maintenance of law and order'. Norway, among others, agreed admitting that it had 'strong objections to the serious violation of human rights committed by the Pol Pot government. However the domestic policies of that government cannot – we repeat cannot – justify the action of Viet Nam'.[8] This line of argument can still be heard today. In 2004, Pakistan argued in the Security Council that the UN should not act to put an end to mass killing in Darfur because 'the Sudan has all the rights and privileges incumbent under the United Nations Charter, including to sovereignty, political independence, unity and territorial integrity'.[9] Activists often put these sorts of arguments down to self-interested political posturing by recalcitrant states who invariably have their own human rights problems. But established democracies also sometimes play the sovereignty card to trump human rights. For instance, in March 2005 the US argued against referring allegations of genocide, war crimes and crimes against humanity in Darfur to the ICC on the grounds that the Court 'strikes at the essence of the nature of sovereignty'.[10]

Given the difficulty of building consensus in the Security Council due to the international community's tendency to privilege sovereigns' rights over peoples' rights, the international legal architecture is often identified as a major barrier to international activism to prevent and halt mass atrocities. This raises important questions about the relative value of international order and the prevention of mass atrocities. But there are grounds for doubting the extent to which international law actually is a barrier to intervention. Simon Chesterman has demonstrated that sovereignty has not in fact inhibited unilateral or collective action to uphold human rights in other countries.[11] Ultimately, he argues, it was not concerns about sovereignty that prevented timely intervention in Bosnia, Rwanda or Darfur, but the basic political fact that no state wanted to pay the price associated with saving strangers. Nevertheless, the law certainly places a premium on international consensus – which is often hard to find – and forces states driven to act without that consensus to prevent or halt mass atrocities to accept a potentially very high price.

Political will

Following on from the insight that effective international action to prevent and halt mass atrocities does not happen primarily because states do not want it to happen, the second major inhibitor of armed intervention is political will. Most states consider themselves to be responsible first and foremost for the well being of their own citizens and are reluctant to spend money and potentially risk the lives of their soldiers and policemen to save strangers from mass atrocities. Some of the worst effects of this lack of will were revealed in the 1999 Report of the Independent Inquiry into the UN's failure to prevent or halt the Rwanda genocide. The report opened with a damning but general criticism, insisting that the Rwandan genocide resulted from the failure of the whole UN system. It is worth citing the report at length on this issue:

> The failure by the United Nations to prevent, and subsequently, to stop the genocide in Rwanda was a failure by the United Nations as a whole. The fundamental failure was the lack of resources and political commitment devoted to developments in Rwanda and to the United Nations presence there. There was a persistent lack of political will by Member States to act, or to act with enough assertiveness. This lack of political will affected the response by the Secretariat and decision-making by the Security Council, but was also evident in the recurrent difficulties to get the necessary troops for the United Nations Assistance Mission for Rwanda (UNAMIR). Finally, although UNAMIR suffered from a chronic lack of resources and political priority, it must also be said that serious mistakes were made with those resources which were at the disposal of the United Nations.[12]

The 'overriding failure', the inquiry argued, was the lack of resources and lack of will to do what would have been necessary to prevent the genocide and protect its victims. The lack of resources and will resulted in UNAMIR not being 'planned, dimensioned, deployed or instructed' in a way that would have 'provided for a proactive and assertive role' in the face of the deteriorating situation in Rwanda. The mission was smaller than recommended by the UN secretariat, slow to deploy owing to the reluctance of states to contribute troops, and debilitated by administrative difficulties. When troops did arrive many were inadequately trained and equipped. All this meant that when the genocide erupted, UNAMIR was not functioning properly. 'A force numbering 2,500' (UNAMIR's strength at the time of the genocide), the inquiry concluded, 'should have been able to stop or at least limit massacres of the kind which began in Rwanda' at the start of the genocide. The Inquiry concluded that the UN's failure in Rwanda was largely created by a critical disjuncture – endemic in many UN operations at the time – between the tasks given to peacekeepers and their conceptual and material tools. For largely political reasons UNAMIR was conceived as a small and cheap operation despite evidence at the time that this would be inadequate. In a tragic coincidence of history, UNAMIR's mandate came onto the UN Security Council's agenda just one week after the killing of American peacekeepers in Somalia in the infamous 'Black Hawk down' incident. The US was understandably in no mood to consider supporting the dispatch of more peacekeepers to Africa and insisted that any force sent to Rwanda be limited in size and dependent on the consent of the conflicting parties.

Prudential considerations

Sometimes, even when states are genuinely concerned about the commission of mass atrocities in foreign countries, prudential considerations or competing priorities may augur against armed intervention. It might be thought, for instance, that robust forms of engagement such as armed intervention will do more harm than good, by provoking a wider conflict or jeopardizing the consent of local actors thought necessary to secure the delivery of vital assistance or a peace agreement. This was part of the rationale behind European objections to the deployment of a UN mission to Somalia between 2006 and 2008 (see Chapter 8). Other times, states might have competing priorities and might calculate that they simply lack the capacity to intervene effectively. The recent debate over whether or not to forcibly intervene in Darfur helps highlight each of these problems. Opponents of intervention argued that it would do more harm than good, might jeopardize other priorities (especially the comprehensive peace agreement between the government of Sudan and the Sudanese People's Liberation Army, which brought a longer-running and more deadly civil war to an end), and that with on-going commitments in Iraq, Afghanistan and the Balkans, the West lacked the political capital and military capacity to assist. Thus, according to Alex de Waal, 'however attractive it might be from a distance, actually providing physical protection for Darfurians with international troops is not feasible'.[13] Likewise, Francis Deng, a well-respected diplomat and the UN Secretary-General's Special Adviser on the Prevention of Genocide agreed that coercive measures would 'complicate and aggravate' the crisis by increasing the level of violence. While these claims are disputable – and we can also dispute the privileging of order over the protection of civilians from mass killing – analysis like this helps illuminate the difficult choices that policy-makers confront when weighing up how to respond when mass atrocities are imminent or underway. When coupled with an absence of national interests, or interests that dictate inaction, it is not hard to see why uncertain prospects tend to produce skepticism about making large investments in preventing or halting atrocities.

None of this is meant to justify inaction in the face of genocide but it goes some way towards explaining why it is, when there is such a clear moral imperative for decisive international engagement to prevent and halt mass atrocities, that governments usually choose to stand aside. It also helps illuminate the difficult choices that policy makers confront and the hurdles that analysts and activists who want to make international engagement more likely and more effective need to overcome.

In 2005, two centuries of political agitation against mass atrocities produced a landmark commitment from heads of state and government when they unanimously declared their responsibility to protect populations from genocide, war crimes, ethnic cleansing and crimes against humanity, to assist one another in achieving this goals and to take 'timely and decisive' action when prevention fails.[14] The Responsibility to Protect (RtoP) principle represents a normative breakthrough that lays down foundations for a new international politics of mass atrocities which prioritizes their prevention and – failing that – the protection of vulnerable populations. Whether and how this potential will be realized is the subject of this book.

Translating the promise of RtoP into decisive action to prevent atrocities and respond effectively to them will be no easy task. It involves preserving, marshaling and managing global consensus whilst maintaining forward momentum. It requires careful thinking about the causes of mass killing and the steps needed to prevent it and provide early warning. It demands the building of international capacities to respond effectively when mass atrocities break out. It requires political courage and consensus in the face of grave and complex emergencies. In short, implementing the RtoP requires nothing less than the reconfiguring of state identities and national interests so that the prevention of atrocities becomes habitual, and decisive responses the norm rather than the exception.

Keeping this long-term vision in mind, this book is about the first tentative steps towards implementing the RtoP. It takes the world – and RtoP – as it is as its starting point and examines the small but important first steps that might be taken towards a world free of mass atrocities. As such, it does not examine some of the underlying theoretical and philosophical debates. Nor do I recount the story of RtoP's evolution and the political battles that were fought to forge the global consensus that emerged in 2005. Nor do I ask whether alternative formulations might have been better.[15] I do examine the different ways governments have interpreted their commitment to RtoP; debates about how to use the principle when crises erupt; and their concerns about how best to implement the principle and the chief priorities. I try to identify where RtoP has made a real impact and avenues where positive impacts might be made in the near future. And I try to articulate an account of RtoP that accommodates non-Western priorities. Some of the arguments are far-reaching, but the emphasis in this book is on understanding the progress made to date and the small first steps that might be taken in the next few years. In all of this, I am guided by insights from Edward Luck, the UN Secretary-General's Special Adviser on RtoP. When he joined us in Bangkok in 2008, to mark the launch of the Asia-Pacific Centre for the Responsibility to Protect of which I was director until 2010, Luck emphasized that the effort to implement RtoP was a marathon, not a sprint. To complete the marathon, we need to successfully navigate the first few kilometers and bring the international community along too. This book is about those first kilometers.

The first part of the book tries to understand how RtoP has evolved from abstract principle into political practice, focusing especially on the period since its formal adoption in 2005. The second part takes its lead from the 2009 General Assembly debate on implementing the RtoP and focuses on four of the key implementation issues, namely the place of economic development and democracy in the prevention of mass atrocities, early warning, the role of regional arrangements, and the question of military intervention and the role of the UN Security Council. In the conclusion, I will summarize my argument and return to the question of whether RtoP carries the potential to remedy the problems of principle, politics and prudence identified above.

1 From idea to norm

This chapter provides a brief account of the evolution of RtoP from an idea coined by the 2001 report of the International Commission for Intervention and State Sovereignty (ICISS) to an emerging norm endorsed by almost all the world's governments. In so doing, it makes two principal arguments. First, that from relatively early on it was possible to discern two strands of thinking about the nature, scope and purpose of RtoP. These strands of thought have continued to characterize debates about the norm and its proper application. The first strand is primarily concerned with persuading states to fulfil their protection responsibilities and providing mutual assistance on a consensual basis. This line of thinking tends to downplay the role of coercive interference (while admitting that such interference may be necessary *in extremis*) in favour of upstream capacity-building and other non-coercive measures aimed at encouraging and enabling states and non-state actors to pull back from the brink when episodes of political instability threaten to deteriorate into mass violence. Proponents of this view typically see RtoP as primarily concerned with the *prevention* of genocide and mass atrocities.[1] The second strand sees RtoP primarily as a response to the dilemmas of humanitarian intervention. Proponents of this view insist that RtoP's most significant added value is in the generation of the international political will necessary to avoid repeats of Rwanda and other large-scale conscience shocking episodes of inhumanity. While most of the world's governments – particularly those in the global south – subscribe to the first view, most academic commentators on RtoP and the principle's critics subscribe to the second, creating dissonance between what states have actually committed to in relation to RtoP and what commentators and critics either believe they have committed to or would like them to have committed to. These two strands of thinking overlap and complement each other (sovereignty as responsibility and ideas about humanitarian intervention directly informed RtoP) but also depart on crucial issues relating to the centrality of armed intervention, the scope of prevention, and the function of RtoP. Some of these complementarities and contradictions will become more apparent in subsequent chapters.

My second argument is that global consensus on the RtoP was not a matter simply of norm entrepreneurs selling the principle to states who, by dint of the persuasiveness of the argument, agreed to endorse the new norm. Instead – and despite protestations to the contrary by some of the key progenitors of the RtoP – the nature and scope of RtoP was contested, negotiated and ultimately revised through the process of norm contestation and diffusion that took place between 2001 and 2005.[2] Key components of the RtoP concept proposed by ICISS did not survive the process: the 'responsibility to rebuild' after an intervention was dropped in its entirety; proposed limits to the use of the veto by the UN Security Council were dropped; criteria to guide decision-making about armed intervention was dropped; and the idea that absent Security Council authorization, intervention for humanitarian purposes might be legitimized by the General Assembly or regional organizations was rejected. The norm that emerged from 2005 was therefore quite different to the concept proposed by ICISS in 2001 and it was precisely these changes that made consensus possible. Therefore if, as I will contend in subsequent chapters, RtoP's greatest strength is the breadth of the consensus around it, it stands to reason that the practice of RtoP should draw exclusively from that consensus and not from earlier proposals such as that put forth by ICISS and others. This view lends support to the first strand of thinking identified above and leaves advocates of the second strand either lobbying for amendments to RtoP or – much more common – confusing the RtoP that governments have actually committed to with the RtoP that they would have liked to have seen. These tendencies are particularly clear in relation to the way in which some commentators have reacted to the implementation of RtoP in the UN system (Chapter 2) and to the way that analysts and some political leaders alike have framed their responses to RtoP crises.

This chapter proceeds in three parts. First, I consider the main antecedents to RtoP, in particular the concept of sovereignty as responsibility and the development of cognate ideas in Africa. Second, I briefly outline the main findings of the ICISS report which first coined the phrase RtoP. Finally, I examine the background to the 2005 World Summit and briefly analyse the commitment to RtoP made there.[3]

Antecedents

Sovereignty as responsibility

During the 1999 Kosovo crisis, UN Secretary-General Kofi Annan wrote a landmark article in the *Economist* magazine in which he contrasted two visions of sovereignty. Traditional accounts, Annan suggested, insisted that states enjoyed the privileges of sovereignty (non-interference etc.) irrespective of the way they treated their citizens. But, the Secretary-General continued:

> [S]tate sovereignty, in its most basic sense, is being redefined ... States are now widely understood to be instruments at the service of their peoples, and not vice-versa. At the same time individual sovereignty – by

which I mean the fundamental freedom of each individual, enshrined in the Charter of the UN and subsequent international treaties – has been enhanced by a renewed and spreading consciousness of individual rights. When we read the Charter today, we are more than ever conscious that its aim is to protect individual human beings, not to protect those who abuse them.[4]

According to this view, sovereignty entailed both rights and responsibilities. Only those states that cherished, nurtured and protected the fundamental rights of their citizens and thereby fulfilled their sovereign responsibilities were entitled to the full panoply of sovereign rights. As such, sovereignty as responsibility rested on two foundations. First, the *inalienable* human rights of individuals.[5] Second, the idea that governments have the primary responsibility for protecting the rights of populations in their care and that when they abuse those rights or fail to protect them due to incapacity, the international community acquires a responsibility to step in, in a manner consistent with the UN Charter.[6]

The immediate catalyst for the articulation of sovereignty as responsibility in the post-Cold War era was the appointment of Francis Deng, a well-respected former Sudanese diplomat, by Annan's predecessor, BoutrosBoutros-Ghali, as the Secretary-General's Special Representative on Internally Displaced People (IDPs) in 1993. Along with his colleague, Roberta Cohen, Deng developed and advocated sovereignty as responsibility. In appointing Deng and highlighting the problem of IDPs, Boutros-Ghali was responding to both urgent humanitarian need and a vexing political dilemma. As wars became less a matter between states and more a struggle between forces within states, so the number of internally displaced people grew. When Deng was appointed there were some 25 million IDPs globally, compared to a little over a million a decade earlier.[7] Because they remained within national borders, IDPs were afforded no special international protection commensurate with that offered to refugees and remained critically vulnerable to the whims or failings of their home state. A combination of violence, disease and deprivation contrived to make mortality rates among IDPs higher, sometimes as much as 50 times higher, than that among the general population.[8]

The principal challenges confronting Deng and his colleague, Roberta Cohen from the Brookings Institution, was how to persuade governments to improve protection for IDPs and find a way to navigate around the potential denial of humanitarian assistance by sovereigns.[9] As Deng himself put it, 'the internally displaced are paradoxically assumed to be under the care of their own governments despite the fact that their displacement if often caused by the same state authorities'.[10] The starting point for sovereignty as responsibility was recognition that the primary responsibility for protecting and assisting IDPs lay with the host government.[11] No legitimate state, they argued, could quarrel with the claim that they were responsible for the well-being of their citizens and in practice no governments did quarrel with this proposition. Where a state was unable to fulfil its responsibilities, it should invite and welcome international assistance.[12] Such assistance helped the state by enabling it to discharge its sovereign responsibilities and take its place as a legitimate member of international community.[13] During major crises, troubled states faced a choice: they could work with international organizations and other interested outsiders to realize their sovereign responsibilities or they could obstruct those efforts and sacrifice their good standing and sovereign legitimacy.[14]

To translate 'sovereignty as responsibility' into protection for IDPs, Deng and Cohen developed 'Guiding Principles' which were released in 1998. They worked with legal experts to define IDPs, identify the rights they already enjoyed under existing human rights instruments, place those rights into the context of displacement, and present them in the form of 'Guiding Principles'.[15] The principles recognized that primary responsibility for displaced people rested with the local authorities but that access to international humanitarian aid should not be 'arbitrarily withheld', especially when the local authorities were unable or unwilling to provide the necessary assistance.[16] They were adopted by the UN's Inter-Agency Standing Committee (IASC), the UNHCR's executive committee, the OSCE and the AU. ECOWAS called upon its members to disseminate and apply them. In addition, several countries (Burundi, Colombia, the Philippines and Sri Lanka) have incorporated them into national law and others are considering following suit.[17]

'Sovereignty as responsibility' focused on the responsibilities of governments towards their own population and maintained that effective and legitimate states were the best way to protect vulnerable populations. In practice, active protection for IDPs required an invitation from the host state and where that was not forthcoming, Deng's arsenal was limited to the power of persuasion. Sometimes, persistent diplomacy paid dividends (for instance, Turkey improved access to displaced Kurds in 2002).[18] In many more situations, however, diplomacy failed.

In the late 1990s, several academics, policy-makers and politicians in Europe and the US put forth their own conceptions of sovereignty as responsibility. For American policy-makers associated with the Clinton and Bush administrations, responsible sovereignty was tied not just to human rights, but also to security imperatives such as WMD non-proliferation and anti-terrorism cooperation.[19] A key advocate of the American conception of sovereignty as responsibility was Richard Haass, President of the Council on Foreign Relations and former Director of Policy Planning in Colin Powell's State Department. Haass argued that sovereignty should be conditional on human rights as well as a commitment to WMD non-proliferation and counter-terrorism. In 2002, he insisted that 'sovereignty does not grant governments a blank check to do whatever they like within their own borders'.[20] Two years later, Stewart Patrick, one of Haass' colleagues at the State Department elaborated, insisting that:

> Historically, the main obstacle to armed intervention − − humanitarian or otherwise − has been the doctrine of sovereignty, which prohibits violating the territorial integrity of another state. One of the striking developments

of the past decade has been an erosion of this non–intervention norm and the rise of a nascent doctrine of 'contingent sovereignty'. This school of thought holds that sovereign rights and immunities are not absolute. They depend on the observance of fundamental state obligations.[21]

This doctrine later became an official part of America's defence strategy, with the 2005 National Defense Strategy declaring that, 'it is unacceptable for regimes to use the principle of sovereignty as a shield behind which they can claim to be free to engage in activities that pose enormous threats to their citizens, neighbors, or the rest of the international community'.[22] These views partly informed Clinton's decision to intervene in Kosovo in 1999, and were subsequently associated with the 2001 intervention in Afghanistan and 2003 invasion of Iraq. Inevitably, this association (especially with Iraq) had a damaging effect on global consensus about RtoP.[23]

The debate surrounding NATO's 1999 intervention in Kosovo provided the impetus for Tony Blair to put forth his own ideas about sovereignty as responsibility. Shortly after NATO intervened in Kosovo, Blair gave a landmark speech in which he argued that sovereignty should be reconceptualized to take account of the transformative effects of globalization. As Blair put it:

> We live in a world where isolationism has ceased to have a reason to exist. By necessity we have to co-operate with each other across nations. Many of our domestic problems are caused on the other side of the world . . . We are all internationalists now, whether we like it or not. We cannot refuse to participate in global markets if we want to prosper. We cannot ignore new political ideas in other countries if we want to innovate. We cannot turn our backs on conflicts and the violation of human rights within other countries if we want still to be secure.

According to Blair, enlightened self-interest created international responsibilities relating to egregious human suffering. Moreover, sovereigns also had responsibilities to the society of states as a whole because problems caused by massive human rights abuse in one country could spread across borders and create instability elsewhere.[24] To balance respect for non-interference with concern for human rights, Blair proposed a series of tests to ascertain the legitimacy of armed intervention – setting in train a debate about the use of criteria to guide intervention which crystallized in the work of the ICISS.

The adoption of variants of sovereignty as responsibility by the US and UK attracted criticism, especially when the doctrine was associated with attempts to justify the 2003 invasion of Iraq. Critics complained that the US and UK were abusing and selectively applying a partial account of human rights to justify armed intervention in weak and mainly postcolonial states.[25] Tellingly, however, such criticisms were aired well before sovereignty as responsibility was picked up by Washington and London, suggesting that they related to the concept itself and not just its selective application. When Francis Deng first started talking about sovereignty as responsibility he attracted withering criticism. During a 1993 discussion on IDPs in the UN's Human Rights Commission, China argued against interference in the internal affairs of states on the grounds of 'self interested' concepts of human rights and ideologies held by 'a few countries'. Argued China:

> [T]he practices of distorting human rights standards, exerting political pressure through abuse of monitoring mechanisms, applying selectivity and double-standards have led to the violation of principles and purposes of the UN Charter, and the impairing of the sovereignty and dignity of many developing countries. Thus the beautiful term of human rights has been tarnished.[26]

Cuba joined the assault, linking Deng's work on IDPs to a doctrine of humanitarian intervention that constituted an attempt 'to forcibly impose certain ideological conceptions of human rights on a number of countries, chiefly, though not exclusively, in the Third World'.[27] Sceptics worried that by advocating sovereignty as responsibility, the West was setting itself up as both judge and jury in relation to a doctrine that lent a veneer of legitimacy to self-interested coercive interference. But the move towards sovereignty as responsibility was not an entirely Western affair, as developments in Africa in the late 1990s attest.

The African Union: from non-intervention to non-indifference

Although many governments outside the West were sceptical about sovereignty as responsibility, seeing it as a potential licence for Western intervention, a significant shift in attitudes was afoot in Africa. Indeed, in some respects, concepts of sovereignty as responsibility and RtoP emerged from Africa. On the one hand, the 1994 genocide in Rwanda was the single most important event in persuading governments that more needed to be done to prevent mass atrocities and protect vulnerable peoples. It is fitting, then, that the post-genocide Rwandan government became a committed advocate of RtoP though revelations in 2010 about its own history of committing atrocities in the aftermath of the genocide became a source of embarrassment. On the other hand, the development of Africa's peace and security architecture from the mid-1990s onwards grappled with many of the same issues later raised in relation to the RtoP and resolved the problems by instituting a doctrine of sovereign responsibilities that included a right of regional intervention to remedy major humanitarian problems.[28] The African Union (AU) itself characterized the shift as one from 'non-intervention to non-indifference' that represented an embrace of sovereignty as responsibility.[29] This alone should dispel the idea that sovereignty as responsibility was an entirely Western notion.

In 2003, the Organisation for African Unity (OAU) was formally replaced by the AU. Among the factors propelling African governments to deepen regional cooperation was a shared belief that the international community had neglected African problems and that the continent must take its own measures to improve peace and security.[30] As the African Heads of State themselves declared: 'the international community has not always accorded due attention to conflict management in Africa, as it has consistently done in other regions, and . . . the efforts exerted by Africans themselves in the area of peacekeeping . . . are not given adequate financial and logistical support'.[31] Under the AU's Constitutive Act, African leaders awarded the new organization a right of intervention balanced by a reaffirmation of non-interference. Article 4(h) established 'the right of the Union to intervene in a Member State pursuant to a decision of the Assembly in respect of grave circumstances, namely war crimes, genocide and crimes against humanity'. The article was amended in 2003 to cover other 'serious threats to legitimate order' and an additional paragraph (Article 4 (j)) formalizing members' right to request intervention was added. Article 4(g), meanwhile, insisted that member states refrain from interfering in the domestic affairs of others. Seen together, these articles reject unilateral intervention while enabling collective regional action. This is an important distinction because Africa's sub-regional organizations have a track record of humanitarian intervention without either the Security Council's or OAU's authorization. Sometimes, as in the case of the ECOWAS intervention in Liberia launched in 1990, legally questionable interventions were welcomed after the fact by the Security Council.[32] Other times however, legally dubious interventions proved quite unhelpful and attracted international criticism, as in the case of the Zimbabwe-led 1998 intervention in the DRC carried out under the auspices of SADC.[33] Thus, Article 4(h) firmly established the AU's right to interfere in the domestic affairs of states in certain circumstances, while Article 4(g) guarantees that this right may only be exercised by the Union as a whole and not by individual members or sub-groups.[34]

It is worth noting that there remains some confusion about the legal relationship between the AU and the Security Council. The Constitutive Act implies that the Union may authorize intervention in humanitarian emergencies without the prior endorsement of the Security Council. As such, the question of whether the AU takes precedence over the UN on matters of African peace and security remains a moot point, but practice since 2003 suggests that the UN Security Council has primacy. In each of its three missions undertaken since that time (AMIB in Burundi; AMIS in Darfur; AMISOM in Somalia) the AU has operated within the framework of the UN Charter, insisting that deployment be contingent on both host government consent and the approval of the UN Security Council. Indeed, some commentators have gone as far as to argue that despite Article 4(h), in practice the AU's efforts may be thwarted by a combination of absent political will, institutional incapacity, and the 'weak bindingness' of the AU's norms.[35] As Paul Williams points out, this is primarily because the practice of RtoP in Africa is embedded within the complexities of African politics.[36]

In summary, the development of a regional peace and security mechanism in Africa and its assertion of a regional 'right to intervene' in cases of genocide and mass atrocities indicates the emergence of support for sovereignty as responsibility in the global south. This conclusion should be tempered somewhat, however, by recognition that the AU has proven extremely reluctant to use its authority in practice and has preferred to defer to host state consent.[37] Nonetheless, while the articulation of variants of sovereignty as responsibility by the US and UK might have discredited the idea in the eyes of many in the global south, by linking it to Western coercive interference (especially the 2003 invasion of Iraq), the adoption of Article 4(h) by the AU dispels the notion that sovereignty as responsibility was a uniquely Western idea. As such, when the ICISS began its deliberations in 2000, it did so within a context where different accounts of sovereignty as responsibility, appropriate guidelines and criteria for intervention, and ideas about the role of regional bodies and UN organs were being actively discussed in diplomatic circles.

The International Commission on Intervention and State Sovereignty (ICISS)

In March 1998, Serbian forces began a campaign of ethnic cleansing in Kosovo. Led by British Prime Minister Tony Blair and US President Bill Clinton, NATO pushed for a decisive international response. It was clear from the outset, however, that the Security Council was unlikely to authorize armed intervention, owing to Russian and Chinese opposition. It was in this atmosphere that Annan took on the role of norm entrepreneur and began to address the problem of intervention head on. The Secretary-General confronted a real dilemma. On the one hand, Annan recognized that the UN's failure to prevent or halt the bloodletting in Rwanda and Bosnia had badly hurt the organization. On the other hand, he believed in the sanctity of the UN Charter, including Article 2(4) which prohibited the use of force without the authorization of the Security Council. In his opening Address to the 1999 General Assembly, Annan challenged world leaders to find a solution:

> To those for whom the greatest threat to the future of international order is the use of force in the absence of a Security Council mandate, one might ask . . . in the context of Rwanda: If, in those dark days and hours leading up to the genocide, a coalition of States had been prepared to act in defence of the Tutsi population but did not receive prompt Council authorization, should such a coalition have stood aside and allowed the horror to unfold?
>
> To those for whom the Kosovo action heralded a new era when States and groups of States can take military action outside the established mechanisms for enforcing international law, one might ask: Is there not a danger of such interventions undermining the imperfect, yet resilient, security system created after the Second World War, and of setting dangerous precedents for future interventions without a clear criterion to decide who might invoke these precedents, and in what circumstances?[38]

Annan maintained that the state was the servant of the people and that the 'sovereignty of the individual' was enhanced by growing respect for human rights. State sovereignty therefore implied a responsibility to protect individual sovereigns. The role of the UN was to assist states to fulfil their responsibilities and realize their sovereignty. This much was clearly set out in the UN Charter, Annan insisted. But in a case like Kosovo, did sovereignty as responsibility require intervention and, if so, who was entitled to decide? Answering his own questions, Annan set out three benchmarks: a principle of intervention should be 'fairly and consistently applied'; it should embrace a 'more broadly defined, more widely conceived definition of national interest; and interventions should only proceed when authorized by the Security Council. To those who would stand in the way of collective humanitarian action, Annan insisted that 'if the collective conscience of humanity . . . cannot find in the United Nations its greatest tribune, there is a grave danger it will look elsewhere for peace and for justice'.[39]

Canada took up Annan's challenge and in early 2000 called for the establishment of an international commission. Foreign Minister Lloyd Axworthy persuaded Annan to endorse the idea, but the Secretary-General maintained that the commission should sit outside the UN so that it could proceed without political interference and controversy.[40] At Canada's invitation, the ICISS was chaired by former Australian foreign minister, Gareth Evans and Mohammed Sahnoun, a former Algerian diplomat who served the UN as special adviser on the Horn of Africa and Special Representative in Somalia and the Great Lakes of Africa. Ten other commissioners were drawn from Europe, North America, Russia, Africa, Southeast Asia, South Asia and Latin America. Quibbles about the under representation of some regions (such as South America, Africa, East Asia and the Middle East) aside, the most obvious imbalance with the Commission's composition was its gender bias. Of the 12 commissioners, only one was a woman. It is not surprising, therefore, that the ICISS was criticized as 'gender blind'.[41] The Commission was overseen by an advisory board and worked with a research directorate led by Thomas Weiss and Don Hubert. Before completing its report, it held 11 regional roundtables and national consultations.

The commission's report, entitled *Responsibility to Protect,* was released in December 2001 and endorsed by Annan, who described it as 'the most comprehensive and carefully thought-out response we have seen to date'.[42] The ICISS insisted that states have the primary responsibility to protect their citizens from genocide, mass killing and ethnic cleansing and that when they prove either unwilling or unable to fulfil this duty, the responsibility to protect is transferred to the international community. According to ICISS, RtoP comprised three interrelated sets of responsibilities: to prevent, react and rebuild.

ICISS described the 'responsibility to prevent' as the 'single most important dimension of the responsibility to protect'.[43] Reflecting long-standing views about the different types of prevention, the Commission divided its recommendations into the areas of 'early warning', tackling root causes, and 'direct prevention'. ICISS noted that failings associated with early warning are often overstated and that the nub of the problem tends to lie not in predicting the outbreak of violent conflict but in generating the political will to act on these predictions.[44] As is now known only too well, the carnage of Bosnia, Rwanda and Darfur were all predicted before the event. However, the Commission found that more accurate analysis of warning signs might identify earlier opportunities for constructive third-party engagement. It recommended that UN headquarters develop the capability to collate this information, including sensitive intelligence, from member states.[45]

The Commission's recommendations on root causes were more opaque. The ICISS called for the Security Council to play a leading role and identified four key dimensions of root cause prevention: political (relating to good governance, human rights, confidence building), economic (relating to poverty, inequality and economic opportunity), legal (relating to the rule of law and accountability) and military (relating to disarmament, reintegration and sectoral reform).[46] These four dimensions also shaped the Commission's recommendations on direct prevention. Here, the political dimension referred to the Secretary-General's preventive diplomacy; the economic dimension to the use of positive and negative inducements by the Security Council; the legal dimension to a range of measures from mediation to legal sanctions; and the military dimension – considered the most limited in scope – to preventive deployments.[47] To implement this agenda, the report called for the creation of a pool of unrestricted development funding that might be used for root cause and direct prevention and the centralization of efforts at UN headquarters.[48]

Despite stressing the critical importance of prevention, the Commission offered little conceptual innovation and stopped short of making far-reaching proposals, focusing instead on a call to centralize the world's conflict prevention efforts and develop early warning capacity. It also stopped short of offering guidelines for prevention equivalent to those set out for guiding decisions about the use of force. What is more, the Commission avoided explicit discussion of the single most pressing dilemma in relation to the 'responsibility to prevent': the question of how to translate early warning signs into a commitment to act and consensus about how to act.

The Commission's treatment of the 'responsibility to react' was altogether more sophisticated, innovative and well-developed. On the question of when to intervene, ICISS adopted the idea, first suggested by Tony Blair, of criteria to guide decision-making. Intervention, it concluded, was warranted in cases where there was large-scale loss of life or ethnic cleansing, 'actual or apprehended', whether deliberately caused by the state or facilitated by neglect or incapacity.[49] In addition to these 'just cause' thresholds, the Commission set out a series 'precautionary principles' to guide decision-making. The question of authority proved particularly thorny and the ICISS was unable to reach a clear consensus on the legitimacy of interventions not authorized by the

Security Council. In its place, the ICISS proposed a three-layered distribution of responsibility. Primary responsibility lay with the host state in line with the general ethos of sovereignty as responsibility. Secondary responsibility lay with the domestic authorities working in partnership with outside agencies. If the primary and secondary levels failed to ameliorate a humanitarian emergency, responsibility transferred to the international community.[50] At this level, the ICISS accepted the view that primary legal authority for intervention was vested in the Security Council. If the Security Council rejected a proposal for intervention in a humanitarian emergency that crossed the just cause thresholds, potential interveners should approach the General Assembly for declaratory support and, if that failed, work through regional organizations or even coalitions of the willing.[51]

To improve the chances of consensus in the Council, the ICISS adopted the idea of a voluntary code-of-conduct first proposed by French foreign minister Hubert Vedrine. ICISS suggested that states always seek Security Council authorization before using force; that the Council commit itself to dealing promptly with humanitarian emergencies involving large-scale loss of life, recognizing that its credibility and legitimacy would be impaired by failing to act; that the permanent members commit to not casting a veto to obstruct humanitarian action where there was a majority in favour unless their vital national interests were involved; and that Security Council members recognize that if they fail to fulfil their responsibility to protect, other states and organizations were likely to take it upon themselves to act.[52] The Commission insisted that the question of military intervention be placed firmly on the Security Council's agenda if either of the 'just cause thresholds' were satisfied.[53] It reasoned that if states committed to these principles, the added transparency would make it harder for them to oppose genuine humanitarian intervention and more difficult for others to abuse humanitarian justifications.

Finally, the ICISS insisted that interveners make a long-term commitment to rebuilding, concluding that potential interveners should have a strategic plan about how they intend to 'rebuild' post-conflict societies.[54] In so doing, interveners were required to consider three areas: security, justice and reconciliation, and development.[55] In relation to security, the ICISS argued that interveners acquired a moral duty to protect those in their care and should also work towards disarming and demobilizing former combatants and establishing effective and legitimate national armed forces. To engender justice and reconciliation, peacebuilders should establish a local judicial system, foster local opportunities for reconciliation and guarantee the legal rights of returnees. Interveners should also use all possible means to foster economic growth.[56] Finally, they should turn responsibility over to local leadership as rapidly as possible.

Few documents have been subjected to the level of academic scrutiny given to the ICISS report. Indeed, more has been said about this report than about the 2005 World Summit agreement. On the whole, the report was highly commended. For instance, Anthony Lewis, former columnist for the *New York Times*, commented that it 'captured the international state of mind'.[57] Where criticism came, however, it came from both ends of the spectrum. At one end were those who thought that in its search for consensus the Commission had sacrificed too much in terms of the moral case for humanitarian intervention and, at the other end, were those who argued that the ICISS had gone too far in advancing an interventionist doctrine that could be abused by the great powers.

The best example of the first type of argument is provided by the Commission's own research director. In a stinging critique of the Commission's stance on prevention, Thomas Weiss argued that 'it is preposterous to argue that to prevent is *the* single most important priority'. He continued:

> [M]ost of the mumbling and stammering about prevention is a superficially attractive but highly unrealistic way to try and pretend that we can finesse the hard issues of what essentially amounts to humanitarian intervention. The ICISS's discourse about prevention is a helpful clarification, but it nonetheless obscures the essence of the most urgent part of the spectrum of responsibility to protect those caught in the crosshairs of war.[58]

This goes to the heart of the question of the place of prevention and rebuilding in the RtoP schema. Weiss rightly pointed to the unsatisfactory way in which the Commission dealt with prevention and it is hard to disagree with his view that prevention and rebuilding were 'tagged on' to RtoP by ICISS in order to make military intervention more palatable.[59] The report was conceptually confused about the nature, scope and place of prevention and added little in the way of new thinking. Much the same can be said of the Commission's findings on rebuilding. There was therefore a gulf between the Commission's sophisticated and nuanced treatment of the question of intervention and its brief take on prevention and rebuilding.

Weiss also argued that when it came to intervention the Commission's just cause thresholds set the bar too high ('large-scale loss of life . . . actual or apprehended' and 'large-scale ethnic cleansing').[60] Indeed, ICISS set the bar higher than actual Security Council practice by excluding the protection of democratic governments from violent overthrow and measures to protect civilians in cases that amounted to less than large-scale or genocidal killing. The ICISS thresholds excluded the overthrow of democratically elected governments despite the fact that in 1994 the Security Council identified the violent overthrow of Bertrand Aristide's government in Haiti as a 'threat to international peace and security' and authorized enforcement measures to restore the elected government. Three years later, ECOWAS intervened in Sierra Leone to restore an elected government, a move subsequently endorsed by the Security Council.[61] In addition, the requirement of large-scale killing or ethnic cleansing precluded Security Council action in circumstances where the threat to civilians was somewhat less. Once again, it appeared that Security Council practice was somewhat in advance of RtoP. Security Council Resolution 1265 (17 September, 1999) stated the Council's readiness to take appropriate steps to protect civilians who were being deliberately targeted, without insisting that this targeting be genocidal or 'large-scale'. In 2005, the Security Council authorized its peace operation in Côte d'Ivoire (UNOCI) to use force to protect civilians even though the level of killing had not reached just cause thresholds. In relation to thresholds, therefore, we can agree with Thomas Weiss that the ICISS took a conservative position and was 'neither forerunner nor pacesetter'.[62] However, we also need to recognize that consensus was an important consideration. The whole purpose of ICISS was to find a position that could command international consensus. The Commission judged rightly that imposing conservative restrictions on the Security Council's room for manoeuvre and embedding coercion within a broader spectrum of measures were necessary in order to build consensus.

At the other end of the spectrum, David Chandler, a left-leaning British academic, claimed that the report advocated nothing short of the forcible imposition of Western values, a view that has come to be widely shared in academic circles.[63] Chandler argued that RtoP ultimately translates into a right of intervention; that 'sovereignty as responsibility' is, in fact, a diminution of sovereignty because it strips states of exclusive jurisdiction; and that far from demilitarizing humanitarianism by embedding intervention within a wider set of responsibilities, 'the Commission makes external intervention more legitimate and extends the rights of a 'continuum' of mechanisms of less and more coercive international interference'.[64] Ultimately, Chandler's critique amounted to a straightforward defence of a traditional account of sovereignty.[65]

These concerns notwithstanding, the ICISS report was clearly a landmark document that helped reframe the terms of the debate about how the world should respond to episodes of conscience shocking inhumanity. Where it missed an important opportunity for innovation, however, was in its halfhearted treatments of prevention and rebuilding. Despite protestations to the contrary, the ICISS report *was* indeed primarily concerned with humanitarian intervention. Thus, while the Commission described the 'responsibility to prevent' as the 'single most important dimension' of RtoP, a view later restated by Thakur, it dedicated only 9 of its 85 pages to prevention.[66] Indeed, the responsibilities to prevent and rebuild received only 16 pages, compared with 32 pages on the question of intervention. The report was therefore clearly more interested in intervention than in prevention or rebuilding. But RtoP succeeded in reframing the debate largely only by situating non-consensual intervention within a wider continuum of measures including prevention, rebuilding and non-forcible means of reaction though the Commission offered little that was substantive or innovative about either prevention or rebuilding and failed to integrate the three components into a conceptual whole.

Getting to 2005

RtoP found itself on the agenda for the 2005 World Summit by virtue of its inclusion in the report of the Secretary-General's UN's High Level Panel and Kofi Annan's endorsement in his agenda for renewing the UN (*In Larger Freedom*).[67] In September 2003, Kofi Annan commissioned the High Level Panel, which included Gareth Evans, to examine contemporary challenges to international peace and security and make recommendations about how the UN might address those challenges more effectively.[68] In its December 2004 report, the Panel endorsed the 'emerging norm that there is a responsibility to protect . . . exercisable by the Security Council'.[69] The Panel endorsed the just cause thresholds and precautionary principles envisaged by ICISS with only minor revisions.[70] The Panel also recommended that the Security Council adopt these guidelines in a declaratory resolution. Also, instead of a commitment not to veto collective action in response to threshold-crossing crises and unless vital national interests were at stake where a majority was in favour, the panel suggested a system of indicative voting whereby Council members would publicly declare and justify their positions prior to an actual vote.[71] Somewhat optimistically, the Panel hoped that members would be reluctant to publicly declare opposition to collective action in conscience-shocking cases.

Annan accepted almost all the Panel's recommendations in his own blueprint for UN reform.[72] He endorsed criteria to guide decision-making about the use of force, seeing in it a mechanism for avoiding the damaging divisions caused by Kosovo and Iraq. The Secretary-General insisted that the Security Council was the sole source of authority for armed interventions under the rubric of RtoP and that criteria should serve as a constraint on its decision-making. The Secretary-General reiterated that primary responsibility lay with the host state, adding that only if a state proved unwilling or unable to protect its citizens would responsibility shift to the international community.[73]

The adoption of RtoP by the High Level Panel and Kofi Annan placed it on the agenda of the 2005 World Summit. In September 2005, world leaders gathered in New York to celebrate the sixtieth anniversary of the UN and debate Annan's proposed reforms, including the commitment to RtoP. The negotiations began in late 2004 when General Assembly President Jean Ping (Foreign Minister of Gabon) began consulting with the permanent delegations. Ping initially anticipated that a final draft would be agreed by late August 2005, well before the summit, but in the end they were concluded only at the last minute, when it seemed that the whole reform agenda would collapse.

It was expected that RtoP would be controversial, because of its association with humanitarian intervention. Early on, there was broad support for setting a high just cause threshold and for the principle that the host state had primary responsibility. The permanent members of the Security Council were solidly against the 'code-of-conduct', a position endorsed by some in the wider UN membership who saw the veto as an important barrier against Western interventionism.[74] As a result, the High Level Panel's proposed 'code' did not survive long in the negotiations.[75] Disagreement persisted on several critical issues. First, the question of whether the Security Council had exclusive authority to authorize intervention. The US and UK argued that unauthorized intervention could not be expressly ruled out but a majority held that if RtoP was to *constrain* Western interventionism then the absolute primacy of the Security Council had to be reaffirmed. Second, there was profound disagreement about criteria to guide decision-making on intervention. Whereas several African states, the High Level Panel and Annan endorsed criteria as essential to making the Security Council's decisions more transparent, accountable (to the wider membership) and hence legitimate, the US, China and Russia opposed them. Finally, several states, notably India, maintained that RtoP was an intervener's charter designed to legitimize Western interference. This view was publicly expressed by only a few states, but it reflected a significant underlying concern in many parts of the world.[76]

Between March and August 2005, steady progress was made towards consensus and by 10 August careful diplomacy had produced a draft outcome document which included a commitment to RtoP and some of its core components. The draft emphasized that RtoP 'lies first and foremost' with the host state and maintained that this responsibility was taken up by external actors when the host government proved itself 'unable or unwilling' to fulfil its responsibilities.[77] The recommendation for criteria was watered-down into a commitment to continue discussing criteria.[78] Ultimately, however, it was recognized that criteria would be a 'bridge too far' and they were quickly taken off the table.[79] Thus, a consensus about the phrasing of the world's commitment to RtoP had begun to emerge in early August. On 3 August, however, John Bolton – a renowned anti-UN hawk – took up position as the US Permanent Representative to the UN and tore this consensus apart.

Less than three weeks before the summit, Bolton called for the redrafting of hundreds of paragraphs (including those on RtoP) and the deletion of many others. Bolton's problems with RtoP itself were relatively minor. He argued that the RtoP paragraph be redrafted to recognize that: 'the responsibility of the other countries in the international community is not of the same character as the responsibility of the host; that the Security Council was not *legally* obliged to protect endangered civilians; and that the commitment to RtoP 'should not preclude the possibility of action absent authorization by the Security Council'.[80] None of these propositions were remarkable in themselves. The sting in the tail came in Bolton's proposed amendments to the wider UN reform project. The US now insisted that the outcome document remove all references to the Millennium Development Goals (MDGs), the 'right to development' and the goal of debt reduction. He also rejected references to disarmament, the control of small arms and called for radical reform to the proposed Peacebuilding Commission.[81] The effect of all this – – especially the inexplicably hard-line on development – was to destroy consensus. Bolton's intervention declared open-season for other spoilers and RtoP was among the casualties.[82]

In late August, China signalled its change of heart on RtoP and announced 'deep reservations'.[83] Russia followed suit, its diplomats maintained that the UN was already equipped to deal with humanitarian crises and suggested that, by countenancing unauthorized intervention, RtoP risked undermining the UN Charter.[84] They were joined by several G77 and NAM states that had made concessions on RtoP and the Human Rights Council in return for the commitment to the MDGs which Bolton was now challenging. The NAM Coordinating Bureau restated its rejection of the 'so-called right' of humanitarian intervention, ominously observing that there were 'similarities' between 'the new expression responsibility to protect and humanitarian intervention'. Algeria argued that RtoP was incompatible with international law while Egypt disputed both the assertion that the international community had a responsibility to protect civilians and that the protection of civilians should trump sovereignty.[86] Most dangerous, though, was the eleventh hour attack launched by India. In one of the many meetings designed to help bridge the widening diplomatic chasms, India's Permanent Representative Nirupem Sen launched a broadside against RtoP, challenging its legal status and moral foundations. Ultimately, however, India was not prepared to scuttle the whole summit by rejecting the RtoP.[87]

With less than three days to go, the negotiations were in disarray and RtoP had been struck from the list of agreed issues. At the eleventh hour Jean Ping and the UN leadership pulled a diplomatic sleight of hand. They had secretly continued to work on the original document, making amendments to take the ebb and flow of debate into account but without going back to first principles.[88] Ping then outmanoeuvred Bolton and the other spoilers by releasing the document to the permanent delegations. Bolton maintained his opposition but was overruled by Secretary of State, Condoleeza Rice.[89]

This final version of the text included the RtoP paragraphs but in revised form: the threshold for when responsibility transferred from the host state to the international community was raised to situations where the state had 'manifestly failed' to protect civilians; UN member states recognized their responsibility to protect their own populations but did not recognize a responsibility to act beyond the use of peaceful means in cases of mass killing, genocide and ethnic cleansing, simply reaffirming their preparedness to use other measures if they saw fit; and the authority to use coercive measures was vested exclusively in the Security Council. Thus, paragraphs 138–9 of the final text declared that:

138. Each individual state has the responsibility to protect its populations from genocide, war crimes, ethnic cleansing and crimes against humanity. This responsibility entails the prevention of such crimes, including their incitement, through appropriate and necessary means. We accept that responsibility and will act in accordance with it. The international community should, as appropriate, encourage and help States to exercise this

responsibility and support the United Nations in establishing an early
warning capability.

139. The international community, through the United Nations, also
has the responsibility to use appropriate diplomatic, humanitarian and other
peaceful means, in accordance with Chapters VI and VIII of the Charter
of the United Nations, to help protect populations from war crimes, ethnic
cleansing and crimes against humanity. In this context, we are prepared
to take collective action, in a timely and decisive manner, through the
Security Council, in accordance with the Charter, including Chapter VII,
on a case-by-case basis and in cooperation with relevant regional organizations as appropriate, should peaceful means be inadequate and national
authorities are manifestly failing to protect their populations from genocide,
war crimes, ethnic cleansing and crimes against humanity. We stress the
need for the General Assembly to continue consideration of the responsibility to protect populations from genocide, war crimes, ethnic cleansing
and crimes against humanity and its implications, bearing in mind the
principles of the Charter and international law. We also intend to commit
ourselves, as necessary and appropriate, to helping States build capacity to
protect their populations from genocide, war crimes, ethnic cleansing and
crimes against humanity and to assisting those which are under stress before
crises and conflicts break out.[90]

The language is surprisingly clear – indeed, clearer and more consistent than
earlier formulations proposed by the ICISS and High Level Panel.[91] The RtoP
that emerged from the World Summit contained three major components: (1)
formal recognition of the responsibility of sovereigns to their own population;
(2) a commitment to develop the institutional capacities and behaviours
necessary to prevent genocide and mass atrocities, assist states in the fulfilment
of their responsibilities, and improve the effectiveness of peaceful and consensual
measures; (3) a reaffirmation of the idea that the Security Council has the
authority to intervene if it sees fit to do so. As such, the Outcome Document
tied RtoP to existing international legal norms.[92] This was much less than
envisaged by the ICISS, but it marked an important milestone in the normative
development of responsible sovereignty and pointed towards a weighty policy
agenda for international institutions, regional organizations and individual
states. It is this agenda that provides the focus for the remainder of this book.

Conclusion

This chapter has briefly charted the evolution of RtoP from ideas of sovereignty
as responsibility articulated by UN officials, academics, and individual governments in the 1990s to its unanimous adoption by world leaders at the 2005
World Summit. While the ICISS can lay claim to having developed the idea
of RtoP, the commission's recommendations followed a path laid out by Francis
Deng and Roberta Cohen (the idea that states have primary responsibility and

when they fail to exercise it, that responsibility transfers to the international community), the British and French governments (the ideas that decisions to use force be guided by criteria and that the Security Council commit to a code of conduct), and echoed parallel developments in Africa. The commission's major innovation lay in shifting the focus onto the victims and the insertion of humanitarian intervention within a broader schema of responsibility that included duties to prevent atrocities and rebuild afterwards. RtoP would have laid dormant had it not been picked up and advocated by the High Level Panel and Kofi Annan, nor would the concept have made it through the 2005 negotiations without resolute support from Annan, Canada and other Western 'friends' of RtoP, and several AU members, especially South Africa and Rwanda.

Although this normative development was incredibly rapid, it was not without its opponents. Indeed, it is fair to say that although the principle enjoyed strong support in Europe and the West, parts of Africa and parts of Latin America, a significant portion of the UN's membership remained cautious and unconvinced. Perhaps a majority among those in the global south that did not advocate the principle merely 'mimicked' support for the norm in 2005 – choosing to accept the new norm rhetorically but without actually changing their behaviour to take account of the norm. Others simply calculated that the principle had been watered down so much as to make it practically meaningless.[94] Finally, some, such as India, Cuba, Sudan, Venezuela, Pakistan and Nicaragua argued that they had not, in fact endorsed the RtoP and that the World Summit agreement only committed states to further consideration of the norm. Taking all this into account, it is not surprising that the consensus on RtoP was only possible because the concept's meaning and scope was revised through the negotiation process. What is more, although the commitment to RtoP was surprisingly clear and unambiguous, governments and commentators continued to argue about the norm's meaning and scope both in general and in relation to specific crises. Even RtoP's supporters began to disagree about what had and had not been agreed to and the proper direction and focus for the new norm, as I will show in the following chapters.

While the World Summit's commitment to RtoP was clear and unambiguous, the consensus that underpinned it was wide but extremely shallow. It could not be taken for granted that rhetorical support for or acquiescence to the RtoP would be translated into behavioural change or the reallocation of resources. The following two chapters tell parallel stories about the evolution of RtoP after 2005. The first focuses on attempts to advance the principle within the UN system and the second considers its use in relation to the dozen or so humanitarian crises that either emerged or were ongoing during this period.

2 Implementing RtoP at the UN

Few would disagree with the proposition that the Responsibility to Protect (RtoP), adopted by heads of state and government at the 2005 UN World Summit, has become a prominent feature in international debates about preventing genocide and mass atrocities and protecting the victims. Five years on from its adoption, RtoP boasts a Global Centre and network of regional affiliates dedicated to advocacy and research, a global coalition of non-governmental organizations, an academic journal and book series, a research fund sponsored by the Australian government, and has spawned a range of off-shoots including the 'IRtoP' (individual responsibility to protect) and 'W2I' (will to intervene) projects, focusing respectively on engaging individuals as agents of change and generating the political will to intervene to put an end to genocide and mass atrocities.[1] More importantly, RtoP has made its way onto the international diplomatic agenda. On the one hand, by appointing Edward Luck as his Special Adviser and publishing a report on implementing the principle, UN Secretary-General Ban Ki-moon has confronted the UN membership with the challenge of translating its 2005 commitment from 'words to deeds'.[2] This challenge was taken up by the General Assembly in 2009, when it agreed to give further consideration to the Secretary-General's proposals and continue dialogue about implementing the RtoP.[3] On the other hand, RtoP has become part of the diplomatic language of humanitarian emergencies, used by governments, international institutions, NGOs and independent commissions to justify behaviour, cajole compliance and demand international action. Governments making use of the principle have included Egypt (calling for an international force to protect the people of Gaza), Russia (justifying intervention in Georgia to prevent 'genocide' in South Ossetia) and India (reminding Sri Lanka of its responsibility to protect all populations under its care), all of whom were initially sceptical about it.[4]

For all this apparent progress, however, evidence of disagreement abounds. Much as they did before 2005, critics complain that the RtoP is a dangerous and imperialist doctrine that threatens to undermine the national sovereignty and political autonomy of the weak. This attitude was evident in the concept note issued by the President of the General Assembly (PGA), former Sandanista,

Miguel d'Escoto Brockmann prior to the UN General Assembly 2009 debate on RtoP. The note intimated that '[c]olonialism and interventionism used responsibility to protect arguments'.[5] Paradoxically, other critics lament that RtoP is nothing more than rhetorical posturing that promises little tangible improvement in the protection of vulnerable people. At first glance, the latter argument appears to carry some weight: despite its commitment to RtoP, since 2005 the Security Council has been hamstrung by deadlock on the protection of civilians in Sri Lanka, Gaza and Zimbabwe and has failed to ensure implementation of protection mandates in Sudan (both in Darfur and in the south), the DRC and Somalia (see Chapter 3).[6] To further complicate matters, profound disagreements have emerged about the meaning and proper use of RtoP and the principle has been employed inconsistently – used, at one end of the spectrum, by France in relation to Myanmar and Russia in relation to Georgia to justify the actual or potential use of coercive force in situations where there was no apparent manifest failure to protect populations from genocide and mass atrocities, while at the other end of the spectrum China has argued that the Security Council should only become engaged in matters that pose threats to *international* peace and security and that RtoP must not be used even in diplomacy to coerce governments to alter their behaviour. Nicholas Wheeler and Frazer Egerton suggest that this means that the meaning and scope of RtoP remains contested, whereas the UN Secretary-General's Special Adviser, Edward Luck, contends that the problem is one of distinguishing between what RtoP is (as agreed by states) and what individual activists and commentators would like it to be.[7]

This is the first of two chapters that tries to make sense of all this by analysing RtoP practice since 2005. There are two parallel stories to tell about RtoP since 2005, one concerning debates about its implementation within the UN system and the other concerning its use in response to humanitarian crises. At times, these parallel stories have overlapped, most notably when the current and former UN Secretaries-General utilized RtoP in their diplomatic effort to end post-election violence in Kenya and when UN peace operations have been charged with developing, interpreting and implementing protection of civilians mandates in a manner consistent with RtoP (see Chapter 3). In general, however, the two stories have remained relatively self-contained, with recent crises having little discernible impact on the debate about implementing RtoP within the UN system and debates about how to respond to various humanitarian crises proceeding without much reference to what was happening at UN headquarters.

This chapter focuses on debates about implementing RtoP within the UN system and the following chapter addresses the principle's use in response to the various humanitarian crises that have emerged since 2005. Initial debates about implementing RtoP in the UN were characterized by a 'revolt' against the principle led by states that remained cautious about the RtoP's implications for state sovereignty. This revolt gained traction in 2006–7, but was stemmed in large part by the work of the Secretary-General's Special Adviser, Edward Luck, whose consultations with Member States, patient diplomacy and conceptual innovation laid the foundations for a renewed consensus to emerge at the 2009 General Assembly debate. This chapter is divided into three sections. The first charts the revolt against RtoP in 2006–7. The second section focuses on the efforts of the Secretary-General and his Special Adviser to clarify the principle, build consensus and set out an agenda for implementation, focusing especially on the Secretary-General's report on implementation. The third section reviews the 2009 General Assembly debate, identifying important points of consensus and a number of areas in need of further clarification. The second part of the book examines some of these areas in more detail.

2006–7: Revolt against RtoP

The debate about implementing RtoP at the UN got off to an inauspicious start. Thanks principally to lingering concerns about its potential to legitimize interference in the domestic affairs of states and fears about abuse, several states displayed what Gareth Evans labeled 'buyer's remorse' and launched a 'revolt' against RtoP aimed at preventing the principle being translated into practice.[8] Before I outline the nature of this revolt, it is important to underscore that prior to 2005, concerns about RtoP were mainly related to its perceived association with humanitarian intervention and coercive interference within a context of heightened sensitivities caused by the perceived misuse of humanitarian arguments to justify the invasion of Iraq.[9] These concerns propelled two of the main battles associated with the post-Summit revolt against RtoP: the (unsuccessful) struggle to prevent the Security Council affirming RtoP and the (successful) attempt to stop the UN Human Rights Council condemning Sudan for its 'failure to protect' Darfuris.

Despite adopting RtoP at the World Summit, it took six months of intense debate for the Security Council to unanimously adopt Resolution 1674, 'reaffirming' the World Summit's provisions 'regarding the responsibility to protect'. The initial UK draft had proposed stronger language 'underlining the importance' of the RtoP.[10] Initially, Russia, China and three non-permanent members (Algeria, the Philippines and Brazil) argued that the World Summit had only committed the General Assembly to deliberation on RtoP and that it was therefore premature for the Security Council to take up the matter.[11] Changes in the Council's non-permanent membership and the softening of the language endorsing RtoP helped forge agreement around Resolution 1674 but it was a hard won consensus. Of the five non-permanent members stepping down in 2005, two (Algeria and Brazil) had openly declared their hostility to RtoP and another (the Philippines) had tended to side with the sceptics, despite its earlier support for RtoP in 2004. Among the new members were Slovakia, Qatar and Peru who had voiced support in the Council's December 2005 debate, Ghana who had not participated in that debate but supported RtoP and Congo who in June 2006 informed the Council of its 'strong support' for the principle.[12] This painful negotiating experience persuaded some of the Council's RtoP advocates to refrain from encouraging the body to make greater use of the principle for fear of creating opportunities for backsliding on the 2005 agreement.[13] Since the passage of Resolution 1674, the Council has referred to RtoP only twice – in the non-operative second preambular paragraph of Resolution 1706 (2006) on the situation in Darfur reaffirming the provisions of paragraphs 138 and 139 of the World Summit Outcome Document and in a 2009 resolution on the protection of civilians in armed conflict (Resolution 1894, 2009). Several Council members expressed discomfort (China abstained in the vote on Resolution 1706) about the diplomatic pressure brought to bear to secure Resolution 1706 and subsequent resolutions on specific crises have shied away from using RtoP language. On Resolution 1706, China abstained on the grounds that Sudanese consent had not been secured. Around the same time, China's position on RtoP subtly hardened and it joined those arguing that it was premature for the Council to deliberate on RtoP because the General Assembly had not conducted its own deliberation as called for in the World Summit Outcome agreement.[14] In 2007, China argued that:

> [T]here are still differing understandings and interpretations of this concept among Member States. The Security Council should therefore refrain from invoking the concept of the responsibility to protect. Still less should the concept be misused. The Security Council should respect and support the General Assembly in continuing to discuss the concept in order to reach broad consensus.[15]

As such, a paragraph referring to the paragraphs 138 and 139 of the World Summit agreement was deleted from Resolution 1769 (2007) on Darfur at the request of council members and Resolution 1814 (2008) on Somalia pointedly referred to the protection of civilians and Resolution 1674 without referring to the World Summit agreement.[16]

Resistance to implementing RtoP was also evident in the UN Human Rights Council. When the Council's High-Level Mission to Darfur reported in 2007 that the government of Sudan was failing in its responsibility to protect Darfuris, the Arab Group, Asia Group and Organization of Islamic Conferences all questioned the report's legitimacy and attempted to prevent deliberation on its findings.[17] On 11 December 2006, the UN Human Rights Council (HRC) decided to dispatch a High-Level Mission (HLM) to Darfur to assess the human rights situation there and the needs of the government of Sudan. This decision was widely applauded as a signal of the members' willingness to compromise in order to make the HRC work. Almost immediately, however, the HLM ran into difficulties. The Sudanese government refused to grant the HLM access because one of its members, the highly respected Bertrand Ramcharan, had earlier criticized the government's behaviour in Darfur. Head of Mission, Nobel Laureate Jody Williams, decided that Ramcharan would remain in the mission and that the HLM would conduct its work without entering Darfur if the Sudanese government did not change its mind. This prompted the HLM's Asian representative, Indonesia's Makarim Wibisono, to leave the group, arguing that without access to Darfur the HLM would be unable to fulfill its mandate.[18]

The HLM then used RtoP as a benchmark for judging the Sudanese government's performance in Darfur. Williams argued that this was appropriate because the World Summit declaration had created a mandate, and because Sudan had endorsed RtoP and pledged 'to act in accordance with it' in.[19] The Mission's findings were conclusive and damning: 'The Mission . . . concludes that the Government of the Sudan has manifestly failed to protect the population of Darfur from large-scale international crimes, and has itself orchestrated and perpetuated those crimes. As such, the solemn obligation of the international community to exercise its *responsibility to protect* has become evident and urgent'.[20] This was a landmark finding. For the first time, a UN commissioned report had applied the RtoP framework as set out at the 2005 World Summit and found that a state had 'manifestly failed' to protect its population.

The backlash was not slow in coming. Sudan, along with representatives of the Arab Group, Asia Group and Organization of Islamic Conferences (OIC) launched an assault on the report's legitimacy in an effort to prevent deliberation on its findings. Underlying their arguments was concern about the use of RtoP to justify international interference in the domestic affairs of states by an entity – the Human Rights Council – that lacked the formal authority to take on this role. Speaking for Sudan, Mohammed Ali Elmardi argued that the report was nothing more than a 'conspiracy' against his government, maintaining that the HLM's failure to visit Sudan rendered the report 'faulty' and 'illegitimate'. Lazhar Soualem (Algeria), speaking on behalf of the Arab Group, agreed that the report was illegitimate and should not be discussed. Speaking for the OIC, Pakistan endorsed Algeria's position and criticized the report's use of RtoP. The HRC had not written RtoP into the HLM's mandate, therefore invalidating the Mission's findings, he argued. Moreover, Pakistan maintained that because RtoP involved political and security matters, it fell outside the HRC's remit. These views were endorsed by Sri Lanka representing the Asian Group, Indonesia, Egypt and Bangladesh, which described the report as 'illegitimate'. China concurred, arguing that the report should not be considered because the HLM's mandate had not been 'faithfully implemented'. Russia was somewhat less forthright in its criticism but it too questioned the report's legitimacy.

Standing against this barrage of criticism were Europe, Canada, Australia, Japan, sub-Saharan Africa and some South American states. Zambia, argued that the critics were wrong to maintain that a mission's inability to visit a country impaired its legitimacy, pointing to the fact that the Human Rights Commission had accepted reports on apartheid South Africa and Israel in very similar circumstances. It warned that if the Council failed to pay attention to the report and allowed technicalities to divert its attention away from the systematic abuse of human rights in Darfur, it would discredit itself much as its predecessor (the Human Rights Commission) had done. These sentiments were echoed by Ghana and Nigeria, which endorsed the report and argued that it should serve as the basis for further action.

In the end, the Council agreed to discuss the report but convened a further group of seven 'mandate holders' to work with the government of Sudan in developing recommendations for further action. The group pieced together a list of 44 recommendations, complete with time frames and 'performance indicators', most – if not all – of which were unlikely to improve the protection of human rights in Darfur.[21] This rather weak consensus on Darfur was bought at the expense of dropping references to RtoP and condemning the government of Sudan's record.

The post 2005 revolt against RtoP was therefore spearheaded by Arab and Asian states and was in large part fuelled by entrenched concerns about 'humanitarian intervention' and the potential for RtoP to justify coercive interference in the domestic affairs of states. However, a significant number of governments from the global south, especially from sub-Saharan Africa and Latin America, joined the West in defending the new principle. In terms of the substance, the debate surrounding Resolution 1674 gave voice to specific concerns relating to intervention. By contrast, at its heart the debate in the Human Rights Council was concerned about that Council's authority to use RtoP as a means of holding states to account. These three points – the root of opposition lying in the continuing association of RtoP with humanitarian intervention and coercive interference, the problem of identifying which bodies had the authority to use RtoP, and the broad constituency of states prepared to defend the principle – suggest that while significant obstacles remained, a new and deeper consensus was possible. As the next section argues, the need for renewed conceptual thinking and dialogue with states was recognized by incoming UN Secretary-General, Ban Ki-moon and underpinned his effort to forge a consensus on the need to translate RtoP from words to deeds.

2007–8: Towards a new consensus?

Even RtoP's friends recognized that in the aftermath of the 2005 agreement, the principle had become 'toxic'.[22] Promising signs began to emerge, however, with the election of South Korean foreign minister, Ban Ki-moon as UN Secretary-General in October 2006. Ban has been repeatedly criticized by some RtoP advocates as being too willing to negotiate with tyrants and for being an American stooge. Prominent RtoP advocate and leading ICISS member, Ramesh Thakur, has been particularly outspoken in his criticism of Ban. Thakur described the Secretary-General as 'hapless' and 'lacking charisma', labelling him the 'model of a mediocre Secretary-General'. His principal substantive charge was that the Secretary-General spent too much time visiting and negotiating with tyrannical regimes in Myanmar and Zimbabwe and has sacrificed the UN's moral authority.[23] Thakur's assessment corresponds with that of Mona Juul, Norway's deputy permanent representative to the UN, whose damaging views were expressed in a leaked internal memo. It is worth noting, however, that shortly before she penned the memo, Juul's husband had unsuccessfully attempted to secure a senior post in the UN secretariat.

Whatever the critics might think, Ban has proven to be an effective norm entrepreneur for RtoP. He has succeeded in forging a wider and deeper consensus, in persuading the General Assembly to take up the question of implementing RtoP, and in setting out a comprehensive implementation agenda. Campaigning under the slogan of 'promise less and deliver more', Ban argued that the UN needed to close the gap between its lofty rhetoric and its often less than lofty performance.[24] Ban was also the only candidate for the post of Secretary-General to make a commitment to implementing the RtoP and upon taking office affirmed his 'deep and enduring' personal commitment to the principle and intention to 'operationalize' it.[25] Other candidates for the position, especially Shashi Tharoor and Jayanatha Dhanapala, mentioned RtoP in response to questions during the campaign – Tharoor describing it as one of Annan's most significant achievements, and Dhanapala as a 'more acceptable means' through which the Security Council can engage in the protection of civilians – but both fell well short of offering a commitment to implement RtoP.[26]

The new Secretary-General appointed the highly regarded UN expert, Edward Luck, as his Special Adviser on RtoP, a move that was also criticized by Thakur on the grounds that Luck lacked expertise in the area and as an American was an inappropriate choice.[27] The initial debate among UN members about Luck's appointment represented a clear low-point for international consensus on RtoP in the post-2005 period. The Secretary-General first proposed appointing Luck in a budget estimates report in December 2007. Ban informed the General Assembly of his decision to appoint a Special Adviser on RtoP to 'operationalize the concept and to develop the doctrine'.[28] He argued that the Special Adviser should complement the work of the Special Adviser on the Prevention of Genocide and provide recommendations about implementing the World Summit agreement. To this end, the Secretary-General requested a modest budget increase for the Office of the Special Adviser for the Prevention of Genocide. The General Assembly's Fifth (Budget) Committee implicitly rejected the proposed appointment and establishment of a joint office for RtoP and Genocide Prevention when it adopted a resolution on the 2007/8 budget without funding for Ban's proposal.[29] The Committee addressed the appointment issue again in March 2008 and several states (Cuba, Egypt, Morocco, Nicaragua, Pakistan and Sudan) used the opportunity to express concern about the appointment and to argue that it was premature because the General Assembly had not begun its deliberations on RtoP as called for in paragraph 139 of the World Summit agreement. Somewhat bizarrely, they argued that the 2005 agreement merely committed the General Assembly to further consider the RtoP.[30] In the end, the Secretary-General exercised his right to appoint advisers and the General Assembly exercised its right to not fund the initiative.[31]

Luck's appointment represented an important turning point in the fortunes of post-2005 RtoP at the UN. Adopting a consultative approach based on a detailed dissection of the 2005 agreement, the Special Adviser engaged in lengthy and detailed dialogue with Member States, many of whom (such as Indonesia) had never been consulted on RtoP and whose concerns had not until then been obviously factored in. Vital to this approach was Luck's sharp distinction between what states had actually agreed to in relation to RtoP, and a variety of alternative formulations such as the doctrine humanitarian intervention and the ICISS recommendations. As Luck explained, 'for the UN and its Member States the principle of a responsibility to protect is what is contained in paragraphs 138 and 139 of the Outcome Document, nothing more and nothing less'.[32]

Early results from these initiatives included a number of conceptual innovations, especially the articulation of RtoP's three non-sequential and equally important pillars (the primary responsibility of the sovereign; the international community's responsibility to assist the sovereign; and the international duty to take timely and decisive action) and what the Secretary-General described as a 'narrow but deep' approach that strictly limited RtoP to what was agreed in 2005 (application to the crimes of genocide, war crimes, ethnic cleansing and crimes against humanity, and their prevention; and implementation in a manner consistent with the UN Charter) but 'utilized the whole prevention and protection tool kit' available to the United Nations system, regional arrangements, states, and civil society.[33] Although criticized in some quarters for emphasizing prevention, capacity-building, and the primary responsibility of states rather than the dilemmas associated with humanitarian intervention that had animated the ICISS, the approach adopted by the Secretary-General and his Special Adviser more closely reflected what states had agreed in 2005 and helped establish a new and stronger consensus upon which to begin discussion about translating RtoP from words to deeds. The Secretary-General invited the Special Adviser to prepare a report on implementing the RtoP which would be tabled in the General Assembly. The report was intended to outline a broad agenda and call upon the General Assembly to pass a resolution indicating its commitment to the on-going implementation of the RtoP. Significantly, the Secretary-General and his Special Adviser, insisted that the General Assembly should be the primary vehicle for moving RtoP forward. It was important, they argued, that all member states be given the opportunity to examine the principle and comment on its implementation. What might be lost in terms of momentum, they rationalized, would be more than compensated for in terms of legitimacy if the principle was moved forward on the basis of consensus.

Implementing the responsibility to protect

The Secretary-General's report, *Implementing the Responsibility to Protect* was released in early 2009 and marked a significant step forward in the normative evolution of RtoP.[34] Based on extensive consultation with Member States and UN agencies, it outlined a comprehensive range of measures that the General Assembly and individual states might consider in relation to implementing RtoP's three pillars. The Secretary-General urged the General Assembly 'to take the first step by considering carefully the strategy for implementing the responsibility to protect described in [his] report'. Specifically, he envisaged the debate as an opportunity for the General Assembly to welcome or take note of his report, to define the nature of the General Assembly's continuing consideration of the RtoP, and to address ways to define and develop the partnership between states and the international community. The Secretary-General argued that, 'the task ahead is not to reinterpret or renegotiate the conclusions of the World Summit but to find ways of implementing its decisions in a fully faithful and consistent manner'.[35] With this in mind, the report began by clarifying the nature and scope of RtoP as agreed in 2005. It maintained that as agreed by member states, the RtoP was embedded in existing international law. It is worth thinking about this in three primary senses. First, the crimes to which the concept relates (genocide, war crimes, ethnic cleansing and crimes against humanity) are crimes that have already been agreed by states and enumerated in international humanitarian and human rights law.

Second, under customary international law, states already have obligations to prevent and punish genocide, war crimes and crimes against humanity; assist others to fulfill their obligations under International Humanitarian Law; and promote compliance with the law.

Third, the mechanisms through which the RtoP can be implemented are consistent with existing international law. Paragraphs 138 and 139 of the World Summit Outcome Document identify four principal ways in which RtoP can be implemented, each of which is consistent with existing international law: (a) the primary responsibility rests with the State itself. This is the cornerstone of sovereignty; (b) the international community may provide assistance, such as capacity-building and mediation. Such assistance may only be provided at the request and with the express consent of the state concerned and is consistent with the state's sovereign right to make bilateral and multilateral agreements; (c) the UN Security Council might take measures in a manner consistent with Chapters VI ,VII and VIII of the UN Charter, the General Assembly might make recommendations on the basis of Article 11 of the Charter, and other Organs of the UN might act in accordance with the Charter; (d) paragraph 139 of the World Summit Outcome Document explicitly envisages a role for regional arrangements. Such roles must, of course, be consistent with the charters, constitutions or guiding principles of the regional arrangement concerned and with the UN Charter. Any other mechanisms that may be called upon in relation to the implementation of the RtoP (such as, for instance, the International Criminal Court) are guided by their own constitutions and statutes which are voluntarily accepted by participating states and their scope and jurisdiction are limited by these agreements and general principles of international law. Although it did not start out this way, the RtoP agreed in 2005 is consistent with the principle of non-interference enumerated in the UN Charter (Article 2(7)). Article 2(7) states that: 'Nothing contained in the present Charter shall authorize the United Nations to intervene in matters which are essentially within the domestic jurisdiction of any state or shall require the Members to submit such matters to settlement under the present Charter; but this principle shall not prejudice the application of enforcement measures under Chapter Vll'. Where states have voluntarily entered into specific international legal obligations, matters relating to those obligations cease to be 'essentially within the domestic jurisdiction of any state'. For example, the UN Human Rights Council (formerly Commission) is authorized through the mechanism set out in Article 68 of the UN Charter. Through their voluntary membership of the UN, states accept that the Economic and Social Council (ECOSOC) has the right to make such provisions for the promotion of human rights. As such, the Human Rights Council's work cannot be considered a breach of Article 2(7) because the matter has ceased to be 'essentially within the domestic jurisdiction' of the state owing to its membership of the UN and accession to the Charter. The same applies to regional bodies to which states voluntarily accede. Of course, such bodies must act only in strict accordance with the provisions of the charters, statutes, treaties or guidelines to which states have voluntarily acceded. Article 2(7) also affirms that the principle of non-interference 'shall not prejudice' the application of enforcement measures by the UN Security Council acting under Chapter VII of the Charter. All of this serves to reinforce the Secretary-General's argument that 'the responsibility to protect does not alter, indeed it reinforces, the legal obligations of Member States to refrain from the use of force except in conformity with the Charter'.[36]

Having demonstrated that RtoP is based on existing law, the Secretary-General went on to forensically examine the 2005 agreement as the basis for his roadmap for implementing the principle. From this, he derived several key insights. Perhaps most important in terms of the principle's conceptual development was the idea that RtoP comprises three pillars. These pillars are non-sequential (one does not need to apply pillars one and two before moving to pillar three) and of equal importance, such that the whole edifice of RtoP would collapse if it were not supported by all three pillars.[37] The three pillars, which will be examined in more detail below, are:

- *Pillar one*: the responsibility of the state to protect its population from genocide, war crimes, ethnic cleansing and crimes against humanity, and from their incitement.[38] This pillar, the Secretary-General described as the 'bedrock' of the RtoP and, in addition to the specific commitments to RtoP, derives from the nature of sovereignty itself and the pre-existing legal obligations of states.[39]
- *Pillar two*: the international community's responsibility to assist the state to fulfill its responsibility to protect, particularly by helping them to tackle

the causes of genocide and mass atrocities, build the capacity to prevent these crimes, and address problems before they escalate in the commission of the crimes.[40]

- *Pillar three*: in situations where a state has manifestly failed to protect its population from the four crimes, the international community's responsibility to take timely and decisive action through peaceful diplomatic and humanitarian means and, if that proves inadequate, other more forceful means in a manner consistent with Chapters VI (pacific measures), VII (enforcement measures) and VIII (regional arrangements) of the UN Charter (para. 139).[41]

In addition, the Secretary-General argued that RtoP 'is an ally of sovereignty, not an adversary', that grows from the principle of sovereignty as responsibility (see Chapter 1) rather than through the doctrine of humanitarian intervention.[42] As such, RtoP focuses on helping states to succeed (pillar two), not just on reacting when they fail (some aspects of pillar three). Furthermore, he found that until member states decide otherwise, the RtoP applies only to genocide, war crimes, ethnic cleansing and crimes against humanity and to their prevention. Expanding the principle to include natural disasters or climate change would undermine consensus and damage the principle's operational utility. As we noted earlier, the Secretary-General also argued that while RtoP's scope should be kept narrow, its implementation ought to be deep, employing all the prevention and protection instruments available to states, regional organizations and the UN system. Finally, Ban Ki-moon made a point of noting that the 2005 agreement contained a specific commitment to strengthen the UN's capacity for early warning.[43]

Having mapped out this legal, conceptual and political terrain, the Secretary-General proceeded to identify a raft of measures for implementing each of the three pillars, drawing on examples of best practices from member states and regional organisations, related work that was already underway within the UN system, and suggestions from states and civil society alike. So as to avoid the appearance that the Secretary-General was telling states what they should do, these proposals were advanced not as a comprehensive framework for implementing the RtoP, but rather as a guide to direct member states in their deliberations about implementation. The report highlighted many of its main recommendations and it is worth setting them out to give us a good flavour of what the emerging implementation agenda looks like.

Pillar one

Pillar one, we noted earlier, refers to the primary responsibility of the state to protect its own population from the four crimes. It is set out unambiguously at the beginning of paragraph 138 of the World Summit Outcome Agreement, in which states agreed that '[e]ach individual State has the responsibility to protect its population from genocide, war crimes, ethnic cleansing and crimes against humanity', including their prevention, and pledged to 'accept that responsibility' and 'act in accordance with it'. The Secretary-General recognized that although this commitment was unambiguous, the question of how states might best exercise their RtoP was more difficult to answer, particularly given the potential for multiple pathways to the same goal. As such, he called for more research on why some societies plunge into mass violence while their neighbours managed to escape this fate and for state-to-state and region-to-region learning processes to generate and share good ideas about pathways to prevention.[44] In addition, the Secretary-General proposed the following measures to implement pillar one:

- The UN Human Rights Council could be used to encourage states to meet their RtoP obligations and the Council's Universal Peer Review (UPR) mechanism could be utilized to monitor their performance.[45]
- States should become parties to the relevant instruments of human rights law, international humanitarian law and refugee law, as well as to the Rome Statute of the International Criminal Court (ICC). They should also incorporate this law into domestic jurisdiction and implement it faithfully.[46]
- In addition to acceding to the Rome Statute, states should also do more to assist the ICC and other international tribunals by, for example, locating and apprehending indictees.[47]
- RtoP principles should be localized into each culture and society so that they are owned and acted upon by communities and not seen as external impositions.[48]
- States, even stable ones, should ensure that they have mechanisms in place to deal with bigotry, intolerance, racism and exclusion.[49]

Pillar two

The second pillar, which relates to the international community's duty to assist states to fulfil their RtoP, is enumerated in both paragraph 138 (asserting that 'the international community should, as appropriate, encourage and help States, to exercise this responsibility') and 139 ('we also intend to commit ourselves, as necessary and appropriate, to helping States build capacity to protect their populations'). The Secretary-General identified four specific elements of this responsibility to assist: (1) encouraging states to meet their pillar one responsibilities (para. 138); (2) helping them to exercise this responsibility (para. 138); (3) helping them to build their capacity to protect (para. 139); and (4) assisting states 'under stress before crises and conflicts break out' (para. 139).[50] These measures should be taken with the consent and cooperation of the host state. The Secretary-General recognized that, of course, this meant that if a state was pursuing a deliberate strategy of genocide and mass atrocities, there would be little that pillar two could do. In these circumstances, pillar three would immediately come into play.[51] In terms of specific measures, the report recommended:

- *Encouraging states to meet their pillar one responsibilities:*
  - Those inciting or planning to commit the four crimes need to be made aware that they will be held to account.[52]
  - Incentives should be offered to encourage parties towards reconciliation.[53]

- *Helping them to exercise this responsibility:*
  - Security sector reform aimed at building and sustaining legitimate and effective security forces makes an important contribution to maintaining stability and provides states with the capacity to respond quickly and legitimately to emerging problems.[54]

- *Helping them to build their capacity to protect:*
  - Targeted economic development assistance would assist in preventing the four crimes by reducing inequalities, improving education, giving the poor a stronger voice, and increasing political participation.[55]
  - International assistance should help states and societies to build the specific capacities they need prevent genocide and mass atrocities.[56]

- *Assisting states 'under stress before crises and conflicts break out':*
  - The UN and regional and subregional organizations could build rapidly deployable civilian and police capacities to help countries under stress.[57]
  - Where the four crimes are committed by non-state actors, international military assistance to the state may be the most effective form of assistance.[58]

Pillar three

By far the most controversial element of RtoP is its *pillar three,* which refers to the international community's responsibility to respond in a timely and decisive fashion to episodes of genocide and mass atrocities. According to the Secretary-General, the wording agreed by states in 2005 suggests that pillar three comprises two steps. The first, set out in the opening sentence of paragraph 139 ('the international community, through the United Nations, also has the responsibility to use appropriate diplomatic, humanitarian and other peaceful means, in accordance with Chapters VI and VIII of the Charter, to help protect populations' from the four crimes), involves an on-going responsibility to use peaceful means to protect populations. The paragraph's second sentence sets out a wider range of peaceful and non-peaceful measures that may be used if two conditions are satisfied: (1) 'should peaceful means be inadequate' and (2) 'national authorities are manifestly failing to protect their populations'. In these cases, states agreed that it may be appropriate to take timely and decisive action through the Security Council, including enforcement measures under Chapter VII of the Charter.[59] The Secretary-General noted that military intervention was just one such measure that the Council may use in such circumstances and it is important to underscore that the application of coercive measures under pillar three is under the authority of the Security Council and UN Charter. Indeed, he outlined a range of measures that states might use to exercise this third pillar:

- The Security Council might use targeted sanctions on travel, financial transfers, and luxury goods, and arms embargoes. In such cases, it is incumbent on the Security Council, relevant regional organisations and individual states to develop the expertise, capacity and political will necessary to properly implement these regimes.[61]
- The permanent members of the Security Council should refrain from using their veto in situations of manifest failure and should act in good faith to reach a consensus on exercising the Council's responsibility in such cases.
- Member states may want to consider developing principles, rules and doctrine to guide the use of force for humanitarian purposes.[62]
- The UN should strengthen its capacity for the rapid deployment of military personnel, including by developing doctrine and training and resolving command and control issues.[63]
- The UN should strengthen its partnerships with regional organisations to facilitate rapid cooperation.[64]

Finally, as we noted earlier, the Secretary-General reiterated his call for the establishment of a joint office for the prevention of genocide and RtoP, arguing that this would help fulfil the specific pledge, made in 2005, to strengthen the UN's capacity for early warning.[65] The significance of this office goes well beyond early warning capacity, however. Its effect would be to give RtoP an institutional home within the UN, allowing the Secretary-General to develop and strengthen the implementation agenda by providing a capacity to generate specific proposals related to implementation and providing a focal point for 'normalising' RtoP across the UN system.[66] Without this focal point, implementation of the Secretary-General's ambitious agenda would be very difficult, if not impossible, to achieve because institutional inertia would give sceptics the cover they needed to kill off RtoP as a practical agenda without ever actually opposing the principle itself.

The report was well received by states, as the ensuing debate in the General Assembly attests. But it received mixed assessments from commentators, especially from some of RtoP's friends. In one of the most strident and widely-publicized critiques, Ramesh Thakur raised three principal concerns that echoed those raised elsewhere. First, he argued that it was untrue to argue that the three pillars were of equal strength and weight. In contrast, he maintained that 'the most important element – the weightiest pillar – has to be the states own responsibility. And the most critical is the international community's response to fresh outbreaks of mass atrocity crimes'. Although it is far from clear how being 'most important' (pillar one) is different from being 'most critical' (pillar three), Thakur was clear in his argument that pillar two was the least important of the three. Second, Thakur complained that the report diluted 'the central defining feature of RtoP' – 'the problem of brutal leaders killing large numbers of their own people'. According to Thakur, 'RtoP's added value is that it crystallized an emerging new norm of using international force to prevent and halt mass killings by reconceptualizing sovereignty as responsibility. It aims to convert a shocked international conscience into timely and decisive collective action'. While capacity building (pillars one and two) is meritorious in itself, he argued, it dilutes this added value. Jennifer Welsh offered a similar critique, suggesting that the report's focus on capacity-building may have been a prudent strategy for securing buy-in from reluctant states, but came at the cost of overlooking questions about how resources will be mobilized to protect vulnerable populations when more peaceful means have failed.[67] What is more, Welsh argued, while the Secretary-General clearly favoured prevention over reaction because he believed it more likely to forge a global consensus around the former, many states are also likely to baulk at preventive measures that interfere in their domestic affairs.[68] Such concerns have already weakened the UN's Peacebuilding Commission and have, historically, made it very difficult to mobilize resources for conflict prevention.[69] Finally, Thakur argued that the report ignored many of the key questions that required urgent clarification, such as: when RtoP should be activated as an international responsibility; 'who makes these decisions'; 'and on what basis'? Other key questions left unanswered, Thakur argued, were: Do RtoP operations require their own distinctive guidelines on the use of force? How and where can we institute systematic risk assessments and early warning indicators to alert us to developing RtoP-type crises? How do we build international capacity to deliver RtoP? 'On these key issues', Thakur lamented, 'we are no further ahead today', concluding that 'we seem to be recreating the 2005 consensus instead of operationalizing and implementing the agreed collective responsibility'.[70] These three criticisms ably capture concerns expressed by advocates and critics alike, so it is worth assessing them in some detail.[71]

The first argument, that pillar two is less consequential than the others, seems out of step with both contemporary practice on the protection of civilians and what states agreed in 2005. In the past decade, the UN and regional organizations have deployed numerous missions tasked with the protection of civilians from RtoP-related crimes. These include: MONUC/MONUSCO and *Operation Artemis* in the DRC, UNMIS and UNAMID in Sudan; UNMIL in Liberia; UNOCI in Cote d'Ivoire; RAMSI in the Solomon Islands; and UNMIT in Timor-Leste.[72] Though many of these operations were authorized under Chapter VII of the UN Charter, *all* were dependent on the consent of the host state and *all* required that peacekeepers *assist* the state in building the capacities and reinforcing the behaviours needed to protect populations into the future. Indeed, it is this building of state capacity and shaping of behaviours that is pivotal to the missions' exit strategy. Although the lines between pillars two and three are unclear, none of these missions involve the second step of pillar three (coercive measures) and all contain significant (if not predominant) pillar two components. What is more, the only case to date where there is consensus that RtoP added value to a protection crisis – the situation in post-election Kenya (see Chapter 3) – fits pillar two better than pillar three, because RtoP was mainly used to encourage political leaders to meet their pillar one responsibilities, which is one of the four main components of pillar two identified by the Secretary-General. Given that the coercive element of RtoP's third pillar has yet to be used to protect populations, and measures related to pillar two have been used often and with good effect, it would be fair to conclude that the Secretary-General's characterization of the three pillars as of equal strength and importance is more accurate than the suggestion that pillar two is less important. In addition, there is nothing in the World Summit agreement to suggest that member states believed the third pillar to be more important than the second.

What of the second argument, that the report diluted the defining feature of RtoP – its framework for responding to situations where states commit atrocities against their own population? It is of course correct that it was this concern that animated the ICISS – despite the commission's hollow protestation that prevention (not intervention) was the most important element of RtoP.[73] But it was states in 2005, and not the Secretary-General in 2009, that changed the focus and balanced questions about forcefully responding to genocide and mass atrocities with their longer-term prevention. Paragraphs 138 and 139 of the 2005 agreement contained seven sentences. Of these, only one sentence referred to measures undertaken to respond to episodes of genocide and mass atrocities through Chapter VII by the UN Security Council and that sentence included important caveats. Five of the remaining six sentences set out pillar one and two responsibilities (the sixth pledged the General Assembly to continue its consideration). Moreover, whether advocates like it or not, states made a specific commitment to capacity building as part of their endorsement of RtoP. In short, therefore, member states clearly paid less attention to pillar three than they did to pillars one and two, and their commitment to pillar three came with caveats the likes of which were absent from pillars one and two. If the focus of RtoP has shifted from the ICISS formulation that was primarily about intervention – and I agree that it has – it was the process of negotiating RtoP among states, and not the Secretary-General that was responsible. The Secretary-General's report was entirely faithful to the spirit, focus and intentions behind the World Summit agreement, as most participants in the 2009 General Assembly debate acknowledged. The difference between the critics and the Secretary-General, therefore, is the difference between what the critics would like RtoP to mean, and what states have actually agreed to. I share the Secretary-General's view that more lives are likely to be saved by implementing what states have already agreed to than by reopening international debate about the meaning and scope of RtoP.

This brings us to the third critique – that the report did not advance the most pressing questions related to RtoP. The first thing we should say in relation to this is that the Secretary-General was clear in arguing that it is for member states to decide how to implement RtoP and many of the questions posed by the critics can only be addressed through further deliberation by states. To argue otherwise would risk RtoP's legitimacy and open a gap between promise and actuality – a common feature of UN practice in the past but something that goes against the grain for the current Secretary-General. Having said that, it is important to note for the record that the report did, in fact, address most of the issues that the critics raised. For example, on whether RtoP operations require their own distinctive guidelines on the use of force, there is nothing in the 2005 agreement to suggest that this is an integral part of RtoP as agreed by states but nonetheless the Secretary-General argued that states may want to consider principles, rules and doctrines to guide the application of force for RtoP purposes (para. 61); on how and where we can institute risk assessments and early warning indicators to alert us to developing RtoP-type crises, the Secretary-General outlined a detailed plan for establishing an early warning capability (annex), the Special Adviser for the Prevention of Genocide has already developed indicators, and the report noted a range of ways in which the Secretary-General can bring matters to the attention of the membership and act without specific authorization (paras. 11(c), 30, 51, 53 and 61); and on how to build international capacity to deliver on RtoP, the report's responses were too numerous to catalogue but many have already been spelled out above. Given all this, it is hard to see the basis for the claim that the report leaves crucial questions unanswered.

The Secretary-General's report largely succeeded in articulating a new way of conceptualizing RtoP (in terms of three pillars) and presenting a broad based policy agenda for its implementation. Its 'narrow but deep' approach connected RtoP to a range of other policy agendas (such as human rights, state capacity, economic development, and the protection of civilians), therefore increasing buy-in from member states, while also demonstrating how these various components comprise a comprehensive system for preventing, and responding to, genocide and mass atrocities. In my view, there can be little doubt that were the Secretary-General's recommendations implemented, there would be a marked reduction in the incidence of genocide and mass atrocities and an equally marked improvement in the world's responses. But it is one thing to present a blueprint and quite another to persuade member states to accept it and commit resources to implementing it. The first step in the effort to do just that was the July 2009 General Assembly debate.

The 2009 General Assembly debate

While Luck privately expressed cautious optimism that a consensus could be reached, a view supported by analysis showing that governments in the Asia-Pacific region, long thought the region most resistant to RtoP, were quite open to the principle and endorsed the Secretary-General's approach, many advocates of RtoP expressed caution about the Secretary-General's approach, fearing that a General Assembly debate could 'provide the opportunity for skeptical governments to renegotiate the norm'.[74] Both prior to and immediately after the debate, it was some of RtoP's self-professed supporters who expressed the most serious reservations about moving towards a General Assembly resolution, fearing that it might add caveats to the 2005 agreement.[75] Indeed, the Global Centre for RtoP suggested that a resolution was not an essential outcome for the debate.[76] Immediately after the debate, several 'friends' of RtoP, particularly European states, argued against moving for a resolution taking note of the Secretary-General's report on the grounds that it could weaken the principle. Thankfully, Guatemala pressed ahead anyway to secure a resolution that creates a mandate for ongoing work on RtoP within the UN system.

The President of the General Assembly (PGA), Father Miguel d'Escoto Brockmann, a former *Sandanista* from Nicaragua did his best to persuade the General Assembly to adopt a critical stance on RtoP and resist making a commitment to implement the principle. In particular, the PGA tried to block consensus on RtoP by: (1) holding off placing RtoP on the agenda for as long possible to give states little time to prepare; (2) failing to cooperate with the Secretariat on the timing of the debate to ensure that the Secretary-General could participate; (3) timing the debate to coincide with an international trip by the Secretary-General and a vacation period when it was thought likely that many permanent missions would be unstaffed, thereby limiting the number of speakers; (4) withholding information about the debate to prevent small and middle powers from participating; (5) appointing one of the most outspoken critics of RtoP, former Indian permanent representative Nirupem Sen, as his special adviser on RtoP; (6) issuing a highly critical concept paper (probably drafted by Sen) which argued that 'colonialism and interventionism used responsibility to protect arguments' and cast doubt on the utility of an early warning capability; and (7) organizing an interactive informal dialogue on RtoP to which he invited two outspoken Western critics of the principle, Noam Chomsky and Jean Bricmont.

These efforts failed and the 2009 General Assembly debate vindicated Luck's cautious optimism, revealing a broad consensus around the approach adopted by the Secretary-General.[77] Ninety-four speakers, representing some 180 governments (including the Non-Aligned Movement) from every region participated in the debate.[78] Of those, only four (Cuba, Venezuela, Sudan and Nicaragua) called for the renegotiation of the 2005 agreement. From the remaining 90 speakers, important points of consensus can be discerned. In particular, the General Assembly agreed with the Secretary-General's inter-pretation of the principle's fundamental elements. They welcomed the Secretary-General's report, noted that the 2005 World Summit represented the international consensus on RtoP and agreed that there was no need to renegotiate that text. The challenge, the General Assembly agreed, was to implement RtoP, *not* renegotiate it – a significant step forward from the position aired by several states just two years earlier. The overwhelming majority also indicated their support for the three pillars and the 'narrow but deep' approach identified by the Secretary-General. Within this context, governments in Asia, Latin America and sub-Saharan Africa were eager to stress six key points about the nature and scope of the RtoP as they understand it. First, *the RtoP is a universal principle that should be applied equally and fairly in a non-selective fashion* – though there was some recognition that decisions about implementation should be taken on a case-by-case basis and that inconsistency should not be a barrier to collective action in response to genocide and mass atrocities.[80] Second, *the RtoP lies first and foremost with the state*. The principle should be understood as an ally of sovereignty (as suggested by the UN Secretary-General).[81] Third, *the RtoP applies only to the four specified crimes and their prevention* and not to other non-traditional security issues such as natural disasters. Attempts to widen the scope of the RtoP, they agreed, would damage efforts to implement the principle. Fourth, *the RtoP must be implemented and exercised in a manner consistent with international law and the UN Charter*. The Non-Aligned Movement in particular stressed that the RtoP must not be used to legitimize unilateral coercive interference in the domestic affairs of states and many others agreed that the principle was embedded in existing international law.[82] Fifth, *measures related to RtoP's third pillar include more than simply coercion or the use of force*. Emphasis, non-Western governments agreed, should be placed on peaceful measures under Chapters VI and VIII of the UN Charter. Finally, *prevention is the most important element of the RtoP*. States uniformly agreed that RtoP's focus should be on preventing genocide and mass atrocities, a point which won support from the few remaining sceptics (e.g. Pakistan and Venezuela).[83] In addition to these substantive points – which reflect basic agreement with the core foundations of the RtoP – many states also voiced their commitment to the General Assembly continuing its consideration of the RtoP. The Philippines, for example, called for the General Assembly to play an 'active and substantive role' in implementing the principle.[84]

The debate also helped identify several areas of concern which are worth setting out in some detail as they represent a work agenda for the future. With that in mind, the second part of this book will examine the first four issues in more detail.

1 Early warning

As we noted earlier, the UN Secretary-General called for the General Assembly to support the strengthening of the UN's capacity for early warning and analysis of impending episodes of genocide and mass atrocities through the establishment of a small joint office for the Special Representative for the Prevention of Genocide and the Special Adviser for the RtoP. Although similar proposals have been presented and rejected before, this time most governments, including several from the global south, lent their support to the idea. However, there remained some important concerns about the operationalization of early warning within the UN system. China, for example, called for further deliberation in the General Assembly and Security Council about the need to create an early warning mechanism and noted that if such a mechanism was thought necessary, it should be predicated on some core principles agreed in advance by the General Assembly. Other governments raised similar concerns about the types and sources of information that the mechanism would use, the transparency and fairness of its assessment procedures, the need for safeguards against politicization, and the mechanism's relationship with regional and sub-regional arrangements and local actors.

2 Role of regional arrangements

The 2005 World Summit agreement included some specific, and some implied, pledges in terms of engaging regional and sub-regional arrangements in the implementation of the RtoP. Since 2005, many governments and civil society actors have called for a stronger focus on regional arrangements. However, relatively little progress has been made on defining what sort of role they should play. Once again, at the 2009 General Assembly debate, governments reiterated the importance of engaging regional arrangements. This time, however, several governments identified specific areas of work for regional arrangements, including: (1) regional arrangements might establish peer review mechanisms to assist states (with their cooperation) in identifying and implementing their pillar one responsibilities; (2) with assistance from the UN, regional arrangements could provide assistance and support for national capacity-building; (3) regional arrangements could develop civilian capacities to assist states under stress when such assistance is requested; (4) regional arrangements could develop regional standby forces that are rapidly deployable in response to episodes of genocide and mass atrocities; (5) regional arrangements could work with the UN on strengthening early warning and assessment; and (6) regional arrangements could provide a useful vehicle for region-to-region learning about the practices and capacities needed to implement the RtoP and for deepening regional partnership with the UN. Although these proposals were put forward by too few states to constitute a consensus about the appropriate role of regional arrangements, they mark a useful starting point for more detailed thinking (see Chapter 7).

3 The role of UN bodies

Several governments called for clarification of the roles of the UN secretariat, funds and programmes, and principal organs – especially the UN Security Council. In relation to the secretariat, funds and programmes, some called for the normalization of the RtoP across the UN system, including its work in humanitarian affairs, peacekeeping, peacebuilding and governance. South Korea went one step further and endorsed a proposal that the Secretary-General be invited to give biennial implementation reports to the General Assembly. This would effectively give the Secretary-General a mandate to normalize the RtoP within the UN system while also providing a mechanism for the Assembly to exercise oversight.

Although a few states (Venezuela and Sudan) argued that the General Assembly should exercise jurisdiction over every aspect of RtoP, by far the most controversial question related to the role of the Security Council and the use of force. Several governments (e.g. Pakistan, Cuba, Sri Lanka) expressed concern about the potential for RtoP to legitimize unwarranted coercive interference in the domestic affairs of states. In general, concerns about the role of the Security Council coalesced around three central questions: (1) the nature of the Council's responsibility; (2) its procedures for determining what action to take in response to emergencies characterized by the commission of the four crimes associated with the RtoP; and (3) reform of the Council's membership.

In relation to the first, several governments argued that the Security Council had special responsibilities under RtoP and that it should exercise these responsibilities in a non-selective fashion. Thirty-five governments argued that the Council's permanent members should refrain from using their veto when a state is manifestly failing to protect its population from the four crimes. Singapore took this logic a step further and stressed that when the Security Council failed to act in a timely and decisive manner, it should become incumbent upon the General Assembly to take such measures it deemed necessary and appropriate for the fulfilment of the RtoP. The second key question revolved around the Council's procedures – particularly in relation to the use of force. There was some support for the view that the Council should articulate policies, principles and rules to guide decisions about when coercive force is needed but the general tenor of attitudes in the global south was that these should be aimed at *limiting* the Council's room for manoeuvre. In particular, China argued that it was important to stress that the Council is entrusted with the protection of 'international peace and security' and should only act when there is a breach of the (international) peace, a threat to the peace or an act of aggression. Situations that did not pass this test should not, in China's view, come before the Council. Finally, a handful of governments argued that the Security Council's membership should be expanded to make it more representative and therefore legitimate – with some (e.g. Jamaica on behalf of CARICOM) arguing that this should be a precondition for full implementation of RtoP.

4 The relationship between RtoP, economic development and capacity building

Many Western advocates of the RtoP continue to resist the idea that there is a connection between the RtoP and economic development. The International Coalition of NGOs, for instance, described as 'unhelpful' calls by governments for RtoP to address the root causes of genocide and mass atrocities such as poverty and economic inequality, despite the fact that the Secretary-General's report had itself recognized a role for economic development.[85] As I will demonstrate in Chapter 5, there is strong evidence to support the view that poverty, economic inequality and severe economic downturns are associated with increased likelihood of genocide and mass atrocities. This point was underscored by many governments from the global south and even a few from the global north. It is clear, though, that much more work is needed to understand the precise contours of the relationship between the RtoP, the prevention of genocide and mass atrocities, and economic development and to develop a tangible strategy to address this issue. In terms of what can be done, some member states noted that multilateral development institutions are well placed to assist states with pillars one and two, called for the allocation of development resources to assist with capacity building, and targeted assistance to improve education in remote and disadvantaged regions.

Of course, this is a long way from a cohesive agenda or even a substantive list of issues for further inquiry but it is important for now to note the view that there is a relationship and that it requires further elaboration. That elaboration needs, however, to heed the note of caution issued by Malaysia that there is a danger that the redirection of aid for RtoP-related capacity building purposes might create further aid conditionalities and the concern raised by the Philippines that RtoP might draw resources away from economic development.

Closely connected to the issue of economic development is the place of capacity-building. The Secretary-General's view that capacity-building is the heart of the RtoP secured broad agreement from the General Assembly. Put simply, this view holds that, first and foremost, the RtoP is about the prevention of genocide and mass atrocities and that the best path to prevention is building the capacity of states and societies. Capacity-building is one element of economic development but it is seen as absolutely pivotal to the RtoP. Of course, capacity-building will need to be tailored for each country's specific situation and so it is unlikely that an overarching blueprint could be developed or that one would be appropriate. Governments (such as UK and Tanzania) voiced their agreement with the proposition that national capacity-building is a central part of the RtoP but raised two important questions about its application: (1) the appropriate *scope* of RtoP capacity-building; and (2) the appropriate *mode of delivery*.

In relation to the scope of capacity-building, several governments from the global north and south made useful suggestions about the most appropriate areas, including: good governance and institution building, rule of law and support for the judicial sector, peacebuilding, conflict prevention – especially the building of civilian capacity to prevent the four RtoP crimes, strengthening civil society, mediation, and peacekeeping. Of these, there was most consensus around measures to build prevention capacity and strengthen the rule of law. Significantly, Japan – the UN's second largest donor – cautioned against an expansive approach to capacity-building, arguing that this could overstretch the RtoP's second pillar. Instead, Japan called for a narrower focus on the rule of law, security sector reform and the protection of human rights.

The second question related to capacity-building referred to its modalities. A handful of governments called for the General Assembly to develop a clear strategy aimed at strengthening capacity-building programmes, and argued that the UN should be given more resources in this area to ensure proper delivery and that capacity-building does not draw resources away from other programs. As noted earlier, regional arrangements clearly have a role to play as well and several states agreed that it was important that the UN provide tangible and practical assistance to regional arrangements to help them build capacity and assist states. Finally, there was broad agreement that, as with all pillar two activities, capacity-building assistance should only be undertaken with the consent and cooperation of the state involved.

Although pillar three has, to date, proven most controversial and states in the global south especially stress that the RtoP lies first and foremost with the state (pillar one), in practice states – sceptics and supporters alike – have proven more reluctant to articulate their own protection obligations and pathways to fulfilling those obligations than they have been to debate pillars two and three. This pattern was evident in the 2009 General Assembly debate, where states reaffirmed the primacy of pillar one but generally shied away from commenting on how they planned to exercise this responsibility. A useful place to start might be to catalogue what states are already doing that contributes towards their pillar one responsibilities and then to engage in comparative analysis, and state-to-state and region-to-region learning processes. Helpfully, South Korea articulated a number of proposals for further consideration, including: (1) establishment of mechanisms for the periodic review of pillar one implementation, possibly under the auspices of the UN Human Rights Council's universal periodic review process; (2) ensure effective mechanisms for handling domestic disputes (clearly related to capacity-building); (3) accession to relevant instruments on human rights law, international humanitarian law, refugee law and the International Criminal Court as called for by the Secretary-General.

After some heated debate among RtoP's group of friends, Ambassador Gert Rosenthal of Guatemala led an effort to secure a General Assembly resolution. Rosenthal argued that a resolution was important as a basis for future dialogue within the General Assembly and a clear sign that the small group of sceptics (especially Venezuela, Cuba, Syria, Sudan, Iran, Ecuador and Nicaragua) could not derail the process.[86] Although these sceptics mobilized to tone down the resolution's endorsement of the Secretary-General's report, the resolution acknowledged the report, noted that the Assembly had engaged in a productive debate, and formally decided that the General Assembly would continue its consideration of the matter.[87] Besides committing General Assembly to further discussion about implementing the RtoP, the resolution also lends substantial political support for the Secretary-General's proposal for the establishment of a joint office for RtoP and the prevention of genocide, though it remains to be seen whether this will be sufficient to overcome the many potential political and bureaucratic roadblocks.

It is here that caution is warranted. Although the debate helped identify a broader and deeper consensus about RtoP than thought possible in the immediate aftermath of the 2005 World Summit, it also exposed a number of critical concerns and a small group of determined opponents. In relation to the former, concerns were expressed about the modalities and need for an early warning capacity, the respective roles of the Security Council and General Assembly, the reform of the Security Council, the scope, nature and mode of capacity-building, the potential for RtoP to legitimize coercive interference, the lack of clarity as to the triggers for armed intervention, and the potential for RtoP to draw resources away from other UN programs without adding additional value.[88] In relation to the latter, while states are obviously reluctant to voice public opposition to a principle promising to prevent genocide and mass atrocities, there is a good chance that sceptics could mobilize to suffocate the principle through institutional inertia. States could do this simply by pointing to the UN's perennial budget crisis and competing priorities in areas such as development in order to starve RtoP of funds. This would reduce the Secretary-General's capacity to bring forward proposals, consult with member states, and hold the General Assembly to its commitments.

Conclusion

These concerns notwithstanding, it is fair to conclude from this survey that the Secretary-General succeeded in stemming the tide of the post-2005 revolt against RtoP, in presenting an account of RtoP that commands a high degree of global consensus, and articulating a manifesto for implementing the principle complete with a first tangible, albeit modest, step – the establishment of a joint office for RtoP and the prevention of genocide. Though this may look like a small dividend on what was agreed in 2005, if we acknowledge the state of play when Ban Ki-moon took office in early 2007 the rate of progress has been rapid and impressive. Through the efforts of the Secretary-General and his Special Adviser, consensus has been built, the General Assembly engaged and a plan for implementation laid out. The vision of RtoP that is emerging from this is significantly different to that envisaged by ICISS, but entirely consistent with what states agreed in 2005. More importantly, if implemented this agenda would almost certainly help prevent genocide and mass atrocities and strengthen the international community's response. The precise contours of what needs to be done and the challenges that stand in the way are outlined in the second part of the book which examines four of the most critical issues raised in the 2009 debate: the relationship between RtoP and economic development, early warning, the Security Council and the use of force, and the role of regional arrangements in implementing RtoP. Before we get to this, however, the following chapter tells the parallel story of RtoP and major international crises since 2005.

3 Humanitarian crises since 2005

Getting agreement on an abstract principle is one thing, translating that agreement into actionable policy that adds value to local, regional and global efforts to prevent genocide and mass atrocities and protect the victims is quite another. Therefore, while it is important to understand the politics behind the RtoP principle, we also need to know about how RtoP is used in practice and what (if any) effects it has had on behaviour. Running alongside the General Assembly's consideration of RtoP, the principle has been used by a variety of different actors in relation to more than a dozen humanitarian crises and cases of acute human rights abuse. Ranging from post-election violence in Kenya, where RtoP was employed by Kofi Annan as part of a diplomatic strategy, to the Russian invasion of Georgia, where the principle was invoked to support unilateral armed intervention, the RtoP has been inconsistently and selectively applied by a wide range of different actors to an equally diverse variety of situations. This chapter briefly identifies the different ways in which RtoP has been used – or not – in relation to humanitarian crises since 2005. In relation to crises in Darfur, Kenya, Georgia, Myanmar/Cyclone Nargis, Gaza, Sri Lanka, the Democratic Republic of Congo (DRC), and Guinea, RtoP has formed part of the debate about how the international community should respond to imminent or actual episodes of genocide and mass atrocities. In relation to a second set of crises, notably south Sudan, Somalia, Afghanistan and Iraq, RtoP has not been invoked or debated despite the commission of atrocities. This is despite the fact that in terms of the number of civilians killed, since 2005 Iraq, Afghanistan and Somalia have been the world's bloodiest countries. In relation to a third set of protracted crises, North Korea and Myanmar, RtoP has been invoked by civil society actors to summon international attention to protracted human rights crises, though with little effect. Covering each type in turn, this chapter examines RtoP's record in practice.

RtoP in action

DRC (1997-ongoing)

The civil war in the DRC had its origins in the Rwandan genocide, involved seven governments and claimed the lives of over 2 million people before a peace settlement was concluded in 2003, which prompted the deployment of the MONUC peace operation.[1] Since then there have been recurrent outbreaks of violence in the country's east targeting mainly civilians and sexual violence against women and girls remains widespread throughout the country. The DRC case is distinctive inasmuch as while there is broad agreement about the applicability of RtoP to this case, there is some division over the appropriateness of viewing the situation through the prism of the principle. On the one hand, some UN officials have used RtoP as a prism to guide their priorities and policies. For example, the Special Representative of the Secretary-General for the DRC, Alain Doss, told the Security Council in 2008 that 'we are doing our utmost to translate the principle of 'responsibility to protect' into 'responsible protection' which means an enhanced, and mobile, military and police presence on the ground'.[2] On the other hand, however, while MONUC was mandated to protect civilians (MONUC was replaced with MONUSCO in 2010), the Security Council has not specifically referred to RtoP in its resolutions on the DRC. And neither is there much evidence to suggest that RtoP played a role in encouraging the Council to expand its engagement with the crisis. MONUC was initially deployed with a civilian protection mandate in 2000, but with only around 3,000 troops it proved incapable of effectively carrying out its mandate. In 2003, the mission was saved from collapse in eastern DRC by a French-led intervention (*Operation Artemis*) and subsequently reinforced (up to a total strength of around 18,000) the following year under a new and more robust mandate. Under this mandate, peacekeepers have tried to neutralize threats to civilians, including by forcibly disarming armed groups (especially the FDLR, which has links to the Rwandan *genocidaires*), with varying levels of success. In 2008, the Security Council authorized the designation of an additional reserve of 3,000 troops but this was slow to materialize. It is important for us to note in all of this that MONUC's expansion, its robust protection mandate, and assistance from Europe all *predated* the RtoP and that RtoP has not generated additional support for the mission since 2005 despite its well-recorded shortcomings.[3]

Darfur (2003-ongoing)

The crisis in Darfur, which erupted in 2003 and saw Sudanese government backed *janjaweed* militia respond to an uprising with a campaign of mass killing and displacement that left around 250,000 people dead and over 2 million displaced, has been consistently viewed through the prism of RtoP and has arguably attracted more RtoP related attention than any other crisis. Indeed, some Security Council members discussed Darfur through the prism of RtoP as early as 2004, well before the principle's adoption at the 2005 World Summit.[4] In 2005, the British Parliament's Committee on International Development exemplified this tendency to view Darfur through the prism of RtoP when it argued that, 'if the responsibility to protect means anything, it ought to mean something in Darfur', insisting that RtoP compelled the international community to apply political pressure on Sudan, deliver timely and effective protection and humanitarian relief, and assist with rebuilding.[5] For many analysts and activists, Darfur represents RtoP's primary test case, a test which the principle is generally reckoned to have failed. Most argue that the world's commitment to RtoP failed to generate sufficient political will to enact a robust response including the deployment of properly mandated and equipped peacekeepers to protect Darfur's civilian population. There is voluminous literature on Darfur and RtoP, much of it making basically the same point about the failure of RtoP to generate sufficient political will.[6] Others take the critique further and argue that it was not the lack of political will to deliver on RtoP that was at fault, but the principle itself. They argue that the attention paid to RtoP encouraged external actors to concentrate on establishing the conditions for the deployment of peacekeepers rather than on tackling the conflict's causes. Thus, Alex de Waal maintains that not only were peacekeepers always unlikely to be an effective source of protection in Darfur, the unwarranted attention given to potential armed intervention undermined efforts to secure a negotiated settlement by encouraging rebel groups to hold out in anticipation of external assistance.[7] In similar vein, Roberto Belloni suggested that RtoP may have actually encouraged the rebellion against Sudan that sparked the mass atrocities by offering the promise of external intervention.[8] This argument draws on the 'moral hazard theory' developed by Alan Kuperman, which maintains that RtoP actually caused genocidal violence in Darfur by encouraging dissatisfied groups to launch suicidal rebellions in the hope of provoking a disproportionate or genocidal response and triggering external intervention.[9] This is obviously a serious challenge to the whole RtoP agenda and I will address this critique in more detail in the following chapter.

Although the critics are right to point out that RtoP has not sufficiently propelled powerful states to reconsider their interests such that they are prepared to contribute peacekeepers to undertake complex and dangerous tasks in strategically unimportant regions, as we noted in Chapter 2, Darfur remains the only case in which the Security Council has chosen to refer to RtoP in a resolution relating to a specific situation (Resolution 1706). It is also important to recognize that judgments about Darfur need to acknowledge the complexity of the situation there. In particular, we need to recognize that the crisis erupted in 2003 and that much of the killing was committed in 2003–4, prior to the world's commitment to RtoP. Moreover, the crisis is closely interrelated with the Comprehensive Peace Agreement (CPA) between the government of Sudan and the Sudanese People's Liberation Army (SPLA) which brought an end to a civil war much bloodier than Darfur's. The conflict is also intimately connected to the situations in Chad and the Central African Republic, meaning that international responses had to be carefully calibrated for their impact on these countries. What is more, the Security Council has, in fact, been consistently seized of the matter and has responded with a raft of relatively innovative measures including targeted sanctions, referral of the situation to the International Criminal Court (which led to the indictment of Sudan's president) and the authorization (under Chapter VII of the UN Charter, Resolution 1769) of a large peace operation (UNAMID) with a clear civilian protection mandate.[10] That said, botched attempts at peacemaking, the international community's failure to deliver on its promises of support packages for the African Union mission (AMIS) deployed to Darfur in 2004, and the reluctance of member states to contribute troops and equipment to UNAMID cannot be primarily ascribed to the situation's complexity but instead demonstrates the limited extent to which RtoP has refashioned national interests.[11]

Kenya (2008)

The diplomatic response to the ethnic violence that erupted in the aftermath of the disputed 30 December 2007 elections in Kenya is widely trumpeted as the best example of RtoP in practice.[12] While up to 1,500 people were killed and 300,000 displaced, a coordinated diplomatic effort by a troika of eminent persons mandated by the AU, spearheaded by Kofi Annan and supported by the UN Secretary-General persuaded the country's president, Mwai Kibaki and main opponent, Raila Odinga, to conclude a power-sharing agreement and rein in the violent mobs. This prevented what many feared could have been the beginning of a much worse campaign of mass atrocities. Reflecting on his successful diplomatic mission, Annan later observed that he:

> Saw the crisis in the R2P [Responsibility to Protect] prism with a Kenyan government unable to contain the situation or protect its people. I knew that if the international community did not intervene, things would go hopelessly wrong. The problem is when we say 'intervention,' people think military, when in fact that's a last resort. Kenya is a successful example of R2P at work.[13]

Ban Ki-moon was also quick to characterize the situation as relevant to RtoP and to remind Kenya's leaders of their responsibilities. On 2 January 2008, the Office of the Secretary-General issued a statement reminding: 'the Government, as well as the political and religious leaders of Kenya of their legal and moral responsibility to protect the lives of innocent people, regardless of their racial, religious or ethnic origin' and urging them to do everything in their capacity to prevent further bloodshed.[14] The Secretary-General's Special Adviser for the Prevention of Genocide, Francis Deng, also called upon Kenya's leadership to exercise their responsibility to protect, reminding them that if they failed to do so they would be held to account by the international community.[15] Several other senior UN officials also weighed in: Under-Secretary-General for Political Affairs, Lynn Pascoe expressed concern about ethnic violence and the High Commissioner for

Human Rights, Louise Arbour, demanded that there be no impunity for those responsible. Significantly, these efforts were given strong diplomatic support by the UN Security Council, which issued a Presidential Statement reminding Kenya's leaders of their 'responsibility to engage fully in finding a sustainable political solution and taking action to immediately end violence'.[16]

It is widely acknowledged that this concerted diplomatic effort prompted the two leaders to back down and saved Kenya from a much worse fate. Reflecting afterwards on this case, Edward Luck told reporters that: 'So the only time the UN has actually applied this [the RtoP], was in the case of Kenya, early in 2008 after the disputed elections. When there's seven or eight hundred people . . . killed, it was not clear there was full-scale ethnic cleansing, but it could well become that or even something greater, and the UN decided to apply R2P criteria and to really make it the focus of the efforts there.[17] But while those involved and analysts such as Francois Grignon contend that Kenya provides an illustration of what RtoP can deliver in terms of preventive action, others, such as Pauline Baker (Fund for Peace) argue that RtoP itself played a marginal role.[18] Another note of caution was sounded by AU Commissioner Jean Ping, the General Assembly President who had guided RtoP through the 2005 World Summit. Ping questioned whether it was appropriate to apply RtoP in this case, suggesting that it raised serious questions as to the threshold of violence that constituted an RtoP situation and about potential selectivity when the response to Kenya is compared with the lack of response to the much more serious situation in Somalia.[19]

Georgia (2008)

In early August 2008, Georgia's nationalist government launched a military assault aimed at restoring 'constitutional order' in the breakaway region of South Ossetia. On the night of 7–8 August, Georgian forces launched a large-scale military offensive on the region's capital, Tskhinvali, supported by artillery. Russia, which had troops in the region as part of the Joint Peacekeeping Force deployed on the basis of a 1992 peace agreement, responded by sending forces into South Ossetia and launching air raids across Georgia. Russian troops and air forces quickly routed the Georgian army and pushed into Georgia proper, taking the city of Gori. A ceasefire was brokered by France's President Sarkozy on 15–16 August, which provided for the cessation of hostilities and staged withdrawal of Russian forces from Georgia proper. Shortly afterwards, Russia unilaterally recognized the independence of South Ossetia and that of Georgia's other breakaway province, Abkhazia.[20]

Among the justifications offered by Russia for its intervention in Georgia was the claim that its action was consistent with the RtoP. The Russian leadership argued that intervention was justified by the commission and imminent commission of mass atrocities by the Georgian army against the South Ossetians. Russia's President Medvedev and Prime Minister Putin insisted that these abuses amounted to 'genocide'.[21] Meanwhile, Russian Foreign Minister, Sergei Lavrov, referred explicitly to RtoP in justifying the intervention. According to Lavrov:

> According to our Constitution there is also a responsibility to protect – the term which is widely used in the UN when people see some trouble in Africa or in any remote part of other regions. But this is not Africa to us, this is next door. This is our area, where Russian citizens live. So the Constitution of the Russian Federation . . . makes it absolutely unavoidable to us to exercise responsibility to protect.[22]

Russia again implied that its actions were consistent with RtoP during a heated exchange with Georgia at the 2009 General Assembly.[23] But these arguments won little international support. RtoP advocates generally saw the Russian argument as an obvious case of misapplication. Two of RtoP's leading Canadian progenitors caricatured Russian arguments as a 'misappropriation' of RtoP, a view shared by the New York-based Global Centre for RtoP on three principal grounds. First, the Centre maintained that the protection of nationals in foreign countries went beyond the scope of the RtoP. Second, it concluded that the scale of Russias intervention was disproportionate to the goals of protecting South Ossetians. Third, the Centre reiterated that RtoP does not provide a justification for the use of force without the approval of the UN Security Council.[24] A similar set of arguments was also put forward by Gareth Evans, though Evans also pointed to the ICISS criteria to support his case.[25] On the other hand, there was some suggestion that Russia's use of RtoP language at least signified a degree of previously absent acquiescence with RtoP and that Western criticism of Russia's military action may have obscured an important diplomatic development.[26] More significant, perhaps, is the fact that a great power tried, and failed, to legitimize the use of force by reference to RtoP, suggesting that concerns that RtoP may be a 'Trojan Horse' supporting unilateral intervention are misplaced. This conclusion is further supported by the failure of another permanent member of the UN Security Council, France, to win support for its call for intervention in Myanmar in the wake of Cyclone Nargis.

Cyclone Nargis in Myanmar (2008)

On 3 May 2008, Cyclone Nargis struck Myanmar, devastating the Irrawaddy delta and leaving much of the region under water. Approximately 138,000 people were left dead or missing and 1.5 million people were displaced by the cyclone.[27] Despite the massive scale of the humanitarian catastrophe and the government's obvious inability to respond effectively, Myanmar's military regime initially denied access to humanitarian agencies, inhibiting the delivery of urgently needed supplies and medical assistance. The disaster occurred shortly before a constitutional referendum aimed at legitimizing the military government, which the regime decided to proceed with. Organizations already present in the country were able to get relatively small numbers of aid workers into the affected areas but reported a tightening of travel restrictions.[28] Other NGOs, UN agencies and states offered assistance but Myanmar was slow to issue visas and insisted on distributing aid itself – raising fears that much of it would be siphoned off by the military and never reach their intended recipients. The junta also insisted on restricting the movement of aid workers, fearing that they might distribute pro-democracy propaganda and encourage social unrest. Independently of one another, some ten days after the cyclone struck, the UN's Office for the Coordination of Humanitarian Affairs (OCHA) and Oxfam reported that, at the most, only a quarter of the required aid was being allowed into Myanmar and that the aid that did arrive was not being effectively distributed.

Frustrated by this lack of progress, French Foreign Minister, Bernard Kouchner, proposed that the UN Security Council invoke the RtoP to authorize the delivery aid without Myanmar's consent. This proposal was reiterated by the French Ambassador to the UN and repeated by commentators, analysts and politicians. When the EU met to discuss its response to the cyclone and the French proposal to invoke the RtoP, France's junior Minister for Human Rights, Rama Yade, told reporters that 'we have called for the 'responsibility to protect' to be applied in the case of Burma'.[30] EU ministers failed to reach a consensus on the French proposal, but the EU's High Representative for the Common Foreign and Security Policy declared that the international community 'should use all possible means to aid through to victims of Myanmar's cyclone'. Some media commentators in the US, UK and Australia echoed Kouchner's call for RtoP to be invoked to justify the delivery of aid without the government's consent. The commentators disagreed, however, about the most appropriate modality for using RtoP. Some suggested that RtoP be invoked to bypass the Security Council, which they believed (correctly) was unlikely to authorize the non-consensual delivery of aid due to opposition from Council members such as China, Russia, Indonesia and South Africa. Some pointed to the international relief efforts in northern Iraq in 1991, when the UK, France and US established 'safe havens' to protect Kurds from Saddam's army without UN sanction. Perhaps most outlandish was the suggestion of one Australian academic, who pointed to Kosovo as a precedent, arguing that the West should invoke RtoP to bypass the Security Council and should fight their way into Myanmar just as NATO fought its way into Kosovo.[31]

Kouchner's proposal was flatly rejected by China and ASEAN, which argued that the RtoP did not apply to natural disasters.[32] ASEAN governments also maintained that Myanmar must not be coerced into accepting humanitarian assistance. This view was shared by senior UN officials who recognized the danger that Kouchner's argument posed to both the relief effort itself (which required Asian cooperation) and the emerging consensus on RtoP. John Holmes, the UN's Under-Secretary-General for Humanitarian Affairs described

Kouchner's call as unnecessarily confrontational. Edward Luck set out the objections to applying RtoP in more detail, arguing that:

> ... it would be a misapplication of responsibility to protect principles to apply them at this point to the unfolding tragedy in Myanmar ... the Outcome Document of the 2005 [World] Summit limited their application to four crimes and violations: genocide, crimes against humanity, war crimes and ethnic cleansing. We must focus our efforts on implementing these principles in these four cases, as there is no agreement among the Member States on applying them to other situations, no matter how disturbing and regrettable the circumstances.[33]

The British Minister for International Development, Douglas Alexander, rejected Kouchner's argument as 'incendiary' and Britain's UN ambassador, John Sawers, expressed his support for the view that RtoP did not apply to natural disasters and therefore should not be invoked to coerce the Myanmar government or justify the forcible delivery of aid.[34] Britain later backtracked somewhat, indicating that it would welcome 'discussion' of the relationship between RtoP, natural disasters and the situation in Myanmar.[35]

In the end, ASEAN and the UN Secretary-General used diplomacy to secure the regime's acquiescence to the delivery of international aid and organized a joint UN–ASEAN relief effort. There has since been speculation that the 'threat' of RtoP encouraged the regime to grant access and anecdotal evidence from multiple sources points in this direction. According to one account, Indonesia's Foreign Minister, Hassan Wirajuda told his Myanmar counterpart that if his government rejected the proposed ASEAN–UN humanitarian relief effort, ASEAN governments would not be able to prevent the UN Security Council from invoking RtoP and authorizing the forcible delivery of aid without the government's consent.[36] If this was indeed the case, it was more likely the regime's paranoid fear of Western invasion rather than a calculated concern about RtoP itself that prompted this shift, given that there was never much chance that Russia and China would do anything other than veto proposals for coercion brought to the Security Council.[37] Although painfully slow, un-coordinated and ad hoc, the diplomatic effort secured humanitarian access and the delivery of relief that helped prevent the much predicted second round of deaths due to disease and malnutrition. However, the restrictions placed on the delivery of aid meant that while it was effective in helping to forestall an impending catastrophe, progress on reconstruction has been much slower.[38]

Gaza (2008–9)

On 26 December 2008, shortly after the expiry of a six-month ceasefire brokered by Egypt between Hamas and Israel, Israel launched an air and land assault on Hamas in Gaza, ostensibly aimed at preventing Hamas from launching rockets into Israel. Israeli forces attacked a wide range of targets including police stations, training camps, port facilities and positions used by Hamas to attack Israel. As the campaign progressed, the target list was expanded to include tunnels between Gaza and Egypt, the homes of parliamentarians, and the full range of Hamas and government institutions, including the Health Ministry. Hamas responded by launching rockets into southern Israel. External observers generally agree that both sides committed war crimes and possibly crimes against humanity. Israel used prohibited weapons against civilian areas, conducted indiscriminate attacks, often failed to exercise due care in distinguishing civilians from combatants, and attacked the UN, humanitarian personnel and the ICRC. According to the detailed 'Goldstone report' commissioned by the UN Human Rights Council, named after its principal author, respected judge Richard Goldstone, the large majority of the approximately 1,200 casualties were Palestinian civilians, killed or injured by Israel. For its part, Hamas launched rockets indiscriminately and used the civilian population as 'human shields'.[39] Unsurprisingly, the Goldstone report was criticized as biased by Israel and its allies, but it remains the most balanced and comprehensive account of the war based on a forensic examination and recounting of the conflict. The General Assembly later adopted a resolution endorsing the Goldstone report. However, many self-proclaimed advocates of RtoP, including Australia, Canada, Germany, and the Netherlands joined Israel's allies in voting against the resolution. Justifying their votes, Canada and Australia erroneously argued that the report held Israel wholly culpable for the harm inflicted on civilians, ignoring the fact that Goldstone found that Palestinian armed groups had conducted indiscriminate attacks which constituted war crimes and possibly crimes against humanity.[40]

At the time of the crisis, the World Council of Churches and Oxfam International reminded the parties of their responsibility to protect civilians.[41] The question of whether RtoP applied in this situation was discussed among the principle's advocates and despite the reported commission of war crimes there was much equivocation, with some arguing that RtoP ought to be robustly applied and others adopting a more cautious view.[42] The matter was not raised by governments until much later. At the 2009 General Assembly debate about RtoP several governments raised the Gaza question. In a thinly veiled reference to Gaza, Qatar argued that priority should be given under RtoP to the protection of populations under foreign occupation. Others used the Gaza experience to point to RtoP's selective application, noting that it tends to be invoked where it suits the interest of Western powers (as in Myanmar) but not in situations where it works against Western interests. As Iran put it, '[w]e have . . . witnessed the repeated failure of the Security Council to leave [*sic*] up to its responsibility and to take appropriate action against Israeli regime's continuous aggression and mass atrocities in the Palestinian occupied territories and in neighboring countries.[43] For its part, the Palestinian authority argued that RtoP required that the Security Council take steps to protect vulnerable populations on a consistent and non-selective basis. Arguing that many Western governments had exhibited double-standards, Palestine argued that 'it should be unacceptable for a country to advocate this concept [RtoP] and similar others, preaching on human rights and calling for intervention while at the same time consistently ignoring abhorrent and systematic breaches of human rights, war crimes and crimes against humanity by others, including its allies. Such selectivity and double-standards have regrettably obstructed any and all attempts in international forums to protect civilian populations entitled to and desperately-needing protection in several cases'.[44]

Sri lanka (2008–9)

In mid 2008, the Sri Lankan government began a military offensive against Liberation Tigers of Tamil Eelam (LTTE). That offensive escalated at the beginning of 2009 as towns and cities fell to government forces. By April 2009, the rebels had been pushed into a small area of jungle near Mutulivu. Alongside the 'Tigers' were approximately 150,000 civilians. Many of these civilians were prevented from fleeing to safer ground by the LTTE, which was determined to use them as human shields and bargaining chips. As a result they were subjected to aerial bombardment and mortar fire directed against the LTTE by Sri Lankan government forces. According to the UN's Office for the Coordination of Humanitarian Affairs (OCHA), by April 2009 around 2,600 civilians had been killed by the fighting. Civilians trapped by the fighting faced a double peril: if they fled, they risked being killed by the LTTE; if they stayed, they were in danger of succumbing to the government's bombardment. To make matters worse, the Sri Lankan government limited the access of humanitarian agencies and the UN to the disputed territory. As a result, trapped civilians had little hope of accessing vital medical assistance and life sustaining supplies. In the end, government forces overran the LTTE in mid-May and the approximately 280,000 civilian survivors were transferred to government run displacement camps, which were sometimes been anything but safe havens. Not only were there scant supplies and medical support, but there have also been reports of 'disappearances' and other violations inside the camps. The government refused to grant humanitarian access to the camps.[45] As such, various UN officials commented that they could not verify or dismiss claims of disappearances and other abuses because the government had not granted access but noted that the denial of access alone implied that all was not well within the camps. These concerns were compounded in September 2009, when the government expelled UNICEF spokesman James Elder for raising concerns about the disproportionate impact of the war on the country's children, speaking out about potential malnutrition among children in the post-war context and noting that the denial of humanitarian access impeded UNICEF's efforts to address malnutrition among children. This expulsion discouraged other aid agencies from publicly raising the myriad protection issues that persist in Sri Lanka.[46]

As the crisis unfolded, it prompted heated debate among RtoP advocates. A few called for the RtoP to be invoked to prompt a robust response from the Security Council. For instance, writing in the *Washington Post*, James Traub, then the Global Centre for RtoP's Policy Director, described Sri Lanka as 'exactly the kind of cataclysm that states vowed to prevent when they adopted the 'responsibility to protect'. Traub called for the UN Security Council to take matters into its own hands by threatening to refer the matter to the International Criminal Court, dispatching a UN envoy and considering the imposition of sanctions.[47] In similar vein, Jan Egeland, the former UN Humanitarian Coordinator, argued that the UN had 'failed' to deliver on RtoP in the case of Sri Lanka. The Global Centre's high-profile advisory board wrote an open letter to the Security Council calling for it to add Sri Lanka to its agenda in order to avert a potential bloodbath for which the Sri Lankan government and LTTE would be held jointly responsible. They wrote, 'the Security Council, according to the terms of the 2005 agreement, must authorize 'timely and decisive measures' to prevent or halt mass atrocities. The Council must be prepared to bluntly characterize the violence in Sri Lanka as mass atrocity crimes; to demand that the government of Sri Lanka grant access to the conflict zone to humanitarian groups and to the media, both of whom it has barred until now; to dispatch a special envoy to the region, and/or to consider the imposition of sanctions. And ultimately, it must help facilitate a durable political solution to the fighting'.[48] In contrast, Mary Ellen O'Connell rejected RtoP as a 'distraction' likely to increase mistrust and provoke opposition to international engagement aimed at protecting the civilians who remained in peril.[49] More provocatively, Ramesh Thakur – a signatory of the aforementioned Global Centre letter – later insisted that 'it was hypocritical and wrong – morally, politically and militarily – of Westerners to fault Sri Lanka' for its conduct.[50]

As the crisis unfolded, several governments suggested that international engagement be viewed through the prism of RtoP. Mexico's Permanent Representative to the UN, Claude Heller, told reporters that 'in the case of Sri Lanka there is a concern of the responsibility to protect the population'.[51] Despite calls from the Global Centre and several Security Council Members, Sri Lanka successfully resisted attempts to place it on the Council's agenda as a protection issue. However, the Council did hold informal meetings on the matter and received briefings from the UN's Humanitarian Coordinator.[52] Perhaps most important in this case, however, was the reference to RtoP made by India's External Affairs Minister, Pranab Mukherjee, in a call for the Sri Lankan government to show restraint. Much as UN officials and the AU's envoys had done in the case of Kenya, Mukherjee reminded the Sri Lankan government that it 'has a responsibility to protect its own citizens', noting that 'we are very unhappy at the continued killing of innocent Tamil civilians in Sri Lanka'.[53] As such, far from being a 'distraction', RtoP helped provide a prism through which the Security Council and India could bring diplomatic pressure to bear by reminding Sri Lanka of its responsibilities and international expectations. Although there is no clear evidence to this effect, it is likely that this pressure encouraged Sri Lanka to show restraint.

Guinea (2009)

On 28 September 2009, government forces in Guinea fired upon demonstrators in the capital Conakry. The demonstrators were protesting the decision of the military regime's leader – Dadis Camara – to run in forthcoming elections. No fewer than 156 people were killed, 1,200 injured and countless others raped and sexually abused, prompting a UN Commission of Inquiry to conclude that a crime against humanity has been committed.[54] In its report on the massacre, Human Rights Watch found that the killing was premeditated and conducted with the prior knowledge of the government. However, there was also evidence to suggest that the government itself was deeply divided on the matter. For example, three government ministers resigned in protest in mid-October and the man widely thought to have instigated the massacre, Aboucar Diakite (Camara's *aide-de-camp*), tried unsuccessfully to assassinate Camara on 3 December. Before he fled, Diakite publicly stated that he tried to kill Camara because the leader was using him as a scapegoat for the massacre. Reportedly shot in the head, Camara was flown to Morocco, ostensibly for medical treatment. In January 2010, he left Morocco for Burkina Faso owing to a dispute with his hosts.

In many ways, the international community's response to the massacre in Guinea was similar to its earlier response to the crisis in Kenya and succeeded in helping to prevent escalation into generalized violence – though significant risks remain. There was, however, one important difference between the two cases. Whereas relevant actors specifically utilized RtoP in the Kenya case, they did not do so in the case of Guinea. The only specific references to RtoP in relation to this crisis came from civil society organizations such as the Global Centre for RtoP. I have included it in this section though, because although RtoP was not specifically referred to, the international response to the crisis in Guinea was squarely in keeping with the principle's spirit.

International actors responded quickly to the 28 September massacre, demanding that it not be repeated and insisting that the government take steps to ensure free and fair elections. Having already suspended Guinea following the military coup that brought Camara to power in 2008, ECOWAS immediately condemned the massacre, established a commission of inquiry, imposed an arms embargo and appointed an envoy to mediate between the government and opposition. Nigeria's absentee president, Umaru Musa Yar' Adua, reportedly defended ECOWAS' response to the massacre by noting that 'we cannot fold our hands and watch the situation degenerate into conflicts of monumental proportion without employing appropriate intervention mechanisms to effectively arrest the drift'.[55] Although deeply divided on the question of whether to interfere, the AU also imposed limited targeted sanctions on the regime, freezing its foreign assets and imposing travel restrictions. Libya, which at that time held the AU Chair, opposed these measures and rejected the idea of establishing a commission of inquiry on the grounds that they constituted interference in Guinea's internal affairs.[56] Elsewhere, the

EU and US joined ECOWAS in imposing targeted sanctions. They also imposed an arms embargo and froze aid.

The UN Secretary-General Ban Ki-moon responded quickly to the massacre. On the day it was first reported, he issued a statement 'deploring' the massacre and urging the government and security forces to exercise restraint.[57] He also used his own authority to establish a UN Commission of Inquiry comprising Mohamed Bedjaoui, Françoise Ngendahayo Kayiramirwa and Pramila Patten, which proceeded with the regime's grudging consent and cooperation.[58] That Commission reported its findings to the Secretary-General and Security Council in December 2009. It concluded that the 28 September violence and its aftermath constituted crimes against humanity and that there were reasonable grounds to prove individual responsibility. It also singled out three people as primarily responsible for the violence: Camara, Diakite, and head of Special Forces Moussa Camara. On the basis of these findings, the Commission made a number of recommendations. These included recommendations that the cases against these three individuals be referred to the ICC, that the UN High Commissioner for Human Rights establish an office in Guinea, that the international community support a process of military reform, that reparations be paid to the victims, and that targeted sanctions be imposed on the alleged perpetrators.[59] As in the case of Kenya, these efforts and sentiments were given political support by the UN Security Council, though the Council stopped short of taking its own measures. The Council held informal consultations on 30 September 2009 and received a briefing from Assistant Secretary-General for Political Affairs, Haile Menkerios. The US, which held the Council presidency, issued a press statement condemning the massacre and expressing the Council's concern, urging the government to end the violence and bring the perpetrators to justice, and supporting ECOWAS and AU efforts.[60] The following month, the Council issued a presidential statement recognizing the potential risk that the situation posed to regional peace and security, supporting the ECOWAS mediation effort and the Commission of Inquiry, and confirming that the Council would remain seized of the matter. However, there was no agreement on the adoption of targeted sanctions, an arms embargo or referral to the ICC.[61] Although observers noted a growing consensus among Council members on the need for activism, the Council did not actively consider passing a resolution or adopting its own measures, due largely to concerns from China and Russia about interference in a state's domestic affairs. Instead, it adopted a further Presidential Statement in February 2010, welcoming the ECOWAS brokered Ouagadougou agreement (below) and reaffirming its condemnation of the massacre.[62]

This combined pressure certainly encouraged the regime – which had replaced the injured and absent Camara with defence minister, Sebouka Konate – to participate in talks brokered by ECOWAS and conclude the Ouagadougou agreement in January 2010. This agreement provided for the installation of a government of national unity, led by a consensus prime minister. It also provided for national elections within six months and forbade military leaders, including Camara, and civilians associated with the transitional government from standing.[63] But it was local factors that inspired the change of thinking in Guinea. Although Konate participated in the coup that elevated Camara, he had always advocated a rapid return to democracy based on the Mali model. The attempted assassination of Camara and his departure to Morocco for treatment, propelled Konate into power, enabling him to restore a degree of order, conclude the peace agreement, and pursue his own agenda.[64] Moreover, as in Kenya, it was the regional security architecture (this time, primarily ECOWAS), largely developed prior to RtoP, which provided the catalyst and institutional framework for external mediation.

The conclusion of the Ouagadougou agreement represents an important achievement for international diplomacy, spearheaded by regional actors and supported by the UN. It remains to be seen, however, whether the agreement will be faithfully implemented. Critical to this is Konate's ability to hold the military together and prevent allies of Camara from disrupting the process Evidence that the government is fracturing and that leaders are establishing/have established their own private militias does not bode well.[65] However, one of the principal players, Guinea's Security Minister Claude Pivi, a noted Camara supporter with a private militia which conducted a bloody crackdown following the assassination attempt, has pledged to support the deal and protect Konate. Whether this transpires remains to be seen. Clearly, the international community has an important role to play – not by placing further pressure on Konate as suggested by the Global Centre for RtoP, but by protecting and supporting him, and offering incentives for compliance. What to do in the event of non-compliance is, of course, another matter and although it is actively engaged in the crisis, it is hard to see the Security Council taking 'timely and decisive' action in that event.

Having reviewed those crises in which RtoP has played a perceptible role, either in framing international responses as in DRC, Darfur, Kenya, Guinea and – to a lesser extent – Sri Lanka, or in prompting sharp debate about its applicability, as in Georgia, Gaza, Myanmar and also Sri Lanka, the next section consider cases characterized by the commission of one or more of the RtoP crimes (genocide, war crimes, ethnic cleansing and crimes against humanity), but where RtoP has not been widely discussed. Asking why RtoP was not used or debated in these cases may prove as illuminating as the cases where it was used or debated.

RtoP: Missing in action

Iraq and Afghanistan (2001–ongoing)

Since 2005, approximately 70,000 Iraqi civilians have been killed in the insurgency there, the large majority deliberately targeted by anti-US insurgents.[66] Civilian casualties in Afghanistan are much lower but increased significantly in 2008. Approximately 5,000 civilians have been killed since 2005 (8,000 since

2001), with more than 2,000 killed in 2008. Blame for civilian deaths in Afghanistan is more evenly shared, with around 55 per cent deliberately killed by insurgents and the remainder killed by a combination of US/NATO air strikes, crossfire and other unintended incidents.[67] Given the scale of civilian suffering in these two cases and the fact that a large portion of it was caused by deliberate attacks constituting war crimes and crimes against humanity, it is somewhat surprising that neither have been discussed in relation to RtoP. There are four principal reasons for this. First, the majority of the attacks on civilians have been committed by non-state actors as part of their campaigns against national governments and US-led coalitions. Thus, even if RtoP were discussed in this context, it is not clear what would be added given that large military forces are already engaged in a protracted, costly and bloody effort to the defeat the perpetrators of the majority of the crimes against civilians. Second, those states actively involved in the two conflicts prefer to see them through the prisms of national security and the 'war on terror' rather than as protection problems. In other words, international engagement in these conflicts is driven primarily by self-interest, not concerns about protection. In that context, it is worth noting that coalition forces are themselves responsible for (albeit mainly unintended) civilian casualties in both contexts. Third, the dubious legitimacy of the 2003 invasion of Iraq especially has made the UN secretariat and other governments reluctant to view it through the prism of RtoP for fear of retrospectively legitimizing unilateral intervention and creating an expectation that the UN should contribute more to these complex, costly and dangerous armed conflicts that it had no role in starting. This tendency was only strengthened by the killing of 17 UN workers, including senior officials Sergio Vieira De Mello and Arthur Helton, by terrorists in Baghdad in 2003. Fourth, given the very real threat that precipitate withdrawal from Iraq and Afghanistan might spark renewed atrocities, one consequence of viewing the conflicts through an RtoP lens might be to give rise to long-term duties to protect civilians, which the coalitions deployed to Iraq and Afghanistan would be reluctant to accept given their eagerness to withdraw as soon as possible.

Somalia (2006–ongoing)

While the international response to the crisis in early 1990s Somalia is often referred to as an important precursor to RtoP, the crisis that has befallen that country since the US-backed Ethiopian intervention that deposed the Union of Islamic Courts (UIC) and ushered in a new period of conflict and anarchy in December 2006 has not commonly been viewed through the prism of RtoP, despite the commission of war crimes, crimes against humanity and ethnic cleansing and the very real threat of escalation.[68] I will examine the UN Security Council's response to the crisis more fully in Chapter 8. Rather than addressing protection issues, international attention has focused more on the external symptoms of the crisis, especially maritime piracy and suspected Somali support for international Islamist extremism. Such engagement has had an almost entirely negative effect. In the two years after December 2006, approximately 16,500 civilians were killed and in 2007 alone up to 1.9 million Somalis were newly displaced.[69] Despite this, UN officials, governments and commentators alike have remained reluctant to link the situation to RtoP. Indeed, Gareth Evans went so far as to argue that Somalia was 'not a classic' RtoP situation, suggesting only that it be placed on a 'watchlist' of countries to pay attention to.[70] The international response to the crisis has been slow and hesitant, and has tended to prioritize the interests of external actors over those of Somali civilians. In line with the problematic doctrine of 'African solutions for African problems',[71] the UN Security Council deferred to the AU which deployed a small and ineffectual peacekeeping force (AMISOM) in 2007. AMISOM's obvious incapacity generated calls, from the US (Bush Administration), Italy and South Africa especially, for the UN to take over peacekeeping duties – though none couched their pleas in RtoP terms or offered their soldiers as peacekeepers. In the absence of clear commitments of troops, equipment and financial support from the West (or elsewhere), the Secretary-General and Secretariat were reluctant to endorse the deployment of UN peacekeepers. Instead, the Secretary-General recommended that UN peacekeepers only be deployed once the security situation had improved, a viable political process had begun, and the state had proven capable of performing basic functions. The Security Council accepted this recommendation in Resolution 1814 (15 May 2008) – a view that enjoys wide support within the Secretariat.[72] In the case of Somalia, therefore, the commission of relevant crimes has not prompted outsiders to view the problem through the prism of RtoP, to prioritize the protection of Somali civilians, or offer resources to foster peace (see Chapter 8).

Sudan (2008–9)

Although the world's attention has been firmly fixed on Darfur, in 2008–9 more civilians were killed in southern Sudan as the Comprehensive Peace Agreement (CPA) between the government of Sudan and SPLA began to unravel.[73] The UN mission charged with assisting implementation of the CPA (UNMIS, established in 2005) has one of the most highly developed plans for the protection of civilians but has had difficulty translating planning guidance into tangible protection.[74] While experts contend that the two major parties still calculate that their interests would not be well served by a return to war, a combination of factors including competition for scarce resources such as water, cattle and land, the return of some 2 million refugees and displaced persons, attempts by the government to destabilize the south, concerns about the implementation of the CPA, and the impending referendum on the south's independence scheduled for 2011 produced a number of violent episodes that left hundreds of civilians dead and more than 250,000 displaced, and create the risk of a wider escalation into violence.[75] The most notable incident to date was the conflict between the SPLA and government forces and their allies over the disputed town of Abyei in May 2008, which forced up to 50,000 civilians to flee and left dozens dead. Despite the very obvious potential for escalation and the clear threat of mass atrocities, except for a handful of vocal NGOs there has been little interest in viewing the situation in southern Sudan through the prism of RtoP and diplomatic efforts to prevent renewed conflict did not begin in earnest until late 2010.[76]

Precisely what these cases tell us about RtoP will be examined in more detail in the following chapter, but at this point it is worth noting the principle's inconsistent usage (the level of civilian destruction does not determine whether or not RtoP will be utilized) and that it has not always succeeded in elevating civilian protection issues to the top of the international agenda. This has not, however, stopped activists from framing their positions in RtoP terms in an effort to generate attention, as the following brief section attests.

RtoP and protracted human rights abuse

The final cluster of cases examined in this chapter are those which, while not reaching a crescendo over the past few years, have seen war crimes and crimes against humanity committed as part of a wider system of chronic human rights abuse by governments. In some ways, these may be described as the 'elephants in the room' of RtoP: North Korea and Myanmar. Once again, though, the level of RtoP-related attention is not correlated with the level of abuse. By any account, the situation in North Korea is far worse, and the abuses more widespread, than that in Myanmar – yet, it is Myanmar that has attracted the attention of RtoP advocates such as the Global Centre while efforts to couch North Korea in RtoP terms have fallen on deaf ears. I will begin with North Korea.

A 2008 report commissioned by Vaclav Havel, Kjell Bondevik and Elie Wiesel found that North Korea had 'failed in its responsibility to protect its own citizens from the most severe violations of international law'.[77] Focusing only on the period 2006–7, the report provided compelling evidence to support its case. In particular it found that regime-induced famine had killed around 50,000 people and left 12 per cent of the whole population undernourished. Moreover, the North Korean military summarily shot and executed hundreds if not thousands of people trying to flee the country and the regime's massive prisons system systematically employed torture and arbitrary killings. If we take the Rome Statute of the ICC as our guide, as most analysts do, each of these practices constitutes a crime against humanity, validating the report's claim that North Korea has failed to fulfil its RtoP. These figures alone, based on just two years of evidence, make North Korea one of the world's worst mass murderers since 2005. But this country is a serial offender, and the past five years have been relatively good by North Korean standards. In total, since 1948 an estimated 1.2 million to 1.7 million people have been killed at the hands of government repression. In addition, between 1995 and 1998, between 2 million and 3.5 million people died as a result of regime induced famine. For good measure, let's also add in the approximately 129,000 civilians that were probably intentionally killed by communist forces during the Korean

War. This, then, is a regime with a long track record of killing, torturing, and starving millions of its own people. The case for arguing that it has manifestly failed to protect its population from war crimes and crimes against humanity appears compelling indeed.

Despite this, the situation in North Korea has been almost entirely overlooked by the RtoP prism. The Havel-Bondevik-Weisel report was largely ignored, neither the Global Centre nor my own Asia-Pacific Centre has picked up the findings and recommendations, and none of the major books to date on RtoP have mentioned North Korea in this context. The Secretary-General's Special Adviser, Edward Luck, argues that this is fitting because RtoP is 'not suited' to dealing with chronic human rights problems not characterized by 'large-scale violence' and because of the availability of other more appropriate mechanisms.[78]

We confront a similar situation in relation to the relationship between the government of Myanmar and many of that country's ethnic minorities, especially the Karen. Here again, there is a considerable amount of evidence to suggest that the government has committed crimes against humanity against ethnic minorities since 2005. In 2006 alone, for example, Human Rights Watch and the Human Rights Documentation Unit reported that government forces killed up to 300 Karen civilians (265 of whom were captured, forced to serve the government and then killed) and forced 25,000 to flee. In total, over 400,000 civilians live in camps on the Thai-Myanmar border having been forced to flee by the regime.[79] Set alongside a longer trajectory of human rights abuse including ethnic cleansing and crimes against humanity and the killing of 5,000–8,000 Karen in the 1980s, a case could be made that Myanmar too has manifestly failed in its RtoP. These statistics have prompted some calls for RtoP to be applied to Myanmar.[80] In 2010, the Global Centre argued that Myanmar was manifestly failing to protect its populations and that the UN Security Council and ASEAN should take timely and decisive action to protect endangered populations – though its recommendations were rather short on detail.[81]

Conclusion

From the preceding analysis it is clear that in the past five years, the RtoP has become a key part of the language used to debate and frame responses to humanitarian emergencies. However, there is little consistency in the way that RtoP is used. The inconsistencies seem to revolve around two axes –scale and scope. In relation to scale, we found surprisingly little correlation between a situation's gravity in terms of the number of civilian casualties and its likelihood of being viewed through the prism of RtoP. Some relatively minor episodes attracted a high degree of RtoP attention (especially Kenya and Georgia) while several deadlier episodes have not (especially Somalia and Iraq). In addition, there is one notable case (Guinea) where international responses were broadly in line with the demands of RtoP but proceeded without reference to the principle. Although this may be construed as a welcome sign of strengthening international engagement with the threat of mass atrocities, it is difficult to know from a case like this whether RtoP is adding value or whether the same (or better) results are being achieved by alternative routes (such as regional security architectures) or whether (as seems most likely) it is a combination of the two.

In relation to scope, although a consensus has emerged that in the abstract, the principle applies to four crimes, in practice states have contested both the substance of that agreement and its application. The key cases in this regard were Georgia and Myanmar/Cyclone Nargis. In both of these cases, permanent members of the Security Council (Russia and France) invoked RtoP to legitimize the deployment or threat of coercive force to stem what they saw as the commission or imminent commission of genocide or mass atrocities. In so doing, they each tested the limits of how RtoP might be used. In the case of Georgia, debate focused on the factual veracity of Russia's claims about Georgia's abuse of civilians in South Ossetia. The debate on Myanmar, however, hinged on the applicability of RtoP to situations where a government fails to provide or permit sufficient humanitarian relief in the wake of a natural disaster. In both cases, the claims advanced were roundly rejected by the international community, effectively placing two limits on the use of RtoP for coercive purposes: (1) a requirement that the use of coercion be preceded by compelling evidence of genocide or mass atrocities; (2) a relatively narrow interpretation of 'crimes against humanity' that excludes crimes not associated with the deliberate killing and displacement of civilians.

In both of these cases, relatively powerful states invoked RtoP to legitimize the use or threat of military force but other states and analysts found their arguments unpersuasive. As a result, Russia failed to translate its intervention into a legitimate basis for recognizing South Ossetia and France failed to galvanize support for the forcible delivery of aid. On a positive note, these failures demonstrates the norm's capacity to inhibit certain types of behavior and the debates generated by Russian and French claims helped to clarify the burden of proof that needs to be satisfied in order to successfully invoke the norm to justify coercive behavior. Moreover, as alluded to earlier these cases lend support to the view that RtoP is not a 'Trojan horse' that legitimizes great power interference in the affairs of the weak, a view which was fuelled by the use of RtoP-related arguments to justify the invasion of Iraq in 2003. In these two cases, permanent members of the Security Council were tempted to use RtoP in this manner, but in both cases they failed to translate RtoP into the legitimization of coercive action.

In cases where there has been little dispute about the applicability of RtoP, the principle has established a patchy track record. With the notable exceptions of Gaza and Sri Lanka, debates tended to hinge not on *whether* international actors should engage, but *how*. Less promising, though, are the limits that were exposed by these cases. Consensus on Kenya and Guinea was possible because engagement was limited to diplomacy with host state consent. There is little evidence to suggest that the Council would have been prepared to adopt a more robust stance had that been required. In relation to

Darfur and the DRC, there have been serious problems in relation to achieving consensus about what ought to be done, as well as a discernible lack of willingness to implement some of the Council's decisions. Although RtoP was utilized in all these cases, it has yet to provide a catalyst for 'timely and decisive' action in the manner envisaged by pillar three. The capacity of RtoP to serve as a catalyst for action is brought into sharper relief by considering episodes of actual or imminent mass killing that have not inspired the use of RtoP, especially Somalia and Sudan.

The challenge now is to consider what these parallel stories, of efforts to implement the RtoP at the UN and the role of RtoP in practice, tell us about the principle itself. It is to this task that we turn in the following chapter, which utilizes the information presented in the previous chapters to address some critically important questions: what is RtoP's function? What is its scope? Is RtoP a norm (and, if so, what sort of norm)? It is effective? And – perhaps most important of all – does it increase the risk of genocidal violence by creating moral hazard?

4   An assessment after five years

In the previous two chapters I noted that while there is growing consensus about the RtoP in principle, in practice RtoP is applied selectively and inconsistently and its use is often contested. As a result, we need to take stock of the emerging politics and practice of RtoP before we can move on to talk about its implementation. Drawing on the analysis in the preceding two chapters, this chapter poses some basic questions about RtoP: (1) What is RtoP's function? (2) What is the scope of RtoP? (3) Is it a norm and, if so, what sort of norm? (4) What contribution has RtoP made to the prevention of genocide and mass atrocities and protection of vulnerable populations? In answering these questions, I am going to argue that RtoP is best seen as an agreed principle that generates policy agenda in need of implementation, that by itself it is unlikely to act as a catalyst for timely and decisive action in response to mass atrocities because its second and third pillars have relatively weak 'compliance pull' owing to their indeterminacy. However, the principle has made a positive contribution to both prevention and protection, in ways that do not tend to grab the headlines.

Before this, however, we need to address what is perhaps the most challenging critique of RtoP, briefly mentioned in the previous chapter. This critique stems from moral hazard theory and claims that RtoP inadvertently *causes* genocide and mass atrocities. If this is true, everything else we can write about RtoP pales into insignificance. But, on closer scrutiny, although they have gained considerable traction in both public and academic debates, these claims are well off the mark.

RtoP as a cause of genocidal violence?[1]

The central claim made by proponents of moral hazard theory is that RtoP 'causes' genocidal violence that would not otherwise occur.[2] RtoP is also criticized for failing to protect at-risk civilians and unintentionally placing others in danger; 'contribut[ing] to the tragedies that it intends to prevent'; 'unintentionally foster[ing] rebellion'; and 'prompting states to retaliate with genocidal violence'.[3] These more general claims are embellished with reference to a small number of specific cases, particularly Bosnia, Rwanda, Kosovo and

Darfur. In each case, genocidal violence is said to have been a '*direct consequence* of the emerging norm of the Responsibility to Protect'.[4] If this claim was true, it would constitute a very serious charge against RtoP and the full range of international activities ostensibly aimed at preventing genocide and mass atrocities and protecting their victims. Indeed, it would suggest that victims of mass atrocities would be better served by international inaction than by the implementation of RtoP. This would lend support to the view that the international community should simply 'give war a chance'.[5]

Derived from economics, moral hazard refers to the phenomenon in which individuals or groups are induced to engage in riskier behavior than they otherwise would by the provision of protection by third parties.[6] This protection, usually in the form of insurance, unintentionally encourages risky behaviour by creating 'perverse incentives' that either reduce the expected costs associated with risky behaviour or actually reward such behaviour.[7] It is a *perverse* incentive because it is not established by the 'insurer' in order to induce the outcome.[8] In the context of world politics, proponents of moral hazard argue that the international community's promise to protect endangered populations provides vulnerable and disenchanted groups with a perverse incentive to provoke the very violence that the international community is trying to prevent.[9] RtoP, it is argued, raises expectations of third party intervention among vulnerable populations and hence creates perverse incentives for them to violently rebel and provoke a genocidal response that they are unable to defend themselves against but which is likely to elicit external intervention. The promise of external intervention is thus said to encourage rebellion by increasing the likelihood of success and lowering its expected cost. By incentivizing risky behaviour and rewarding provocative rebellions, RtoP is said to unintentionally cause genocidal violence.[10] From this perspective any action undertaken with the purpose of protecting the civilian victims of armed conflict – including military intervention, robust peace operations, traditional peacekeeping, sanctions (general and targeted), judicial interventions, diplomacy (coercive and non-coercive), mediation, and public criticism of genocidal regimes – helps establish moral hazard.

This theory is underpinned by two additional assumptions. First, that a significant majority of genocidal violence is provoked by violent and often suicidal rebellions against governments. In other words, 'most ethnic groups that fall victim to genocidal violence are responsible for initially militarizing the conflict'.[11] If we accept this assumption, and there are powerful empirical reasons for not doing so, the most important question about the cause of genocidal violence becomes: why do vulnerable groups choose to rebel, bringing the anticipated genocidal response down upon the people they claim to represent? The second assumption is that the answer to this question can be deduced from theories of deterrence in International Relations. From this perspective, owing to the massive asymmetries of power that usually inhere between states and rebels, vulnerable and oppressed groups usually choose to not rebel because they expect to fail and suffer badly as a result. To understand the cause of genocidal violence, therefore, the theory suggests we need only know why deterrence fails in some circumstances. Kuperman offers five alternative hypotheses: (1) oppressed groups do not believe that the state's threat to retaliate is credible; (2) they expect to be victimized irrespective of their behaviour; (3) they expect victory at a tolerable cost without third party intervention; (4) they expect third party intervention to enable victory at a tolerable cost; (5) they do not behave as rational unitary actors. Proponents of moral hazard use case study analysis to conclude that option four – the expectation of third party intervention – provides the most plausible answer and therefore explains the cause of genocidal violence.[12]

Kuperman argues that Western intervention in northern Iraq in 1991 was the first relevant case and that, since then, interventions have proliferated, creating negative precedents that established perverse incentives.[13] During this time the RtoP norm (and its associated perverse incentives) gained ground through a combination of occasional negative precedent-setting activities (interventions) and 'irresponsible rhetoric; and was spurred on with the release of the 2001 ICISS report.[14] The effects were magnified in 2005 when the UN General Assembly unanimously affirmed RtoP.

Although moral hazard theory makes major general claims about RtoP as a remote cause of genocidal violence, to date, detailed evidence has only been presented in relation to its role as a proximate cause in a very limited subset of cases: Bosnia, Rwanda, Kosovo and Darfur. Not only does this raise issues of selection bias and spurious findings, but close examination of the empirical details of these cases reveals significant problems with, and limits to, the interpretations offered by proponents of moral hazard theory.[15]

In order to test these claims empirically, I examined them with my colleague Paul D. Williams. First, is there evidence to link the rise of RtoP as charted in the previous three chapters of this book with an increase in the prevalence and severity of armed rebellions and genocidal violence? Second, taking the first case study (Bosnia), does moral hazard provide a plausible account of the causes of genocidal violence? What is presented here is a brief summary of an early version of our assessment, we can give clear and negative answers to both questions. In short, despite the vociferousness of its proponents, we found very little evidence to support the claim that RtoP causes additional genocidal violence.

Moral hazard theory assumes that most genocidal violence is provoked by armed rebellions launched by vulnerable groups. Williams and I do not think that this claim is accurate, but for the purpose of our analysis here we will assume that it is. From this, the theory holds that by establishing perverse incentives through its promise of third party intervention, RtoP causes vulnerable groups to launch suicidal rebellions by altering the balance of deterrence. If moral hazard theory is correct in this regard, the development of RtoP should be associated with an increase in armed rebellions against established

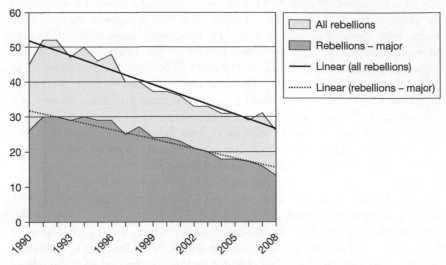

Figure 4.1 Rebellions against established governments 1990–2008 (all years)

governments because of the added incentives to rebel. In order to test this proposition, we used the Uppsala Conflict Data Program (UCDP) database of state-based conflicts and identified those conflicts between 1990 and 2008 that pitted at least one non-state rebel group against an established government. We excluded cases of state collapse (e.g. Somalia) and cases where the state did not exercise authority over its territory prior to the episode (e.g. the second war in the Democratic Republic of the Congo, post-2003 Iraq, post-2001 Afghanistan). The results are set out in Figure 4.1 and summarized in Table 4.1.

These results contradict the expectations from moral hazard theory. Most obviously, between 1990 and 2008 there was an overall decline in all forms

Table 4.1 Number of rebellions against established governments 1990–2008 (summary at three-year intervals)

Year	Rebellions	Rebellions involving over 1,000 battle-related deaths in any given year
1990	45	26
1993	47	29
1996	48	29
1999	37	24
2002	33	21
2005	31	18
2008	26	13

of armed rebellion against established governments. In terms of major rebellions, the number of cases declined by half between 1990 and 2008, and there was a decline of 44 per cent across all rebellions. Far from being encouraged to launch armed rebellions against their governments, therefore, vulnerable groups have proven significantly less likely to rebel since the emergence of RtoP. The emergence of RtoP has therefore been associated with a clear general pattern of decline in the number of rebellions. Significantly, that decline has been sharpest in relation to the more serious rebellions where genocidal violence is, presumably, most likely. The principal mechanism through which RtoP is said to act as a cause of genocidal violence (inducing provocative rebellions) is therefore invalid.

It is worth also considering the relationship between RtoP and mass atrocities more directly because it might be argued that although moral hazard is wrong about the mechanism through which RtoP causes genocidal violence (inducing rebellions) it is correct in its broader proposition that RtoP is associated with increased genocidal violence. If moral hazard were correct, the development of RtoP would be associated with a corresponding increase in episodes of genocidal violence. To test for this, we compiled a list of episodes of mass atrocities between 1945 and 2008 where the *lowest* casualty estimates put the toll of civilians *intentionally killed* at greater than 5,000 (Appendix A). If moral hazard theory were correct, we would expect to see an increase in the number of new episodes of genocidal violence as governments were provoked into acts of violence by rebels induced by RtoP's perverse incentives. Figure 4.2 charts the number of new episodes of genocidal violence in each year from 1945 to 2008.

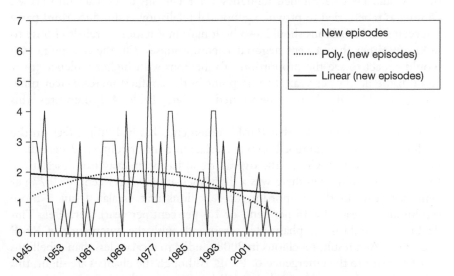

Figure 4.2 Number of new episodes of 'genocidal violence' (with more than 5,000 intentional fatalities), 1945–2008

Clearly there is no upward trend in new episodes corresponding with the emergence of RtoP. Across the period, the annual number of new episodes fluctuated between six and zero. When we add trend lines to this chaotically fluctuating diagram they both suggest a downwards trend since the emergence of RtoP. The linear trend line identifies a straightforwardly negative trend whereas the polynomial trend line indicates a slight upwards trends from the 1940s until the late 1970s/early 1980s, followed by a more pronounced decline that has accelerated in the first decade of the twenty-first century. This finding is consistent with research showing a marked reduction in the overall number of new armed conflicts over the same period. Writing in 2007, for instance, Harbom and Wallensteen found that '[w]hile more than half (67) of the 122 armed conflicts active between 1989 and 2006 started after 1989, the highest number of new conflicts erupted just at the start of the post-Cold War period. In the early 1990s, the annual count of new conflicts ranged from 8 to 11, compared from 1 to 3 in the late 1990s and early 2000s. No new conflicts erupted in either 2005 or 2006. Thus all currently ongoing conflicts have a history, many of them a long one'.[16] Far from encouraging new episodes of genocidal violence as anticipated by moral hazard theory, therefore, RtoP's emergence correlates with a reduction in the incidence of new cases.

This brings us to an associated claim made by moral hazard theory: that RtoP inadvertently increases civilian suffering by exacerbating and prolonging genocidal violence. The theory suggests that RtoP creates a perverse incentive for rebels to hold out on a negotiated settlement in the expectation that external intervention will deliver their political objectives for them. If this were correct, there would be a heightened tendency for rebellions to escalate into armed conflict as rebels tried to provoke genocidal retaliation and induce third party intervention. Rebellions should also be longer in duration as rebels choose to hold out rather than accept negotiated compromises. On the first point, we would expect to see the proportion of rebellions with higher violence (over 1,000 battle deaths per year at some point in the conflict) increase over time. Using the UCDP dataset mentioned earlier, Table 4.2 illustrates this relationship.

Table 4.2 demonstrates that RtoP's emergence has had little effect on the likelihood that an armed rebellion will escalate into major conflict. Where there has been an effect, however, the overall trend has been away from escalation. Between 1990 and 1999 there was a slight increase (by 7 per cent, or 0.77 per cent per year) in the proportion of rebellions that escalated but a more significant decrease (by 15 per cent, or 1.6 per cent per year) thereafter. This decline, it should be emphasized, corresponds with the emergence of RtoP after 2001. As a result, rebellions in 2008 tended to escalate less than rebellions in 1990, prior to the emergence of RtoP. Although the changes are slight, this data supports the conclusion that RtoP has not created remote incentives to escalate rebellions.

Table 4.2 Proportion of rebellions that escalate into armed conflict 1990–2008 (three-year summary)

Year	Total	Major	Major (%)
1990	45	26	58
1993	47	29	62
1996	48	29	60
1999	37	24	65
2002	33	21	64
2005	31	18	58
2008	26	13	50

A second way of testing the proposition that RtoP prolongs suffering is to consider the *duration* of episodes of genocidal violence. If moral hazard theory was correct, all other things being equal we should expect episodes of genocidal violence to increase in duration as rebels are induced to hold out by the perverse incentives associated with RtoP. The temporal duration of conflict is notoriously difficult to measure and still more difficult to compare across time. The temporal factor makes simple averages misleading, because the data for later dates is more heavily distorted by a small number of long-running episodes than data for earlier dates. To take account of this problem, we adopted a broad approach based on the modified UCDP list of cases used above that simply compares the duration of episodes across 'Cold War' and 'post-Cold War' cases. This simple analysis yielded useful results (see Table 4.3).

Episodes of genocidal violence that erupted after the Cold War tended to be considerably shorter than episodes that erupted during the Cold War: 44 per cent of post-Cold War episodes were resolved in three years or less, compared with only 5 per cent of Cold War episodes. The figures are an equally marked 58 per cent and 10 per cent respectively if we draw out the analysis to seven years or less. This suggests that post-Cold War rebels are significantly less likely to be able or willing to fight protracted conflicts. This contradicts moral hazard theory's proposition that post-Cold War rebels have additional

Table 4.3 Duration of episodes of genocidal violence

	3 years or fewer	4–7 years	8 years and over	Unresolved
Cold War (1946–89)	2 (5%)	2 (5%)	21 (57%)	12 (33%)
Post-Cold War (1990–2008)	24 (44%)	8 (14%)	9 (16%)	14 (26%)

incentives to hold out. Indeed, the reverse seems to be true: for whatever reason post-Cold War rebels are *more likely* to resolve conflicts and *less likely* to hold out.

In summary, therefore, the evidence suggests that the claim that RtoP constitutes a remote cause of additional genocidal violence by creating moral hazard cannot be empirically sustained. Where moral hazard would expect the emergence of RtoP to be associated with an increased number of rebellions against established governments, increased frequency of new episodes of genocidal violence, a greater tendency for rebellions to escalate into armed conflict, and the prolonging of episodes of genocidal violence, the rise of RtoP has been associated with fewer rebellions, fewer new episodes of genocidal violence, a slight reduction in the likelihood that a rebellion will escalate and a marked reduction in the expected duration of genocidal violence. These findings are consistent with a wide range of other studies.[17] They lead us to reject the claim that RtoP constitutes a remote cause of genocidal violence. This brings us to the question of whether RtoP might constitute a cause of genocidal violence in a small selection of cases. To consider this, much more modest proposition, we will briefly consider the case of Bosnia.

Moral hazard theory holds that RtoP and the norms that contributed to it helped cause genocidal violence in Bosnia by establishing perverse incentives that induced the Bosnian Muslim leadership to deliberately provoke the Serbs into committing genocidal violence. Apparently, they did this in order to trigger the third party intervention that was necessary to deliver their stated goal of a unified and independent Bosnia. This explanation suggests that the Bosnian Muslim leadership developed its plan in June 1991, at the time when Croatia launched its secession from the Yugoslav federation.[18] According to proponents of moral hazard theory, the Bosnian government accepted and then rejected two peace plans – the 'Belgrade Initiative' (August 1991) and the 'Cutileiro plan' (March 1992) – in order to make themselves appear reasonable while secretly holding out for external intervention by provoking the Serbs into genocidal violence. As part of this plan, we are told that the Bosnian Muslims refrained from developing their own militia until international recognition was guaranteed in order to preserve their image as helpless victims. Once recognition was promised they moved quickly to establish a militia of 100,000 fighters, armed with 50,000 weapons.[19]

This account of the proximate causes of Bosnia's war suffers from a number of major problems.[20] Most notably, it cannot satisfactorily account for why RtoP related norms created expectations of third party intervention sufficient to induce provocative behaviour from Bosnia's Muslims but did not deter the Serbs from genocidal behaviour. In addition, the theory's account of the Belgrade Initiative and Cutileiro plan overlook important pieces of information which significantly downgrade the role that expectations of third party intervention played in shaping Bosnian government decision-making. Space constraints prohibit a thorough assessment of all these points.[21] We will therefore limit ourselves to briefly examining the first question – the source of the Bosnian Muslim leadership's expectation of third party intervention.

Moral hazard theory's account of the causes of the Bosnian war hinges on the claim that the Bosnian government expected that Serbian genocidal violence would be met with third party intervention. The theory needs to be able to show that these expectations were not simply 'hopes' or 'preferences' but sufficiently powerful beliefs to have the causal effect of inducing a democratically elected government to provoke genocide against its own people. Proponents of moral hazard theory argue that these expectations derived from three principal sources: the precedent set by the Western intervention in northern Iraq in April 1991, direct encouragement by the US, and the deployment of UNPROFOR to Croatia in February 1992.[22] The theory holds that it was increased Western involvement in the crisis, after June 1991, that encouraged the Bosnian Muslim leadership to abandon the search for a negotiated compromise in favour of pursuing independence, provoking genocidal violence, and securing external intervention.[23] Thus, 'had it not been for the expectation of international intervention, the Muslims might not have seceded at all, or at least not without first agreeing to a cantonization plan, so the bloody Bosnian war might have been averted'.[24]

But this account runs into an immediate problem in relation to timing. The Bosnian Muslim leadership's intention to secede from Yugoslavia in the event that Slovenia and Croatia seceded was openly declared as early as September 1990 and the Bosnian nationalist party (SDA) took this policy to the November 1990 parliamentary election. At a widely reported speech in Velika Kladuša, the leader of the Bosnian nationalist party, Alija Izetbeović insisted that: 'there are three options for Bosnia: Bosnia in a federal Yugoslavia – an acceptable option; Bosnia in a confederal Yugoslavia – also an acceptable option; and finally an independent and free Bosnia. I must say here openly that if the threat that Croatia and Slovenia leave Yugoslavia is carried out, Bosnia will not remain in a truncated Yugoslavia. In other words, Bosnia will not tolerate staying in a greater Serbia and being part of it. If it comes to that, we will declare independence, the absolute independence of Bosnia and we will decide then in what new constellation will find itself, as a sovereign republic that will use its sovereignty'.[25] It is this policy – seeking independence in the event of Slovene and Croatian secession – that moral hazard theory claims was inspired in the second half of 1991 by the emerging promise of third party intervention in the event that the Serbs perpetrated genocidal violence. The problem, of course, is that Bosnia's intention to secede in the event of Slovene and Croatian secession was stated well in advance of Western engagement with the crisis in Yugoslavia. More specifically, the declared intention to secede predated all three of the factors that, according to moral hazard theory, motivated it. It was stated seven months before *Operation Provide Comfort* in Iraq, at least ten months before the US abandoned its policy of insisting that Yugoslavia remain united,[26] and 18 months before the deployment of UNPROFOR. Izetbegović's preference for secession in the event of Slovene and Croatian secession thus cannot have been motivated or encouraged by perverse incentives associated with what would later become RtoP. Analysts agree that there was no humanitarian intervention norm or doctrine of sovereignty as responsibility in September 1990 and none of the sources of perverse incentive identified by moral hazard theorists were in place at this time.[27] As such, expectations about third party intervention could not possibly have motivated the Bosnian Muslim's intention to secede in the event of Slovene and Croatian secession because that intent *predated* the emergence of perverse incentives.

Despite the vociferousness with which the claim that RtoP causes genocidal violence is sometimes made, the claim is an ill-founded one. The rise of RtoP has been associated with a decline in armed rebellions and genocidal violence and a cursory examination of one of the theory's most prized examples, the war in Bosnia, reveals that the account it offers is logically implausible and not supported by the evidence. We can therefore be quite confident in arguing that there is very little to the claim that RtoP causes additional genocidal violence and proceed to consider what the preceding chapters tell us about RtoP's function, scope, international status and effectiveness.

RtoP's function

The discussion in the preceding two chapters suggests that RtoP is conceptualized by different actors as fulfilling two functions, which are not necessarily complementary. The first manner in which RtoP is used is to describe a political commitment accompanied by a policy agenda in need of implementation. This is the manner in which RtoP is most commonly referred to by the UN Secretary-General and diplomats at UN headquarters (see Chapter 2). Based largely on a plain text reading of paragraphs 138 and 139 of the World Summit Outcome Document, this position makes two general propositions. First, as agreed by member states, the RtoP is universal and enduring. In other words, it applies to all states, all of the time. From this perspective, there is logically no question of whether RtoP 'applies' to a given situation because the RtoP does not arise and evaporate with circumstance. As such, much of the debate about RtoP in practice covered in the previous chapter, focused as it was on the question of whether RtoP applies to a given situation, poses the wrong question. The question should not be whether it applies, but how it is best exercised. Second, it follows that as a universal and enduring commitment, RtoP gives rise to a comprehensive policy agenda that needs to be identified, articulated and implemented. The UN Secretary-General's 2009 report and the ensuing General Assembly debate marks the first step towards defining that agenda but, as the Secretary-General recognized, there is much more work to be done in this field. The report and General-Assembly debate that followed it mark out a framework in terms of the three pillars, but implementation has yet to begin in earnest.[28] Precisely what should be included in this policy agenda is still to be debated.

The Secretary-General's report sets out some of the parameters and while academics dispute the precise contours, there is broad agreement around a dozen or so key factors that ought to be addressed as part of a comprehensive strategy to prevent genocide and mass atrocities under pillars one and two of RtoP.[29] Likewise, there is an emerging body of evidence about the most effective forms of protection which might inform the development of capacities to better exercise pillar three responsibilities.[30] The effect of this approach is to emphasize RtoP as a broad based policy agenda focused on the 'upstream' prevention of genocide and mass atrocities through capacity-building and international cooperation, though without downplaying the significance of pillar three, and to focus attention on the capacities for effective response within the prevailing normative framework that underpins international community.

In my view, this interpretation of RtoPs function accurately reflects what was agreed by states in 2005 and it is therefore no surprise that it is this view that has been most commonly expressed by governments, especially from the global south. Critics, however, complain that it fundamentally weakens the principle's normative value. For example, Gareth Evans has argued that the preventive component of RtoP should be confined in scope to situations where mass atrocities are imminent and should not extend to longer-term prevention efforts.[31] 'To widen the focus' of RtoP in this way, he argues, 'is dangerous from the perspective of undermining R2P's utility as a rallying cry. If too much is bundled under the R2P banner, we run the risk of diluting its capacity to mobilize in the cases where it is really needed'.[32] The problem with this critique is that most of the world's governments and most scholars who work on the prevention of genocide and mass atrocities seem to agree that a commitment to prevention needs to take root causes seriously. Moreover, in the majority of cases, by the time that mass atrocities are imminently apprehended, the window for prevention is closed or extremely narrow. The oft-touted case of Kenya, where late-in-the-day prevention succeeded, is a rare exception and even here up to 1,500 civilians were killed.[33] But even if we accept Kenya as a model, we are left with a doctrine that requires the killing of hundreds, if not thousands, of civilians before its 'prevention' arms kicks in. A preventive tool that is only activated after the massacre of civilians is morally troubling and not particularly useful.

Evans' argument brings us to the second putative function of RtoP language. Drawing on 'Copenhagen School' theories of securitization, Eli Stamnes has shown that the intention behind the RtoP principle is to generate a speech act which has the effect of elevating certain issues above normal politics as a catalyst for decisive international action.[34] In other words, RtoP is a label that can be attached to particular crises in order to generate the will and consensus necessary to mobilize a decisive international response. According to Evans, 'the whole point of embracing the new language of 'the responsibility to protect' is that it is capable of generating an effective, consensual response in extreme, conscience-shocking cases, in a way that 'right to intervene' language simply was not'.[35] This is how RtoP has most obviously been used by diplomats and activists in response to humanitarian crises. In the case of Darfur, advocates used RtoP to generate the political will to intervene; in Myanmar, Kouchner invoked 'RtoP' to legitimize forcible aid delivery; in Georgia it was used to justify the use of force; in Gaza, activists referred to RtoP to generate international attention to the commission of war crimes; and in relation to North Korea and Myanmar it was invoked as part of efforts to persuade the international community to pay attention to acute human rights situations. It is this mode of thinking that frames debates as being about the applicability of RtoP in a given situation rather than about the most appropriate manner of preventing mass atrocities and protecting vulnerable populations. Although many commentators and some diplomats switch between the first mode ('RtoP as policy agenda') and this, the two are largely incompatible, contributing to much of the confusion about the way in which RtoP is used. As Stamnes points out, one cannot sustain a commitment to the long-term prevention of genocide and mass atrocities as part of RtoP while also conceptualizing RtoP as a quasi-securitizing catalyst for immediate action, because referring to RtoP outside a context of imminent crisis weakens its capacity to highlight exceptional emergency situations. Employing a 'securitized' version of RtoP in relation to the structural prevention of genocide and mass atrocities is likely to generate significant opposition from states concerned about the slippery slope to coercive interference that would be implied by every utterance of RtoP.[36] Therefore, analysts, activists and advocates need to make a decision about which vision of RtoP they want to pursue.

While the speech-act account ('RtoP as catalyst for international action') dominates public discussion about RtoP and humanitarian crises, and may certainly be consistent with the concerns that animated the ICISS, it is hard to find support for it in paragraphs 138–9 of the World Summit Outcome Document. On the one hand, the commitment made by states was open-ended not time or context sensitive. The declaration makes clear that a government's RtoP does not arise or evaporate with each individual crisis. By saying that RtoP does not apply to Sri Lanka or Myanmar, for example, commentators are inadvertently suggesting that the government does not have an obligation to protect its populations from the four crimes. This is plainly inconsistent with the World Summit agreement. Of course, what the commentators mean to say is that coercive interference by external powers is unlikely to win international support or to strengthen the protection of vulnerable populations. By saying the former and not the latter (which is what they actually mean), however, they inadvertently help to reinforce the association between RtoP and coercive interference which has so stymied efforts to build consensus on the principle (see Chapters 1 and 2). On the other hand, the World Summit agreement made it plain that RtoP related crises would be dealt with through the UN's *normal* peace and security mechanisms and did not require 'exceptional' measures such as armed intervention without the authorization of the Security Council. We will return later to the question of how effective the use of RtoP as a call to action is. For now, it is important to note that actors have a choice about the way in which they employ RtoP language, that the two options cannot be used conjointly with coherence, and that this choice affects how we understand the principle's role, impact and effects.

RtoP's scope

There is evidence of clear progress towards a shared understanding of what RtoP refers to and as I noted in the previous chapter the debates about Myanmar and Georgia have helped to further clarify the situation. In Chapter 1, I pointed out that the ICISS was surprisingly opaque on this question. The Commission's list of 'basic principles' described the overall RtoP problem as involving cases where 'a population is suffering serious harm, as a result of internal war, insurgency, repression or state failure'. Its 'just cause thresholds' focused on large-scale loss of life and ethnic cleansing. Its description of prevention, however, covered 'the root causes and direct causes of internal conflict and other man-made crises putting populations at risk'. The World Summit performed an immense service by clarifying that the principle was concerned with genocide, war crimes, ethnic cleansing and crimes against humanity and this consensus was reaffirmed in the 2009 General Assembly debate. To date, outside academic circles, the only significant attempt to widen this scope was Kouchner's argument that the Myanmar regime's failure to grant humanitarian access provided grounds for international coercion undertaken under the rubric of RtoP. This claim, we noted, received very little international support and the whole debate may have had the effect of actually reinforcing the more limited understanding of RtoP's scope that emerged from the World Summit. Besides this case, diplomatic use of the principle has been surprisingly uniform. In the Georgia case, for example, Russia invoked RtoP in relation to genocide and crimes against humanity. In this case, it was the facts of the case that were contested (i.e. whether Georgia was actually committing genocide and mass atrocities in South Ossetia) not the principle's applicability to the alleged crimes. Nonetheless, this case helped establish a benchmark of evidence required to justify utilizing RtoP for coercive purposes – there must be an evident pattern of widespread killing or forced displacement, even though not all war crimes and crimes against humanity require this.

What this means in terms of the sorts of activities and issues than can be discussed under the rubric of RtoP depends on what we think about the principle's function, bringing us back to our earlier discussion. Those who view RtoP as a policy agenda can follow the UN Secretary-General in articulating a 'narrow but deep' approach focusing on the four crimes and their prevention but mobilizing the full weight of human knowledge and international institutional capacity to that end, producing programs of work in areas as diverse as interfaith dialogue, equitable economic development, and security sector reform that may appear tangentially related to atrocity crimes but which are the building blocks of prevention. Those who want to preserve RtoP as a catalyst for decisive action, however, will reject the depth of this agenda and prefer instead to use the four crimes as a checklist to judge which situations deserve RtoPs attention, resources and some form of international intervention or engagement and, by extension, which do not. Within this schema, there will almost always have to be actual massacres before RtoP can be invoked, as we noted earlier. One way to resolve these issues is to look carefully at what governments have agreed to and at their practice since 2005. Another is to ask where RtoP can best add value. The multiple crises of the past five years provide us with an evidentiary base to begin making judgments about that.

RtoP as a norm

Is RtoP a norm and, if so, what sort of norm is it and what does it require? Simply put, norms are shared expectations of appropriate behaviour for actors with a given identity.[37] There is general consensus that RtoP is a norm, but much less agreement on what sort of norm it is.[38] There are two elements to this particular problem. First, RtoP is not a single norm but a collection of shared expectations which have different qualities. On the one hand, RtoP involves expectations about how states relate to populations under their care. These expectations predate RtoP and are embedded in international humanitarian and human rights law.[39] Although there are arguments at the margins about their scope (especially concerning crimes against humanity) and the extent to which they are embedded or habitual, the basic proposition that states are legally and morally required to not intentionally kill civilians is well established.[40] RtoP's first pillar is therefore best understood as a reaffirmation and codification of already existing norms.[41] On the other hand, as we noted in Chapter 2, RtoP also places demands on states as members of the international community: to assist and encourage their peers in the fulfilment of their RtoP (pillar two) and to take timely and decisive action in cases where a state has manifestly failed to exercise RtoP (pillar three). It is much less certain that this aspect of RtoP constitutes a norm and, if it can be so-called, there remains a serious question as to whether it is a sufficiently determinate norm to exert a compliance-pull that alters state behaviour.[42]

The test of whether pillars two and three are properly called norms is the extent to which there is a *shared expectation* that governments will exercise this responsibility such that they recognize a duty and right to do so and that failure to act this way attracts criticism from the society of states. There is some evidence to support the view that such positive duties exist: in the case of *Bosnia vs. Serbia*, which concerned Serbia's alleged complicity with the commission of genocide in Bosnia, the International Court of Justice found that states have a legal obligation to take all measures reasonably available to them to prevent genocide. In addition, international humanitarian law requires that states 'ensure respect' for the law as well as follow the rules themselves. Moreover, the International Law Commission's Draft Articles on the Responsibility of States for Internationally Wrongful Acts give states a duty to cooperate to bring an end to breaches of the law. Finally, the UN famously recognized its failure to prevent the Rwandan genocide as a failure of the whole UN system – implicitly recognizing a shared norm of intervention in cases of genocide.[43] But these claims require a very liberal interpretation of the law.[44] Also, the case history documented in the previous chapter suggests that mutual recognition of a positive duty to exercise pillars two and three is inconsistent at best. While there is evidence of these norms at work in creating expectations about the world's responses to the crises in Kenya and Myanmar/Nargis, states were not criticized by their peers for failing to do more to protect civilians in Sudan, Somalia, and the DRC, the norm did not prevent politically motivated objections to Goldstone's finding that Israel committed war crimes in Gaza from overriding concerns about indiscriminate and disproportionate attacks on a civilian population, and international engagement with the crisis in Guinea was mobilized without reference to RtoP.

The case of Guinea is particularly interesting in this regard because it is so difficult to assess. On the one hand, an RtoP optimist might argue that this case demonstrates the internalization of RtoP. In other words, it shows that the international community has reached a point where it responds to massacres as a matter of habit with condemnation, punitive measures and engagement aimed at fostering peace and preventing further violence. That those actors do not refer to RtoP may be construed as demonstrating the norm's internalisation. Thus, this kind of response is considered habitual so that there is no need to invoke specific doctrines or norms to justify behaviour, because the society of states considers it to be routine. On the other hand, however, sceptics may argue that this case demonstrates that RtoP is superfluous because it does not add value. Or, worse, that because RtoP is associated with controversial ideas such as intervention, international engagement is more effective when RtoP language is avoided altogether. The reality is probably somewhere in between these positions. RtoP is itself a manifestation of the sorts of political and humanitarian sensibilities that generated the international response to the crisis but the response was not dependent on RtoP itself and neither, in this case, was RtoP used as a diplomatic lever – though the sorts of arguments in relation to international expectations about the roles that ought to be played by political leaders employed in relation to Kenya can certainly be discerned in the background of the Guinea too.

Returning to the broader question about RtoP as a norm, even if pillars two and three can be described as norms they are fundamentally weakened by the problem of indeterminacy. While norms shape shared understandings and limit the behaviours that can be justified by reference to them, such that actors will be inhibited from acting in ways that cannot be plausibly justified, what a norm prescribes in a certain situation is never fixed or absolute.[45] All other things being equal, the more precisely a norm indicates the behaviour it expects in a given situation, the stronger its compliance pull.[46] RtoP's first pillar, for example, is a relatively determinate norm: it demands that states refrain from perpetrating four specific crimes. By comparison, the demands imposed by pillars two and three of RtoP are indeterminate. In this context, beyond a minimum expectation that states should not actively assist genocidaires, it is seldom – if ever – clear what, exactly, the RtoP requires in a given situation. This is partly because of the indeterminacy of the norm itself, a product of disagreement among its authors evidenced by the concerns raised at the 2009 General Assembly debate,[47] and partly due to the inevitable effects of intervening variables such as competing judgments about the facts of the case (e.g. about the cause, existence and scale of mass atrocities) and different assessments about the most prudential courses of action. Thus, for example, it is possible to plausibly attempt to legitimize both sides of debates about forceful intervention in Darfur, no-fly zones in Sudan, the indictment of Omar al-Bashir, international peacekeeping in Somalia, heaping criticism and sanctions upon Sri Lanka, criticising Israel and/or Hamas, the deployment of Western troops to the DRC, Sudan and Somalia, sanctions, engagement or the status-quo in relation to North Korea and Myanmar, and much else besides by reference to the RtoP. The indeterminacy of what RtoP requires in these cases weakens its compliance pull because it is difficult, if not impossible, to know with any certainty what is required by RtoP and therefore the extent to which actors are satisfying shared expectations of appropriate behaviour. Of course, as Quentin Skinner argued, actors 'cannot hope to stretch the application of the existing principles indefinitely; correspondingly, [the actor] can only hope to legitimate a restricted range of actions'.[48] It is fair to say, therefore, that active support for *genocidaires* and arguments in favour of complete inaction in the face of mass atrocities would be obviously inconsistent with RtoP. But once states agree that *something* ought to be done, the indeterminacy of pillars two and three severely restricts RtoP's compliance pull, and hence its ability to pull states to agree as to what needs to be done and who should contribute. This gets us to the question of RtoP's effectiveness and added value.

How effective is RtoP?

To date, assessments of RtoP's effectiveness have tended to fall into one of three camps. As we noted earlier, the most extreme, put forth by proponents of moral hazard, holds that RtoP has actually 'caused' genocidal violence that would not have otherwise occurred by encouraging rebels into risky armed uprisings that provoke genocidal responses from governments. A less radical variant on this theme suggests that RtoP can encourage external actors to pay undue attention to military responses to mass atrocities rather than focusing on more promising political solutions.[49] An alternative critique, posed above, suggests simply that the indeterminacy of RtoP's second and third pillars limit the extent to which it can exert tangible effects on behaviour, especially in response to crises.[50] On the other hand, as we noted earlier, some point to Kenya as a good example of RtoP in practice and argue that in this case RtoP helped galvanize international attention and bring diplomatic pressure to bear on that country's political leaders.

Systematic analysis of RtoP's effectiveness should be prefaced on a clear understanding of what it is that RtoP is meant to achieve. This takes us back to the principle's function. The 'RtoP as policy agenda' approach lends itself to the view that the primary aim of RtoP is to prevent genocide and mass atrocities from occurring in the first place whilst also strengthening the world's capacity to respond. For this approach, while it is important that the world responds to mass killing in a timely and decisive manner, the key test in the long-run is whether there are fewer cases of mass killing to respond to. What is more, this account would suggest that it is too early to pass judgment on the principle because RtoP has not yet been implemented. In relation to prevention, though, although it is too early to offer definitive answers to this question, we noted earlier that the general information is mainly positive: the Uppsala Conflict Data Program recorded a sharp reduction in the number of fatalities caused by one-sided violence between 2004–7 and my own survey of episodes of mass killing involving the intentionally caused deaths of over 5,000 civilians shows an equally sharp decline, with no new episodes after 2005.[51] These downward trends in relation to attacks on civilians are especially important because they come within a context of an increase in armed conflict overall between 2004–8, suggesting that belligerents are generally less likely to use atrocities than they were previously.[52] Taken together, this data suggests that RtoP has been associated with a general decline in mass atrocities, though we cannot conclude that RtoP *caused* this effect or even contributed significantly to it. Each of the trends were evident prior to 2005 and it is impossible to know from global figures whether international activism was prompted by RtoP, and whether it was this activism or local factors that encouraged actors to refrain from mass atrocities. Nevertheless, these figures do give us good grounds for thinking that international efforts to prevent mass atrocities can help deliver an overall reduction and that RtoP hs been part of an international context that has helped support a reduction of mass killing.

One way around the problem of general causation would be to analyze cases individually. Of the cases outlined in the previous chapter, six (Kenya, Myanmar/Nargis, Sri Lanka, Gaza, Sudan/CPA, and Guinea) were/are crises characterized by credible fears of mass atrocities occurring in the future. In three of these cases (Kenya, Myanmar/Nargis and Sri Lanka), diplomats reminded governments of their RtoP and of the fact that the world was paying attention to their behaviour, and/or the UN and regional organizations helped broker political agreements, and/or humanitarian agencies delivered aid and assistance. In an additional case (Guinea), diplomatic pressure was placed on a regime though without reference to RtoP explicitly. Although compliance was neither complete nor unhindered, the feared mass atrocities did not eventuate in any of these four cases. Of course, in the case of Myanmar the invocation of RtoP by France was widely rejected and criticized, so it would be difficult to credit the principle with fulfilling a useful function in that case.[53] Although there were calls for the Security Council to step into the fray in all three situations, in neither case did the situation get so bad that the costs associated with non-consensual measures were outweighed by the gravity of the situation. In relation to the other cases there is little evidence to suggest that international concerns about RtoP persuaded either Israel or Hamas to moderate their behaviour. It is too early to tell whether international engagement with the CPA in Sudan will help prevent the potential slide back into civil war in that country. RtoP has, therefore, been associated with the use of diplomacy to prevent crises escalating into mass atrocities and those attempts have enjoyed a reasonable degree of success. In two of the six relevant cases (Kenya and Sri Lanka), diplomats used RtoP language to good effect to encourage political leaders to refrain from the use of mass atrocities. In a third (Guinea) a similar diplomatic strategy was employed to good effect, though without specifically referring to RtoP. Of course, we cannot definitively know whether more atrocities would have been committed had RtoP language not been used.

This approach only captures part of the contribution that RtoP might make to preventing mass atrocities. The further upstream we go in terms of structural prevention, the more difficult it is to demonstrate that RtoP is having a positive preventive effect, yet it is here that the principle might have its greatest effect. Upstream, RtoP may prevent mass atrocities in three principal ways: by encouraging the internalization of the principle of discrimination within armed forces, state leaders and societies; by helping states and societies to build the capacities they need to resolve differences without recourse to violence and atrocities; and by persuading political leaders that they are likely to pay material and reputational costs for the commission of mass atrocities thereby encouraging them to adopt alternative strategies. These three factors may persuade potential belligerents to not employ mass atrocities. This is an inevitably long-term agenda that involves changing identities and interests, and it is impossible to draw a direct causal connection between these processes and the prevention of specific atrocities at a later date. Moreover, as mentioned earlier, these upstream effects are contingent on RtoP's implementation. For these reasons we should not expect to see the principle having an effect until it is implemented. However, there are numerous examples of armed conflicts in the past five years that have not produced mass atrocities, despite having occurred in regions that have endured recent episodes. In addition to the case of Guinea, discussed earlier where (at the time of writing) mass killing was limited to a single episode, this list includes, but is not limited to, Chad, Mali, Pakistan, Cote d'Ivoire, and Timor-Leste. In these cases, a combination of the internalization of the principle of non-combatant immunity, international monitoring and assistance, and rational calculations about the potential costs and benefits associated with mass atrocities, encouraged actors to refrain from committing atrocities in situations where doing so might have secured short-term gains such as punishing insurgents or toppling governments. That it is here that RtoP and associated norms are having some effect is supported by the fact, noted earlier, that the incidence of mass killing is declining while the incidence of armed conflict more generally has increased, suggesting that active belligerents are more often choosing to not commit atrocities.

This brings us to the second function of RtoP – as a speech act that provides catalyst for timely and decisive international action in the face of emergencies characterized by the commission, or imminent commission, of one or more of the four RtoP crimes. The effects of RtoP in this regard are easier to measure, but the results are less promising and suggest that the principle has had little success in mobilizing timely and decisive international action.[54] Since 2005, the five largest crises in terms of the numbers of civilians intentionally killed are Iraq (c. 75,000 civilians killed violently since 2005), Somalia (c. 17,000), Sudan (Darfur and south, c. 5,000), DRC (c. 5,000), Afghanistan (c. 5,000) and Kenya (c. 1,500).[55] Of these, Iraq and Afghanistan have not been viewed through the prism of RtoP but through the prism of military occupation and the war on terror. In relation to Somalia, there has been little RtoP talk, the UN and AU have proven reluctant to act decisively, and the West tends to focus more on the situation's external symptoms (piracy and links to Islamist terrorism) than its civilian protection dimension (see Chapter 8). Despite talk of operating through the prism of RtoP, international engagement with Sudan (UNAMID and UNMIS) and the DRC (MONUC/MONUSCO) has not perceptibly changed as a result of RtoP. In these cases, the most significant development – the ICC's indictment of Omar al-Bashir – needs to balanced against continued under-resourcing of the UN's peace operations. As a result, MONUC/MONUSCO and DRC government forces have thus far failed to bring the murderous Hutu FDLR to heal, UNAMID continues to struggle to protect itself and civilians in its care, and UNMIS has proven unable to stem the tide of local conflicts. Finally, while Kenya is a notable success for RtoP we need to be clear about RtoP's role in this case. While RtoP was utilized by diplomats, it is not clear that RtoP itself caused or contributed to the relatively high levels of international engagement. In this case, RtoP was more a diplomatic tool than catalyst for action. It was the emergence of the AU's peace and security architecture that provided the immediate catalyst and institutional setting for preventive diplomacy in this case. More general data seems to support these assessments. In the past few years, the RtoP's Western champions have proven less, not more, willing to contribute to UN peace operations and have almost uniformly tightened their domestic regimes governing asylum for people displaced by violence.[56] The most charitable conclusion from all this is that it is too early to tell whether RtoP can be an effective catalyst for timely and decisive action in the face of mass atrocities. But this assessment may be too generous in the face of the principle's consistent inability to generate heightened international activism or change behaviour.

The best explanation as to why RtoP's third pillar has thus far failed to generate additional political will relates to the problem of indeterminacy discussed earlier. Because it is difficult to determine with any degree of certainty what RtoP's third pillar requires in any given situation, it is unlikely that – without a requisite transformation of national interests – the principle will 'pull' governments towards making larger commitments to protecting civilians in danger. It is important in this regard to recognize that there are different reasons why actors want to legitimize their behaviour by reference to a shared norm. At one end of the spectrum, norm compliance is caused by instrumental decisions: actors obey a norm not because they think it has inherent value (i.e. it is 'internalized'), but because they believe that norm-violation will impose prohibitive costs. Close to this is 'non-instrumental conformism' or 'mimicry', where compliance is generated not by overt calculations of costs in relation to particular actions but by a more generalized concern about social exclusion.[57] When a norm is indeterminate, actors who comply for instrumental or mimicry-related reasons are unlikely to be pulled into changing their behaviour. Instead, they are likely to adopt the norm's language while persisting with established patterns of behaviour. They are able to do so precisely because it is so difficult for other members of the society to determine whether or not they are acting in a manner consistent with the norm. In none of the RtoP related cases whose origins predated RtoP have actors – be they RtoP supporters or critics – adjusted their behaviour to take account of the new norm, lending support to the view that RtoP's indeterminacy permits states to commit to the principle in rhetoric without changing their practice. Alarmingly, evidence from the cases studied in the previous chapter suggests that even RtoP's most ardent supporters have not internalized the norm to the extent that it affects the way they actually behave.

Given that indeterminacy makes it unlikely that RtoP will serve, in the near future, as a catalyst for international action in response to genocide and mass atrocities, it seems reasonable to argue that the most prudent path is to view the principle as a policy agenda in need of implementation. This view would certainly be consistent with the evidence thus far that RtoP is best employed as a diplomatic tool or prism to guide efforts to prevent and stem the tide of mass atrocities and has little utility in terms of generating additional international political will to intervene in response to such episodes. Over the long-term, if national, regional and global institutions support the behaviours and build the capacities envisaged by the UN Secretary-General, this will make it easier and less costly to prevent and respond effectively to genocide and mass atrocities. This may also have the effect of reducing the tendency of states to view prevention and protection work as inimical to national interests and increasing the likelihood that they will undertake prevention work as a matter of habit and make use of the response capacities they have created when needed. Of course, there should also be fewer overall cases to respond to because of the effects of the prevention work. We need to recognize that, by itself, RtoP is unlikely to stimulate greater international activism in response to immediate crises in Darfur, Somalia, the DRC or, indeed, the next Rwanda. Where enhanced activism has been apparent, for instance in relation to Kenya and Guinea, it has been led by other developments such as regional security architecture that complement the RtoP agenda. The effect of implementing the agenda outlined by the Secretary-General would be to strengthen these parallel and complementary processes and thereby establish the institutional frameworks and capacities needed to deliver on RtoP. If that were done, there is a good chance of reducing the likelihood of future Rwandas and ensuring that future responses are indeed 'timely and decisive'. For this reason, it may be more important that the UN Secretariat establish a joint office for RtoP and the prevention of genocide – thus embedding RtoP within the UN system – than that the Security Council refers to the principle in the next resolution it passes on the protection of civilians.

Conclusion

In its first five years, RtoP has become an important part of diplomatic and academic debate about how to prevent and respond to genocide and mass atrocities. The rise of RtoP has prompted some to claim that far from preventing genocide and mass atrocities and protecting the victims, the principle actually *causes* genocidal violence that would not otherwise happen and prolongs the suffering of civilian populations. It was important to deal with this question before looking more systematically at RtoP itself because the critique goes to the very heart of what the principle is trying to achieve. Working with my colleague, Paul D. Williams and examining evidence relating to the frequency, scale, and duration of rebellions and mass atrocities, and by examining a prominent case that is often mobilized in support of this theory, I demonstrated that there is no empirical validity to this claim. In addition to withstanding these outlandish claims, the principle has survived a revolt against it in 2006–7, attempts by the French and Russian governments to use it to legitimize coercive intervention, and heated debates about its applicability and utility. In the process, it has been discussed in relation to a dozen crises and stimulated a lively General Assembly debate in 2009 in which almost the whole membership participated (180 governments had their views expressed by 94 participants).

This short, but immensely rich, history provides us with good grounds for some initial assessments about the function, nature and scope of RtoP and its effectiveness. At the deepest level, debates about RtoP have given rise to two accounts of the principle's function, the first which views it as a broad based policy agenda in need of implementation and the second which sees it primarily as a catalyst for international action in response to genocide and mass atrocities. I argued that the first account corresponds more closely to what states agreed in 2005 and that it is in this area that RtoP has proven most effective. While

RtoP has proven incapable of generating additional international political will in the face of humanitarian emergencies, it has been employed as a diplomatic tool with some good effect and is part of a normative context that has contributed to a downward trend in the overall commission of one-sided violence against civilians. The increased clarity and consensus about RtoP's scope has certainly helped in this regard. But the main reason for RtoP's inability to generate additional political will to respond to crises is the indeterminacy of its third pillar, which stands in sharp contrast to the relative determinacy of pillar one. To date, in practice all states have to do to appear compliant with pillar three in the face of an episode of mass killing is not support *genocidaires* and accept the proposition that international community should do *something*. Beyond that, it is not clear what RtoP demands in any particular case. Navigating around this problem requires a long-term commitment to implementing all three pillars of RtoP in the hope that by building national, regional and global capacities, the upstream prevention of genocide and mass atrocities becomes habitual – reducing their incidence – and the costs associated with effective responses are reduced thereby increasing the likelihood that states will not find such action inimical to national interests. It is to this task that we now turn. Taking a cue from the issues raised at the 2009 General Assembly debate, the following chapters examine four critically important implementation issues: the place of economic development and democratization, early warning, the role of regional arrangements and the UN Security Council and the use of force.

5 Economic development and democratization

The question of whether economic development and democratization have a legitimate place within the RtoP framework has proven controversial. The ICISS took a broad brush to this issue. It argued that 'root cause' prevention, an integral part of the 'responsibility to prevent', 'may also mean tackling economic deprivation and the lack of economic opportunities' and suggested that this might involve development assistance to address economic inequalities, the promotion of economic growth, better terms of trade, and the encouragement of economic reform.[1] In his subsequent book, Gareth Evans included a similarly broad range of economic measures in his 'preventive toolbox' for RtoP.[2] Since then, however, Western advocates of RtoP have tended to express caution about or outright reject the inclusion of economic development, broad based capacity building and democratization under the rubric of RtoP. As I noted in Chapter 3, the International Coalition of NGOs described calls by some states to include measures to address the root causes of conflict (which they defined as poverty and inequality) under the rubric of RtoP as 'unhelpful', claiming that such arguments 'subordinate RtoP to decades-old political disagreements' about the place of development in the UN's agenda. The Coalition expressed its preference for Japan's view that RtoP should address only the direct and imminent causes of genocide, war crimes, ethnic cleansing and crimes against humanity.[3] In late 2009, Evans expressed a similar view, arguing that RtoP's preventive component be limited to addressing the immediate threat of the four crimes.[4] These sentiments are based on an understandable eagerness to defend RtoP's putative capacity to serve as a catalyst for timely and decisive international responses to mass atrocities against perceived attempts to broaden the principle to such an extent that it loses this mobilizing capacity. For some proponents of this view, there is no legitimate reason to include economic development and democratization within the RtoP framework because they simply deal with different problems. Others, including the International Coalition, worry that RtoP sceptics might argue for the sequencing of economic development and RtoP, with the implication that RtoP would only be implemented once global poverty was eradicated.[5]

A significant number of states, however, have argued that economic development should be an integral part of the RtoP agenda and some analysts have argued that the same can be said for democratization. At the 2009 General Assembly debate, several governments raised the issue of economic development, arguing that the root causes of armed conflict and the four RtoP crimes lay in poverty and underdevelopment and that the international community should address these issues as part of its commitment to RtoP. New Zealand argued that development assistance and development agencies were central parts of the agenda; Australia agreed, arguing that development aid should focus on building preventive capacity; South Korea maintained that underdevelopment was a critical cause of conflict; and Viet Nam stressed the connections between development assistance and prevention.[6] These arguments have yet to win much support in the academic world, though Michael Newman recently argued that humanitarian intervention and economic development need to be seen as two sides of the same coin.[7]

This debate seems to be simply the latest act in what Conor Cruise O'Brien once described as the 'sacred drama' of debates among UN members.[8] The drama tends to follow a familiar script: the global North, comprised of industrialized states, privilege military security and human rights issues; the global South, comprised of developing countries, privilege development issues. UN bargaining requires an accommodation between the two, which is brought about by horse trading: 'Northern' gains on security and human rights require concessions on development, and vice versa. This posturing is one of the principal reasons for the lack of progress in so many of the UN's agendas.[9] In this case, fuel has been poured on the fire by some members of the civil society support cast. This leads to a view of RtoP as an exclusively human rights/ security issue and attempts to insert an economic dimension are viewed with extreme suspicion. We should remember, though, that Kofi Annan's reform agenda, of which RtoP was part, was driven by the idea that security, human rights and development were complementary, not antagonistic goals.[10] With that in mind, it is worth examining the case for including economic development and democratization within the RtoP framework on their merits.

In his 2009 report on implementing the RtoP, the Ban Ki-moon tried to find a mid-point between the two positions. He did so by incorporating economic development into his schema but limiting its role and striking a cautious tone. Democracy and democratization were overlooked entirely. On economic development, he maintained that 'chronic underdevelopment does not in and of itself cause strains among different ethnic, cultural and religious communities. But it can exacerbate the competition for scarce resources and severely limit the capacity of the State, civil society and regional and sub-regional organizations to resolve domestic tensions peacefully and fully'.[11] The solution, the Secretary-General maintained, was to increase general development assistance. Placing limits on the scope of relevant assistance, however, Ban argued that RtoP-related development programs should be 'carefully targeted' to giving poor and minority groups a stronger voice, raising their education levels, permitting greater political participation and building specific capacities (such as indigenous mediation, security sector reform and strengthening the rule of law) that would enable countries to avoid the path towards genocide and mass atrocities.[12]

In order to better understand the most appropriate relationship between RtoP, economic development and democracy, I begin with first principles. The first part of the chapter examines what, if any, relationship there is between economic and regime conditions and the onset of genocide and mass atrocities. Surprisingly, given the sharp lines of debate outlined above, there is a relatively strong academic consensus around two basic propositions. First, that most episodes of mass atrocities occur in the context of civil wars and that there is a strong correlation between underdevelopment, economic stagnation and the risk of civil war. Second, that almost all of the cases of mass killing that occur outside the context of civil war involve non-democratic states. The remaining parts of the chapter focus on two questions that flow from this insight. First, *why* is there such a strong link between these two factors and the risk of genocide and mass atrocities and what is the nature of that connection? Second, what sorts of policies should be included in the RtoP agenda to address these problems and reduce the overall risk of mass killing?

To avoid misunderstandings, it should be stressed here that I am not saying that the presence of one or both of these factors makes genocide and mass atrocities inevitable. Nor that poverty, inequality and non-democratic regimes directly *cause* mass killing. There are few, if any, causal arguments in the social sciences that can make such direct claims (which is why Ted Gurr prefers to speak of 'symptoms' rather than causes) but this does not mean that no relationship exists.[13] Drinking and driving does not make a specific car crash inevitable, but it does make it much more likely. As such, we can safely say that alcohol causes car crashes that would not occur otherwise and develop public policy accordingly. My point is that economic underdevelopment and stagnation and particular types of regime are important preconditions for genocide and mass atrocities. They do not make mass atrocities inevitable, but they do make them much more likely. Viewed the other way, atrocities are *extremely* unlikely in the absence of underdevelopment and authoritarianism. A world of wealthier, more equitable and more democratic states would be one with far fewer atrocities. Every aspect of public policy is based on judgments about the likelihood of certain eventualities. Because it involves the setting of priorities and allocating of resources, public policy deals in trends, averages and likely outcomes. Lifting societies out of economic deprivation and authoritarian government may not prevent a specific case of mass atrocities, but it is very likely to reduce the overall number of cases. We need to focus our attention on the factors that make mass atrocities more likely and adopt measures to mitigate those factors. This is how we reduce mass atrocities overall.

Preconditions of genocide and mass atrocities

Mass killing is a means to an ends – a way in which actors get what they want. Therefore, we first need to understand the context in which they take place. Most of the mass atrocities committed since 1945 were perpetrated by states (92 of the 122 primary perpetrators).[14] A state was the primary perpetrator in all but one of the episodes where the estimated death toll exceeded 1 million.[15] In total, 53 *different* states perpetrated mass atrocities in this period, meaning that around a quarter of the states that exist today have committed at least one episode of mass killing since 1945.[16] In all but a handful of cases, the primary victims of state-based mass killing were the state's own populations.

It is generally assumed that there is a close relationship between war and mass atrocities.[17] Indeed, it is commonly argued that between half and two-thirds of twentieth century episodes of mass killing took place in the context war.[18] The evidence presented here suggests a slightly lower correlation but supports the general finding. Of the 103 episodes, 65 (63 per cent) occurred during wartime and 38 (37 per cent) occurred outside war. Importantly, however, since the end of the Cold War there has been a strong trend towards mass atrocities being committed only in civil wars and a corresponding decline in other contexts. Of the 22 episodes that erupted after the fall of the Berlin Wall, 19 (86 per cent) were associated with civil wars that pitched at least one rebel army against a government. Of the remaining three, one (the Armenia-Azerbaijan war) occurred in tandem with the participants' birth as sovereign states, another (communal clashes in Nigeria) pitched religious communities against one another, and the third (the North Korean famine) was a famine induced by an authoritarian government with a long record of past offences. It is therefore fair to say that mass atrocities in the post Cold War era have almost always occurred during civil wars. To prevent them, we need to know the causes of civil war. To understand how to prevent atrocities committed outside of war, we also need to know why some governments might massacre their own populations. Once we have answers to these questions, we can begin to understand the relationship between the RtoP, the prevention of genocide and mass atrocities, economics and democracy.

In the past few years there has been an outpouring of quantitative and qualitative research on the causes of civil war. One recent study identified 47 separate quantitative studies, generating 64 separate tables of findings, 99 statistical models and covering 203 independent variables.[19] As one would expect, there is significant variation across the studies and many of the variables have been hotly contested. Much of this variation is caused by the fuzziness of the social phenomenon under examination (what constitutes a civil war? what about other forms of violence? What about countries with exceptionally high homicide rates, such as Mexico, whose annual rate of drug related murders (15,000) exceeds that of many civil wars?), the use of different definitions, different ways of measuring the key variables and interpreting proxies.[20] Allowing for these problems, across the 47 separate studies, there is a strong consensus around three clusters of variables that make a country more 'prone' to conflict: low levels of economic growth and prosperity, regime type and stability, and the number of years a country has been at peace.[21] A country whose economy is growing, is democratic and stable and has been at peace for more than five years is extremely unlikely to experience civil war. In contrast, a stagnating or shrinking economy, undemocratic or factionalized government, and recent history of violence makes a country as much as 30 times more likely to experience civil war in any given year. We concentrate here on the first of these, and turn to regime type below. There is not much that policy makers can do about past history.

There are many studies showing a link between economic stagnation and the likelihood of civil war. At its simplest, researchers agree that the risk of civil war varies with per capita income. Data drawn from Paul Collier and Anke Hoeffler's study found that countries at $250 GDP per capita had a 15 per cent risk of war within five years, those at $600 GDP per capita had a 7.5 per cent risk of war within five years and that countries at $5,000 GDP per capita had a less than 1 per cent risk of war within five years.[22] Separate studies by Fearon and Laitin and Nicholas Sambanis differed on the precise thresholds but identified the same basic trends. Fearon and Laitin found that at $579 GDP per capita, there was a 17.7 per cent risk of war within one year; at $2,043 GDP per capita there was a 10.7 per cent risk of war within one year; and at $9,466 GDP per capita there was less than a 1 per cent risk of war within one year.[23] Likewise, Sambanis found that the average GDP per capita for countries that experienced war in the previous five years was $2,176, while the average for those that did not was $5,173. As such, a country on the bottom of the global economic pile might enjoy several years of economic growth but still confronts a higher risk of conflict than middle income countries. No other variables exhibited this degree of consistency with the onset of civil wars and exhaustive testing of this basic relationship, using different methods, proxies and datasets, have only further confirmed the statistically significant relationship between per capita income and the risk of civil war.[25] There is also evidence that relative economic wealth drives conflict at the sub-state level too. According to one study, which focused on sub-state regions, armed conflict was more likely in relatively deprived areas than in relatively wealthy parts of the same country.[26]

This general finding is open to a number of charges. Some make the point that the analysis is undermined by the fact that economic information about the least developed countries is inaccurate.[27] This is no doubt correct, and while this would certainly affect the precise figures it is hard to see how it would impact the general finding. A more potent critique is that it gets causation back to front – that it is not low income that causes conflict, but conflict that causes low income. Of course, the latter proposition is true. In what Paul Collier describes as the 'conflict trap', civil war significantly reduces economic growth.[28] But analysis of countries that have enjoyed an identical number of years at peace shows that those with worse performing economies are more likely to experience civil war than those without.[29] This is why conflict creates a 'trap' and is also one of the reasons why the number of years at peace is the other important variable: bad economies create the preconditions for conflict, conflict damages the economy, further heightening the risk of future conflict. This creates a downwards spiral from which it is very hard (but not impossible) to escape.[30] Countries at the bottom have to increase their per capita income significantly to even begin to reduce the risks.

Various analysts have found that there is some relationship between specific economic factors and the risk of civil war. If this were the case, it would certainly speak to the UN Secretary-General's call for a targeted approach to development assistance as part of RtoP. Factors such as drought, diamond export based economies, low levels of investment, and the level of trade as a proportion of GDP have all been identified as being related to the onset of civil war, but the results here are mixed.[31] Moreover, the Political Instability Task Force found that there was very little relationship between a wide range of economic variables and the likelihood of instability.[32] Of all the economic factors studied none was more closely associated with the onset of civil war than GDP per capita. However, there was one important national income related event that correlated strongly with civil war. In addition to the overall level of GDP per capita, a *fall* in national income further increased the risk of civil war.[33] The tragedy for those at the bottom of the pile is that growth has to be sustained over a number of years to reduce the risk of war, while decline can have an immediate and negative effect in the other direction.

In addition, studies of genocide have identified three further economic factors that increase risk. First, countries that have low economic interdependence are more likely to experience genocide and mass atrocities than those with higher levels of interdependence.[34] These countries are also less susceptible to economic inducements and sanctions. Second, activities aimed at depriving a particular ethnic or religious group from equal access to employment, wealth attainment or property ownership are a clear warning of the possibility of future genocide or mass atrocities.[35] The 1971 genocide in Bangladesh (formerly East Pakistan) was preceded by two and a half decades of economic exploitation by West Pakistan, evidenced in East Pakistan's main export commodity (jute) for which all investment and all profit remained in the West. This was part of a greater transfer of wealth which resulted in substantial economic inequality between east and west, to the extent that many Bengalis felt that they had replaced one colonial ruler for another.[36] A third connection relates to horizontal economic inequalities. This theory holds that it is not so much a country's overall level of wealth that determines its risk of civil war, though that is an important consideration, but rather the relative economic position of groups within that country.[37] This refers to *horizontal* inequalities (across groups) rather than the more commonly measured *vertical* inequalities (referring to relative wealth of rich and poor measured by Gini coefficients). This account has been advanced using detailed qualitative case studies which seem to support the theory, but is hindered by a paucity of relevant and accurate data, selection bias (each case selected included horizontal inequality), and definitional problems (on what basis to identify a 'group').[38] In addition, although income inequalities can play a crucial role in generating the grievances necessary to cause civil war, there is little statistical evidence of a direct connection between inequality (measured in terms of the Gini coefficient) and the onset of civil war.[39] These problems notwithstanding, the idea of horizontal inequalities begins to offer insights into *why*, in some circumstances, income levels influence susceptibility to civil war.

From this discussion it seems clear that civil war is more likely in countries that have a poor, stagnating or declining economy measured in terms of GDP per capita. According to Paul Collier, the people of the 'bottom billion' have a one in six chance of enduring war in any given year. The growing number of 'middle income' and developing (literally growing) countries are at risk of civil war, but that risk is much lower – about 1 in 17. At the top end of the global economic pile, there is virtually no risk of civil war. This relationship operates independently of other variables such as ethnic fragmentation, natural resources, or past conflicts and of all the potential economic factors that might be associated with the onset of civil war, it is overall income that is most strongly correlated. Of course, a poor and declining economy does not in itself trigger war and atrocity but it is the single most important precondition, without which the various other causes and triggers would most likely fail to materialize.[40] To reiterate this point – a poor, stagnating or declining economy may provide the precondition for civil war but they do not directly motivate or trigger them.[41] Instead, they might be thought of as creating a 'permissive' environment that enables violence.[42] This suggests that instead of adopting a narrowly targeted approach to economic development, which, for example, focuses on inequalities within countries, RtoP could more profitably demand that development assistance focus on increasing national income more generally – something on which the neo-liberal Paul Collier and 'unorthodox Marxist' Christopher Cramer agree. Paul Collier estimates that for each percentage added to economic growth, the likelihood of conflict declines by a percentage point.[43] While such estimates are likely to be wrong, the general idea that growth reduces risk is well supported. In sum, to end mass atrocities once and for all, we need to prevent civil wars. The principal thing that would reduce the overall global risk of civil war is economic growth in the world's poorest countries.

This brings us to the second context: genocide and mass atrocities committed outside the context of civil war. Cases of mass atrocities committed outside a context of armed conflict share one thing in common – they all occur in a context of authoritarian government.

The relationship between authoritarianism and the commission of genocide and mass atrocities is highly controversial. At one end of the spectrum, some analysts such as R. J. Rummel insist that the four crimes associated with RtoP

Table 5.1 Atrocities outside war by regime type 1945–2010

	No. cases	Proportion (%)
Autocracy (−10 to −6)	26	68
Anocracy (−5 to +5)	10	26
Democracy (+5 to +10)	1	3
No data	1	3

are simply not committed by democratic states. At the other end of the spectrum, other analysts such as Alexander Downes argue that there is no relationship between democracy and mass killing, and that democratic states are just as likely to commit massacres as non-democratic states. A third position, taken by the Political Instability Task Force, suggests that while democratic states are much less likely to experience genocide and mass atrocities than non-democratic states, the process of democratic transition is a particularly dangerous period and highly factionalized partially democratic states are the most vulnerable of all.[44]

To investigate these claims I used the Polity IV dataset, which rates countries on an authority scale ranging from +10 (the most democratic) to −10 (the most authoritarian). It describes scores ranging from −5 to +5 as 'anocracies', in that the political system includes some elements of democratic government. Scores of −5 to 0 can be considered 'weak authoritarian' regimes and those of 0 to +5 can be considered 'weak democracies'. The simple results are set out in Table 5.1 and are quite striking.

Most atrocities committed outside of war (slightly over two-thirds of all major cases since 1945) were perpetrated by fully authoritarian states and over a quarter

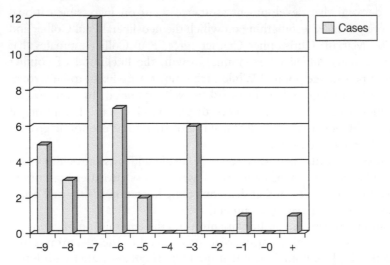

Figure 5.1 Democracy and atrocity 1945–2010

by anocracies. There was only episode of mass killing in a democratic country outside the context of war – the communal violence associated with Indian partition in 1947. Other than this singular case, which occurred in a context of extraordinary social upheaval, it is safe to say that atrocities do not occur outside of war in democratic countries. An even stronger correlation between authoritarianism and atrocities is revealed, however, if we look inside the categories. Figure 5.1 presents the number of cases in relation to the individual Polity IV score for each, placing all the cases on the positive side of the democracy ledger (0–10) in a single column.

This figure is instructive because it shows that within the band of ten cases that occurred in 'anocratic' states, all ten were rated more authoritarian than democratic. Not one episode was perpetrated by an anocratic state that could be described as a 'weak democracy' (scoring 0 or better). Two of the ten were only borderline anocracies, scoring –5 which place them very close to being fully authoritarian. Considering that these countries were Duvalier's Haiti in the 1950s and Sukarno's Indonesia in the early 1960s, we might conclude that it is rather generous to not describe them as fully authoritarian. A further six were much closer to the authoritarian end of the scale (–3, missing by 3 points) than the democratic end (missing by 8 points). This leaves only one – Laos in the early 1960s (scoring –1) near the 'weak democracy' end of the spectrum, but still much closer to being fully authoritarian than fully democratic.

This suggests that not only are mass atrocities outside a context of armed conflict associated with an absence of democracy but that the risk of atrocities declines as states become more democratic. We might therefore hypothesize a link between the sharp reduction of mass atrocities outside the context of war since the end of the Cold War and the increase in the number of democratic states mapped by Polity IV since 1990.[45] Before we get too carried away, though, we should stress that the Political Instability Task Force has identified a particular type of anocratic state – partial democracies characterized by high levels of factionalism – as being more susceptible to political instability than any other type of regime. Partial democracies without such factionalism, however, are much more stable.[46] In addition, when authoritarians hold elections without enacting other democratic reforms (e.g. constraining the executive, establishing a free press, abolishing intimidation, winding back patrimonialism) those elections tend to be associated with heightened instability and an increased risk of civil violence and war.[47] While transitions to democracy are not themselves directly associated with heightened risk of mass atrocities, it is important to acknowledge the potential risks associated with factionalized weak democracies and authoritarian elections, and to calibrate democracy assistance accordingly.

To summarize, although there are a handful of notable exceptions, it is possible to identify patterns that tell us important things about the pre-conditions for genocide and mass atrocities. Around two-thirds of all cases since 1945, and around 85 per cent of all cases since the end of the Cold War, have occurred in the context of civil war. The causes of individual wars are idiosyncratic and context bound but there is a very strong relationship between the risk of civil war and per capita income. The wealthier and more vibrant the economy, the less the risk of civil war and therefore of mass atrocities. Where mass atrocities were committed outside the context of war, they were almost always perpetrated by non-democratic regimes against their own people. The less democratic the regime, the greater the risk that it will perpetrate atrocities. Although they can sometimes foster instability when characterized by factionalism or fake elections, transitions to democracy reduce the risk of a government massacring its own people in peacetime. From this, therefore, we can make a bold statement. If it is serious about preventing genocide and mass atrocities, the implementation of RtoP should endorse two large policy agendas: stimulating economic growth in the world's poorest countries and supporting transitions to democracy. Before we get into the question of what specific policies should be incorporated into the RtoP agenda, we need to know more about *why* economic deprivation and authoritarianism have the pernicious effects that they do.

Why income and democracy?

While there is broad agreement that national income levels influence the risk of civil war, there is much less agreement on *why* this is the case. In contrast, there is relatively little debate about why democracies are much less likely to massacre their own population than authoritarian states. We will therefore review this latter question first before moving on to a more detailed examination of the first question.

If we look at mass killing since 1945 perpetrated by non-democratic states outside the context of war, we find two basic types of case. The first involved *revolutionary communist governments* implementing their plans for radical trans-formation. Over one-third of all the relevant cases (14 of the 38 episodes) were perpetrated by communist governments.[48] According to Benjamin Valentino, communist governments were so exceptionally violent because the social trans-formations they attempted to engineer required the material dispossession of vast numbers of people. The most radical of these regimes, in China, Cambodia and North Korea, attempted to completely reorient society, eradicating traditional patterns of life and forcibly imposing a new and alien way of life. Communist objectives, Valentino points out, could only be achieved with violence and the scale of the transformation dictated a massive amount of violence.[49] Of course, communist revolutions also elicited resistance, prompting the state into massive and bloody crackdowns and generating a culture of paranoia which led many regimes to periodically purge their own ranks (China's 'cultural revolution' being a good example). In communist ideology, the good of the party was associated with the national interest, individuals were divested of rights and subordinated to the will of the party leadership, and entire groups (e.g. *kulaks* in the Soviet Union, merchants and intellectuals in Cambodia) were deemed 'class enemies' that could be eradicated *en masse* to protect the revolution.[50]

The second type involved military dictatorships, theocracies, and kleptoc-racies or 'shadow states' using mass violence to protect themselves and/or group interests or to deter or avenge opposition. A relatively small number, such as Argentina's military junta, Pinochet's Chile, and Indonesia's crackdown on communism in the 1960s were intimately linked to the Cold War and involved the commission of mass atrocities against leftists and suspected communists.[51] Most, though, simply involved the use of extreme violence by authoritarian leaders to maintain power and protect privilege.

Assuming that there are situations in which governments of all stripes might be tempted to think that mass atrocities may help them achieve their objectives, there are four principal reasons why authoritarians use mass atrocities, while their democratic counterparts do not. First, authoritarian governments are less dependent on the consent of the governed than democratic governments and their right to rule is not conditioned by their performance. Democratic governments earn their right to rule and by making government accountable, electoral competition ensures that if they manifestly fail to deliver on their promises they will be ejected from office.[52] This is no idle claim. Studies show that all other things being equal, democratic government provide more and qualitatively better public services (health, education etc.) than their non-democratic counterparts, presumably because of the accountability associated with democracy.[53] Authoritarian governments rule irrespective of performance. Typically, they draw their support from a narrow section of the community and do not need to secure the loyalty of other groups. Instead, they often find that extreme violence provides a more efficient means of keeping marginalized groups in check. Second, democratic systems decentralize political power and impose institutional constraints on the executive, reducing opportunities for them to abuse their own people.[54] These inhibitions are further strengthened by the plethora of international institutions and regimes to which democratic states are generally tied. The third explanation is normative and holds that because democratic governments are selected by the people they enjoy domestic legitimacy. This makes it very difficult to mobilize sufficient arms against them to challenge the prevailing order, reducing the frequency and intensity of domestic existential threats to the state.[55] As such, democracy reduces a government's perceived need to terrorize a section of the population. Finally, democracy provides a process for the peaceful transfer of power. Transfers of power in authoritarian states are often violent, with the individuals at the top paying the ultimate price for failing to stay in power. As such, authoritarians have greater personal incentives to cling to power by any means possible than democratic leaders.

The question of *why* economic wealth is associated with heightened risk of civil war is more hotly contested. This is probably inevitable because the effects of deprivation, economic stagnation and decline in any given setting are mediated by a wide range of other historical, political, cultural, social and geographic factors. As such, we are not looking here for a unified theory but rather for an account of the different ways in which income levels influence the risk of civil war. I argue that low income, stagnation and decline are preconditions for civil war because they underlie the establishment of *motives* and *opportunities* for violence.[56] Precisely how will differ from country to country, but some general insights are possible as a guide.

Motives

Why do people turn to violence? Much of the debate generated by the economic work we have referred to above revolved around the question of whether economic greed or political and social grievances 'caused' civil war. The debate was prompted by arguments presented by Paul Collier and his collaborators based on their research showing the connection between economic wealth, civil war and a third factor – the existence of lootable natural resources. From this, they concluded that most civil wars were caused by 'greedy' rebels who used violence to loot and sell natural resources for personal profit.[57] This interpretation was criticized on a number of grounds. Most significantly, critics pointed out that Collier's account was based entirely on statistical analysis and that while such analysis might point to general relationships between variables, it could not tell us anything about human motives and causation. Collier's conclusions were based not on 'objective' numbers but subjective interpretations of them. These interpretations are open to challenge. Why, for instance, would the link between economic wealth and civil war point towards a greed based argument rather a focus on economic grievances?[58] As David Keen perceptibly explains, the salient question is not whether 'greed' or 'grievance' cause civil war, but how economic factors and political factors *interact*.[59] We know from other research that perceptions of injustice are a prime motivator of war and that regardless of other calculations, belligerents tend to sincerely believe in the legitimacy of their cause.[60] Even if misplaced, such sincere beliefs must have some basis in lived experience.

The most direct form of interaction is in the way that low income, stagnation and decline creates political grievances. This interaction can operate in a number of ways, but three stand out. First, a decline in overall per capita income stimulates heightened inter-group competition for scarcer resources. In a context of declining wealth, the relative position of groups matters more, the acquisition of resources is more important for survival, and groups need to secure a higher proportion of overall resources to maintain their standard of living.[61] The role that the increasing scarcity of water and grazing land, both necessary for survival in Darfur, played in sharpening the conflict there is a case in point.[62] Conversely, where absolute wealth is growing, relative wealth across groups seems less important, it is easier to secure resources, and groups need a smaller proportion of overall resources to maintain their standard of living.[63] Sometimes, however, the picture is made more complex by economic windfalls caused by natural resource booms. In these cases, stark wealth differentials can cause significant grievances. For example, although the Nigerian economy has grown relatively well in the past decade (averaging annual growth of around 4 to 8 per cent) this growth was caused almost exclusively by the export of oil. Other sectors of the economy, such as agriculture and industrial production stagnated or declined (e.g. industrial production declined by 1.8 per cent in 2009). Coupled with the government's failure to redistribute oil wealth, this resulted in large income inequality in the Niger delta region and is a clear source of grievance.

Second, civil wars can only get off the ground if rebels secure a core group of dedicated supporters and a degree of sympathy in parts of the wider population. Acute individual hardship, dissatisfaction with one's situation, and the belief either that war can improve that situation or will impose few additional costs, are among the principal reasons why individuals lend their support to violent rebellion.[64] In Sierra Leone, for example, informants told David Keen of their anger at their low status and lack of opportunities.[65] Other studies found similar grievances at work in places as diverse as China, Guatemala and Uganda.[66]

A third factor, which amplifies the first two, is that countries at the bottom of the economic pile often have a large youth population – a 'youth bulge'. Demographers agree that the poorest sections of a community tend to have more children, mainly due to a combination of poor (or non-existent) sex education, limited (or non-existent) access to contraception, the disempowerment of women, high infant mortality rates, and expectations that children will provide insurance to care for elderly relatives.[67] As a result, around 60 per cent of the world's poor are under 25 years old.[68] There is a clear statistical relationship between countries with youth bulges and civil war, with one study showing that of all recent episodes of mass violence, a youth bulge was evident in every case except one – the former Yugoslavia.[69] Collier and Hoeffler argue that a youth bulge increases the risk of conflict by increasing the stock of potential rebel fighters, but this is only half the story. Youth bulges also magnify grievances and expand the population of aggrieved. If the population is growing but the economy is not, or is growing unevenly, then a large and increasing group of marginalized and economically depressed young people is established.

Another problem with an exclusively 'greed' based explanation is that it misses an important part of the puzzle: the state. In addition to causing grievances directly, poor economies tend to generate a type of state formation that creates grievances. The problems caused here are exacerbated by the presence of lootable natural resources and by international financial policies that encourage states to withdraw from the provision of public services.[70] The problem is that in low income settings, the state itself often operates in a fashion not too dissimilar from rebel groups. In many post-colonial settings where the state suffered legitimacy problems owing to the poor fit between the state and other forms of identity and where regimes are non-democratic, political leaders are more likely to use violence and other forms of intimidation to manage the economy for their own economic and political gain. Described as 'shadow states', 'kleptocracies' and 'protection racket states', these regimes siphon off public resources to elevate the personal wealth of their leaders and establish patronage networks to protect their position. A country's economic resources are diverted away from the provision of public goods (like security, health education, and infrastructure).[71] And, according to Karen Ballentine, 'the relative capacity of the state to perform core functions . . . has a direct bearing on the incidence of armed conflict'. Clearly, when the state behaves in this manner, it loses legitimacy and establishes grievances against it. Patronage and corruption work by granting special favours to certain groups which means that other groups are marginalized and unfairly treated. Irrespective of how the economy as a whole develops, marginalized groups are likely to face hardship and have few opportunities to change these facts. The problem is compounded when the redirection of resources away from public goods increases hardship, inhibits growth and reduces opportunity. In the absence of democracy, the marginalized have little hope of achieving peaceful change.

Low income therefore sows the seeds of grievance, which is a necessary but not sufficient cause of civil war. Globally, there are many more seriously aggrieved groups than armed conflicts, partly because in most cases aggrieved groups simply lack the capacity to challenge the state. The second way in which low income economies increase the risk of conflict is by establishing *opportunities* for violence. Although the precise configuration of how this works remains disputed, three principal mechanisms have been identified. First, 'shadow states' are also hollowed states, incapable of preventing the establishment of armed groups and resisting opposition without recourse to massive violence. Many civil wars result from a breakdown of state authority and arise in regions where authority is weakest.[73] One of the most significant recent studies on civil wars shows that one of the key drivers is the state's inability to deter and defeat insurgencies.[74] Because 'shadow states' use their resources inefficiently and secure loyalty through patronage rather than legitimacy they tend to have a fragile grasp on authority, especially in regions that are far from the regime's power base. As such they are more vulnerable to rebellion, and even small rebellions can gain significant traction as the government and its allies become factionalized or disintegrate.

Second, opportunities are established by the presence of incentives for armed groups. Although much of the literature focuses on rebel, i.e. non-state, groups, it is important to recognize that many government behave in precisely the same fashion – indeed as we noted earlier the 'theft' of resources for personal gain is one of the hallmarks of the 'shadow state'. In general, in this context powerful incentives are created by the relatively low costs associated with challenging the state and the presence of high potential benefits that may accrue from successfully challenging the state. For political leaders, it is the potential benefits and the relative ease with which state power can be used to secure resources for personal gain that creates the incentive. This is especially true in poor countries endowed with lootable natural resources, a feature of many of the regions that have suffered from war and atrocities since the end of the Cold War. In West Africa, Angola and the DRC, lootable high value resources helped fuel protracted wars characterized by mass atrocities. For the presence of lootable resources to constitute a realistic opportunity, though, two external conditions must be met. First, there must be international traders prepared to buy the resources from non-state armed groups or authoritarian states. Second, those groups or states must be able to acquire sufficient arms to capture natural resources and then translate newly generated income into enough arms to sustain a protracted conflict. This requires a combination of internal actors (usually in the army) willing to sell the state's armaments and international actors prepared to sell and export weapons, sometimes in breach of UN arms embargoes. If these conditions are satisfied, actors (both non-state and state) are presented with strong incentives to use violence and given the means of sustaining an armed conflict.[75]

Finally, opportunities present themselves by virtue of the absence of alternative pathways out of hardship and marginalization. It is significant that there is a correlation between low income levels, the absence of democracy, low levels of education, and war. Wherever data is available, evidence shows that there is a connection between relative wealth and educational attainment: the poor are always less well educated than the rich. The Political Instability Task Force identified a connection between falling secondary school enrolments and heightened risk of political crisis, and approaching the problem from the other direction, Collier and Hoeffler found that as enrolments increased, the average risk of conflict declined significantly.[76] The level of available education serves as a good proxy for opportunity levels more generally and when young, poor, men (mostly) have limited or no economic opportunities, the meagre chance of betterment presented by joining an armed group is transformed into a credible incentive. As education levels rise, the poor are presented with pathways out of poverty, creating disincentives for violence. This logic was clearly at work in Sierra Leone, where most recruits to the various armed groups were largely young and poor, and 80 per cent had not finished school.[77] Staying with Sierra Leone for a moment, this last point tells us something important about how the motives and opportunities discussed above interact. One of the reasons why so many young Sierra Leoneans did not finish school was because schools were closed as the 'shadow state' wound back funding for public services in line with international demands that the government cut spending.[78] Reducing spending on schools, satisfied the World Bank's neo-liberal 'small state' agenda, allowed the government to weaken what was left of an independent civil service that had imposed some constraints on patronage, and maintained the flow of funds and favours to the government's allies. The result was a fundamentally weakened state, sharpened grievances and the incentivization of violence.

In summary, there are multiple pathways by which poor economies and an absence of democracy can lead to armed conflict and mass atrocities. Although there will be significant differences across cases, some general themes and patterns can be identified. Authoritarian regimes are plagued by domestic illegitimacy, face few internal constraints and sometimes use massive violence to either enforce a radical transformation of society or exterminate real or potential threats to the regime. The disarmingly simple antidote to this problem is democratization but not only is that much easier said than done, we also know that certain types of weak democracies characterized by high levels of factionalism or authoritarian democracies characterized by fraudulent elections can actually increase the risk of political instability and civil war. When it comes to economics, things are more complicated still. Although the precise configuration of effects alters from case to case, there are a range of ways in which low income enables the establishment of both the motive and opportunity for violent conflict. Importantly, though far from inevitable these effects are often mutually reinforcing, creating a spiral into war. The disarmingly simple antidote here is economic growth, but again that is easier said than done. Not only is growth difficult to achieve, but it has to be managed in such a way as to address the specific motives and opportunities outlined above in order to ensure, at the very least, that the pursuit of growth does not exacerbate conflict. This, of course, was precisely the point made by the UN Secretary-General in his 2009 report on RtoP. The challenge now is to identify the sorts of measures that could be adopted.

What is to be done? The RtoP agenda

I have argued that the principal precondition for civil wars, in which the majority of mass atrocities are committed, is a country's national income and that the principal precondition for atrocities committed outside the context of war is authoritarian government. I have also identified some of the reasons why this might be, while noting that the preconditions will produce different effects in different contexts. One or both of low income and authoritarian government was evident in almost every episode of mass killing since 1945. From this, we can suggest that if RtoP is to be about 'ending mass atrocities once and for all' and not simply hosing down the fires a little more quickly, then its implementation needs to incorporate measures designed to reduce the number of countries acutely affected by these two preconditions. Of course, these are large and complex policy agendas but we should not shy away from the challenge, and the empirical evidence, just because it is difficult. There is no space here to offer anything other than a broad framework for thinking about how to incorporate support for economic growth and democratization into the RtoP framework but I hope to at least stimulate some thinking and debate about these two issues.

Before getting into some of the specific policies, it is important to recognize two key prerequisites – the local political conditions necessary for effective reform and the necessary international institutional setting. First, and most importantly, these two agendas require indigenous *national political leadership*. The pursuit of economic growth and democratization is difficult, complex and potentially painful – especially for entrenched elites who have few obvious incentives to pursue either agenda. But neither can be imposed from the outside against the wishes of national leaders and attempts to do so usually make matters worse. For example, in the 1980s and 1990s externally imposed growth agendas designed to stimulate investment by privatizing and shrinking the state's share of GDP, facilitated 'crony capitalism' (the 'sale' of state assets to political allies and their ensuing dismemberment) and the collapse of public services and infrastructure. These effects hollowed out the state, sowed the seeds of economic decline and sometimes paved the way to civil war and even genocide.[79] They were primarily caused by a combination of the inherent limits of neoliberal economics and insufficient attention paid to local agency. With hindsight, it is fairly obvious that authoritarian leaders would manipulate externally imposed economic agendas for their own enrichment and empowerment. Research shows, for instance, that aid given to weak and 'shadow states' to strengthen infrastructure, health, education and economic growth leaks into military spending. Alarmingly, one study which tracked foreign aid delivered to Chad to support frontline health care, found that 99 per cent of the aid failed to get to the health sector.[80] Another estimate suggests that up to 40 per cent of military spending in sub-Saharan Africa is inadvertently funded by foreign aid.[81] Foreign aid may therefore inadvertently fund the procurement of military hardware. Precisely the same sort of process happened in relation to many externally imposed democratization processes. As Paul Collier has convincingly demonstrated, of all the various ways of governing and extracting rewards, elections and democratization is the least promising for authoritarian leaders. Confronted with post-Cold War expectations about democratization, authoritarian leaders gradually bowed to external pressure and called elections. Many found that they were not as popular as they thought, but only a tiny minority accepted the results and stood down. Instead, authoritarian leaders and other members of the political elite who wanted to challenge those leaders found a variety of ways to win – and failing that, steal – votes, including ethnic mobilization, bribery and patronage, intimidation and violence, and simple vote rigging. The result was a form of politics democratic only in name (and only in the fact that there are periodic elections) but that was more unstable than authoritarian government. Ethnic mobilization, for example, helped *produce* the factionalism that, we noted earlier, significantly heightened the risk of civil war. It was very much in evidence during the disputed 2007 election in Kenya discussed in Chapter 3, where almost all the votes were cast along ethnic lines.[82] Moreover, this form of democracy exerts none of the constraints on the executive that I argued earlier explains the tendency of democratic states to not massacre their own populations. The key lesson here is that economic growth and democratization can only take hold if national leaders are genuinely committed to pursuing these paths. If they are not, externally driven agendas will probably fail and might make matters worse.

Beneath this anodyne conclusion is an extremely controversial policy proposal – but one that has gained such traction that variants have been proposed by African economist Dambiso Moya, former World Bank economist Paul Collier, and former Medecins sans Frontieres practitioner and analyst Fiona Terry.[83] Because aid and assistance given to countries that lack the necessary well-intentioned leadership is essentially wasted money, and may actually help prop up authoritarian 'shadow states', it should be directed only to those countries that are genuinely committed to pursuing growth and democratization. Elsewhere, where authoritarianism and patrimonialism pervade and there are few signs of a serious commitment to reform on the part of leaders, external assistance would do just as much good – and much less harm – if it was limited to providing life sustaining humanitarian assistance to the neediest.

This brings us to the second important prerequisite. An international institutional setting is required in order to develop coherent and context-specific plans for national economic growth and democratization and marshal international assistance. I think that the UN's Peacebuilding Commission (PBC) fits the bill quite well, but that it needs reforming and strengthening. The PBC was formally established in 2005 by concurrent Security Council (Resolution 1645, 20 December) and General Assembly (Resolution 60/180, 30 December) resolutions. It was given three primary functions:

1   To bring together all relevant actors to marshal resources, to provide advice, and propose integrated strategies for post-conflict peacebuilding.
2   To focus attention on the necessary reconstruction and institution-building efforts to ensure post-conflict recovery and sustainable development.
3   To provide recommendations and information to improve coordination of all relevant actors.

Formally, the PBC is an 'advisory body' that operates on the basis of consensus among its 31 state members and the governments it is engaged with. Significantly, other agencies with an important stake in the process, such as the World Bank and IMF and relevant regional bodies (such as the African Development Bank) are also included in the Commission's deliberations. Countries may come onto the PBC's agenda at the request of the Security Council, the ECOSOC or General Assembly with the consent of the state concerned, and in exceptional circumstances at the request of the concerned state, or at the request of the Secretary-General.[84] The idea is that the PBC provides a forum that enables governments under stress to develop strategic plans in partnership with other states, the UN and other relevant agencies and which also allows external partners to coordinate and complement one another in delivering meaningful assistance. As an example of how it might work, it is worth briefly considering the PBC's work on Sierra Leone. In relation to Sierra Leone, the Commission encouraged foreign governments to broaden the overall donor base, provide secure assistance, relieve government debt and meet consolidated peacebuilding objectives.[85] In the first half of 2007, for instance, the Commission focused on preparations for the country's presidential elections. In particular, the PBC served as a forum for the UNDP, the UN's Integrated Office in Sierra Leone (UNIOSIL) and Sierra Leonean officials to identify potential risks to the election and those that might be generated by the election. The PBC hosted discussions on the development of strategies to reduce those risks, including measures to ensure that the election itself was managed fairly, transparently and effectively; a process of dialogue and confidence building involving the electoral commission and political parties; measures to ensure freedom of speech in the media while also guarding against hate speech through the instigation and supervision of a government sponsored Code of Conduct for the media; and measures to uphold the recommendations of the Truth and Reconciliation Council in order to discourage opposition spoilers. In addition to these measures already adopted by the government of Sierra Leone, the PBC advocated a range of other initiatives aimed at reducing the risks related to elections. The PBC argued that the government should establish a National Human Rights Council to address grievances raised by political parties and individuals, develop a strategy for decentralizing public policy and the electoral commission to make them both better able to respond quickly and effectively to regional concerns, and initiate a process of dialogue with political parties that would continue after the election.[86] Taken together, these measures constituted a comprehensive plan for dealing with the inherent risks associated with elections in post-conflict societies such as Sierra Leone. The outcome was a generally positive electoral process. European Union observers gave a positive assessment of the election and Ban Ki-moon noted that it had proceeded in a 'generally orderly and peaceful atmosphere, in spite of the tensions and violence that marred the campaign period'.[87] Early indications from Sierra Leone's presidential elections suggest that these measures succeeded in ensuring a largely free, fair and non-violent electoral process.

On a small scale, this example demonstrates what the PBC is capable of achieving simply by providing a space for dialogue between national reformers and international assisters, and for coordination between the different actors. For the PBC to extend its work and become an institutional vehicle for tackling the preconditions of genocide and mass atrocities, however, several significant political and bureaucratic hurdles would need to be overcome. Most importantly, the PBC's remit would need to be expanded from its currently narrow focus on the immediate aftermath of armed conflict. Indeed, the body that first proposed establishing a PBC, Kofi Annan's High Level Panel, had originally envisaged a broader scope for the Commission. The Panel had recognized that there was 'no place in the United Nations system explicitly designed to avoid State collapse and the slide to war or to assist countries in their transition from war to peace' but nevertheless noted a clear international obligation to assist States in developing the capacity to perform sovereign functions effectively and legitimately.[88] This, the Panel argued, should be the task of the PBC. The Panel recommended that the PBC be given broad-ranging tasks and should be charged with enabling the UN to act in a 'coherent and effective way' on everything from preventive action to post-conflict reconstruction. It envisaged that the PBC would identify countries at risk, organize and coordinate assistance, and oversee the transition from risk to peace.[89] In so doing, the PBC would facilitate joint planning across the UN system and beyond, provide high-level political leadership, and marshal the necessary resources.[90] In the flurry of negotiations that followed, the Panel's vision underwent two major changes: one which strengthened the proposal and situated it within the UN system more appropriately, the other that gave it an unnecessarily narrow remit and thereby cut off its capacity to contribute to prevention.

The first amendment came from Kofi Annan himself. Well aware that giving the UN a standing capacity to monitor member states and identify those in need of support would prove highly controversial and could weaken support for the whole proposal, Annan expressed his preference for a voluntary system whereby the UN would provide assistance on request.[91] The Secretary-General rightly reasoned that the UN already had offices and functions designed to address early warning and the prevention of imminent crises. It would be better to strengthen these capacities, Annan argued, than overlay them with new offices. Moreover, he argued the development of additional offices might lead to inadvertent duplication and unhelpful interference in politically sensitive peacemaking activities.[92] Annan's preference was that the PBC would take a longer-term view, playing an advisory role, working with national governments and other stakeholders to develop action plans, and providing ideas and inputs to the Security Council, General Assembly, and ECOSOC.[93] It is precisely this vision that could be harnessed for RtoP purposes. The consent aspect is important because while it will undoubtedly reduce the number of governments that come before the Council, it will ensure that participation is voluntary – an important prerequisite as we noted earlier. Unfortunately, however, even this modest proposal proved too much for the General Assembly. Through the second major change to the High Level Panel's vision, the PBC's mandate was limited to bringing together 'all relevant actors to marshal resources and to advise on and propose integrated strategies for post-conflict peacebuilding and recovery'.[94] Effectively, the General Assembly demanded that a country have a war before it could approach the UN to provide a forum to develop plans for peace.

Clearly, amending the PBC's remit to allow all interested states to take advantage of coordinated plans for peace backed up with international assistance is the necessary first step. But even if this were achieved, other obstacles would remain. First, the PBC lacks the formal authority to ensure the envisaged level of coordination between UN bodies and agencies. As one commentator put it, 'its influence within the UN stems entirely from the quality of its recommendations, the relevance of the information it shares, and its ability to generate extra resources'.[95] The PBC is not operating in a 'policy vacuum' but in an area already crowded with UN agencies and bodies, regional organizations, individual government donors and NGOs. Developing the authority and legitimacy to coordinate agencies with much larger budgets presents a major challenge. Second, and related to this, the bureaucratic infrastructure supporting the PBC would need significant augmentation. As conceived by Annan, the Peacebuilding Support Office (PBSO) was to be given the role of preparing substantive inputs for Commission meetings, providing inputs for the planning process and conducting best practice analysis and policy guidance where appropriate.[96] This modest proposal called for an office staffed by 21 new appointments funded by the regular budget. Once again, however, the UN membership had a more circumscribed view, limiting the PBSO's role to 'gathering and analysing information relating to the availability of financial resources, relevant United Nations in-country planning activities, progress towards meeting short and medium-term recovery goals and best practices'.[97] Most notably absent was the policy guidance role envisaged by the Secretary-General. Nor, as noted earlier, were the members convinced by Annan's case for new appointments to staff the PBSO. Under pressure, the UN's budget committee insisted that the PBSO's needs be met from existing resources. To address both problems, the PBSO would need to be enlarged and mandated to play a more prominent role in informing and guiding the Commission's work.

With the engagement of national leaders and international assisters, the PBC could help develop context sensitive plans for preventing civil wars and mass atrocities. There is clearly no single blueprint that can guide this process but there are a number of policy levers that are worth noting and which deserve closer examination. This brings us to the question of the type of policies that might be pursued in order to promote equitable economic growth and sustainable democratization. Both issues have been the subject of a significant amount of research and there is certainly no shortage of advice and recommendations. As such, we will limit ourselves to briefly reviewing some of the steps that might be adopted to support country-specific programs that would ideally by marshalled through the PBC. This discussion is by no means exhaustive.

What can outsiders do to assist and encourage economic growth in highly vulnerable countries? Financial aid by itself has done very little to stimulate growth in these settings, with some going so far as to argue that it actually impedes growth by crowding out private investment.[98] Simply increasing the amount of aid, for instance by doubling aid to Africa as committed by the G8 at the Gleneagles conference in 2005, might have a marginally positive effect but it is unlikely to lift the poorest countries out of their acute vulnerability to civil war. Moreover, aid is subject to diminishing returns, so additional aid is unlikely to have significant effects.[99] This finding is subject to an important caveat, however. Financial aid is significantly more effective in better governed and more democratic countries. Therefore, in a context where a government is genuinely committed to pursuing both growth and democratization, and progress is made on the latter, increased amounts of aid is likely to be effective in promoting growth, providing public goods and strengthening institutions. With these points in mind, there are a range of more modest measures that could be adopted to assist the pursuit of growth.

The first cluster relates to foreign aid and here draws upon insights from research by Paul Collier and his colleagues. The key lesson here is that aid needs to be targeted to where it will have best effect. We noted earlier that aid given to authoritarian and 'shadow' states bleeds away from its intended purpose and is used instead to support patronage and military spending. Moreover, where democratic governance is not consolidated, large increases in aid can increase the risk of a coup and thereby the risk of armed conflict and mass atrocities. As such, without appropriate structures of governance the flow of aid money does little to stimulate growth and can actually help to sustain non-democratic government.[100] The first step, therefore, is to ensure that in order for it to have greatest effect aid is *targeted* at supporting those countries whose political leaders have committed to economic and political reform.[101] This is not to say that all forms of aid to the world's poorest countries charac-terized by authoritarian governments should be wound back but that in these countries aid should be focused on meeting humanitarian needs. There is some evidence that major donors are beginning to move in this direction. The UK, for example, has donated money to the World Bank to be held in a fund specifically targeting countries undertaking indigenous reform. Likewise, the US' Millennium Challenge Corporation marshals aid and generates private investment for the world's poorest democracies.[102]

What form should this aid take? In general terms, effective aid is likely to begin with the provision of technical assistance to establish the skill base necessary to manage reforms and build indigenous capacity. Once the requisite skills are in place, aid can take the form of 'budget support' – injecting money directly into the state's budget. This approach has the obvious advantage of ensuring that aid targets national priorities rather than the donors' priorities but comes with some major pitfalls. Most especially, budget support can promote leakage and patronage. By relieving governments of the financial burden of providing public goods, aid may encourage the diversion of money to political clients and the military.[103] To ensure that this does not happen, two things are needed. First, while national governments should determine their own spending priorities, there should be tighter supervision of national budgets so that donors have a precise idea about how their money is spent. This is not about telling governments what to spend their money on, but simply ensuring that they spend it on what they say they will.[104] When money is improperly used or cannot be accounted for, aid should be withdrawn. Moreover, donors could create disincentives for military spending by tying it to aid such that increased expenditure on the military would prompt a decline in external aid and vice-versa.[105] Second, government expenditure needs to be made accountable to national citizens.[106] Critics have argued that World Bank and IMF led policies of neo-liberal 'structural adjustment' in the 1980s and 1990s, which called for the retreat of states from the provision of services, undermined state accounta-bility and led to the 'internationalization of welfare' wherein basic services were provided more by international NGOs than governments.[107] Although the extent of this has been disputed, there is now recognition of an important link between accountability, taxes and service provision. Citizens need to be able to see how public funds are expended and be given opportunities to work within the political system to ensure the provision of public goods. There have been a variety of proposals for achieving this but there is an obvious connection to democratization and especially the establishment of strong institutions capable of monitoring government expenditure. But strong institutions by themselves do not necessarily increase a government's accountability to its people. The clearest pathway to this is to increase the proportion of government revenue derived from direct taxation. Evidence suggests that tax creates demand for accountability and increases the extent to which citizens 'buy-in' to the state. To achieve tax revenue, of course, governments first need to facilitate the generation of private income.[108] Another model, proposed by Collier, is the establishment of 'independent service authorities'. These would be funded by external donors, national governments and NGOs and be responsible for the provision of public goods (e.g. health, education, water etc.) The authority would provide funding to whichever service provider (government, private sector, civil society etc.) delivered the most effective and efficient results, thereby creating accountability channels and improving service delivery.[109]

In terms of the specific measures that foreign aid directed towards stimulating economic growth as a means of reducing the risk of mass atrocities could support, there are several key elements. First, investment in public services, especially the provision of education and basic health services. Second, investment in the national infrastructure needed to stimulate growth (roads, railways, ports). Third, measures to encourage savings and private investment. Fourth, measures to create incentives for the establishment of labour-intensive industry, making economies less dependent on commodity exports. Fifth, the development of financial institutions aimed at delivering credit to those on low-incomes to stimulate economic activity. Sixth, governments should pursue land reform to improve access and guarantee land tenure. Seventh, once opportunities for investment and economic activity are created, governments should gradually reduce trade barriers to allow productive firms to flourish and diminish the capacity of 'crony capitalist' firms to crowd out the economy. Finally, steps should be taken to improve natural resource management with a focus on increasing transparency and accountability.[110] Overarching all of these initiatives should be investment and technical assistance to the state's core institutions to strengthen their capacity and establish accountability and transparency.

The second cluster of measures relate to the international norms and institutions necessary to promote economic growth and discourage abuse, corruption and patrimonialism. Chief among these are international policies to level the terms of trade and improve market access. As Paul Collier argues, 'it is stupid to provide aid with the objective of promoting development and then adopt trade policies that impede that objective'.[111] Two aspects of the trade policies pursued by the world's richest countries (OECD) are in particular need of reform. First, US and EU grant sizable agricultural subsidies which discourages their farmers from diversifying and places severe restrictions on the agricultural sectors of low income countries. Removing subsidies would allow the world's poorest farmers to sell their goods to richer countries, generating income and stimulating growth. Second, OECD countries charge higher tariffs on processed goods than on unprocessed goods. This encourages the export of unprocessed raw materials from the world's poorest countries and discourages investment in processing industries in those countries. This locks the world's poor into commodity exporting and inhibits the growth of higher value activities such as processing and manufacturing, leaving them vulnerable to dramatic changes in world commodity prices and unable to sustain steady economic growth. The key to economic growth in today's globalized world is for poor countries to trade with richer ones. The first cluster of measures described earlier will help generate and diversify local economic activity, but this can only deliver growth if the world's rich countries permit it to by liberalizing their own trade laws. What is more, encouraging trade strengthens democratization by encouraging new actors into the political arena, while giving vulnerable governments a credible voice in international trade negotiations might strengthen their domestic legitimacy.[112]

More specific international measures include the establishment of certification schemes (such as the Kimberly Process for diamonds) governing the transfer of natural resources, international laws governing the payment of bribes by multinational companies, regulations to promote banking transparency and therefore limit illegal capital flight, and strengthened international cooperation to track the proceeds of criminal activity.[113] These measures would make it more difficult for states and rebels alike to redirect resources for their own personal gain, sustain patrimonial relations and fund protracted armed conflict.

Matters are equally complex when it comes to promoting and sustaining democratization. According to one study, of 123 democratic regimes created between 1960 and 2004, 67 had survived and 56 had been reversed, more than two thirds within five years.[114] Given the importance we accorded to national leadership, it seems sensible to focus on why processes of democratization sometimes fails and what the international community can do about it, rather than on how to make democracies out of authoritarian states. Democratic reversals usually take place in one of two ways: a military coup against the incumbent government or a decision by the government to 'steal' an election. They are more likely when one or more of three background conditions are present: poverty, mineral wealth and ethnic fragmentation. However, background conditions do not determine the fate of democratization in a particular country and an important political factor has been found to heavily influence the likelihood of success: the extent to which executive power is dispersed or concentrated. In short, the more concentrated executive power is, the more likely is democratic reversal. This appears to be true irrespective of the form of system adopted (presidential or parliamentary) or the regime's economic performance. The likelihood of reversal diminishes significantly after five years of democracy, and still further after ten years. Democracies that are over ten years old tend to be durable and not susceptible to reversal.[115] From this brief analysis, it seems clear that international assistance for democratization needs to focus on (1) safeguarding against coups and stolen elections, (2) encouraging the dispersal of political power and (3) intensively protecting democracy for up to ten years.

The first, and most obvious, challenge is to protect new democracies from coups and fraudulent elections. Many vulnerable countries have a tradition of non-constitutional regime change and many unelected leaders know that they are more likely to lose than win a free and fair election. These problems are exacerbated in countries endowed with natural resources which enable the rapid translation of political power into economic wealth. Even in those countries where democracy is appearing to take root, significant structural challenges remain. First, in impoverished and fragmented societies especially, trust is seriously lacking and new democratic leaders have difficulty making credible promises. In order to build trust and maintain a slim electoral majority, leaders may resort to patrimonial or populist politics. This entrenches fragmentation and creates powerful incentives to forgo democratic politics to protect the interests of kin groups or clients.[116] Second, low levels of information, knowledge and education means that in the world's poorest countries, voters are unable to judge a government on the basis of its performance. Instead, votes are determined either by ethnic loyalty or the transmission of money or goods. This pattern of voting lends itself to the use of intimidation and bribery and raises the stakes of victory by delivering the spoils of government to the successful group and diverting them away from the losers.[117]

Part of the solution lies in the dispersal of political power, which is discussed below. In terms of more immediate steps that the international community could take, the most obvious involves taking a tougher stance on coups and fraudulent elections in order to reduce the perceived incentives. One of the most intriguing and ambitious proposals was recently suggested by Paul Collier. Collier proposed inviting governments to sign up to a voluntary charter setting out the requirements of democratic government backed up by rigorous external monitoring. In return for this voluntary commitment, governments would be offered not economic assistance but what they want most of all: a security guarantee. In return for their commitment to democracy, the international community would promise to protect elected governments and remove any regime brought to power by a coup, by force if necessary. The security guarantee would encourage governments to sign up, but the guarantee would be withdrawn if the government tried to steal an election, leaving it vulnerable to being ousted by a coup. Coups would be deterred by the threat of intervention and governments would be deterred from stealing elections.[118] By supporting new democracies and raising the costs of anti-democratic behaviour, the proposal's structure and ambition is ideal. However, it would be almost impossible to actualize any time soon, primarily because potential interveners would be reluctant to commit their troops and treasure to a potentially un-limited number of foreign interventions, including in some states with significant military capacities (e.g. Pakistan). In the interim, more feasible approaches to raising the costs of democratic reversal include: (1) a commitment to not recognize or deal with governments brought to power by unconstitutional means; (2) liberal democratic states should agree to immediately suspend all forms of aid that pass through states (mainly budget support and technical assistance) in the event of a coup or stolen election; (3) those same states should promise to impose targeted sanctions. Most importantly, they should refuse to buy commodities, making anti-democratic behaviour somewhat less lucrative. Obviously, these measures would not have the same impact as Collier's proposal, but they would reduce the expected payoffs associated with anti-democratic behaviour.

The second way in which the international community could support the consolidation of democracy in vulnerable countries is by providing assistance that encourages the dispersal of political power. The dispersal of political power also invariably disperses economic power, helping to address the horizontal inequalities discussed earlier. Even allowing for such factors as poverty and ethnic fragmentation, institutional composition and capacity is the single most important factor in determining whether democratization consolidates or reverses. The key lies in the extent to which the political system constrains executive power. Where constraints are weak, few barriers exist to patrimonialism, coups and election stealing. The dispersal of executive power involves four main elements. First, irrespective of whether a parliamentary or presidential system is developed, decision-making needs to be decentralized and made accountable. Second, the executive should be subject to the rule of law (requiring a strong and independent judiciary) and accountable to both elected bodies (requiring a sufficiently mandated and informed legislature) and the wider citizenry (requiring: a free press, measures to prevent intimidation, good public education, and a vibrant civil society). Third, there should be limits on the exercise of arbitrary power, most obviously in relation to property rights. Fourth, government policy should be implemented in an efficient, effective, impartial and non-corrupt fashion whether by a professional civil service, 'independent service authorities' or other entities.

Of course, what is needed to achieve these four goals will differ from country to country, which is why a consensual process involving all the stakeholders, such as the one mediated by the PBC, is an invaluable tool. In general, though, Kapstein and Converse have suggested two core principles to guide assistance.[119] First, assistance (whether budget support or technical assistance) should be careful to not empower the executive at the expense of the other arms of government. Where support is given to strengthen the executive, donors should ensure that they are also strengthening the other arms – especially the legislature, judiciary, media and civil society. Second, an interim solution may be to lock newly democratizing countries into international institutions. One of the most significant differences between cases of successful and unsuccessful democratization is geography: almost all new democracies in Eastern Europe survived while only a third of new democracies in Africa did. Part of the explanation is their relative economic wealth, but another significant component is the socializing and enabling effects of regional organizations. Because most East European governments wanted to join NATO and the EU, they were socialized into choosing democratization. Moreover, those institutions provided assistance in support of democratization and related reforms (such as security sector reform). Of course, sub-Saharan Africa is not so well endowed with attractive regional arrangements, but support and socialization could be funnelled through the arrangements that there are and through global institutions such as the World Bank, World Trade Organization, and UN bodies such as the PBC.

The third component addresses their critical vulnerability during their first decade. We know that democratic reversals are most likely in the first decade and that factionalized democracies are highly unstable and increase the risk of civil war. To counter these effects, external actors eager to assist democratization should pay attention to underwriting security. Most obviously, as discussed earlier, they should be prepared to protect fledgling democracies against military coups, but the commitment to security may need to go deeper than this. In post-conflict and fragile environments, external actors may need to provide public security and respond forcefully to armed challenges to elected governments (as in Timor-Leste in 2006). This implies the need for the deployment of robust military and police forces to keep the peace, uphold the law and deter and combat potential spoilers. Elections are particularly unstable periods. International security assistance may be needed to provide protection against intimidation and guard against attempts to use violence to overturn the voters' decision.[120] This requires an intensive but not open-ended commitment and offers significant dividends because the likelihood of democratic reversal diminishes significantly after the first decade. Nevertheless, persuading external actors to commit the necessary resources is another matter entirely.

Conclusion

In this chapter I have made three basic arguments. First, there is a sufficiently strong relationship between a country's economic performance, regime type and risk of mass atrocities to justify the inclusion of economic development and democratization as core components of the preventive aspect of RtoP. Indeed, I go as far as to claim that continuing to leave economic development and democratization in the cold restricts RtoP's contribution to the prevention of mass atrocities and risks making the principle a 'fire-fighting' tool. This, of course, is a vision of RtoP championed by some of its advocates (see Chapter 4) but one with an unpromising record thus far. If the goal really is to 'end mass atrocity crimes once and for all', then economic development and democratization need to be a significant part of the agenda. Second, the incorporation of economic development and democratization into the RtoP agenda should be based on two prerequisites: international support is only likely to deliver results when prefaced on the voluntary commitment of national leaders and this support should be planned and coordinated through a consultative process involving all of the major stakeholders. I argued that with some modest reforms the UN's new Peacebuilding Commission could provide the ideal venue for this sort of process. Finally, while recognizing the need for context-sensitive programs, I identified some of the measures that might be taken. In relation to economic development we highlighted three clusters of measures: general principles, targeted aid, and international reform. The general principles were that aid should be targeted at those countries where it is likely to have greatest effect, that it should be prefaced on the delivery or building of capacities needed to ensure effectiveness, and that aid and government spending more generally should be made accountable to citizens. In terms of specific areas for assistance and investment, I identified public services, infrastructure, manufacturing base, financial institutions and land reform. In relation to international reform, I argued that OECD countries should reform their subsidy and tariff rules to enable access to markets and that the international community should develop and strengthen international certification regimes for natural resources, develop legislation outlawing corruption, strengthen financial regulation to detect and prevent unlawful capital flight, and enhance international cooperation to fight the various other forms of criminal activity that fuel wars. In relation to democratization we emphasized three ways in which external actors could support indigenous reform processes: by protecting democratic regimes and promising to punish coup leaders; by focusing on aid and assistance that disperses political power; and by providing security during the critical transformation period.

This analysis is open to three obvious criticisms. The first, and most fundamental, questions the link between income, regime type and mass atrocities. Obviously, specific episodes of mass killing have numerous direct causes and triggers. I am not arguing here that poverty and authoritarianism directly *causes* mass killing. My claim is the more modest one that low income and regime type impact upon the *risk* of mass atrocities. Simply put, while they do not directly cause mass killing, such killing rarely occurs in their absence. Each year, a combination of these two facts places approximately 30 countries at risk, with on average between 0 and 5 of them succumbing to atrocities in any given year. While economic development and democratization will not insulate at risk countries from the danger of mass atrocities, they should reduce the overall number of countries at risk and therefore the overall incidence of mass killing. The alternative is to focus attention exclusively on preventing at risk countries from realizing that risk. That approach would not reduce the overall level of risk, exposes communities to mass killing when it fails, and does not necessarily require fewer resources.

The second criticism is that my argument expands the scope of RtoP so far as to make the principle indistinguishable from other normative goods. In a recent review of Gareth Evans' book on RtoP, Michael Barnett complained that expanding RtoP beyond humanitarian intervention meant that it 'now means everything and anything, which can potentially reduce the very idea of a responsibility to protect to an empty symbol, little more than a clarion call to undertake various kinds of intervention in the name of human rights'.[121] Barnett's argument gets things a little upside down inasmuch as expanding the scope of RtoP would probably diminish its capacity as a clarion call rather than draw attention to it (see Chapter 4). But the argument chimes well with those that see RtoP as a speech act that provides a catalyst for international intervention in humanitarian emergencies. This gets us back to the question of RtoP's function and my argument in Chapter 4 that the principle is better seen (in that it better reflects what states have agreed and is more likely to be effective in terms of saving lives) as a principle implying a broad policy agenda than as a clarion call for urgent action in the face of emergencies. But it is important to stress that even an expanded vision of RtoP does not bring in 'anything and everything' which is why I went to such great lengths earlier to demonstrate a clear linkage between income, regime type and mass atrocities. I am not here calling for more effort to be expended on economic growth and demo-cratization simply because I think they are goods in themselves (which, of course, they are), but because I think that the weight of evidence suggests that doing so will help reduce the incidence of mass atrocities.

Finally, it may be objected that the measures I have called for are unrealistic. In particular, the world's richest states are unlikely to alter their trade laws, reconfigure their aid programs, commit to punishing coup leaders and (possibly) forcibly removing them, and make a decade long commitment to providing security to fledgling democracies. There is no doubting that we are indeed a long way from an international community that would do all of this as a matter of routine. But there are already examples of some these policies in practice. For example, some OECD governments, notably Australia, argue for a reduction of agricultural subsidies and tariffs; both the UK and US have recognized the need to channel aid and assistance to countries undergoing indigenous-led reform programs; in 1994 the UN Security Council authorized armed intervention in Haiti to reverse a coup and more recently the AU has taken economic and political measures against coup leaders in Guinea; and the West made a fruitful decade-long commitment to providing security in the new democracies of Bosnia and Kosovo. Although the measures envisaged here require the commitment of new resources, they are not unprecedented.

6 Early warning[1]

The first part of any system for directly preventing genocide and mass atrocities (as opposed to reducing the background risks) is its early warning mechanism. It is therefore appropriate that the UN Secretary-General has focused on early warning as the first stage of his implementation agenda for RtoP. Simply put, international actors, states and local communities have a better chance of preventing the escalation of conflict into violence and mass atrocities if they are warned about the impending threat.[2] Advance warning provides decision-makers with evidence to support priority-setting and informs debate about appropriate responses to the threat of violent conflict.[3] Early action tends to be associated with a higher level of success and lower financial cost than late action or action that waits to respond only once violence has broken out. According to James Sutterlin, effective early warning mechanisms must have three components – access to information, analysis capabilities, and a communication channel to decision-makers capable of authorizing timely and effective preventive measures.[4] The need to see early warning as encompassing more than simply the acquisition of information is made clear by the fact that some of the worst recent atrocities, such as the war in Bosnia and genocide in Rwanda, were predicted in advance – the former by the CIA in reports that were only made public after the war had begun and the latter with startling clarity by the commander of the UN's mission in Rwanda, General Romeo Dallaire. The problem in both cases was that the warnings were issued on an *ad hoc* basis to institutions that were not specifically tasked with preventing atrocities. The US government chose not to share the CIA's advice with others, and General Dallaire was advised by the UN's Department of Peacekeeping Operations (DPKO) that preventive measures such as the disarmament of militia groups were beyond the scope of UNAMIR's mandate.[5]

Early warning is not without its problems, however. We noted in Chapter 2 that while the UN General Assembly included a specific reference to strengthening the UN's capacity for early warning in its 2005 commitment to RtoP, states were continuing to raise concerns about it in 2009. In particular, states worried about the potential for early warning to be a catalyst for interference in domestic affairs, its potential politicization, and about the very principle of the UN collecting sensitive information about its member states. There are also significant technical problems. Although it is relatively straightforward to identify countries at risk of political turmoil or humanitarian disaster in general terms, it is much more difficult to predict precisely when conflicts will escalate into genocide and mass atrocities and it is politically problematic (to say the least) to issue alerts identifying states at risk – especially if those alerts are given formal diplomatic status by being issued by a UN office or regional organization.[6] This problem is magnified by the fact that RtoP triggering crises can develop quickly – for instance in the immediate aftermath of a contested election, as in Kenya in 2008 – and while warning mechanisms might identify dozens of 'at risk' countries, those risks will only manifest themselves in a relatively small number of cases.[7] This has prompted at least one prominent critic – Stephen Stedman, a key architect of Kofi Annan's UN reform agenda which included the RtoP – to argue that as policy makers do not have 'crystal balls' we should not be too optimistic about the possibility of effective early warning.[8] The danger is that a cavalier approach to early warning (sounding the alarm whenever a country is deemed at risk) is likely to generate false alarms making it more difficult to engage political actors and eliciting opposition from the governments that are subjects of those alerts as well as from their friends. It is unsurprising, therefore, that many governments have expressed concern that moves to develop an international 'culture of prevention' might undermine principles of sovereignty and territorial integrity by legitimising external interference in the domestic affairs of states.[9] When the Security Council debated conflict prevention in November 1999, several states argued that preventive action should never violate sovereignty.[10] Sovereignty concerns also explain why it took two years for the General Assembly to negotiate a resolution endorsing a 2001 report by the Secretary-General on the prevention of armed conflict, and why although early warning was specifically mentioned in the 2005 commitment to RtoP concerns were still being raised about it four years later.[11] Finally, some analysts have also raised concerns that precipitate external intervention prompted by early warning could exacerbate political conflicts by encouraging rebels to take up arms in order to attract international attention, a variant of the moral hazard argument analysed in Chapter 4.[12]

Taking up the challenge thrown down by the 2009 General Assembly debate on RtoP, this chapter examines the potential and the pitfalls of early warning. It does so in three parts. First, it briefly outlines different methods of early warning analysis and provides an overview of international capacity in this area. Second, it reviews the UN's past experience with early warning, focusing on why recurrent commitments to strengthen early warning have not been translated into practice. Finally, it examines progress towards the establishment of a Joint Office for the Prevention of Genocide and RtoP, which would provide early warning advice directly to the UN Secretary-General.

Approaches to early warning

This section briefly outlines some of the key approaches to early warning operated by governments, inter-governmental organizations and non-state actors. The various systems in which these approaches operate provide warning of slightly different phenomena (e.g. political instability, armed conflict, international crises, humanitarian crisis etc.) and provide different services ranging from the simple issuing of warnings or alerts, to the provision of detailed country-studies and policy recommendations. Indeed, it is worth noting that there is some debate within the field as to whether early warning ought to be in the business of recommending response options, with some arguing that early warning systems should divorce themselves from the response framework in order to protect their independence and integrity, while others argue that response options are a crucial part of early warning.[13] In addition to the type of actor that operates them (international organization, state, NGO etc.), early warning systems can be categorized by reference to the methodology they employ. Alex Austin, for example, has identified four distinct methodological approaches (qualitative, quantitative, hybrid and networks) each of which has distinct advantages and weaknesses.[14] Table 6.1 provides an overview of some of the most prominent systems and identifies their 'type'.

Qualitative frameworks tend to be based on field research and involve the real-time collection of information and analysis. This tends to be done by organizations that enjoy a significant field presence (e.g. International Crisis Group), but the methods used are often not wholly transparent and systematic.[15] Qualitative approaches have the advantage of providing detailed contextual information which is easy to absorb and translate into actionable policy options. They also tend to incorporate local stakeholders in the process, ensuring that both the framework and information gathering are context specific. On the downside, their contextual specificity makes it hard to generalize across cases or conduct global or regional analysis, making it difficult to use to establish global priorities. In addition, the application of qualitative methods tends to be less transparent and systematic than quantitative methods and is more subject to the interpretations and judgments of the individual analyst. Finally, it cannot be assumed that qualitative data is less partial and more complete than quantitative data.[16]

There are a variety of *quantitative* frameworks, which tend to adopt one of four general approaches: structural models, process/accelerator models, pattern analysis and response models. Structural models simply highlight conditions under which conflict might erupt and develop indicators to measure their presence. Such indicators will seek to measure the extent of existing threats by comparing them with previous conflict.[17] Process models assume the existence of stages in the conflict cycle. The identification of accelerators for particular types of conflicts give clues to the probability of a certain stage of conflict (or pre-conflict) developing.[18] With pattern analysis, large amounts of conflict data is collected and divided into a number of indicators that highlight both structural and events-related conditions. These indicators interact (using algorithms to match patterns) in a way that shows signs of 'negative developments' leading to conflict.[19] Finally, response models focus on the influence that intervention, or other kinds of preventive or reactive responses have on a particular

Table 6.1 Early warning systems

Actor/Qualitative	Quantitative	Hybrid	Network
National government	• BMZ – Crisis Early Warning (Germany) • State Department and National Intelligence Council Instability Watch List (US)		
Intergovernmental • OSCE Conflict Prevention Centre • Continental Early Warning System (AU) • EU External Affairs Commission watchlist	• Country Indicators for Foreign Policy	• CEMAC – mechanisme d'Alerte rapide • West Africa Early Warning and Response Network (ECOWAS) • CEWARN (IGAD)	• Humanitarian Early Warning System (OCHA) • Refworld (UNHCR) • Reliefweb (OCHA)
Non-governmental • Crisis Watch (International Crisis Group) • GPPAC Early Warning, Early Response Programme	• Centre for International Development and Conflict Management (Maryland) • Political Instability Task Force • Minorities at Risk • Kansas Events Data System • Global Peace Index • Conflict Early Warning Systems • PANDA/IDEA • Future of Global Interdependence • SIPRI Early Warning Indicators Database	• FAST (Swisspeace) • PIOOM • Fund for Peace Conflict Assessment System Tool	• FEWER

conflict. The aim of such models is to identify when it is best to respond, and what strategies are the most effective.[20] Many quantitative models are very accurate in their predictions, for example the Political Instability Task Force reports a success rate in excess of 80 per cent.[21] The use of quantitative data that is generated for most countries permits comparison and the establishment of 'watchlists' that facilitate priority-setting. In addition, the identification of variables that correlate with instability, violence, and/or mass atrocities provide useful insights about prevention priorities.[22] However, it is important to recognize the limits of what quantitative approaches can tell us. While they can indicate general levels of risk, quantitative analysis cannot provide guidance as to whether the risk is likely to become manifest or *when* a conflict or crisis is likely to erupt.[23] Quantitative approaches also tell us little about the political dynamics in a given country and do not provide much of a basis for developing policy options that are context sensitive. As a result, decision-makers may be reluctant to trust the analysis and there may be a disconnect between the factors that are identified as contributing to instability and politically feasible policy options.[24] Finally, quantitative models are limited by their data. Relevant data for the most troubled countries is likely to be non-existent or highly unreliable, and there are significant time lapses between the period described by the data and the time that data is released for analysis.[25]

The third type is a *hybrid* framework that comprises quantitative and qualitative components. Some organizations run the two methodologies concurrently. This is usually a combination of event data analysis and field work or expert analysis.[26] Datasets can point to areas at risk, or areas experiencing escalating tension, and the more direct approach or field-based or expert analysis has the potential to yield insights and details that computerized modelling possibly overlooks. Another approach is to use the methodologies sequentially, using predominantly (though not exclusively) quantitative methods to conduct risk analysis and identify those countries that have heightened risk and then utilizing qualitative research to monitor and provide deeper analysis of the situation in those countries. It is important to stress that although a hybrid approach may provide a more complete picture than either the quantitative or qualitative approaches, and permit triangulation to verify or discount evidence provided by one or other method, it does not escape the limitations associated with either approach. However, the sequential hybrid approach does provide a framework for thinking about the operationalization of early warning within a UN office for the Prevention of Genocide and RtoP.[27]

Finally, some early warning systems operate as *networks*, cooperating with other agencies to compile and systematize their information. This provides a repository of information on a particular type or types of crises that various actors can draw on.[28] This has the distinct advantage of tying early warning into the local context by including stakeholders and incorporating local interpretations of the relevant data, but still confronts the challenges noted earlier as well as problems of coordination and benchmarking to ensure consistency across different actors.

This brief survey suggests that there are many ways of doing early warning. Moreover, as Table 6.1 demonstrates, there are many early warning systems. One notable point about these systems is that many of them have had limited life spans (e.g. FAST) and failed to deliver on their promises, largely because of funding and capacity problems. It also shows that the systems are not consistent in what it is they aim to provide warnings about, with topics including natural disasters, refugee movements, political instability, armed conflict, and genocide and mass atrocities. Indeed, there are a relatively small number of systems dedicated to genocide and mass atrocities and those that do exist either focus exclusively on genocide or have yet to fully operationalize their methodologies. On a more positive note, the proliferation of systems in both the governmental and non-governmental sectors is testament that sufficient open-source information is available to make early warning viable without access to secret intelligence information. The amount of information in the public realm is more than sufficient to provide adequate early warning, and makes redundant the concerns that some member states had about UN early warning amounting to the acquisition of intelligence information. As such, the biggest technical challenge for early warning in the UN system is not acquiring relevant information, but building the capacity needed to analyze that information and assess risk. The key challenge that policy makers face is no longer a shortage of information, but an excess. This creates a predicament of deciding what information to use and what to overlook and how to use the information to develop better prevention strategies.

In comparison to humanitarian and conflict early warning, early warning for genocide and mass atrocities is underdeveloped. In particular, the early warning systems that currently operate focus on genocide at the expense of other mass atrocities. Other mass atrocity crimes have a presence inasmuch as they are indicators of impending genocide. Consequently, these early warning systems have limited use when it comes to providing warnings for war crimes, ethnic cleansing and crimes against humanity. Recently, early warning for genocide has begun to broaden to incorporate 'genocide-like crimes' that include crimes against humanity and ethnic cleansing. Thus, Barbara Harff has pointed out that providing early warning for genocide and 'politicide' naturally incorporates a number of non-genocidal atrocities, as the conditions that heighten the risk of genocide also heighten the risk of similar crimes that nevertheless lack genocidal intent.[29] Thus the same causal frameworks are utilized. While the broadening of emphasis is significant, and is a reflection of RtoP's influence on the research community, frameworks for addressing mass atrocity crimes remain imprecise. Although such frameworks do provide important insights into the relationship between genocide and other mass atrocity crimes, more work needs to be done to ensure that the range of conditions that contribute to all these crimes are adequately accounted for.

Finally, in addition to noting the absence of systems directed at providing warning of genocide, war crimes, ethnic cleansing and crimes against humanity, four other important limitations need to be acknowledged before we move on to examine the UN's experience with early warning. Without significant advances in information gathering, communication and capacity, these limitations are unlikely to be overcome but they are important to recognize as a guide to what can be reasonably expected from early warning. First, although relevant data is available, there will always be a time lapse between the production and analysis of good quality data and the publication of early warnings. It is largely unavoidable that key data covering issues such as income, horizontal inequalities, trade openness, licit and illicit trades in arms, democratic governance, and press freedoms, will take time to collect, verify and analyse, with the result being that the picture painted of a particular country is likely to be considerably out of date when it is released. Second, risk analysis and early warning cannot account for every case and must acknowledge the potential for unexpected events that cannot be predicted in advance. Although most atrocities are usually foreseen, there will always be unforeseeable cases. Often, such cases are products of rapid and violent regime changes that are difficult to predict. For example, the slaughter of suspected communists in Indonesia in 1965–6 was rapidly organized as a response to an attempted coup that enjoyed the tacit support of President Sukarno. To predict it would have required prior knowledge of the coup (of course, kept a secret), an assessment that the coup would fail (difficult given the president's tacit support), and information that the army would respond with mass atrocities (for which there was no precedent and no prior evidence). Other episodes such as the coup and subsequent rightist atrocities in Chile were similarly difficult to predict in advance. It is for this reason that the Political Instability Task Force's accuracy rate of 80 per cent probably represents the limit of what can be achieved. Third, as I noted earlier, in some of the most troubled countries, the data needed to conduct risk analysis is unlikely to be accurate and in some cases may be non-existent. This raises questions about how to interpret inaccurate and missing data and challenges researchers to remain open to substituting different kinds of data. Finally, it is important to note that while most early warning systems operate at the level of the state, many conflicts, including those involving mass atrocities, are local or regional in nature. For example, country-level analysis of Sudan may have identified national risks but would not have identified Darfur specifically. Likewise, country-level analysis of Nigeria would fail to predict the communal atrocities around the city of Jos. Country-level analysis is also likely to give an inaccurate picture of conflicts and atrocities once started. For instance, since 2003 the conflict in the DRC has been limited mainly to the east of the country, with sporadic eruptions of violent conflict elsewhere. Most of the country did not experience armed conflict during this period, yet country-level analysis identifies the whole country as being at war, papering over significant regional variation within the century.[30]

Early warning in the united nations: a brief history

Calls for the establishment of an international conflict early warning mechanism go back many decades. Quincy Wright floated a proposal in 1957 for a 'world intelligence center', which coincided with President Eisenhower's decision to approve a UN satellite reconnaissance capability – ideas that did not progress very far.[31] In the 1960s, one of the pioneers of peace studies, Kenneth Boulding, appealed for the establishment of networks with the capacity to monitor and provide information about places at risk of conflict.[32] Independent of governments, its intended purpose was to collect and analyse information on the relations between states, with updates and forecasts published on a yearly basis.

Within the UN, the idea of developing a form of early warning capacity was first touted in the 1960s by Secretary-General, Dag Hammarskjöld. In a context where Cold War rivalries inhibited the organization from playing its intended role in relation to international peace and security, Hammarskjöld argued that the UN could play an important role in what he termed 'preventive diplomacy', by which he meant preventing the escalation of local conflicts into regional or global wars involving the superpowers.[33] This view of the UN's role in international peace and security was premised on the assumption that the organization would develop the capacity to discern the existence of such threats before they materialized.[34] Hammarskjöld himself acknowledged that such international engagement was most effective when conducted early.[35] Despite this, little progress was made on developing an early warning capacity within the UN system until the 1980s. Thus, more than 20 years after Hammarskjöld claimed that preventive diplomacy was a core function of the UN, Secretary-General Perez de Cuellar was still appealing for states to allow the organization to develop such a capacity.

In 1981, a report by Prince Sadruddin Aga Khan for the UN Human Rights Commission called for the creation of an early warning system within the UN.[36] Following up on this, in his first annual report to the General Assembly in 1982, Perez de Cuellar out the case for establishing an early warning office, arguing that, 'if the [UN Security] Council were to keep an active watch on dangerous situations and, if necessary, initiate discussions with the parties before they reach the point of crisis, it might be otherwise possible to defuse them at an early stage before they degenerate into violence'.[37] Keeping an active watch meant the Security Council having access to early warning resources. To achieve this, the UN secretariat would need the capacity to access information on dangerous situations, to analyse that data, and transmit it to decision-makers. While early warning in relation to famines and natural disasters had gained currency in the 1970s, the fact that the outbreak of the Falklands War in 1982 took the Secretary-General by surprise exposed the UN secretariat's analytical weakness in this area.[38] This was not the first time that the UN Secretary-General had not received warnings from the secretariat on the emergence of major crises. Prior Secretaries-General had learned of both the 1948 Communist coup in Czechoslovakia and Bangladesh's declaration of independence in 1971 through media reports.[39] Perez de Cuellar's support for early warning, demonstrated by his 1981 speech to the General Assembly, coupled with the secretariat's failure to provide advance warning of the Falklands War, provided new impetus and helped generate some political support for the establishment of a loose early warning capacity. Calls mounted for the UN to establish a capacity to collect information and provide timely reports on escalating crises that heightened the possibility of armed conflict. After a number of consultations in the Security Council between 1983 and 1987, consensus was reached on the need to set up a 'UN system for monitoring developments worldwide to aid the preventive role of the Council'.[40] The result was the establishment of the Office for Research and the Collection of Information (ORCI).

Office for Research and the Collection of Information

Based within the Office of the Secretary-General (the forerunner to the Department of Political Affairs (DPA)), ORCI was mandated to provide the organization's security and humanitarian arms with information about the potential causes of conflict and notification of emerging warning signs by 'conducting research, assessing global trends, and bringing potential trouble spots and critical security situations to the attention of the Secretary-General'.[41] With an initial staff of 20 professionals and a further 20 research assistants and secretaries, the Office aimed to develop an early warning system that utilized both qualitative and quantitative analysis. This included the anticipated use of computer modeling for early warning and the fostering of research to identify conflict trends. The office tried to develop an approach to early warning that drew on traditional techniques of information gathering and analysis as used by foreign ministries as well as developing 'numerical indicators' that would help to codify and strengthen qualitative approaches. This would lead to the establishment of a database that would direct analysts to the most current information and assist in identifying situations that were likely to lead to conflict or instability if ignored. It was anticipated that the office would provide advice directly to the Secretary-General, who would in turn employ his good-offices (for example by despatching special representatives or envoys) and communicate with relevant states and regional bodies or, when thought necessary, bring matters to the attention of other UN organs such as the Security Council, as provided for by Article 99 of the UN Charter.[42]

Most of these ambitious objectives were never achieved, primarily due to budgetary and staffing constraints, which were themselves a direct product of unease among member states about the UN playing a role in something akin to 'intelligence gathering'. Several key states, including both superpowers, were concerned by what they saw as the development of an independent intelligence-gathering capacity by the UN. Conservatives in the US Congress viewed it as inconsistent with the UN's role as a neutral body, some even describing ORCI as a 'communist conspiracy'. Soviet ire was attracted when it was discovered that ORCI's interests included signs of political conflict in the Baltic.[43] Although both American and Soviet attitudes improved, neither was prepared to support the dedication of new resources to the initiative. This compounded ORCI's problems. At the time, there was a freeze of new appointments at the

UN, forcing de Cuellar to second staff from other departments. This caused delays and inter-departmental resistance – creating the impression that the office was unable to fulfill its ambitious mandate.[44] Moreover, secondment worked in the opposite direction too and the office's capacity was not helped by the frequent movement of staff members to other parts of the organization. In some cases, outward secondments halved the office's staffing level.[45] Plans to establish a computerized database that assessed emerging crises stalled. The office also faced a persistent shortage of basic materials such as computers, books, periodicals, and audio-visual equipment, which inhibited its capacity to gather information and provide advice. There were also no mechanisms for the sharing of information between UN departments and agencies and many were hostile to cooperating with UN headquarters in such an overtly 'political' enterprise, in some cases because they were precluded by their mandates from reporting on political matters.[46] In addition, UN representatives in the field worried that early warning indicators might jeopardize their relations with the local authorities.[47] These setbacks rendered the office's medium-term plan (1987–92), which focused on developing its capacity to collect and disseminate information, unworkable, making it difficult to discern any positive contributions stemming from the office.[48] Shortly after taking over as Secretary-General, Boutros-Ghali closed ORCI down in 1992 as part of a broader program of staff cuts forced on the UN by its major donors.[49]

ORCI's short life and the political and bureaucratic problems it encountered inhibited the development of an early warning framework, let alone its implementation. In particular, ORCI was blocked from providing recommendations on early action, as no resources were allocated for developing response options. In addition to the aforementioned concerns of the superpowers, a significant portion of the wider UN membership was also concerned about the potential impact of the office. As a result, the office was never endorsed by the General Assembly and was therefore a prime target for closure when budget cuts had to be made. Thus, Simon Chesterman noted a 'profound ambivalence' among states towards the idea of the UN having the capacity to collect information and provide analysis,[50] and Connie Peck points to the evidence of growing suspicion among 'southern' states especially of a post-Cold War UN having access to intelligence that could ultimately be used against them, possibly in the strategic interests of the global north.[51] Such suspicions were fanned in part by the Palme Commission on Disarmament and Security Issues, whose 1989 report recommended that member states 'undertake to provide national data to United Nations experts' and that the Secretary-General be given the necessary personnel and technology to deal with this information.[52] Given this, it is hardly surprising that member states drew connections between the operations in ORCI and potential infringements on sovereignty.

Despite the apparent consensus on the need for an early warning capacity within the UN, the obstacles experienced by ORCI demonstrated a significant degree of residual political and bureaucratic opposition to the idea. There was great reticence to combine information gathering and analysis in the one office (the separation of which made early warning largely ineffective) and this trans-lated into a reluctance to support and fund the office, rendering it ineffective. Additional investment would have required the endorsement of the General Assembly, thought unlikely given the degree of suspicion that member states held towards the Office's activities.[53]

Despite ORCI's closure, the idea that the UN should have an early warning capacity continued to win support in some quarters. In *An Agenda for Peace*, first released in 1992, Boutros-Ghali recognized the growing need for early warning in the UN system, noting that the UN should 'seek to identify at the earliest possible stage situations that could produce conflict and to try through diplomacy to remove the sources of danger before violence erupts'.[54] The Secretary-General maintained that there was a need to strengthen the UN's capacity to determine the existence of a threat to peace, and to provide analysis that would inform decision-makers about the appropriate response options in such situations. In 1995, a Ford Foundation report appealed for the creation an early warning and threat assessment capability within the Secretary-General's office.[55] In the same year, the UN Joint Inspection Unit (JIU) called for the creation of a specialized unit within the Department of Political Affairs (DPA) to identify emerging crises and coordinate the 'anticipatory planning' of 'appropriate actions' by the Secretary-General.[56] In one of his first reports to the General Assembly as Secretary-General, Annan criticized the JIU for underestimating the concerns expressed member states, pointing out that a majority of UN members had rejected his predecessors' attempt to create integrated UN offices on the grounds that this was an attempt to 'obtain polit-ical reporting on Member States' internal affairs'. Annan also criticized the JIU's expansive understanding of prevention as including root causes and eco-nomic development, arguing instead that conflict prevention was an 'essentially political' activity.[57] Unsurprisingly, given the extant political concerns and the Secretary-General's criticisms, the General Assembly chose not to adopt the JIU's recommendation. Nonetheless, some UN officials continued to press the case. One of the many reports on the Rwandan disaster identified the absence of an early warning system as a contributing factor, noting that there was no way of channelling evidence gathered by UN agencies in the field to the key decision-makers.[58] Likewise, Marrack Goulding, former head of UN peacekeeping, pressed the case for consolidated early warning analysis and policy development.[59] In 2000, the high profile and well-regarded Brahimi report on peace operations proposed the consolidation of various departmental units into a single entity designed to gather, analyse and disseminate information – the Information and Strategic Analysis Secretariat for the Executive Committee for Peace and Security (EISAS).[60] In 2005, the High Level Panel commissioned by Annan to provide recommendations for reforming the UN system recom-mended that a proposed UN Peacebuilding Commission serve as a focal point for conflict prevention, including early warning.

In summary, therefore, although the end of the Cold War helped forge some consensus about the need to invest more fully in measures to anticipate and prevent crises from escalating into violent conflict, is was not enough to allay the suspicions of some key member states, including the US and Soviet Union. Some of these concerns, especially relating to the gathering of information, have become progressively redundant as the global communications revolution expanded the amount of publicly available information about conflicts and countries, allowing a growing number of NGOs to collect information and conduct early warning without the need to draw on classified and sensitive intelligence. As a result, although the UN has, until now, resisted calls for the establishment of a dedicated office for early warning, elements of early warning practice have become part of the work undertaken by several UN offices.

Department of Political Affairs (DPA)

When ORCI was disbanded, its information collection and analysis functions were dispersed to the Department of Political Affairs (DPA) and the Department of Humanitarian Affairs (known since 1992 as the Office for the Coordination of Humanitarian Affairs (OCHA)). The DPA was charged with being the primary conduit to the Secretary-General in relation to countries at risk of conflict. Among other functions, such as peacemaking, peacebuilding, liaising with regional arrangements and assisting member states, the DPA gradually came to function as de facto coordinator of the UN's preventive activities. The first step along that road was taken in 1995 when, in response to findings that one of the sources of the UN's failure to prevent or respond effectively to the Rwandan genocide was poor communication between UN offices that were privy to early warning signs, the Policy Analysis Team was established in the DPA. The team had a mandate to improve the department's capacity to conduct early warning and analysis, as well as to make recommendations with regards to possible responses to such signs.[61] Based on initiatives spurred by the Policy Planning Team and regional divisions of the DPA, the Under-Secretary-General for Political Affairs, Kieran Prendergast created the DPA Prevention Team in 1998. Its function was to identify situations that were most at risk of escalating into violent conflict and which might require a preventive response from the UN.[62] This involved the creation of 'prevention teams' within the DPA. Each of the DPA's four regional divisions was required to provide the Secretary-General with early warning of emerging crises in their area, based on information gathered from open sources and other UN departments and agencies.[63] Another task it was given was to plan a *system* for early warning and prevention, based on extensive in-house consultations in order to learn the lessons from ORCI. These efforts produced made progress by establishing regular consultation between key UN agencies on the subject of prevention and early warning.[64] To further strengthen inter-agency consultation, Annan also established the Executive Committee on Peace and Security (ECPS). Convened by the DPA, the ECPS meets twice a month and provides a forum for 'high-level discussion and decision-making' with regards to early warning and prevention.[65]

Despite these improvements in information sharing, the DPA has been disadvantaged by the reluctance of some member states to afford it the capacity to conduct early warning analysis due to persistent fears that such capacity would compromise sovereignty. To be more effective in prompting prevention, the DPA requires the capacity to analyse risk situations, something that it currently lacks.[66] This lack of progress was recognized in Kofi Annan's two reports on prevention, written five years apart (in 2001 and 2006). In his 2001 report, Annan stated that desk officers in the DPA were 'well placed to detect changes and developments that may lead to crisis'.[67] However the department lacked capacity for analysis and crafting policy recommendations. He therefore recommended that the General Assembly improve the DPA's capacity in these areas so that it could become a 'focal point' for prevention within the UN system.[68] The General Assembly responded with a resolution in 2003, which acknowledged the need to strengthen early warning capacity throughout the UN, noting that this included both the collection and analysis of information.[69] However, it failed to follow up with additional resources and Annan's 2006 report observed that no real progress had been made. It identified three interlinked problems: (1) an ongoing lack of capacity for the analysis and integration of information from various parts of the UN system; (2) the inability to integrate data from the various bodies and agencies within the UN to formulate regular early warning reports; (3) the problem of 'insufficient' and 'insecure' funding.[70] According to the Secretary-General, without a centralized unit in the UN system, resourced with the capacity for data collection, analysis, and information sharing, progress in the field of operational or direct prevention was unlikely. Yet, at first glance it is difficult to see how such these predicaments can be overcome. It has traditionally been thought that greater capacity for risk analysis would require a greater field presence to collect the information needed, and it is the prospect of such capacities that provokes the resistance of many states, on the grounds that it would violate their sovereign rights. One way around this, proposed by Rubin and Jones, is to increase collaboration with outside groups that can provide the UN with the relevant information without the need to engage directly in activities that can be perceived as intelligence gathering.[71] Another approach, adopted as part of the proposed joint office for genocide prevention and RtoP, is to use only data already gathered by the UN system. This could potentially be supported by other initiatives spearheaded by the 'Framework Team' and UN Staff College.

The Interdepartmental Framework for Coordination (Framework Team) provides a forum for early warning that draws insights from 14 agencies and bodies from across the UN system. Formed in 1995, it brings key agencies together to share information and analysis of 'at risk' situations and discuss integrated responses.[72] Also aiding this process is a UN training project on developing capacity in early warning and preventive measures. Taught by the UN Staff College in Turin, a number of training courses were developed with the aim of building 'institutional capacity by significantly improving professional and analytical skill and awareness of UN staff in the area of early warning and preventive action'.[73] More specifically, they aim to assist the mainstreaming of early warning analysis across the UN system by providing UN staff with skills relevant to identifying causes and stages of conflict, undertaking early warning analysis, identifying preventive measures, and improving their understanding of the mechanisms that exist for coordination across the UN system, thereby creating better policy recommendations.[74]

Therefore, the idea of developing an early warning capacity within the UN system has a long history. However, although many states, analysts and secretariat officials recognize the need for a focal point for early warning, concerns among some states that such a capacity might lead the UN towards collecting sensitive information and issuing politicized reports that might constitute a breach of the principle of non-interference have thus far prevented the development of such a capacity. However, as we noted in the first part of the chapter, the globalization of information means that ample open source data is freely available for risk analysis purposes. In addition, some UN departments have begun to develop their own *de facto* early warning capacities. When viewed alongside the clear commitment to early warning made as part of the international community's adoption of RtoP, these developments suggest that it might now be politically feasible to establish an early warning focal point within the UN system. In Chapter 2, I pointed out that the Secretary-General argued that the establishment of a joint office for genocide prevention and RtoP, which would conduct early warning, should be the first tangible step towards implementing the RtoP. In the final part of this chapter, I will consider the development of this capacity in a little more detail.

Towards a joint office for genocide prevention and RtoP

In 2004, on the tenth anniversary of the genocide in Rwanda, the Secretary-General established the position of the Special Adviser for the Prevention of Genocide. This position was tasked with (1) collecting information on massive and systematic violations of human rights that, if not prevented or halted, might lead to genocide; (2) providing early warning advice to the Secretary-General; (3) making recommendations on actions to prevent genocide; and (4) liaising with the UN system on measures to prevent genocide. Critically, the Special Adviser was tasked with providing early warning advice directly to the Secretary-General, bypassing the need to filter it through various policy committees and ensuring (in theory, at least), that the Secretary-General receives clear advice untarnished by political or bureaucratic interests. The Special Adviser was not, however, to be in the business of determining whether particular crises constituted genocide. Political support for this work, and for the role of early warning within it, was strengthened when as part of their commitment to the RtoP at the 2005 World Summit, Heads of State and Government unanimously supported the Special Adviser's work (para. 140) and committed to strengthening the UN's capacity for early warning (para. 139).

The appointment was broadly welcomed, with the first Special Adviser, Juan Méndez, reporting that he had received 'clear signs of support' for the development of an early warning capability in relation to genocide.[75] However, funding restrictions meant that Méndez was appointed only on a part-time and year-by-year basis – severely limiting the extent to which he could do more than act as a vocal figurehead. Méndez set to work quickly, contributing to the Secretary-General's plan for preventing genocide, which was announced in April 2005. The plan called for the prevention of armed conflict in general, because war usually provides the context for genocide; the protection of civilians; the ending of impunity through international criminal proceedings; early warning; and swift and decisive responses including the use of force as a last resort. Méndez explored the early warning indicators that might point to impending genocide, consulting with NGOs in identifying four clusters of indicators including the existence of groups at risk, violations of human rights, hate speech, and histories of genocide.[76] Indeed, Méndez himself described his role as 'com[ing] up with ideas for early action that are relatively less costly, but also produces a result'.[77]

The Special Adviser devoted much of his attention to Darfur, but also wrote notes to the Secretary-General on Côte D'Ivoire and DRC, and made his concerns known on the situations in Colombia, Myanmar, West Papua, Togo, northern Uganda and Somalia. He visited Darfur several times, criticizing governments for their 'insufficient' response to the suffering there – describing it as 'very eerily reminiscent' of the world's reaction to the Rwandan genocide. Méndez also provided the Secretary-General with policy recommendations, focusing on the physical protection of vulnerable populations through the deployment of peacekeepers, the provision of humanitarian assistance, legal accountability, and efforts to advance the peace process.

After Méndez retired in March 2007, three NGOs (Amnesty International, Human Rights Watch and the World Federalist Movement) – expressed concerns at reports that the new Secretary-General, Ban Ki-moon planned to either downgrade the appointment or merge it out of existence by tying it to a new advisory position on RtoP.[78] There is some evidence that Ban came under pressure to alter the Special Adviser position. American envoy Andrew Natsios indicated his disquiet with using the term 'genocide' in the position's title and a UN official informally advised that concerns had been raised about the Special Adviser's title because states had expressed a reluctance to permit the adviser to visit, opining 'who would want to let into their country an office with genocide in the title?'[79] However, Ban confounded the sceptics' expectations by appointing the highly regarded Francis Deng and by augmenting this work with the appointment of Edward Luck as Special Adviser on RtoP. The strengthening of the Office of the Special Adviser has helped to significantly advance work on early warning and plans in 2010 emerged for a joint office for genocide prevention and RtoP, with a critical role in early warning.

In the last two years, the Office of the Special Adviser has developed and strengthened significantly, increasing its capacity to fulfill the various elements of its mandate. Three aspects of this work are particularly relevant here. First, the Office has developed an 'analysis framework' as a guide in the monitoring and assessment of the risk of genocide. Second, it is developing an inventory of information sources including the various UN departments and agencies that collect information relevant to the monitoring of the risk of genocide. Third, there is ongoing consultation with the Special Adviser for the RtoP, but it should be stressed that the Office remains focused exclusively on the prevention of genocide and not the other RtoP related crimes. I will briefly examine each of these in turn.

In October 2009, the Special Adviser released an 'analysis framework' as a guide to assist staff in recognizing and assessing the risk of genocide in various situations. The framework lists eight criteria, or 'categories of factors' that may indicate the risk of genocide and as such constitutes the closest thing the UN has ever developed to a risk analysis framework for genocide. It is a rudimentary framework, however. The factors are not ranked, and the framework acknowledges that information about all categories may not be available in any given place or situation. But as the Special Adviser points out, risk is not determined by a ticking of the boxes of all eight categories, but rather by the 'cumulative effect' of the factors that may be present.[80] The first category focuses on two elements – the nature of intergroup relations and the existence of discrimination or human rights violations targeting a particular group. It calls for assessment of the relations between these groups in terms of economic, social and political power, and examines the perceptions that exist among the various groups in these relations. This is then viewed in terms of the existence of any tensions or conflict, either ongoing or in the past (including past genocide), to determine whether patterns of discrimination or inequality are entrenched.

The second category focuses on circumstances that may result in a diminished capacity to prevent potential genocide. These include the absence or weakness of judicial independence and human rights institutions, as well as the extent to which any international presence may be able to protect targeted groups, as well as the extent of impartial law enforcement bodies and independent media. This involves analysis which scrutinizes existing legal structures and practices, access to legal and civil protection for vulnerable groups, and the extent to which impunity for past crimes against targeted groups persists.

The third category assesses the presence of illegal weapons and militia groups. The aim here is to determine whether the capacity for mass killing exists. This involves identifying any armed groups and assessing their strength in terms of their own access to arms, as well as any support or connection they may have with state authorities.

The fourth category focuses on the motives and behaviour of key government actors, in reference to impact they have on inciting 'divisions between national, racial, ethnic, and religious groups'. This involves examining the use of exclusionary language and policies, which establish an adversarial sense of 'us' and 'them'. Such rhetoric, seen most commonly in the use of propaganda, often depicts the targeted group as inferior, or even sub-human. The presence of any such sign will indicate the connections between the government and potential genocide.

The fifth category seeks to identify escalatory factors, or those which 'facilitate the perpetration of genocide'. These include sudden changes to the military, such as an increase in arms acquisitions, and greater support to militia groups, efforts to 'eliminate diversity' within the military, preparing local populations to support or perpetrate acts of violence, legislation that further limits the rights of target groups, increase in hate propaganda, and a 'permissive environment' that facilitates the use of violence, usually in the context of war.

The sixth category focuses on 'genocidal acts'. These include a number of acts of violence, as outlined in the Rome Statute of the International Criminal Court, which include 'killings, abductions and disappearances, torture, rape and sexual violence, ethnic cleansing and pogroms'. It also includes a range of actions that are less overt in their violence, but clearly aimed at the eventual destruction of a particular group. These include the deprivation of vital resources, such as food, clean water and medical supplies, as well as the denial of basic facilities such as adequate shelter and clothing. Enforced hard physical labour, forced sterilization and abortion, long term separation of men and women, and the forcible transfer of children are all indicators of such genocidal ends.

Category seven looks for evidence of the intent to 'destroy in whole or in part'. Indicators include hate speech, the systematic nature of violent acts against a victim group in the context of violent conflict, widespread discrimination against a victim group outside of the context of violent conflict, the nature of violence against a particular group, (including dismemberment of corpses and systematic rape), destruction of cultural symbols and property, and elimination of key group leaders.

Finally, the eighth category focuses on the presence of a range of triggering factors that may rapidly 'aggravate conditions' and could possibly spark violence very quickly. Triggers can be unpredictable, and include a wide range of events, such as elections, natural disasters, unconstitutional change of government, outbreak of violent conflict, or the increase in opposition activity, which could be regarded as a threat, attracting violent reprisal.

As the UN's first attempt to establish a framework for early warning for genocide, the framework is highly significant and marks an important step forward. However, the framework only indicates general risk and does not provide a basis for predicting when and where genocide might erupt. Nor does it provide much guidance about what information should be used to make determinations in each of the categories, which of the categories is most important or how information should be evaluated in order to determine the risk of genocide. As an essentially qualitative framework, it grants wide leeway to individual analysts. Finally, as is made clear by category seven, the framework focuses specifically on genocide, and is not tailored to identify the risk of war crimes, ethnic cleansing and crimes against humanity.

In addition to a framework of analysis, an early warning mechanism requires sources of information. Responding to traditional concerns about 'intelligence gathering' as a violation of state sovereignty, the Office of the Special Adviser has focused on identifying sources of information that already exist within the UN system. There are a number of UN departments and agencies that have the prevention of genocide as part of their mandate. These include the Office of the High Commissioner for Human Rights (OHCHR), the DPA, the Department of Peacekeeping Operations/Department of Field Support, the Office of Legal Affairs (OLA), OCHA, the Department of Public Information, UNICEF, UNHCR and UNDP. Throughout 2008, the Special Adviser and his Office liaised with their counterparts in these departments to consider ways to foster collaboration and information sharing. One particularly useful aspect of this collaboration is the development of an inventory of sources relevant to early warning and prevention. With the sharing and overlapping of prevention responsibilities, a parallel project developed involving the collection of 'monitoring and information collection systems within the UN', related to the prevention of genocide. Given that several hundred staff within the UN are involved in the gathering of information on a variety of themes and locations relevant to the assessment of the risk of future genocide, most of the information needed by the Special Adviser is already being gathered. Contacts with various departments are maintained by an 'information management officer' to ensure that Office resources are effectively used to tap into and gather existing sources of information in the UN system relevant for the prevention of genocide.

As I noted in Chapter 2, in 2007 Ban Ki-moon appointed the highly regarded UN expert, Edward Luck, as his Special Adviser on RtoP to 'operationalize the concept and to develop the doctrine'.[81] The Secretary-General mandated that the Special Adviser should complement the work of the Special Adviser on the Prevention of Genocide and provide recommendations about implementing the World Summit's commitment to RtoP. In his 2009 report on *Implementing the Responsibility to Protect*, which was drafted by his Special Adviser on RtoP, the Secretary-General called for the establishment of a joint office for the prevention of genocide and RtoP, arguing that this would help fulfill the specific pledge to strengthen the UN's capacity for early warning made at the 2005 World Summit.[82] The joint office would act as a focal point that would gather information, assess and analyse it, and mobilize the UN system in developing a coordinated response to reduce risk.[83] Although similar proposals have been presented and rejected before, at the 2009 General Assembly debate on RtoP, most governments, including several from the 'global south', lent their support to the idea but there remained some important concerns about its operationalization. China, for example, called for further deliberation in the General Assembly and Security Council about the need to create an early warning mechanism and noted that if such a mechanism was thought necessary, it should be predicated on some core principles agreed in advance by the General Assembly. Other governments raised concerns about the types and sources of information that the mechanism would use, the transparency and fairness of its assessment procedures, the need for safeguards against politicization, and the mechanism's relationship with regional and sub-regional arrangements and local actors. Nonetheless, no government opposed the basic idea of establishing a joint office with an early warning function. Therefore, this represents the UN's best chance of finally establishing an early warning capacity.

Although the modalities for this new capacity are still to be worked out, some of the basic principles have already been established by the Office of the Special Adviser on the Prevention of Genocide. The new joint office would liaise with focal points in the UN's departments and agencies to collate relevant information based on data already gathered by the UN system. It would then use an early warning framework – probably one based on the framework outlined above but refined to accommodate the three other crimes – to analyze this information, possibly producing an annual risk assessment report. Having identified countries facing heightened risk, the office would then conduct more intensive qualitative research, probably including fieldwork or a longer-term mission.[84] The Office would also maintain regular contact with the various focal points so that it could be alerted to imminent emergencies. It might also be expected that the Office would establish links to relevant regional arrangements, especially those that conduct early warning analysis but it is not yet clear how this would be operationalized.

Another question that remains to be answered is what the Office will do with its early warning advice once generated. There are two main elements to this question. First, should the analysis be made publicly available? The Global Centre for RtoP took the view that the Office's work should be made public so that the Secretary-General and Security Council might be held accountable by civil society. There is a certain appeal to this line of thinking but it does not take political realities into account. This is also true of proposals that the reports go directly to the Security Council or General Assembly. Publicizing early warning reports, even sharing them privately with member states, politicizes them immediately. The subjects of those reports are likely to be embarrassed and will probably respond in a hostile fashion, mobilizing friendly states to oppose the findings. In this scenario, the chances of fruitful early action by the Secretary-General or other arms of the UN are damaged from the outset, and the legitimacy of the whole system impaired. This is why many UN officials would prefer that the reports not be made public and not be passed directly to member states. From this point of view, early warning reports are there to advise the Secretary-General and, ultimately, the Secretary-General will be held to account if the organization fails to prevent genocide. It is for the Secretary-General to decide how best to act on the reports, given their substance and the circumstances. He may opt for quiet diplomacy, or may work through a group of friends; he may pass the information on to the Security Council, either formally or informally; and, if he chooses, he may decide that publicizing the report is the best strategy. Because we cannot know the best strategy without knowing the circumstances, it is important that the Secretary-General have the ability to determine how best to use the information he receives. The second question relates to how the information should be handled within the UN. Again, there are two views. The DPA would prefer that the Office provide advice to it, which would then be passed on to the Secretary-General. DPA officials argue that this is the best way to ensure coordination and context sensitivity. However, the danger here is that the DPA would face a conflict of interest in that it would be difficult for it to maintain good diplomatic relations with governments while also examining the extent to which they posed a threat of genocide.[85] As such, the DPA might face pressure to 'massage' the early warning reports, so that the Secretary-General heard only what was politically convenient to hear and not what he needed to hear from a prevention perspective. As such, outside the DPA there is a strong preference for the office sitting outside any existing department.[86] The alternative is that the joint office report directly to the Secretary-General. One way of doing this would be through the Secretary-General's 'Policy Committee' which is chaired by the Secretary-General and includes senior UN officials. Another would be simply to establish a direct line between the Office and the Secretary-General, ensuring that the advice given was completely unadorned.

It is clear, therefore, that the UN is beginning to develop an early warning and analysis capacity and that RtoP has helped give this effort fresh impetus and legitimacy. The Office for the Prevention of Genocide has laid some solid foundations but its focus on genocide, the Office's small staff, and the somewhat unsystematic nature of its framework indicates that more work needs to be done. Moreover, although member states are more willing to support a UN early warning mechanism than they were in the past, evidence from the 2009 General Assembly debate suggest that the consensus is quite fragile and that some significant concerns remain. In addition to the political hurdles, there are also innumerable bureaucratic hurdles to be overcome too.

Conclusion

The UN has experienced a number of false starts in relation to early warning since its first attempt with ORCI in the late 1980s. However, with developments in the DPA, the Office of the Special Adviser on the Prevention of Genocide and the proposed joint office of genocide prevention and RtoP, there is some evidence that early warning efforts are becoming more coordinated and centralized, and that long-standing political concerns are easing. While the DPA and Special Adviser still lack the capacity to conduct their own fieldwork, and the precise nature and institutional location of the proposed joint office remains unclear, there are grounds for optimism that the UN system is developing ways of better utilizing the information that it already gathers for early warning purposes. Moreover, although concerns remain among member states as to whether the UN should be in the business of early warning, opposition has become less pointed for two main reasons. First, the amount of publicly available information has increased dramatically over the last 20 years, meaning that ample information can be gleaned from open-sources in order to conduct early warning analysis. As a result, there has been a proliferation of non-state actors conducting their own early warning analysis from open source information. Second, the unanimous commitment to RtoP signals an international consensus that sovereignty does not provide a veil to protect the perpetrators of genocide, war crimes, ethnic cleansing and crimes against humanity and that it is legitimate for the international community to concern itself with their prevention. The specific commitment to early warning made as part of this removes some of the political obstacles. Despite the false starts, therefore, there have been a number of improvements in the capacity for early warning in the UN system. With the emergence of RtoP and the office for the prevention of genocide, the question is increasingly becoming not one of whether the UN should be engaged in early warning and preventive action, but of how it should conduct that early warning analysis and translate it into timely and decisive preventive action. Establishing a focal point for early warning within the UN system, with a direct line to the Secretary-General, is a crucial part of the effort to implement the RtoP.

7 Regional arrangements

With Sara E. Davies

It is widely recognized that regional arrangements have an important role to play in assisting states to build the capacity to protect their populations, preventing responding to genocide and mass atrocities, and adding value to the UN's efforts.[1] Indeed, the World Summit Outcome Document specified at least seven distinct roles for regional arrangements. They should: (a) encourage and help states to fulfil their primary responsibility to protect (para. 138); (b) support the UN in establishing an early warning capability (para. 138); (c) help states build the capacity to protect their populations from genocide, war crimes, ethnic cleansing and crimes against humanity (para. 139); (d) assist states under stress before a crisis breaks out (para. 139); (e) support the mission of the Special Adviser of the UN Secretary-General on the Prevention of Genocide (para. 140); (f) utilize peaceful measures under Chapter VIII of the UN Charter to respond to crises involving genocide, war crimes, ethnic cleansing and crimes against humanity (para. 139); (g) cooperate with the Security Council in the application of measures, including Chapter VII measures, when peaceful means are inadequate and national authorities are manifestly failing to protect their populations (para. 139).[2] Of course, it is for regional arrangements themselves to determine precisely how they will fulfil these roles, taking into consideration relevant regional needs, capacities, and norms of behaviour and we should therefore expect to see significant regional differences in the roles taken up by regional organizations.

Governments have repeatedly voiced their support for the idea that regional arrangements have an important role in implementing the RtoP. Indeed, there have been calls from within regional organizations such as AU and ASEAN for deeper partnership with the UN's various agencies on matters pertaining to conflict prevention, early warning, disaster preparedness and peacekeeping.[3] However, little work has been done to precisely identify what measures might be taken and what challenges regional arrangements might confront.[4] This chapter will attempt to remedy this problem in three stages. First, it examines the emergence of regional arrangements in the post-1945 order, focusing on persistent dilemmas relating to the relationship between regional arrangements and the UN and the role of such arrangements in articulating and advancing the principle of sovereignty as responsibility, which underpins RtoP.

Second, it considers the potential role of regional arrangements in implementing the RtoP, noting particular challenges and opportunities. Third, it evaluates the Regional Assistance Mission to the Solomon Islands (RAMSI) as a good example of regional arrangements fulfilling pillar two responsibilities through a comprehensive package of assistance to a country in crisis.

Regional arrangements and international order

There was a tendency during the Cold War period to see regional arrangements as 'secondary' institutions to the UN Security Council. Indeed, the precise relationship between regional arrangements and the Security Council proved highly contentious. During negotiations about the creation of the UN, several governments favoured a regional rather than global approach to managing international peace and security whereby the great powers would assume responsibility in their respective spheres of influence.[5] Others, especially South American governments, expressed deep reservations about the potential for regional hegemony implicit within such an approach and argued that great power responsibility for peace and security should be constrained by global rules and overseen by the membership as a whole. Ultimately, this vision carried the day and the Security Council was given primary responsibility for the maintenance of international peace and security (see Chapter 8). The role of regional arrangements was set out primarily in Chapter VIII of the UN Charter, which provided that regional arrangements may deal with matters related to international peace and security (Article 52), pursue peace measures prior to referring a matter to the Security Council (Article 52), may undertake enforcement actions under the authority of the Security Council but not without such authority (Article 53), and must keep the Security Council fully informed of their activities (Article 54). However, this did not resolve critical questions relating to the primacy of the UN Charter over regional arrangements within the given region or the modalities for cooperation between the UN and regional arrangements. Although progress has been made in both areas, and matters today are much less contentious than they were during the Cold War, serious questions remain. For example, is the African Union's 'right to intervene' in the domestic affairs of its members in the event of a major humanitarian crisis as set out in Article 4(h) of its charter dependent upon the prior authorization of the UN Security Council? Likewise, does the principle of 'non-interference' – a central norm in Asia – override the Security Council's authority to authorize enforcement action in situations where there is no immediate threat to *international* peace and security? Despite the broad international consensus about the need to engage regional arrangements in the implementation of RtoP, questions about the relative authority of regional and global norms and institutions remain.

Given this, it is hardly surprising that the question of where authority resides in relation to the adoption of enforcement measures, deployment of troops for protection purposes, or the leadership of diplomatic endeavours has often proved controversial.[6] For example, the issue arose over Palestine in 1948 (in relation to the Arab League), Hungary in 1956 (in relation to the Warsaw Pact), and the Dominican Republic in 1965 (in relation to the Organization of American States, OAS).[7] In 1948 the League of Arab States claimed that it was acting to uphold the principles and purposes of the UN Charter when its forces entered Palestine in response to Israel's declaration of independence. This plea was rejected by the United States and not discussed further within the Security Council. In 1956, the Soviet Union justified its intervention in Hungary to suppress a pro-democracy movement not by insisting that it was upholding the principles and purposes of the UN but by arguing that within the Warsaw Pact zone, the pact took precedence over the UN Charter. Once again, though, the Security Council did not discuss the question at length owing to the Soviet veto. The OAS operation in the Dominican Republic in 1965 is more instructive precisely because the Security Council discussed it at some length. As violence spread following a coup, US soldiers were deployed, ostensibly to protect US citizens. Following criticism from both OAS members and the wider UN membership, the US pushed for the mission to be brought under OAS auspices. It succeeded despite the deep misgivings of some of the organization's members, notably Brazil. In the Security Council, the Soviet Union, France, and the Asian and African representatives were highly critical of the United States, insisting that only the Security Council had the authority to mandate military actions. The US argued that Chapter VIII of the Charter gave the OAS a legitimate role to play, but it failed to persuade the Council of its case. Nevertheless, the US continued to argue that it was legitimate for regional organizations to take action within their sphere of influence without UN authorization.[8]

After these early debates, regionalization did not emerge as a significant issue at the UN until the early 1990s. Indeed, between 1945 and 1990, Security Council resolutions contained only three references to regional organizations.[9] This situation changed dramatically after 1991, giving rise to calls for 'regional' solutions to 'regional problems'.[10] Diehl and Cho have shown, for example, that before 1975 regional organizations conducted only an average of approximately two mediations each year. Between 1989 and 1995, however, regional organizations conducted 116 attempts at mediation, representing almost 20 attempts per year.[11] These trends were also evident in relation to post-Cold War international peacekeeping, peacebuilding and conflict prevention efforts.[12] Thus, in the past two decades, the AU has undertaken operations in Burundi, Sudan, the Comoros and Somalia, the Russian-led Commonwealth of Independent States (CIS) in Georgia and Tajikistan, ECOWAS has undertaken enforcement operations in Liberia and Sierra Leone in addition to other operations in Cote d'Ivoire and Guinea-Bissau, NATO has undertaken operations in Bosnia, Kosovo, Macedonia and Afghanistan and in the Pacific, the Pacific Islands Forum deployed an assistance mission to the Solomon Islands (RAMSI) that bore the hallmarks of a second pillar RtoP endeavour – and this does not exhaust the range of regional activism in this area.[13]

Unsurprisingly, the rise to prominence of regional arrangements has produced greater recognition of their contribution to international peace and security but also of the challenges of strengthening cooperation. In 1992, Boutros-Ghali urged the UN to make better use of regional arrangements but stopped short of calling for a formal relationship with them or offering a blueprint for deepening cooperation. Instead, the UN and regional organizations were to engage in informal consultations and joint undertakings in the hope that such cooperation would imbue regional efforts with a greater degree of legitimacy and simultaneously generate the impression of greater participation in international decision–making.[14] With an increase in practical cooperation between the UN and regional arrangements, Boutros-Ghali's *Supplement to An Agenda for Peace* described the forms that such cooperation was taking, namely, consultation, diplomatic support, operational support, co-deployment and joint operations. The Secretary-General also instigated a series of high-level meetings between the UN and regional organizations. By 2007, seven such meetings had been convened.[15] The growing prominence and potential of regional arrangements was also recognized in the World Summit Outcome Document. As I noted earlier, paragraphs 138 and 139 afforded specific roles to regional arrangements in implementing the RtoP and paragraphs on peacekeeping and peacebuilding recognized the role of regional arrangements.[16]

The growing prominence of regional arrangements has not, however, brought resolution to the questions of authority and modalities of cooperation highlighted earlier. In particular, regional activism in enforcement has proven highly controversial. The most notable examples here are the Economic Community of West African States (ECOWAS) intervention in Liberia (1990) and NATO intervention in Kosovo almost a decade later. ECOWAS created its first Nigerian-led peace enforcement force (the ECOWAS Monitoring and Observer Group (ECOMOG)) in 1990 in response to the Liberian civil war, which erupted the previous year. Deployed into an ongoing armed conflict at the request of the recently ousted government, its formal role was largely limited to ensuring a (non-existent) cease-fire, restoring law and order and creating the conditions for free and fair elections. In practice, as Mark Malan notes, this involved taking sides and becoming actively embroiled in the civil war. Though suffering significant losses, and plagued by funding shortages, repeated accusations that its troops committed atrocities, abused locals, stole goods and colluded with Liberia's warring factions, the mission maintained a presence in Liberia, and became part of the UN mission (UNMIL) in 2003.[17] Although ECOWAS intervened without Security Council authorization, and its claim to legitimacy based on a request by the ousted government was deeply problematic, the intervention did not prove controversial outside the region and was retrospectively welcomed by the Council.[18]

By contrast, NATO's 1999 humanitarian intervention in the former Yugoslavia, proved highly controversial and brought questions about authority to the fore once again. However, the international debate about Kosovo also helped highlight a degree of consensus around the basic ideas of sovereignty as responsibility that underpin RtoP. Indeed, the sharpest disagreements concerned not the principle itself but the most appropriate way of acting upon it. From the outset of the crisis, the European response, if somewhat indecisive, was rapid and based on the presumptions that ethnic cleansing and other human rights abuses were illegitimate and that external actors had a legitimate role to play in bringing such abuses to an end. These efforts were supported by a relatively early UN Security Council Resolution 1160 (31 March 1998). For our purposes, the significance of Resolution 1160 lay not in the specifics of what it said about the crisis but in its recognition that the situation in Kosovo warranted international engagement because the Yugoslav authorities were failing in their sovereign responsibilities. To be sure, the Resolution's adoption at a relatively early stage in the crisis caused significant unease within the Russian and Chinese governments in particular, both of which abstained arguing that the situation in Kosovo was a domestic matter that fell within Yugoslavia's jurisdiction.[19] China argued that Security Council intervention in internal matters such as this was likely to set a negative precedent for the future. On the other hand, the majority of Council members argued that human rights abuse in Kosovo constituted a clear threat to regional peace and security.[20] Although Russia had expressed concerns about international engagement in what it saw as a domestic matter, its position began to change after the passage of Resolution 1160 leaving China alone in arguing against Council activism on the grounds of domestic jurisdiction. In September 1998, the Council passed a tougher resolution with Russian support (Resolution 1199, 23 September 1998). Resolution 1199 was passed under Chapter VII and identified the 'deterioration' of the situation in Kosovo as a threat to international peace and security. The resolution demanded (rather than requested) a cessation of hostilities and demanded that the leadership of both sides take urgent steps to 'avert the impending humanitarian catastrophe'. The Council also insisted that it would consider further measures in the event of non-compliance. Although Russia supported the Resolution, it stressed that the Resolution did not authorize military force or impose further sanctions.[21] China was now alone in arguing that it could not support the resolution but felt the need to supplement its argument that the crisis in Kosovo was a domestic matter and therefore not a threat to international peace and security with the pragmatic argument that threatening Yugoslavia with punitive measures 'would adversely affect the possibilities of a peaceful settlement to the conflict'.[22]

My point here is that prior to NATO's intervention in Kosovo there was a broad consensus (though not unanimity) that Yugoslavia was not entitled to treat its citizens however it saw fit and had a duty to alleviate human suffering in Kosovo. Specifically, Resolution 1199 imposed on Yugoslavia obligations to 'cease hostilities' and 'take immediate steps to improve the humanitarian situation' and made the Yugoslav authorities accountable to the Security Council by deciding that further measures would be considered in the case of non-compliance. Of course, the consensus that Yugoslavia had sovereign responsibilities did not translate into agreement on the most effective and legitimate means of ensuring that the Yugoslav government complied with its responsibilities. This point was made abundantly clear by the debate that followed the launch of NATO's intervention in early 1999. NATO and its allies defended the intervention by arguing that continuing Serbian abuses created a moral imperative to intervene to enforce the Security Council's wishes as set out in Resolution 1199.

In response, on 24 March 1999, Russia introduced a draft resolution demanding an immediate cessation of hostilities against Yugoslavia. In line with Russia's position on Resolution 1199, the draft resolution limited itself to criticizing the use of force as a breach of Article 2(4) of the Charter and recalling the Council's primacy on matters of international peace and security and did not imply a position on the question of Yugoslavia's actions in Kosovo (S/1999/328, 26 March 1999). Nonetheless, the resolution was heavily defeated by 3 to 12, with only Russia, China and Namibia voting in favour. Among the states voting against the resolution were Argentina, Bahrain, Brazil, Gabon, Gambia and Malaysia. While the vote cannot be understood as retrospective endorsement or authorization for the intervention, it was indicative of broader sentiment regarding Yugoslavia's failure to fulfil its responsibilities in Kosovo. Russia's criticism of NATO centred on two arguments, both of which focused on the intervention's modalities rather than on the appropriateness of international engagement with domestic human rights issues. The first was that NATO did not have the authority to make determinations about when to use force in circumstances like this.[23] Stressing that it did not condone 'violations of international humanitarian law by any party', Russia's second argument was that NATO's intervention was likely to make the humanitarian crisis in Kosovo worse and hinder attempts to broker a peace settlement.[24] This basic claim – that it was not the principle of sovereign responsibility but the modalities of unilateral armed intervention that was the nub of the problem – was further emphasized by Namibia, who joined China in supporting Russia.[25] Among NATO's prominent critics, only China continued to question the legitimacy of international engagement in what it saw as an essentially 'domestic' matter, though in the March 1999 debates China augmented this claim with arguments about the primacy of the Security Council on matters of international peace and security.

NATO's intervention therefore helped sharpen the debate about the relationship between the UN and regional arrangements. On the one hand, there was broad (though not universal) agreement that the international community should take measures to halt the ethnic cleansing and killing of Kosovar Albanians. On the other, however, there were profound disagreements about what measures should be taken and which bodies were empowered to act. UN Secretary-General Kofi Annan declared that though he wished action had been authorized by the Security Council, NATO's actions may have been 'legitimate in the pursuit of peace'.[26]

These cases were touted as examples of how Chapter VIII of the UN Charter might be used to implement the RtoP but they both demonstrate the continuing debate about the relative authority of the Security Council and regional arrangements.[27] In both cases, regional arrangements claimed the authority to conduct enforcement operations without the explicit authorization of the UN Security Council, a move commonly thought to be contrary to the UN Charter. However, in neither case was the Council moved to condemn the putative violation – issuing a retrospective welcome to ECOMOG and convincingly rejecting Russia's proposed condemnation of NATO.

In addition to the obvious problems associated with authority, these cases also demonstrate a distinct lack of clarity about how cooperation between regional arrangements, the Security Council and the UN more generally, should be managed. As a guide, on the eve of NATO's intervention in Kosovo, the DPKO's Lessons Learned Unit identified 18 principles it hoped would shape the relationship between the UN and regional organizations in relation to peacekeeping. These principles were designed to ensure that:

- primary responsibility for maintaining international peace and security remains within the Security Council;
- cooperation is viewed as a dynamic process which is enhanced by clear and concise mandates based on realistic timetables;
- cooperation be based on consultation that involves effective information sharing;
- all cooperating parties share a common understanding of basic doctrine and operational rules of engagement;
- personnel are sufficiently trained and equipped; and,
- attempts to maintain peace and security do not end with the departure of a UN or regional operation but entail long-term efforts to strengthen civic associations committed to democracy, human rights and the rule of law.

The report also suggested a variety of mechanisms for implementing these principles. These mechanisms can be summarized as: ensuring multiple channels for regular communication; establishing a strategic-planning group and relevant planning cells that would involve regular, senior-level meetings; intensifying joint training; and engaging in international conferences or meetings of a 'Group of Friends' in order to foster communication and develop a common code of conduct.[28]

Although this represented a useful starting point, these principles related only to peacekeeping operations and not the full range of potential activities relevant to implementing RtoP. The need to strengthen the wider partnership between the UN and regional arrangements is widely recognized and has fostered the emergence of a thematic discussion on the issue in the Security Council. In early 2010, China – which held the Council presidency at the time – issued a concept paper on 'Cooperation between the United Nations and regional and sub-regional organizations in maintaining international peace and security'. According to the Chinese paper, 'in a rapidly changing world, strengthening cooperation between the United Nations and regional organizations will both promote multilateralism and boost the international collective security mechanism'. The paper continued by setting out the key themes that are relevant to developing this partnership and are worth setting out in full:

> 2.3. A collaborative partnership between the United Nations and regional organizations are crucial in the effective prevention, management and resolution of conflicts. How best to utilize the advantages of regional organizations, including early warning mechanisms, to enable early responses to disputes and emerging crises, and to encourage countries concerned in the region to resolve differences and problems peacefully through dialogue, reconciliation, negotiation, good offices and mediation?
>
> 2.4. Taking into account the surging needs for United Nations peacekeeping operations, and building upon the achievements of Security Council debates on support to African Union peacekeeping operations authorized by the United Nations, what are the additional measures that the United Nations and regional organizations may undertake to respond collaboratively to situations in pressing need of deployment of blue-helmets?
>
> 2.5. How to more closely involve regional and sub-regional organizations in peacebuilding, post-conflict stabilization and reconstruction processes, including through the framework of the Peacebuilding Commission?[29]

China recognized that cooperation should extend across a range of issues including early warning, peacebuilding and peacekeeping, but like many of those that have broached the subject before, stopped short of identifying specific modalities.

To summarize the argument thus far, it is widely recognized that regional arrangements have an important role to play in implementing the RtoP and the idea has widespread support. The relationship between the UN and regional arrangements has been complicated by questions about (1) the relative authority of the Security Council and regional arrangements within their own locality and (2) the modalities for cooperation. While progress has been made on these questions, the relative authority of the Council remains contested and the precise modalities for cooperation ill-defined. We need to bear both of these factors in mind when we move to examine precisely what role regional arrangements should play and the extent to which they have the capacity to act effectively. It is to this that we now turn.

Regional arrangements and the implementation of RtoP

When it comes to identifying precisely what role regional arrangements might play in implementing RtoP, a useful place to start is the Secretary-General's 2009 report, *Implementing the Responsibility to Protect*. To date, as the previous section makes clear, attention has focused mainly on the role of regional arrangements in peacekeeping, peace enforcement and related activities. Given the scope of RtoP, however, the role of regional arrangements is likely to be much broader than this and the Secretary-General has identified potential avenues in relation to all three pillars.

In relation to RtoP's first pillar – the primary responsibility of the state – the Secretary-General noted the important role regional organizations may play in promoting 'state-to-state learning processes – often neighbours helping neighbours' in the promotion of best practices.[30] Referring to the African (Union) Peer Review Mechanism and the membership standards for joining the European Union, he suggested the inclusion of compliance with responsibility to protect principles into criteria governing membership of regional organizations and establishment of peer review mechanisms.[31] In relation to pillar two, the Secretary-General identified three important functions that regional arrangements may play in assisting states to deepen their responsibility to protect. First, there is much value to be found in region-to-region cooperation. The lessons learned by regional organizations in the field of preventive diplomacy or peacekeeping should be shared not only within the region itself, but also with regional counterparts. Second, the preventive capacities of regional arrangements should be strengthened. There are particular advantages that regional arrangements bring to preventive diplomacy such as local affiliation, cultural awareness, and a vested long-term interest in regional stability, which (in theory at least) lends credibility and capacity to these organizations.[32] Third, regional arrangements might consider developing rapid response units dedicated to assisting states to restore 'effective sovereignty' and meet their responsibility to protect, preferably prior to the commission mass atrocities but also in response to mass atrocities if needed. While the focus should remain on the UN's capacity to develop and deploy rapid response units, the Secretary-General argued that regional arrangements should pay attention to questions about how they could assist such deployments – the RAMSI experience in the Solomon Islands being a good example.[33]

Finally, in relation to pillar three, the Secretary-General was emphatic in emphasizing that timely and decisive response falls under the purview of regional arrangements when their members are committing mass atrocities. First, the Secretary-General recommended that regional arrangements be proactive in engaging their member-states with non-coercive responses, which do not require Security Council authorization, in situations where mass atrocities are occurring.[34] However, when the state is unable or unwilling to halt the commission of atrocities, then the member states have a responsibility with the rest of the international community to respond. In relation to the thorny questions about authority described in the previous section, the Secretary-General stated bluntly that 'the more robust the response, the higher the standard for authorization'.[35] Enforcement operations required both the acquiescence of the regional organization and the explicit authorization of the UN Security Council.[36] In addition to military enforcement, the Secretary-General identified two critically important areas relating to timely and decisive response: diplomatic sanctions and arms embargoes. In relation to diplomatic sanctions, the Secretary-General pointed out that regional arrangements were vital for the effective implementation of bans on travel, financial transfers, and luxury goods authorized by the Security Council.[37] Historically, such sanctions have rarely been effective because they are seldom enforced by the target's neighbours. In addition, regional arrangements can play a pivotal role in restricting the flow of arms and police equipment (which may be used by repressive regimes or in situations where conflict escalation may lead to commission of large-scale crimes) or ignoring UN sanctions regimes, rendering them ineffective.[38] The most important step is that neighbours refuse to sell arms to states that are manifestly failing to protect their populations from the four crimes. Other important elements include preventing the transfer of illicit arms through the duplicity or complicity of a neighbouring state which allows the transfer across its border, or the use of its flag and certification licence for arms purchase(s).[39] As the Secretary-General noted, '[w]hile the General Assembly has at times called for arms embargoes, only the Security Council has the authority to make them binding. Finally, under Article 53 of the UN Charter, regional arrangements may take enforcement action with the authorization of the Council. In practice, however, as we noted above it has not been uncommon for regional or subregional bodies or ad hoc groups of states to undertake such measures without formal prior authorization from the Council.[40]

As we noted in Chapter 2, the Secretary-General's proposals on implementing RtoP were warmly welcomed by most UN members at the 2009 General Assembly debate. Not only did the General Assembly generally endorse the implementation recommendations of the Secretary-General, there was particular support for the strengthening of regional arrangements in the areas of early warning, stand-by capabilities, and mediation.[41] In fact, many states – including those of the global south – specifically referred to the implementation tasks set aside for regional arrangements by the Secretary-General. For example, the Philippines emphasized the importance of region-to-region learning and South Korea referred to the need for peer review mechanisms that included RtoP criteria.[42] African states such as Sierra Leone, Ghana, and Gambia called for closer cooperation between AU and UN in the development of peacekeeping and standby capacities and suggested that regional arrangements might spearhead the establishment and implementation of legally binding instruments relating to the four crimes.[43] For their part, several EU members pointed out that regional organizations are well positioned to assist member states in upholding their responsibility to protect due to their existing work on 'capacity-building in [the] areas of conflict prevention, development and human rights, good governance, rule of law and judicial and security sector reform'.[44] In total, approximately 60 states gave voice to the importance of regional arrangements in implementing RtoP. While this hardly represents universal endorsement, and it is notable that there was little agreement on the specific role of regional arrangements, the lack of opposition to the general idea that regional arrangements had a role to play and the stated readiness of states to develop such regional capacity, suggests sufficient consensus on moving forward.

To date, relatively little attention has been paid to the capacity of regional arrangements to implement RtoP and the role that regional norms might play in constraining and enabling implementation.[45] Early studies on this topic, however, have elicited some important findings. Studying seven regional organizations, David Carment and Martin Fischer identified three critical issues. First, despite the UN Secretary-General's call for enhanced region-to-region cooperation, there are important limits on the transfer of knowledge and 'positive lessons' between regional arrangements. This is principally due to the fact that many regional arrangements (i.e. ASEAN, OAS, SAARC) are prefaced on the principal of non-interference in the domestic affairs of member states affairs, which inhibits the learning of lessons from regions with more relaxed attitudes to this principle (e.g. AU, EU, OSCE).[46] Lesson learning and practical region-to-region co-operation may be difficult in a context where regional norms dictate different priorities, set different thresholds and determine different courses of action. In that context, it is worth noting that within the ASEAN Regional Forum (ARF), even the seemingly harmless and consensual practice of preventive diplomacy has proven highly controversial.

Second, many of the regional organizations assessed by Carment and Fischer –especially those in the global south – lacked the analytical capacity to conduct early warning assessment, construct mediation efforts to prevent conflict escalation, and – we might add – cooperate in a meaningful fashion with the UN. Sometimes, as in the case of ASEAN and other Asia-Pacific arrangements such as the ARF and APEC, this lack of bureaucratic capacity is an intentional product of an approach to multilateralism predicated on non-interference and scepticism about international institutions. Obviously, overcoming political obstacles to the establishment of regional capacities is the thorniest task because it involves the 'localization' of RtoP, which could itself prove to be a protracted endeavour. According to Amitav Acharya, new global norms are not situated in a normative *tabula rasa* but emerge in a context of pre-existing regional norms and beliefs which are considered legitimate in a given region. When new global norms emerge they interact with pre-existing beliefs with one of three potential outcomes – (1) resistance: local actors employ existing norms to resist the new norm and prevent its transmission; (2) localization: a negotiated compromise where the new norm is interpreted and implemented through the prism of existing norm; here, both the new norms and existing norms are altered by the process of negotiation; (3) displacement: the new norm is institutionalized and displaces the old.[47] Localization means that global norms are rarely implemented identically in different parts of the world. As such, the political obstacles to regional capacity building are only likely to be overcome through a process of negotiation which recognizes regional differences and permits different solutions to common problems. The tricky thing is recognizing regional difference while ensuring that the world is not divided into a two or three track system where some regions are highly capable of preventing and halting mass atrocities, while populations in other region remain deeply vulnerable.

In other cases, especially the AU and ECOWAS, this is more a product of limited resources driving incapacity. In the case of the AU, for instance, Carment and Fischer note that there have been very clear institutional and Charter commitments to intervention to restore peace and security since 2004, but not nearly enough resources dedicated to risk assessment and key deployment capacities such as standby forces, training, and logistics.[48] Such critical capacity issues are not easily remedied. Even with the best of intentions, there are stark differences in the capacity of regional arrangements to conduct early warning and analysis and to translate political decisions taken on the basis of these warnings into timely and decisive action. Here we come back full circle to the role of region-to-region cooperation and the idea that the provision of assistance to regional arrangements should be a key component of the implementation of RtoP. In this, it is worth recalling that several Southeast Asian governments argued that while regional arrangements had an important role to play in implementing RtoP, it was incumbent on the UN to help them build requisite capacity.[49]

Third, a point mentioned in passing by Carment and Fischer but which warrants highlighting, is the need to pay attention to the fact that many regional organizations have to juggle competing concerns and priorities such as economic development, military security (both internal and external), food and water security, human rights, rule of law, and democratization. Because many regional arrangements, especially in Africa and Asia, are in an 'embryonic' stage, the rapid addition of new mandates and responsibilities has helped only to keep them at this stage by preventing them from developing effective capacities in a smaller range of issue areas. In this context, external pressure on embryonic organizations may prove counter-productive. For example, SAARC's membership comprises Afghanistan, Bangladesh, Bhutan, India, Maldives, Nepal, Pakistan and Sri Lanka – four member states have been embroiled in civil conflict since the adoption of the SAARC Charter in 1985 (Afghanistan, India Nepal, Pakistan and Sri Lanka), the majority have populations that subsist on $2 or less a day, and the two hegemonic forces in this regional organization – India and Pakistan have experienced four wars in the last 50 years. Despite there being much obvious need for SAARC to take up the RtoP agenda, not only is the rapid adoption of an RtoP agenda politically unlikely, but if SAARC were to take it up it would likely only further slow the body's ability to address its current seven areas of work, without adding significant new RtoP capacity.[50] Learning from Acharyas's work on localization, advocates of RtoP need to recognize that there is no 'one-size-fits-all' approach to implementation, that it cannot be assumed that RtoP trumps other regional priorities, and that if it is to be localized, RtoP needs to be made consistent with regional priorities and to add palpable value to those priorities.

Perhaps partly owing to the focus on different cases (she includes NATO, but not SAARC or ECOWAS), Kristin Haugevik's analysis is generally more positive. Haugevik finds that the EU, NATO and OSCE have strong prevention and reconstruction capacities and that the AU is attempting to build such capacities, but lacks the resources and political clout needed to hold states to account.[51] She maintains that ASEAN and OAS actually have the tools and resources they need (possibly to a greater extent than the AU), but that the emphasis that both organizations place on consensus decision making – a by-product of their commitment to non-interference – allows a small number of recalcitrant member states to block progressive action to implement RtoP. Across regional organizations, Haugevik argues that the key problem is political will. In other words, she finds that there is no consistency across regional organizations as to when they will become actively involved in cases where a member state is abusing its own population or the form such involvement will take. This inconsistency is produced by a combination of factors already discussed, including uneven localization, which means that some arrangements prioritize consensus and non-interference over timely and decisive action, uncertainty about the relationship between regional arrangements and the UN Security Council – and especially the question of authority, and uneven bureaucratic capacities.[52]

From this brief discussion, therefore, we can discern three key challenges to the positive engagement of regional arrangements in the implementation of RtoP. First, regional norms such as non-interference and consensus-based decision-making, evident especially in Asia and South Africa but also to some degree in Africa, inhibits the development of institutional capacity relevant to pillars two and three of RtoP and prevents some regional arrangements from playing a proactive in the prevention and alleviation of mass atrocities. In these circumstances, the Security Council will remain the first port of call and, if anything, regional arrangements might constrain the Council's room for manoeuvre. Navigating around these norms through processes of localization is therefore a key challenge, and indeed a prerequisite for the building of capacity. Second, and directly following on from this, is that regional institutional capacity is very uneven. As a result, too much emphasis on the regional dimension of implementation could produce a multi-tiered system whereby some regions (especially the global north) enjoy the benefits of comprehensive and effective mechanisms for preventing mass atrocities, while others have to continue to rely on ineffective prevention mechanisms and inconsistent responses marshalled by the Security Council. That said, there is clearly a need for serious attention to be paid to the capacities that different regions require, the capacities they actually have, and ways in which gaps between the former and latter might be bridged. In line with our first point, however, this needs to be done in a way that recognizes the politics of localization. Third, implementation agendas need to be aware that many regional arrangements are nascent and still developing regional identities, norms and capacities. The AU Charter is only eight years old, the ASEAN Charter was agreed to in 2005, and while the OAS Charter dates back to 1967, that organization has been traditionally hampered by discord between the US and its allies and the others. The embryonic status of these organizations is reflected in the value members place on their sovereignty and on membership to the organization, decision-making processes, and the organization's capacity to implement its extant agenda. Where implementing RtoP would constitute a radical departure from existing agendas or place massive new burdens on still weak bureaucracies, there is little chance of a rhetorical commitment to the principle being translated into determined practical action. It is critical that external advocates and governments ensure that their lobbying for RtoP is consistent with local norms as far as possible, respectful of regional priorities, and realistic in its expectations. How, then, might this be achieved? The following section examines an example of a comprehensive regional approach to assisting a troubled state – the RAMSI mission in the Solomon Islands.

From words to deeds: the case of RAMSI

Having identified some of the opportunities and challenges associated with utilizing regional arrangements to implement the RtoP, this final section reviews potential practical areas of development. We do this by briefly examining the case of the Regional Assistance Mission to the Solomon Islands (RAMSI) as a good example of how regional arrangements might contribute to preventing mass atrocities by implementing pillar two of RtoP. As we noted earlier, the UN Secretary-General identified the need for the UN and its various agencies and donor states to support regional organizations in identifying the prevention, capacity-building and protection strategies that could be tailored to their specific geographic location and building the required capacity. As a clear example of how consensual capacity-building spearheaded by regional arrangements can prevent the escalation of conflict and thereby the commission of atrocities, RAMSI demonstrates both the utility of regional arrangements and highlights areas where they may in need of augmentation.

The Solomon Islands achieved independence from Britain in 1978. Through the 1980s and 1990s, however, the local economy gradually deteriorated thanks largely to a combination of corruption, mismanagement and global economic factors. Within this context of growing economic hardship, ethnic resentment was fuelled by the ongoing migration of Malaitan populations from the island of Malaita to the island of Guadalcanal (which contains the national capital of the Solomon Islands, Honiara). In late 1998, the Guadalcanal Revolutionary Army/Isatabu Freedom Movement (IFM) embarked on a campaign of violence and intimidation against Malaitans, forcing some 20,000 to flee. Malaitans responded by forming the Malaita Eagle Force (MEF) which countered IFM attacks and demanded – and sometimes violently claimed – compensation for the destruction of Malaitan owned property. In 2001, Australia brokered the Townsville Agreement which provided for provincial elections overseen by an International Peace Monitoring Team (IPMT), comprising 49 people. Sir Allan Kemakaze was elected Prime Minister, but the IPMT failed to prevent the ex-militias from continuing to form criminal gangs and withdrew in June 2002. The situation continued to deteriorate into lawlessness and in July 2003, Kemakaze requested Australian assistance in restoring law and order and disarming the IFM militia and criminal gangs.[53] It is crucial to stress at this point that the impetus for RAMSI came from the Solomon Islands government itself, responsibly recognizing that it required international assistance to maintain the rule of law and protect the population in its care.

The catalyst for Australia's decision to work with the Pacific Islands Forum in assisting the Solomon Islands, was the release of a report in June 2003 by the Australian Strategic Policy Institute (ASPI).[54] The report claimed that the collapse of the government in the Solomon Islands posed an important threat to Australian security because it would make the Solomon Islands a potential haven for organized international criminals and, more worryingly, terrorists. A few days after the report was released, the Australian government called for the establishment of the Regional Assistance Mission to the Solomon Islands (RAMSI), augmenting the security arguments put forward by ASPI with a humanitarian case for action.[55] To strengthen the mission's legitimacy and capability, Australia proposed a multinational force, comprising elements from New Zealand as well as other Pacific Island states (Fiji, Papua New Guinea, Samoa, Tonga, and Vanuatu). The mission was launched pursuant to the Biketawa Declaration, adopted by the Pacific Islands Forum in 2000, which set out a regional framework for security cooperation which included mutual support for good governance and democratic processes, recognition of indigenous rights, and a process for addressing crises. In addition to RAMSI, the Biketawa Declaration has been invoked in relation to the Pacific Regional Assistance Program in Nauru (PRAN, established in 2005) and regional election observation missions in Bougainville, the Solomon Islands and Fiji have been conducted under this framework. As such, through the Biketawa Declaration, the Pacific Islands Forum has established a regional mechanism for providing assistance to states and addressing emerging crises in a consensual fashion, creating a regional capacity for exercising pillar two of the RtoP. The Australian government recognized that more forceful measures undertaken under pillar three would have required the authorization of the UN Security Council, as set out in the World Summit Outcome Document.

The international deployment was authorized by an agreement signed by the Solomon Islands government and each of the contributors to the mission on 24 July 2003. The agreement noted that the peace operation had been formally requested by the Solomon Islands government and endorsed by the PIF, encompassing all the region's island states. It went on to precisely delineate the new force's mandate, chain of command, and rules of engagement. Both the agreement and RAMSI itself had the strong support of the overwhelming majority of Solomon Islanders.

RAMSI began work on 24 July 2003. The initial RAMSI operation comprised 2,225 military, police and civilian personnel. Among their number were 325 police officers. The political head of the mission was Nick Warner, a well-respected diplomat from Australia's Department of Foreign Affairs and Trade. RAMSI had two primary phases. In phase one, it was tasked with restoring law and order. This involved ending criminal impunity and disarming the militia and criminal gangs. Although the whole mission was characterized as 'police led', the reality is that during this first phase, different parts of the mission were led by different agencies.[56] The military contingent of RAMSI led efforts to disarm the militia and criminal groups. By November 2003, they had removed from circulation 3,700 weapons, including 660 high-powered weapons. In August 2003, one of the most notorious criminal leaders and destabilizing factors in the country, Harold Keke surrendered to RAMSI – effectively removing the risk of armed conflict. Meanwhile, RAMSI's police contingent focused on investigating crimes committed by militias and criminals with the aim of ending impunity and strengthening the Royal Solomon Islands Police (RSIP) as a precursor to enhancing its capacity to maintain law and order. By the end of 2003, 733 people had been arrested on 1,168 charges.[57] Restoring order, disarming potential belligerents, and weeding out corruption – the first phase of the operation – was therefore completed relatively successfully.

Phase two was more complex and protracted. This aimed to build the capacity of the Solomon Islands government to maintain law and order and facilitate the resolution of the conflict. During this phase, the military component was withdrawn almost entirely and the focus of the mission came to rest on 200 or so police officers. Their mission was further broken down into eight distinct phases, which included:

- detailed specification of institutional problems in the Solomon Islands' law and justice system;
- community-relationship building measures;
- identification, mentoring and coaching of key RSIP personnel;
- identification of gaps between what the authorities ought to be able to accomplish in an effective and legitimate manner and what they could actually accomplish given present capacity;
- establishment of transparent institutional processes;
- development of a meaningful exit strategy.[58]

Throughout 2005, steady progress was made. High-profile cases were successfully brought to trial and the RAMSI police component handed over primary responsibility for policing almost entirely to the RSIP. The wider nation-building and conflict resolution parts of the mission proved less successful, as the April 2006 riots demonstrated.

In April 2006, riots broke out in the capital city of Honiara. These were fuelled by a mixture of political intrigue and racism which sent the capital city into a temporary states of lawlessness. The unrest, which went largely unchecked for days by the RSIP, exposed the limits of capacity-building and it was left to the international police contingent to protect parliamentarians and gradually restore order. With assistance, the RSIP was able to prevent the spread of violence but the international contingent sustained 31 casualties, including 5 serious injuries, and the destruction of 11 vehicles.[59] In the aftermath of the riots, capacity-building efforts resumed and several prominent Solomon Islanders were prosecuted for their part in the violence. This alone suggests that progress was made in relation to capacity-building in the justice sector but that the system remained fragile and required external assistance to respond to crises such as rioting and widespread disorder.

The RAMSI experience illustrates many of the benefits of regional assistance aimed at helping states exercise their RtoP, thereby strengthening their sovereignty and capacity. Some specific operational lessons are detailed below. The mission proved relatively successful largely due to its rapid deployment, significant capabilities and the consent and cooperation of the Solomon Islands government.[60] In the case of RAMSI, both the military and police contingents fared relatively well in the Solomon Islands because they were able to rapidly remove potential troublemakers and bring prominent criminals to trial. Similarly, the 2006 riots did not escalate or spread beyond Honiara because RAMSI was able to provide timely support to the RSIP. Most significant, however, was the way in which effective regional assistance was mobilized in response to a request from the Solomon Islands government and that this assistance was specifically aimed at strengthening state capacity. Although significant problems remain in the Solomon Islands, RAMSI helped the government restore the rule of law and build its police and justice capacity, reduce violent conflict and the risk of escalation, while improving the government's capacity to respond to new and emergent challenges.

It was precisely this type of activity that was envisaged by the UN Secretary-General in relation to pillar two of RtoP. The Solomon Islands acted as a responsible sovereign by requesting international assistance when it recognized that it would be unable to stem the descent into violence alone and the Pacific community discharged its duty to assist. The result was a significant improvement in conditions in the Solomon Islands, the strengthening of the state, and an equally significant reduction in the likelihood of violence and harm to the civilian population. Although it continues to confront significant challenges, RAMSI provides an excellent example of how a comprehensive regional approach to implementing pillar two, adopted in full partnership with the state concerned, can play a significant role in averting crises and supporting capacity building. In addition to this general point, there are several specific operational lessons that can be learned that might inform cooperation between the UN and regional arrangements in the future.

First, success depends on rapid deployment and high levels of capacity. The military and police contingent fared relatively well in the Solomon Islands because both were able to rapidly remove potential trouble-makers and bring prominent criminals to trial. Similarly, the 2006 riots did not escalate or spread because RAMSI was able to provide immediate support to the RSIP.

Clearly, for the RAMSI experience to be replicated elsewhere, therefore, regional arrangements need to focus on developing rapidly deployable capacities to assist states under stress. Second, in building regional deployable capacities, regional arrangements should pay attention to the need to integrate civilian, police and military units – paying particular attention to the training and generation of civilian capacities essential for building long-term capacity. Third, it needs to be recognized that capacity-building is a long-term and complex endeavour. Although rapid gains can be made, fragile justice systems, security sectors and state bureaucracies are likely to require external support for extended periods and hard won progress comes with the potential for rapid reversal. Long-term support is likely to involve the provision of training, funding and equipment and usable capacity to ensure effective governance and crisis responses. This finding is also supported by other experiences in the region, especially in Timor-Leste. If authorities and international agencies are able to respond rapidly to crises and outbreaks of violence, these episodes are less likely to have a negative impact on overall rule of law and civilian protection. If, however, the state fails to respond in a timely, decisive and legitimate manner, crises such at the 2006 riots in Honiara can rapidly spiral out of control. Fourth, success for pillar two endeavours such as this is defined by capacity-building. Ultimately, the effectiveness of international assistance is measured by the ability of national authorities to prevent instability and protect populations. Finally, operating in pillar two mode, regional arrangements can play a crucial role in assisting states in the near-term by disarming and demobilizing armed groups, acting as impartial mediators and providing technical expertise to augment the state's own efforts. The Solomon Islands experience tells us that this type of engagement can have an immediate and positive effect, and help states under stress prevent the commission of genocide and mass atrocities. Of course, though, it does nothing to stand in the way of states that are determined to abuse their own population.

Conclusion

This chapter contends that regional arrangements have an important role to play in implementing the RtoP but that issues relating to the locus of international authority, the modes of cooperation between regions and between regions and the UN, and varying levels of political will and institutional resources still need to be tackled. The danger of pursuing a regional approach to implementation in the absence of measures to address these issues is that a form of 'protection apartheid' would emerge whereby some parts of the world develop comprehensive systems for preventing and halting mass atrocities, while others do not. Political will and different regional norms are key obstacles, but just as challenging has been a lack of institutional knowledge about how to assist states, institutional capacity to generate such assistance, and the absence of modalities for effective cooperation with the UN. However, there are clear signs of improvement and in the past few years a number of regional arrangements, including ASEAN, the AU and PIF have begun to develop capacities that could be used to implement RtoP. In particular, our study of RAMSI in the Solomon Islands shows that regional arrangements can work effectively with member states to prevent conflict escalation and build state capacity. Clearly, though, much more needs to be done to identify how regional arrangements can add value to the global effort to implement RtoP.

8 The UN Security Council and the use of force

When all else fails, RtoP insists that the buck stops with the UN Security Council. To paraphrase paragraph 139 of the 2005 World Summit agreement, when a state is manifestly failing to protect its population from genocide, war crimes, ethnic cleaning and crimes against humanity, and peaceful means have failed, the Security Council has a responsibility to use its authority to protect endangered populations by imposing measures, including the use of force if necessary. The Security Council's subsequent affirmation of RtoP (Resolution 1674 (2006) and Resolution 1894 (2009)) implies that it accepts this special responsibility. Of course, it was profound international disagreement about the circumstances in which the use of force or other coercive measures may be used for human protection purposes generated by NATO's 1999 intervention in Kosovo that animated the ICISS and provided the immediate impetus for the development of RtoP, though as I noted in Chapter 1 the concept itself drew on ideas that were not directly connected to the question of intervention. The ICISS, recall, was established to address a critical challenge identified by Kofi Annan. Reflecting on the controversy surrounding the Kosovo intervention, and noting the damage that the UN's failure to act in Rwanda had done to the organization, Annan asked whether: 'On the one hand, is it legitimate for a regional organization to use force without a UN mandate? On the other, is it permissible to let gross and systematic violations of human rights, with grave humanitarian consequences, continue unchecked?'[1] The Secretary-General challenged member states to avoid 'future Kosovos' (cases where the Security Council is deadlocked about whether to intervene to prevent humanitarian crises from worsening) and 'future Rwandas' (where states lack the political will to take decisive action in the face of genocide, mass murder and/or ethnic cleansing).[2]

In examining the extent to which RtoP provides solutions to these two problems, it is important to not confuse what some advocates would like the RtoP principle to be with *what it actually is* – in terms of what states have actually signed up to.[3] Although a recurrent theme in this book, this is a particular problem when it comes to the use of force because many commentators and advocates seem to confuse what RtoP actually says or fail to distinguish between the ICISS recommendations and the 2005 commitment made by heads of state and government. It is all too common to read that RtoP establishes a new right of intervention in certain circumstances. The ICISS, it is worth noting, pointedly commented that it was 'quite premature' to argue that RtoP might become a customary principle of international law and constitute a legitimate exception to the legal ban on the use of force contained in Article 2(4) of the UN Charter.[4] Nonetheless, although the World Summit Outcome Document specifically identified the Security Council as the sole source of authority for coercive measures, Alicia Bannon argued that 'the [2005 World] Summit agreement strengthens the legal justification for limited forms of unilateral and regional action –including military action – if the United Nations fails to act to protect populations from genocide and other atrocities'.[5] The following year, Stephen Stedman, a former senior adviser to Kofi Annan, argued that Annan's agenda had included, 'a new norm, the responsibility to protect, to legalize humanitarian intervention' and then claimed that the Summit had succeeded in establishing 'a new norm to legalize humanitarian intervention'.[6] More recently, Robert Jackson argued that 'the responsibility to protect doctrine, in order to shield or rescue people from mass atrocity crimes, calls for a departure from the basic legal norms of the United Nations pertaining to war, namely an expansion of the right of military intervention and a restriction of the corresponding right of non-intervention'.[7] It is hard to see where the World Summit Outcome Document does anything other than reaffirm the Security Council's primacy on use of force decision-making, but commentaries such as this help reinforce the belief that RtoP could be used as a 'Trojan horse' to support great power interventionism.

A close examination (see Chapter 1) of what states have *actually* agreed to shows that RtoP sets out responsibilities that states have to their own citizens (the primary responsibility to protect), responsibilities that all states have as members of the international community (responsibilities to help build capacity and use peaceful means to prevent and protect), and responsibilities that certain institutions have (the Security Council's responsibility to use all appropriate means when necessary, in partnership with relevant regional organizations). RtoP does *not* set out criteria for the use of force, suggest that there are 'just causes' that justify the use of force beyond the two exemptions of the UN Charter', offer pathways for intervention not authorized by the Security Council, amend the way the Council does business, apply more widely that to the four specific crimes, or promise military intervention in every case.[8]

Bearing all this in mind, this chapter evaluates the Security Council's role in preventing future Kosovos and Rwandas, focusing on the use of force. It does so in three parts steps. First, given the ubiquity of the association between RtoP and the idea of criteria to guide decision-making about the use of force in academic debates about the principle, I begin by examining the question of criteria. I argue both that the rejection of proposed criteria by the Permanent Five members of the Security Council (China, France, Russia, UK, US) was politically inevitable and that it is practically inconse-quential because criteria are very unlikely to produce consensus or manufacture political will in real cases. Second, I evaluate the Council's practice, examining lessons learned from the 1990s and then focusing in detail on its handling of the crisis in Somalia which erupted in 2006. Here I find that despite its commitment to RtoP, the Council has remained reluctant to adopt non-consensual measures when confronted with evidence of mass atrocities or their imminent threat. But on closer inspection we find that Council decision-making is a complex business that requires harmonizing differing interpretations of the situation, judgments about the most appropriate and effective courses of action, and beliefs about the likely consequences of particular actions. Given this complexity, attention should be directed primarily towards the effective implementation of Council decisions rather than to the decision-making process itself. In the final section, I identify two areas in which RtoP can play a role in the work of the Council: (1) by helping to identify a broader continuum of protection measures available to the Council and (2) by providing an impetus for the development of protection doctrine and training and for new thinking about generating troops for protection operations. A third area, cooperation between the UN and regional arrangements, was discussed in the previous chapter.

The limits of criteria

As I noted in Chapter 1, one of the centrepieces of the ICISS report was its proposal for criteria (just cause thresholds and precautionary principles) to guide decision-making about the use of force for human protection purposes. These criteria, which have become almost synonymous with RtoP itself in some circles, were meant to fulfil three primary functions. First, in an attempt to avoid future cases like Rwanda where the world stood aside as 800,000 people were butchered in genocidal violence, the just cause thresholds were intended to create expectations about the circumstances in which the international community – primarily the UN Security Council – should become engaged in major humanitarian catastrophes and consider intervening with force, and to constrain permanent members from casting pernicious vetoes for selfish reasons.[9] Second, responding to a need to avoid future situations like Kosovo where the Security Council was blocked by veto, the criteria provided a pathway for legitimizing justifiable intervention for protection purposes not authorized by the Security Council.[10] Third, criteria were intended to serve as constraints on the ability of powerful states to 'abuse' RtoP and limit the scope of potential Security Council interventionism.[11] According to Thakur, the criteria would 'make it more difficult for coalitions of the willing to appropriate the language of humanitarianism for geopolitical and unilateral interventions' while making the Security Council's deliberations more transparent.[12] Consensus on criteria, he insisted, would make it more, not less, difficult for states to claim a humanitarian mantle for armed intervention.[13]

Before assessing the extent to which criteria fulfil these functions, it is important to stress how little serious political support they received. Most of the Security Council's Permanent Five members were sceptical about criteria from the outset. At the Security Council's annual retreat, in May 2002, the US rejected them outright on the grounds that permanent members should not constrain their right to cast their veto whenever they saw fit.[14] Russia and China expressed concern that criteria could be used to bypass the Security Council.[15] Although the British government had earlier presented its own version of criteria to guide decision-making and circumvent a Security Council veto, along with France it worried that agreement on criteria would not necessarily deliver the political will and consensus required for effective responses to humanitarian crises.[16] Negative attitudes towards criteria were only hardened by the US-led invasion of Iraq in 2003. Fearing that criteria might be used to justify the invasion, a forum of social democratic governments rejected a British proposal to endorse the idea.[17] In the post-Iraq context, the Canadian government recognized that a full-scale effort to persuade the Assembly to endorse criteria could 'backfire terribly', destroying potential consensus on RtoP.[18]

To be fair, there was some international support for a limited role for criteria. The proposal was endorsed by the UN's High Level Panel convened by Kofi Annan and in Annan's own blueprint for reform.[19] Significantly, however, Annan separated the commitment to RtoP from the proposed criteria, placing the former in a section on the rule of law and leaving the latter in a section on the use of force. He did this to reinforce the view that RtoP was not only about the use of force and to protect RtoP from the almost inevitable rejection of criteria.[20] The AU's 'Ezulwini Consensus' on UN Reform endorsed the High Level Panel's criteria for guiding the Security Council but, at the insistence of South Africa, observed that these guidelines 'should not undermine the responsibility of the international community to protect'.[21]

It was clear from the outset of the negotiations preceding the 2005 World Summit that there would be no consensus on criteria. Whereas several African states endorsed the view that criteria were essential to making the Security Council's decisions more transparent, accountable (to the wider membership) and hence legitimate, the US, China and Russia opposed them – though for very different reasons: the US because it believed that criteria would limit its freedom of action and the others because they feared that criteria might be used to circumvent the Council. Many other influential states, most notably India, shared this latter view. This view was publicly expressed by only a few states, but Canada's regional consultations had revealed that this was a significant underlying concern in many parts of the world, especially Asia. As such, the recommendation for criteria was watered-down into a commitment to continue discussing criteria, in order to keep the Americans, Chinese, Russians and Indians on board.[22] Ultimately, however, the diplomats charged with selling RtoP to the world recognized that criteria would be a 'bridge too far' for the Americans and the proposal was not strongly argued for.[23]

It was always unlikely that members states would be persuaded to adopt criteria and there was a real danger that persisting with the linkage of criteria to RtoP could have undermined the 2005 consensus on the principle.[24] Moreover, a diplomatic effort to persuade states to adopt criteria in the future would require a significant investment of political capital with little chance of success. In his 2009 report, the Secretary-General doffed his cap to ICISS by suggesting that member states might want to consider discussing criteria, but this was a deliberately half-hearted reference which was not seriously taken up in the ensuing General Assembly dialogue.[25] In addition to these political problems, it is not at all clear that RtoP would be strengthened by the addition of criteria to guide decision-making about the use of force. In what remains of this section, I will examine the three putative functions of criteria in a little more detail.

The first function of criteria – creating shared expectations about the assumption of international responsibility – is most easily dispensed with because although the 2005 World Summit did not endorse criteria, it did identify the crimes that governments had a responsibility to protect populations from and the circumstances in which that responsibility ought to be taken up by the international community. World leaders, it will be recalled, insisted that states have a responsibility to protect their populations from genocide, war crimes, ethnic cleansing and crimes against humanity and that this responsibility should be taken up by the Security Council in cases where a government was 'manifestly failing' to protect its government. There is broad agreement that the Security Council should be engaged in such circumstances. For example, the Chinese government's 2005 position paper on UN Reform agreed that 'massive humanitarian' crises were 'the legitimate concern of the international community'.[26]

It is important to recognize, however, that agreement on thresholds does not guarantee agreement on whether the thresholds have been breached and the most appropriate responses.[27] This problem has been evident in practice both before and after 2005. In relation to Kosovo and Georgia/South Ossetia, disagreements between the West and Russia boiled down to judgments about the sufficiency of evidence of mass atrocities – the West thought mass atrocities were sufficiently evident and grave to warrant intervention in Kosovo and not in the case of Georgia; Russia thought the exact reverse.[28] In relation to Darfur and Somalia, governments more or less agreed on the gravity of the threat but disagreed about the most appropriate and prudent courses of action (see Chapter 3). Indeed, even advocates of RtoP disagreed on whether the just cause thresholds and precautionary principles justify armed intervention in different cases. Debate among advocates has been particularly sharp over Darfur, Sri Lanka and Myanmar/Cyclone Nargis.[29] On the other hand, agreement has been reached on the deployment and use of force in less high-profile cases such as the Democratic Republic of Congo (DRC), and on measures short of enforcement in the cases of Kenya and Guinea, without the need for criteria and thresholds.[30]

Nor is there much evidence to suggest that the thresholds could constrain the use of the veto. It has been suggested that Russia and China might have been 'compelled' into abstaining on a vote authorizing non-consensual intervention in Darfur were such a resolution tabled in the Council and backed by the argument that intervention would be the only means of relieving the humanitarian catastrophe.[31] But China's actual performance in the Council suggests that it would be more than willing to use its veto in such cases. In relation to Darfur, China threatened vetoes on measures far less intrusive than non-consensual military intervention, such as comprehensive targeted sanctions and no-fly zones.[32] Given that China's position on Darfur enjoyed the support of a significant portion of the Non-Aligned Movement, the League of Arab States and the Organization of Islamic Conferences, and was broadly in line with the AU's position, it is not clear where the pressure to abstain in such a vote would have come from. 'Naming and shaming' only works if a state's position is out of step with that of the international community – or at least that part of the international community from which it draws its legitimacy. China draws its legitimacy in part from the Non-Aligned Movement and in part from being in step on a particular issue with the relevant regional organization. On the issues of Darfur, Zimbabwe or Myanmar, where its position was at variance with the West, China has tended to make a point of aligning itself with the relevant regional bodies (AU and ASEAN respectively). In this context, 'naming and shaming' will only work if China's position is out of step with the relevant regional organization and there has yet to be an instance of this since 2005.

What, then, of the second function of criteria – to provide a way of legitimizing armed intervention without Security Council authorization? We should note at the outset that this has been the most oft-cited function of criteria since they were first mooted in the 1970s.[33] Interest in criteria was reignited by the Security Council's failure to reach a consensus over Kosovo. In the wake of the storm over Kosovo, Tony Blair outlined five tests to guide intervention decisions and the Foreign Office circulated a draft paper on the subject among the Permanent Five members of the Security Council.[34] Blair's view that criteria would provide guidelines for when regional organizations and coalitions of the willing may legitimately intervene without the authority of the Security Council was endorsed by the Independent International Commission on Kosovo (IICK). Working towards its finding that the intervention in Kosovo was 'illegal but legitimate', the IICK lent support to the idea of using criteria as thresholds for determining whether or not to use force to alleviate humanitarian emergencies. The Kosovo Commission recognized that while the UN Charter's restrictions on the use of force contributed to international peace and security by prohibiting aggressive war, there may be circumstances – as in Kosovo – where intervention was needed as a last resort but is not likely to be authorized by the Security Council because of a threatened veto. Criteria, the Commission reasoned, might create pathways for states to intervene legitimately in the most extreme emergencies without Council authorization.[35]

There was never much likelihood that the UN membership would have endorsed guidelines providing a pathway to intervention not authorized by the Council. Moreover, it is not altogether clear what such a pathway would contribute. After all, states already have moral arguments that they can employ to justify armed intervention without Security Council authorization.

For example, the US used moral rather than legal language to justify its participation in *Operation Allied Force,* arguing simply that the moral imperative to protect people from ethnic cleansing overrode the legal ban on the use of force.[36] Critics did not respond by arguing that ethnic cleansing did not, in some circumstances, provide grounds for intervention. Instead, as mentioned earlier, they quibbled over the gravity of the threat and the prudence of intervention.[37] It is difficult to see how criteria would have helped in this case. NATO would have argued that the criteria were satisfied and therefore legitimized their actions; critics would have contended that the criteria were not satisfied. In the end, it is for the international community to make judgments about the legitimacy of armed intervention and individual states are left making up their own mind on the basis of their perception of the facts of the case and relative importance of the relevant norms, including sovereignty, non-intervention, the protection of human rights, and prudential calculations.[38] International law relating to the use of force and crimes such as genocide already provides a common language for this debate. It is not clear what criteria would add.

This brings us the third putative function of criteria: restricting abuse. This concern has become somewhat redundant in the wake of the World Summit's adoption of RtoP. The danger of abuse is raised whenever there is a pathway to legitimate intervention that circumvents a deadlocked Security Council. Paragraph 139 of the World Summit agreement clearly declares that it is for the Security Council to determine whether enforcement measures are necessary in the event of states manifestly failing to protect their populations. As such, the constraining function of criteria would be a constraint only on Security Council decision-making and the Council already contains mechanisms for guarding against abuse – not least the need for a majority vote and the veto.[39] The closest historical case we have of Council sanctioned 'abuse' was its endorsement of the French *Operation Turquoise* at the end of the Rwandan genocide. The French intervention was widely regarded as 'abusive' because France's primary aim was not humanitarian and the intervention could have done more to save lives.[40] The problem in that case was not that France intervened, but that it did not do enough to protect Rwandans. Given that this is the best case we have of Council authorized 'abuse', it seems safe conclude that the Council's own operating procedures are sufficient guard against potential future 'abuse'.

Thus, the argument that criteria are to be valued because they make it harder to put forward humanitarian justifications for intervention is only plausible in one of two circumstances. First, if criteria are connected to a pathway for legitimizing intervention not authorized by the Security Council. By specifying that coercive measures must be authorized by the Security Council, RtoP clearly does not offer such a pathway. Second, if we believe that the Security Council has become *too* proactive and should be constrained. This is not an argument that is often aired and with good reason – the problem at hand is not a surfeit of intervention aimed at protecting populations from genocide and mass atrocities, but a deficit.

Therefore, it is difficult to see what just cause thresholds and precautionary principles would add to RtoP or contribute to decision-making about armed intervention to protect populations. As agreed by governments, RtoP clearly identifies its scope and its thresholds (genocide, war crimes, ethnic cleansing and crimes against humanity) and the international bodies responsible for discharging the responsibility. Although RtoP thresholds are unlikely to generate political will by themselves in relation to particular cases, the endorsement of RtoP demonstrates a broad consensus that international community should be engaged in protecting populations from grave harm. Beyond this basic admission of responsibility, criteria are unlikely to foster consensus on how to act and deter the use of vetoes, and provide anything other than a self-serving pathway to the legitimization of intervention not authorized by the Security Council. Moreover, although they may be able to constrain interventions not authorized by the Council, criteria add nothing to the Council's mechanisms for preventing 'abuse'.

If this analysis is correct, then advocates of RtoP should not invest political capital persuading governments to endorse criteria for the use of force. Endorsement in the short or medium term is highly unlikely, and even if the campaign was successful criteria would probably not improve decision-making about the use of force. Rather than trying to amend RtoP by calling for the addition of criteria, therefore, advocates should instead focus on the steps needed to implement the principle as it is. In relation to the UN Security Council, a good place to start is by examining the way the Council does business and the challenges it confronts when responding to mass atrocities.

Learning lessons from the 1990s

This section is the first of two that reviews Security Council practice relating to the deployment of forces for protection purposes. Here I briefly examine some of the lessons learned from the 1990s and in the following section I consider the Council's response to the crisis in Somalia that erupted in 2006. A review of the cases examined in Chapter 2 suggests that the focus for debate in the Council has moved on from the 1990s, inasmuch as the critical questions revolve not around the legitimacy of Council activism but rather around the appropriateness of different courses of action. Moreover, it suggests that in practice the Council is rarely confronted with situations *exactly* like Rwanda, where clearly identifiable perpetrators attack large numbers of victims and where the Council faces a choice between authorizing armed intervention and standing aside, or like Kosovo where a group of states seek a mandate for humanitarian intervention in a context where there is little international consensus about its merits. Since 2005 at least, patterns of conflict and mass killing in places such as Somalia, Sudan, the DRC, Sri Lanka, Kenya and elsewhere have been more complex than either of these scenarios, the most appropriate course of action has been far from self-evident, and the Council has tended to be actively seized even if it has not always adopted robust measures.

In such a context, it is difficult to see how using RtoP as a speech act to provide a catalyst for (undefined) 'action', a view of the principle preferred by some of its advocates (see Chapter 4), has a useful role to play. Moreover, attempts to squeeze analysis of specific conflicts into this framework has tended to obscure more than it illuminates, promoting simplistic and reductionist accounts of complex problems, offering little in the way of novel policy recommendations, and failing to deliver additional international political will that might be translated into resources for peace operations, even among states that consider themselves to be RtoP's 'friends'.

In addition to the fact that conflicts themselves rarely exhibit the internal or international characteristics of a Rwanda or Kosovo, four trends within the Council itself have helped to shift the manner of international engagement with RtoP related crises. First, learning some of the lessons of failed engagements in the 1990s, the Council has become noticeably more circumspect about what it can achieve. The most obvious general indicator of this trend has been the steady reduction in the overall number of decisions taken by the Council each year, with the number taken in 2009 the lowest since 1991.[41] Second, and somewhat conversely, Council engagement has become deeper and more complex. The Council has tended to use a wider variety of instruments (sanctions and embargoes, legal instruments, peacekeeping, support for political processes), to work cooperatively with relevant regional and sub-regional arrangements, and when it does take decisions in the form of resolutions, these tend to be longer, more complex and more specific than in the past. Third, in cases where there is little dispute about the commission of one or more of the four RtoP crimes, Council members have become more cooperative and less confrontational and the political divisions between them have become more context specific, with lines agreement and discord differing from case to case.[42] Therefore, in the case of Somalia, which I discuss in more detail below, while the permanent members disagreed on the merits of particular courses of action, there was plenty of evidence of a genuine intent to pursue consensus and most members remained open to potential compromises. As a result, the resolutions passed on Somalia between 2006–10 enjoyed unanimous support and involved compromises among the permanent members. Moreover, the debates and political alignments sometimes crossed traditional Security Council divides. Whereas in the 1990s, debates about engagement with major crises usually pitted the Western permanent members (arguing for interventionism) against Russia and China (defending sovereignty), since 2005 those lines have been less clear. In the case of Somalia, the US and China backed the AU's call for the deployment of UN peacekeepers, while the European members expressed grave reservations about intervention. Fourth, the Council has exhibited a much greater willingness to task peace operations to protect populations under threat, obviating the need for humanitarian intervention outside Council auspices. In two cases, Sudan and the DRC, the Council gave UN peacekeepers (in UNAMID, UNMIS and MONUC) robust Chapter VII mandates to protect civilians and supported this by authorizing the deployment of relatively large (by UN standards) operations. Moreover, the Council has exhibited willingness to authorize non-UN operations where it thinks they are more appropriate. For instance, in relation to Somalia, the UN secretariat argued that the Council should authorize a robust (non-UN) stabilization force led by a strong lead-nation. Council members accepted this recommendation but the force failed to materialize because no government was prepared to serve as lead-nation. Perhaps partly as a result of these changes to Security Council practice, since 2005 the Council has not been confronted with a Rwanda-like situation and its engagement with crises characterized by the commission or threat of one or more of the RtoP crimes has not been characterized by straightforward debates between interventionists and anti-interventionists.

Before we come to the Council's response to the crisis in Somalia, it is worth briefly reflecting on the lessons learned from the 1990s as these provide the institutional context for Council decision-making since 2005. As the Cold War came to an end, the Security Council's engagement with armed conflict and humanitarian crises underwent a 'triple transformation'.[43] There was a *quantitative transformation* as the Security Council became more activist, authorizing more new missions between 1988 and 1992 than had been authorized in the previous 40 years combined. There was a *normative transformation* catalysed by a growing belief among some member states that the Council should protect vulnerable populations and promote positive peace in one way or another. And there was a *qualitative transformation* in that the UN was asked to carry out a complex range of new tasks often in hostile environments, marrying peacekeeping with the delivery of humanitarian aid, state-building, local peacemaking and peace enforcement. By 1995, catastrophic mission failures in Angola, Somalia, Bosnia and Rwanda, characterized by the failure of UN peacekeepers to protect themselves and those under their care, had damaged the legitimacy of both peace operations and the UN more generally. The number of UN peacekeepers deployed around the world fell dramatically as member states expressed a preference for working through regional organizations and alliances, such as ECOWAS and NATO, and the Security Council became reluctant to create new missions. This ushered in a period of hesitant introspection and lessons learning at the UN, which saw the production of reports detailing its failings in Rwanda and Bosnia and the landmark 'Brahimi report' on the future direction of UN peacekeeping. Each of these identified failings on the part of the Security Council and the lessons learned have helped to shape Council behaviour in the twenty-first century.

The 1999 Report of the Independent Inquiry on the UN's inability to prevent and respond effectively to the 1994 Rwandan genocide concluded that the genocide resulted from the failure of the whole UN system.[44] The 'overriding failure', the Inquiry argued, was the lack of resources and lack of will to take on the commitment that would have been necessary to prevent the genocide and protect its victims. The UN mission (UNAMIR) deployed to oversee implementation of the Arusha Accords was smaller than recommended by the UN secretariat, slow to deploy owing to the reluctance of states to contribute troops, debilitated by administrative difficulties, and when troops did arrive many were inadequately trained and equipped.[45] Among the Inquiry's many criticisms and recommendations were several relating directly to the Security Council. First, UNAMIR's mandate was unsuited to the situation in Rwanda. This was a product of a lack of will on the part of member states to properly resource the mission but also the secretariat's failure to accurately inform the Council about the situation in Rwanda prior to the genocide. Once deployed, UNAMIR should have done more to alert the Security Council to the inadequacy of its mandate. Second, the Council failed to ensure that UNAMIR was sufficiently resourced to implement its limited mandate. At the time of the genocide, the mission had only five roadworthy Armed Personnel Carriers, one helicopter and insufficient medical supplies for its personnel. Third, the secretariat failed to provide important pieces of information to the Security Council, including a now infamous warning about the impending genocide issued by UNAMIR commander Romeo Dallaire, and the flow of information to the Council was weak once the genocide began. The Inquiry concluded that the UN's failure in Rwanda was largely created by a critical disjuncture between the mandate and resources given to the peacekeepers, and the situation on the ground. Because of political dynamics in the Council (especially, the US refused to support a large complex operation so soon after the 1993 'Black Hawk Down' incident in Mogadishu) UNAMIR was conceived as a traditional peacekeeping mission deployed to monitor compliance with a peace agreement, even though its operational context lacked the basic prerequisites for traditional peacekeeping (stable peace, viable political process, commitment of parties, cantonment of forces etc.). These conclusions echoed those of the UN's report on the 1995 Srebrenica massacre, issued a month earlier.

The report on the 1995 massacre in the UN 'safe area' of Srebrenica found that operational problems with UNPROFOR were rooted in deeper political problems in the Security Council. Once again, the Security Council was focused on trying to keep the peace when there was no peace to keep and delivering humanitarian aid in the false belief that this would help remedy the situation.[46] Moreover, decisions about the nature and direction of UNPROFOR were taken on the basis of false assumptions about Serbian war aims.[47] As a result, the Council put peacekeepers into situations where they might be required to use force but without the mandate or resources to do so effectively.[48] The report identified a series of lessons for the future, two of which are particularly important here. First, it stated that when peace operations are deployed without the general consensus of the Security Council, and as a substitute for such consensus, they are likely to fail. Peace operations must only be deployed with clear mandates and clear support from the UN membership, backed up with the commitment of adequate resources.[49] Second, it concluded that it was important to recognize that a strategy of genocide and ethnic cleansing could only be met 'decisively with all necessary means, and with the political will to carry the policy through to its logical conclusion'.[50]

Building on these insights, in March 2000 the UN Secretary-General appointed the Panel on United Nations Peace Operations to identify the principal weaknesses of UN peace operations and make practical recommendations to overcome them. What became known as the 'Brahimi Report' contained important lessons for the Security Council. In particular, the Report made four recommendations that related to the way in which the Council took decisions about deploying peacekeepers. First, the UN Secretariat should give realistic advice to the Security Council about the situation on the ground, the potential for a peace operation to work effectively, and the resources needed. UN officials should be prepared to spell out precisely what the UN could and could not realistically hope to achieve and to argue against the deployment of peacekeepers if they did not believe that the conditions for success were satisfied.[51] In other words, the Secretariat should tell the Council what it needs to hear and not simply what it wants to hear. Second, the Security Council should ensure that mandates are clearly worded and realizable. The Security Council and Secretariat should avoid writing 'blank cheques' by establishing wide protection mandates without fully examining what would be required to implement them. Third, the Security Council should not authorize an operation until it is confident that it has the means to accomplish its goals. Finally, the Report recommended that the way peace operations were financed should be reformed so that financial arrangements are in place before a mission is deployed. The UN membership – including all five of the Security Council's Permanent Members – welcomed the Report.[52] Although the Secretary-General experienced considerable difficulty persuading member states to implement its main recommendations, especially those that required the establishment of new offices or institutions, many of the recommendations relating the way that the Council goes about its business have been informally implemented in practice.

It is important to understand that the way in which the Council addressed post-2005 crises in Somalia, Sudan, the DRC and elsewhere was framed against the backdrop of these lessons learned from some of the mission failures of the 1990s, and especially shared recognition among members and the secretariat of the centrality of Council consensus, the need for clear and realistic mandates, the need to calibrate policy with the situation on the ground, and the need to ensure that Council mandates are supported by sufficient resources. In the following section I focus on Council decision-making in response to the crisis in Somalia and show that these lessons helped shape deliberations.

Security Council decision-making: Somalia 2006–10

As I noted in Chapter 2, approximately 16,000 civilians have been killed and over 2 million people displaced in Somalia since early 2006. The Security Council's re-engagement with this crisis has bucked most of the identifiable trends associated with Council politics. Most especially, China, the US and the AU have consistently pushed for greater UN activism and the deployment of a UN peace operation, while European members of the Council and the UN secretariat have expressed persistent scepticism about this move. What has blocked the deployment of UN peacekeepers in this case has not, therefore, been concerns about sovereignty but prudential concerns about the absence of conditions thought necessary for successful peacekeeping, the funding and composition of any such force, and whether peacekeepers would do more harm than good. Moreover, the Council's engagement with Somalia has been further complicated by four pressing concerns. First, there are multiple armed groups and significant doubts about the capacity and legitimacy of the Transitional Federal Government (TFG). What is more, all of groups (including the TFG) have been responsible for war crimes and/or crimes against humanity.[53] As a result, Council members have adopted divergent views on the extent to which the UN should support the TFG at the expense of a more inclusive political process and the extent to which support for the 'government' would be read as partiality by other armed groups, undermining the UN's peacemaking role and making potential targets of deployed peacekeepers. This would be particularly harmful were the TFG to collapse, which has been a realistic prospect throughout. Second, the conflict in Somalia is closely associated with wider regional tensions involving Ethiopia, Eritrea, Djibouti and, to a lesser extent, Kenya and Yemen. In violation of an arms embargo imposed by the Security Council in 1992, Ethiopia and Yemen provided arms to the TFG, while Eritrea (Ethiopia's long-standing opponent) armed and aided various Islamist organizations including the Union of Islamic Courts (UIC) and al-Shabaab. Third, the conflict has been associated with the US-led 'war on terror' owing to links between the Islamists and al-Qaeda and US concerns that al-Qaeda might take advantage of the authority-vacuum in Somalia to establish facilities which replace those lost in Afghanistan. This linkage explains the Bush administration's eagerness to see the deployment of UN peacekeepers, as well as the US use of force in Somalia and support for Ethiopian intervention. Finally, the conflict has been associated with an exponential increase in maritime piracy off the east coast of Africa, which poses a major threat to international shipping. It is this complexity that has encouraged some advocates of RtoP to argue that Somalia is not a 'classic' case or that RtoP does not directly apply.[54] At every stage, hopes of progress were checked by setbacks on the ground and, as I noted in Chapter 2, the Council's understandably cautious approach left it reacting to events on the ground. Except where otherwise stated, the account draws upon Council's minutes, the excellent work done by the NGO, *Security Council Report*, which has provided monthly briefings on the Council's response to the crisis in Somalia.

In 2004, the Intergovernmental Authority on Development (IGAD) negotiated a peace agreement of sorts for Somalia which saw the establishment of the TFG, whose parliament (then based in Nairobi) promptly elected Abdillahi Yusuf Ahmed as President, and established its base in Baidoa.[55] The selection of Yusuf, a notorious Somali warlord, was controversial from the outset. Because of his long-standing ties with the regime that seized power in Ethiopia in 1991 (between 1984–91 Yusuf was imprisoned by the Ethiopian government, and was released when the Ethiopian People's Revolutionary Front seized power), Yusuf was deeply unpopular in many parts of Somalia and compounded that unpopularity by immediately calling for the deployment of a 20,000 strong AU peacekeeping force, a move read by many Somalis as indicating his intention to impose his will on the rest of the country.[56] Despite the reservations expressed by many Somalis, the following year, at the request of the AU and the new government, IGAD agreed to deploy a peace operation (IGASOM) to support the new government. However, the proposed mission ran into a number of roadblocks which ultimately prevented its deployment. In particular, there were serious disagreements about the composition of the force, with several armed groups in Somalia insisting that IGASOM not use troops from neighbouring states, meaning that only Eritrea, Sudan and Uganda could contribute. In addition, though, were questions about IGAD's capacity to deploy, fund and sustain an operation of this kind and questions about its impartiality. The Security Council enjoyed significant leverage over these questions because under the terms of the 1992 arms embargo, IGASOM was not entitled to transfer arms to Somalia or provide active support to the TFG without an exemption.

In early 2006, amidst an increase of fighting around Mogadishu between the Union of Islamic Courts (UIC) and an anti-Islamist group of warlords calling themselves the Forces of the Alliance for Peace and Fight Against International Terrorism, which some reported to be the heaviest since the early 1990s,[57] the Security Council broadly supported the IGAD initiative though some members (especially European) worried that the TFG was little more than an alliance of warlords and that granting an exception to the arms embargo could undermine the embargo regime, given the presence of persistent violators (Ethiopia and Eritrea).[58] These same Council members were also unsure about whether, if deployed without the consent of all the parties including the Islamic Courts, IGASOM would promote peace or cause an escalation of the conflict. A combination of AU's support for the IGAD's and mounting US concerns about Islamism (shared to some extent by the UN Secretary-General) and piracy created some impetus for the Council to respond positively on the request to lift the arms embargo. However, by mid-2006 a division had begun to emerge, based on different assessments of IGASOM's likely impact, between those states that were willing to grant the exemption (China, Russia, AU) and those that remained reluctant to do so (UK, France, Denmark, Qatar). As a compromise, the Council invited IGAD to submit a detailed plan for its proposed operation and indicated in a presidential statement that it would not lift the embargo until a satisfactory plan was submitted. In addition, concerned that peace operations are unlikely to succeed in the absence of a viable political process, the Council used the same presidential statement to call upon the TFG to submit a plan for national security and stability that comprised a viable political process.[59]

At the same time, on the ground in Somalia the UIC continued to advance, taking control of Mogadishu and other important cities (e.g. Jowhar), while several states – including the US – stepped up the supply of arms and other assistance to anti-Islamist groups, culminating in the deployment of Ethiopian troops to support the TFG in Baidoa.[60] For its part, the TFG delivered its national security strategy and agreement was reached that Sudan and Uganda would provide around 7,000 troops for IGASOM, obviating the need for troops from neighbouring countries. However, in response to the deployment of Ethiopian troops in Baidoa, the UIC rejected the government's plan and threatened to wage 'holy war' on Ethiopia.[61] All of this encouraged some Security Council members, such as the UK and Russia, that had been sceptical about IGASOM to briefly take a more favourable view and to begin backing the idea that the UN provide security sector support to the TFG while at the same time encouraging the establishment of an inclusive and viable political process.[62] But this sense that the Council should respond to the escalation of violence was tempered by evidence of divisions within the TFG about the merits of the Ethiopian intervention, the government's failure to deliver plans for a political process that would involve the UIC, evidence of emerging divisions within IGAD itself over the merits of intervention, and IGAD's failure to set out a viable plan for IGASOM.[63]

The Security Council's refusal to grant an exemption for IGASOM unless certain conditions were met proved useful in terms of putting pressure on the TFG to initiate dialogue with the UIC. In September 2006, the parties agreed an interim settlement which included a pledge to work towards a power-sharing agreement and establishment of a joint security force.[64] The AU and IGAD took advantage of this apparent progress to once again call upon the Council to endorse IGASOM and grant an exemption to the embargo. The plea won informal support from China and Tanzania, but other Council members continued to express concerns. Not least, they remained sceptical about the veracity of the talks given evidence of persistent fighting, the UIC's steady expansion (UIC seized Kismayo on 25 September) and the TFG's counter-assaults supported by Ethiopian forces. They also worried that without the UIC's consent, the proposed deployment could undermine the nascent peace process and also raised questions about how the projected force would be funded and sustained, questions which the IGASOM plan had apparently paid little attention to.[65] In October 2006, the UN Secretary-General weighed into the debate by underscoring that the Council had set out the conditions under which it would consider lifting the embargo and calling on the AU and IGAD to follow the steps set out by the Council (submission of a detailed mission plan consistent with the TFG's national security plan).[66]

Despite the interim settlement, UIC forces encircled the TFG in Baidoa and began to threaten the autonomous regions of Puntland and Somaliland to the north. The Islamists also rejected any proposed peacekeeping force, effectively blocking the political process.[67] Concerned about the TFG's impending collapse and the potential for an outright victory for the Islamists, the Bush administration defected from the Council's cautious approach and circulated a draft resolution giving IGASOM an exemption from the arms embargo and a mandate to support the TFG.[68] The draft enjoyed the support of China, who accepted the US argument about the need to support a military solution by backing the TFG against the Islamists, and of Russia and the African members. On the other side, the UK, France and the Special Representative of the UN Secretary-General, Francois Lonseny Fall, continued to argue against granting IGASOM a mandate. Lonseny Fall advised the Council that IGASOM's deployment could hasten the TFG's collapse and also noted a number of shortfalls in the mission's plan. Not least, there was no consensus within IGAD and the operation was based on the assumption that external donors would pay the annual US$335 million price tag. Although it was pushing for a speedy resolution, the US was notably not offering to fund the mission to any great extent. Moreover, the Special Representative noted that the mission plan made the potentially fatal mistake of assuming that it would be deployed into a consensual environment, despite the UIC's clear pronouncements that this would not be the case.[69]

Events on the ground in late 2006 forced the Council's hand. The TFG's imminent defeat prompted Ethiopia to intervene with US backing and forced the Council to authorize IGASOM and grant it an exemption from the arms embargo despite the aforementioned misgivings on the part of some Council members. In grudgingly accepting the resolution, European members – who still believed that the intervention was likely to worsen the situation – insisted on a number of revisions to the text, especially the imposition of limits on the mission's mandate, the exclusion of troops from neighbouring countries (especially aimed at Ethiopia), and encouragement of political dialogue between all the parties. These revisions were incorporated into Resolution 1725 (6 December 2006), which authorized the deployment of IGASOM to establish a 'protection and training' mission and granted it an exemption from the arms embargo. Specifically, IGASOM was tasked to: (a) monitor implementation of agreements between the TFG and UIC; (b) ensure safe passage for those involved in the political process; (c) maintain security in Baidoa; (d) protect members of the TFG; (e) train TFG security forces. Council members that had previously expressed scepticism about IGASOM hoped that the resolution would provide a roadmap for the withdrawal of Ethiopian troops and their replacement by IGAD forces.

European concerns about the potentially negative impact of Ethiopian intervention and the authorization of IGASOM on the peace process and humanitarian situation in Somalia were soon realized. By the end of December 2006, full-scale fighting had erupted around Baidoa, prompting Ethiopia to step-up its military involvement. Ethiopian forces rapidly defeated the UIC, relieving Baidoa and forcing the Islamists from their major strongholds, including Mogadishu (on 28 December). On 10 January, the US joined the fray by launching air strikes against suspected al-Qaeda sites in southern Somalia. The US followed up with the deployment of a ground team to conduct damage assessment, a second round of strikes at the end of January, and a third round in June 2007.[70] In addition, the nascent political process collapsed and the Islamists and other opponents of the Ethiopians launched an insurgency. Equally troubling was the fact that the intervention damaged the future potential for the deployment of peacekeepers thought impartial by all sides. The insurgents argued that given that both Ethiopia and IGASOM (and, for that matter, the US) supported the TFG, there was no meaningful difference between Ethiopian forces and other foreign peacekeeping forces.[71] All would be viewed as hostile and treated accordingly. As such, although the intervention delivered some short-term benefits to the TFG, it severely reduced the Council's options and made its earlier strategy of linking the deployment of peacekeepers to progress towards a viable political process moribund.

Within the Security Council, attention now turned to what measures could be taken to support the TFG. Given the divisions within IGAD, its association with the Ethiopian intervention, and its lack of resources (due mainly to the fact that external donors remained unconvinced about its capacity to execute an effective mission), on 19 January, the AU's Peace and Security Council authorized the deployment of a peacekeeping mission (AMISOM) comprising 8,000 troops that would obviate the need for the deployment of IGASOM. Significantly, the AU's resolution stated that it would be deployed with the 'clear understanding that the mission will evolve to a UN operation' despite the facts that there was no consensus in the Security Council about the merits of the UN taking on the operation and that the UN secretariat remained deeply sceptical about the prospect.[72] Heeding the lessons from the Brahimi report – especially that the secretariat should give frank advice to the Council and should acknowledge the limits of what it can realistically expect to achieve – over the coming years, the UN Secretary-General repeatedly cautioned against the authorization of UN peacekeepers on the grounds that the conditions for peacekeeping (ceasefire, security, political process, viable exit strategy etc.) were not in place. In this context, the inclusion of the reference to the UN taking over peacekeeping duties in Somalia in the AU resolution was highly premature and is probably best interpreted as an attempt to put pressure on the Council to move in that direction. This was arguably the first time that a regional organization had looked to put such overt pressure on the Security Council to authorize a UN mission.

Although the AU reiterated its call several times over the coming years, sceptics in the Council and the UN Secretary-General remained relatively unmoved. Instead, the Council reached a consensus that it should give support to AMISOM and duly authorized the mission under Chapter VII of the Charter (Resolution 1744, 21 February 2007). AMISOM was authorized to use 'all necessary means' to provide security to the participants in political dialogue and to support TFG in developing effective security forces. In an attempt to distinguish AMISOM from the Ethiopian intervention, the Resolution 'welcomed' Ethiopia's decision to withdraw its forces and called upon AMISOM to create conditions for the withdrawal of all foreign forces. The cautious wording on this issue reflected divergent views in the Council about the merits of the intervention, with the US reluctant to demand Ethiopian withdrawal and the Europeans seeing withdrawal as a prerequisite to political progress. The Council also remained divided on the prospects for a transition from AMISOM to a UN Mission. In informal consultations, the US, China and African members argued that the resolution should include a paragraph requesting recommendations about the potential for a UN peace operation but other members remained sceptical about the merits of the proposed takeover and urged against including language implying that the Council thought this to be a viable path.[73] In addition to concerns, expressed before, about whether conditions in Somalia were suitable for a UN peace operation and the absence of a viable political process, sceptics now began expressing doubts about potential force generation and overstretch problems given the Council's on-going consideration of another potentially large and complex deployment, in Darfur.[74]

Support for AMISOM was clearly aided by the perception among some members that an 'African solution' might obviate the need for UN peacekeepers. However, members more positively inclined to the AU's proposal for a UN follow-on force succeeded in persuading the Council to task the secretariat to send a technical team to Somalia to help draw up plans for a potential UN mission.[75] That said, the US and EU were slow to provide assistance to AMISOM, at first donating around $33 million (or around 10 per cent of the mission's estimated cost) and attaching political conditionalities, including a deadline for the launching of an inclusive and viable political process.[76] African members such as Ghana (which also held the AU presidency at the time), began pushing for the UN to take over the mission and, crucially, its funding. Ghana's President, John Kufour, told the high-level plenary session of the General Assembly that, 'it cannot be overemphasized that the enormity of the challenges in Somalia go well beyond the capacity of the AU and requires the concerted support of the UN'.[77]

As the insurgency deepened into 2007, the humanitarian situation in Somalia deteriorated.[78] TFG, Ethiopian and AMISOM troops were all targeted by insurgents and responded with sometimes heavy-handed force, leading observers to complain that all sides were committing war crimes and/or crimes against humanity. In April/May 2007, the TFG and Ethiopian forces launched an offensive to reassert its control of Mogadishu, which led to indiscriminate attacks on civilians and caused displacement.[79] In response, anti-TFG/Ethiopian elements, including Islamists and various warlords, began organizing themselves more systematically, establishing the so-called 'Alliance for the Re-Liberation of Somalia' with backing from Eritrea in September 2007.[80] The anti-Ethiopian insurgency also aided the rise to prominence of al-Shabaab, a radical Islamist militia with suspected links to Al-Qaeda, which had previously been associated with the UIC.[81] The insurgency's radicalization contributed to an increase of attacks on humanitarian workers. Twenty-two humanitarian workers were killed in 2008 prompting many agencies, including Medecins sans Frontieres, to withdraw their international staff and limit operations.

Under intense international pressure from the Security Council, the TFG launched a political process and held an AU-supported 'national reconciliation conference' in July–August 2007. Although clan leaders agreed in principle on issues such as a ceasefire, disarmament and the restitution of property, the 45 days of talks did not progress onto implementation issues. Moreover, core issues such as power sharing and Ethiopian withdrawal were not canvassed and some opposition groups including moderate Islamists and several important clans (especially the Hawiye clan) did not participate on the grounds that the withdrawal they saw of all foreign forces as a prerequisite for negotiations.[82] The Council's assessment of the TFG was further damaged by reports that it was obstructing the delivery of humanitarian assistance (control of food aid was thought crucial to public support) and that TFG forces indiscriminately targeted civilians.[83]

Amidst all of this, AMISOM was also confronting a number of serious operational problems. Although the first contingent of 1,700 Ugandan troops was deployed in early March, the mission soon ran into serious force generation problems.[84] By July 2008, only around 2,500 of the projected 8,000 troops had actually been deployed, and although this grew to around 5,200 by early 2010 – some three years after the mission had been mandated – the mission seriously short of its target. There were multiple reasons for this shortfall. First, although the Security Council agreed that AMISOM was the best vehicle for peacekeeping in Somalia, donors were reticent about furnishing it with the financial support that it required. Among the multiple reasons for this were budget constraints, competing priorities (especially Darfur), and concerns about the mission itself – especially the lack of a viable political process, the mission's perceived partiality, and the absence of a clear exit strategy. Second, lacking financial and other forms of support from the UN (in early 2008, the mission had funding for around 5 per cent of its projected annual budget), the mission was chaotically organized around a loose command structure which undermined mission unity and emphasized national command and control. Third, the mission's perceived partiality encouraged insurgent attacks on AMISOM forces, deterring potential troop contributors. In June 2007, for instance, Ghana argued that the security situation and logistical problems prevented it from deploying troops as part of AMISOM, reinforcing its view that the mission should be taken over by the UN.[85] Fourth, like IGAD, the AU was somewhat divided on the force's merits with some states (Eritrea, Libya) outright opposed, others (Ethiopia) pursuing separate lines of action, and a third group of neighbours (Kenya, Uganda, Djibouti, Sudan), concerned about the potential implications for them if the situation deteriorated.[86]

The slow deployment allowed Ethiopia to delay its withdrawal and placed the question of whether and when AMISOM might hand over to the UN at the forefront of the Council's deliberations.[87] On the one hand, the AU pushed hard for a speedy transfer, seeing it as crucial to the mission's long-term political viability and financial sustainability and to efforts to persuade states to contribute. In early March, the AU's Peace and Security Commissioner, Said Djinnit, rather optimistically stated that AMISOM would be deployed for 'five, six or seven months, and it would be followed by a larger United Nations operation'.[88] In supporting this view, the TFG insisted that the UN's assessment of the security and humanitarian situation was too negative and disputed OCHA's estimates about the number of people displaced by the resumption of fighting.[89] At a meeting in Jeddah (Saudi Arabia), the TFG concluded an agreement with clan leaders which called for the deployment of a joint African-Arab force under UN auspices.[90] On the other hand, the UN secretariat and several Council members continued to resist owing to the concerns outlined earlier. In April 2007, the Secretary-General reported on the findings of the assessment mission mandated by Resolution 1744 (discussed earlier). He concluded that conditions necessary for a UN peace operation to be effective (in particular broad-based support for the transitional political process and the consent of major clans) were not in clearly place and that given a scenario of continuing instability and limited political progress, 'the deployment of United Nations personnel would not be possible or appropriate'.[91] The Secretary-General set out two scenarios that offered potential pathways to the Council. First, in the event that hostilities ceased and a political process was put in place, the conditions might become ripe for the deployment of a UN mission, although even in those circumstances any operation would face immense operational challenges. Second, if instability persisted and the political process continued to falter, the only viable intervention path for the Council was for it to authorize the deployment of a 'coalition of the willing' to undertake enforcement action. Although France subsequently offered to provide maritime support to protect the delivery of humanitarian supplies (Canada later performed a similar function for the World Food Program), there was little support among potential contributors for the idea of a coalition of the willing to conduct an enforcement operation.[92] In response, therefore, the Council accepted the Secretary-General's basic argument that certain conditions (especially a viable and inclusive political process and credible and enduring ceasefire) must be in place before the authorization of UN peacekeepers and that the focus should be placed on supporting AMISOM (though not to the extent that the mission be bankrolled from the regular UN budget) but, paying heed to those governments that wanted the UN to proceed with deployment, tasked the Secretary-General to conduct contingency planning for a potential operation – though without indicating that it believed a UN mission to be a viable option.[93]

In his contingency plan, set out in June 2007, the Secretary-General noted that any mission would face a number of major threats stemming from the approximately 50,000–70,000 clan militia and other armed groups operating in Somalia. Thus, even assuming that the conditions thought necessary for the deployment of a UN mission were in place (cessation of hostilities and formal consent of the major parties) the Secretary-General argued that any mission would need to be robust and highly mobile and include significant air and maritime components. In total, the Secretary-General estimated that the necessary size of the force would exceed 20,000 military personnel and a 'sizable and comprehensive' civilian component.[94] This assessment was not well received by the Council.

New impetus came with the appointment of Ahmedou Ould-Abdallah as Special Representative in September 2007. In his first report drafted by Ould-Abdallah, the Secretary-General stated more bluntly his assessment that 'the deployment of a United Nations peacekeeping operation cannot be considered a realistic and viable option'. Instead, he suggested that further consideration be given to the deployment of a (non-UN) multinational enforcement mission to improve security and pave the way for the complete withdrawal of Ethiopian forces.[95] For his part, Ould-Abdallah used his first briefing to the Council to argue that the UN's 'business as usual' approach had failed to improve the situation and that the Council should adopt a more proactive stance on both the political and security fronts. On the political front, he indicated his intention to play a role as mediator and with the support of key states in the region helped broker a political agreement (the 'Djibouti agreement', 9 June 2008) that included many (but not all) of the key factions.[96] At a press conference in Nairobi, he also suggested that the Security Council refer the situation in Somalia to the International Criminal Court (ICC).[97]

The Secretary-General's suggestion that the Council consider authorizing a non-UN enforcement mission was supported by both the TFG and AU, which renewed their call for the UN to take over peacekeeping duties and support AMISOM in the meantime.[98] As before, however, there was little support elsewhere for a multinational force or for the UN to provide direct financial assistance to the AU (on the grounds that it might set a precedent of regional arrangements expecting to be bankrolled by the UN) and although Council members were open to bilateral and multilateral arrangements being used to support AMISOM, no concrete proposals to this effect were brought forward.[99] On the question of finances, however, progress was made possible by a proposal that the Council establish a voluntary trust fund to support AMISOM.

The situation in Somalia continued to deteriorate in the first half of 2008, with the estimated number of displaced increasing to 700,000, an escalation of attacks on civilians and humanitarian workers, and renewed US bombing (3 March) of suspected al-Qaeda sites which, of course, further reduced the likelihood of any UN force being seen as impartial. At the request of the Security Council, the Secretary-General set out a roadmap identifying three steps towards the deployment of a UN peace operation. The roadmap represented something of a compromise between the different positions expressed by Council members but also exhibited the secretariat's reluctance to deepen the UN's engagement in Somalia, fearing that the organization could once again find itself deployed in Somalia without the mandate or means to succeed in an exceptionally difficult environment. The first step involved the establishment of a UN office, enhanced support for AMISOM including a deployment by a 'coalition of willing partners' to secure parts of the country, and the development of an agenda for political dialogue. Once the peace process was under way, the second step would involve moving the UN office to Mogadishu and establishing a timetable for Ethiopian withdrawal. The third step would be marked by the conclusion of a comprehensive political agreement among all the parties, a phased withdrawal of Ethiopian forces, and the deployment of an interim 8,000 strong force to complement AMISOM. Assuming that the peace agreement held, the security situation stabilized and the parties granted their consent, the final stage would see the deployment of a 30,000 strong, robustly mandated, UN peace operation.[100] A few days later, Ould-Abdullah followed up by renewing his calls for the deployment of a multinational force to assist AMISOM and the referral of Somalia to the ICC.[101]

The Secretary-General's approach broadly reflected the Council's wishes inasmuch as it acknowledged the need for the organization to play a role in the crisis but exhibited considerable caution. It was therefore welcomed by most members. Most agreed that the conditions were not ripe for the deployment of UN peacekeepers, but some privately expressed dissatisfaction that the Secretary-General had not presented the Council with a range of short-term options and scepticism about the merits of a non-UN stabilization force operating alongside AMISOM. To address these concerns, Ould-Abdullah subsequently added the possibility of simply rehatting AMISOM as a UN mission to the existing list of options (multinational force, UN mission).[102] Moreover, while the African members lamented that the UN had agreed to support the AU directly in Darfur but not in Somalia, three permanent members (France, US, Russia) expressed their opposition to using the UN budget to fund an AU operation.[103] Finally, differences remained as to whether the Council should clearly signal its intent to authorize a UN mission in the future (a position favoured by the US, China and African members) or whether it should maintain its focus on contingency planning (a position favoured by the Europeans, including Russia).[104]

The 'Djibouti agreement' reached between the TFG and the 'Alliance for the Re-Liberation of Somalia' in June 2008 generated renewed discussion of the peacekeeping options. Some of the non-African states that had pushed for a UN mission (especially the US) informally expressed disquiet about the Secretary-General's proposal for a large and robust mission comprising up to 30,000 troops, arguing that this sort of commitment was unfeasible and that the secretariat should have provided a range of options for a UN peace operation, including a smaller mission which would focus on specific regions (such as Mogadishu) and a more limited range of tasks (such as support for humanitarian agencies).[105] Of course, from the secretariat's perspective it was precisely this type of graduated response (relatively small missions with limited tasks deployed to volatile regions) that had failed in the 1990s. Its clear preference for a large and robust mission, in line with the recommendations brought forward by the Brahimi report, was meant to ensure that the UN had the capacity it needed to fulfil its mandated tasks. From the perspective of some of the Council members, however, the secretariat's plan was simply unrealistic given the UN's other commitments and they placed the onus back on the Secretary-General to deliver a plan that could be resourced.[106]

There was even discord within the UN secretariat about what to advise the Security Council. Ould-Abdullah, who had played a role in brokering the Djibouti agreement, argued that the Secretary-General should advise the Council to authorize a UN mission to support the agreement, maintaining that because it would be monitoring an agreement reached by the parties themselves the force would not need the resources previously recommended by the secretariat. A smaller force, he reckoned, was more likely to attract sufficient resources from Member States. The DPKO disagreed with this assessment and provided a detailed briefing to the Council in which it argued that the security situation remained extremely volatile because the Djibouti accord did not include the largest insurgent groups, the country was awash with weapons, and al-Shabaab had threatened to attack all foreign forces. As such, the DPKO argued, any force would need to be sufficiently large and robust to defend itself from concerted attack. Because UN peace operations were not well configured for this kind of task, the DPKO advised that the Council authorize a non-UN 'international stabilization force' of at least 8,000 troops to perform peace enforcement duties and facilitate the withdrawal of Ethiopian troops. This force would help create the conditions necessary to facilitate the deployment of a follow-on UN peace operation. The stabilization force, it argued, should be led by a strong lead-nation and be prepared and configured to conduct counter-insurgency operations. The Council accepted this recommendation and tasked the Secretary-General with developing a concept of operations for a stabilization force and to begin approaching potential troop contributors.[107] Of course, given that no government had expressed the remotest interest in playing the role of lead state, this exercise was never likely to produce a viable alternative to AMISOM. This reality encouraged states that supported the deployment of a new peacekeeping force (e.g. US and South Africa) to argue that a UN force was more likely to attract troops than a non-UN stabilization force because of the funding attached to the UN route.[108] Moreover, the differences between Ould-Abdullah's approach and that of the DPKO did little to create confidence in the Special Representative or the secretariat's approach more generally.[109] Nonetheless, as the Djibouti agreement unravelled towards the end of 2008, Council members became more accepting of the DPKO's view that in the absence of a durable peace negotiated and implemented by Somalis themselves, a robust stabilization force was a necessary precursor to any UN peace operation though the US and South Africa continued to argue that the UN route should be pursued if the stabilization force failed to materialize.[110] As France told the Council in December 2008, 'a conventional peacekeeping operation would not be realistic in Somalia today. There would have to be tens of thousands of troops equipped and trained in specific urban combat techniques, totally self sustaining, with very heavy military equipment'.[111]

As expected, the prospects for a stabilization force were quickly dashed because no government responded positively to the Secretary-General's request for a lead nation and other troop contributors. With the in-coming Obama administration thought to have a view more in line with the Europeans (in-coming Permanent Representative, Susan Rice, told a Senate Confirmation hearing that she was sceptical about the merits of deploying UN peacekeepers), the US launched a final effort to persuade the Council to authorize a UN peace operation. The AU signalled its clear support for the initiative by authorizing AMISOM for only a further three months to create an expectation that it would hand over to the UN. Once again though there was insufficient support in the Council and the UK submitted a competing draft resolution which omitted the UN option in favour of enhanced support for AMISOM. In the end, a compromise was brokered and Resolution 1863 (2009) expressed the Council's intention to review the establishment of a UN peace operation by June 2009, extended the UN's material support for AMISOM and established a trust fund for the AU mission.

Positive signs in Somalia at the beginning of 2009 seemed to lend support to the idea of deploying UN peacekeepers. At the end of January, Ethiopia completed its withdrawal. In addition one of the country's major divides, between the TFG and the Hawiye clan, was bridged by the appointment of Omar Abdirashi Ali Sharmarke, a prominent Hawiye who had indicated his intention to negotiate with al-Shabaab, as the prime minister. However, these positive moves – which Ould-Abdullah reckoned brought Somalia 'back from the brink' – were soon cancelled out. The insurgents established a new united front led by al-Shabaab, stepped up attacks on AMISOM, killing 11 Burundian peacekeepers on 22 February, and marshaled demonstrations led by clerics in Mogadishu demanding AMISOM's withdrawal. Meanwhile, the Council's decision to extend financial assistance to AMISOM met resistance from the General Assembly's Fifth (Budget) Committee which was already trying to finance an escalating peacekeeping budget, delaying the finalization of plans for support. A support package worth around $81 million, increased to $138 million in June 2009, was agreed and the Council also agreed to establish a UN office to marshal logistical and technical support for AMISOM (UNPOA). This remained less than half the total annual projected cost of AMISOM, with much of the rest funded bilaterally through the trust fund.[112]

After the flurry of activity in late 2008-early 2009, debate in the Council settled down into a familiar pattern. In March 2009, the Secretary-General reiterated his assessment that the conditions for a UN peace operation were not in place, identifying five necessary prerequisites: (1) the formation of an inclusive government; (2) effective operation of security forces in Mogadishu; (3) a credible ceasefire; (4) the consent of all the major parties to the deployment of UN peacekeepers; and (5) sufficient pledges of troops and equipment by Member States.[113] The head of the DPKO, Alain Le Roy, advised the Council that these conditions were not yet satisfied making a UN force inappropriate and noted that while some countries (Bangladesh, Indonesia, Pakistan and

Uruguay) had responded positively to the call for commitments of troops for the potential mission, this remained insufficient. The generally negative assessment was borne out in May 2009 when conflict erupted in Mogadishu between TFG forces and insurgents, with the government accusing Eritrea of supporting the rebels.[114] In light of these events, the Council's review of the UN option mandated by Resolution 1865 reaffirmed the Secretary-General's approach, with the new US administration dropping its predecessor's calls for a UN mission.[115] Although some members expressed dissatisfaction with this approach, complaining that it did little to improve the situation in Somalia, there was general recognition that there were no viable alternatives.[116] In September, a further 17 peacekeepers, including the deputy force commander, were killed in a suicide attack, strengthening the Council's reticence and prompting it to maintain its view that the conditions for UN peacekeeping were not in place and that in the absence of a viable alternative, the focus should be placed squarely on supporting AMISOM.

It is easy to see the Brahimi report's main recommendations for the Security Council at work in its deliberations on the crisis in Somalia. Learning that it works most effectively when it is united, Council members tried to find consensus wherever possible and both sides of the debate were open to compromises. The secretariat's advise to the Council emphasized the difficulties associated with mounting a peace operation in Somalia based upon a realistic (some would contend overly-pessimistic) analysis of the situation on the ground, a modest assessment of what a peace operation might be able to achieve, and an account of the resources likely to be made available. In considering the various options and the type of mandate that it might hand down, Council members and the UN secretariat paid careful attention to the tasks that peacekeepers would be asked to do and to the question of what resources they would need to accomplish those tasks given the conditions in Somalia. What all this suggests is that, at least in relation to this case, the way the Council does business has progressed significantly since the 1990s.

Most noticeably, the Council's reluctance to pursue stronger measures was driven primarily by prudential considerations, different interpretations of the facts on the ground, and beliefs about the likely consequences of different courses of action. Cautious Council members worried that without stable conditions, a viable peace process, the consent of the belligerents or an exit strategy, a conventional UN peace operation was unlikely to succeed. While there was some recognition that a robust non-UN enforcement operation could try to create more suitable conditions for UN peacekeeping, the likelihood of success was thought sufficiently low and potential costs sufficiently high to deter more detailed consideration. Calculations about high costs and limited payoffs no doubt also conspired to inhibit the emergence of a lead nation. This caution was almost uniformly echoed by the UN secretariat, and especially by the Secretary-General and DPKO. Given the unstable situation, the reluctance of member states to make a large commitment of troops to any potential mission, and the UN's previous experience in Somalia, the UN secretariat came to the view that a UN mission was unlikely to succeed and quite likely to prove costly.

In this context, what could an RtoP lens contribute? Clearly, absent a viable strategy for intervening to protect vulnerable populations (and recall it was the absence of a viable strategy rather than sovereignty concerns that prevented this), using RtoP as a catalyst for action would not have contributed much to the debate. However, an RtoP lens could have made two contributions to the Security Council's deliberations. First, it could have given the Council a clearer protection focus. Although protection issues were addressed, they were not central to the Council's work and none of the proposed peace operations had protection as a core role. This in itself is problematic given the importance of protection to the legitimacy of peace operations in general and the likelihood than any UN mission deployed to Somalia would be judged primarily on its record in civilian protection.[117] This issue aside, a protection focus would have encouraged the Council to deliberate on Ould-Abdallah's proposal that the matter be referred to the ICC and follow-up on its calls for the parties to comply with international humanitarian law with a plan for ensuring such compliance. Second, an RtoP lens could have encouraged the Council to play a more proactive role in the political process both within Somalia itself and in relation to neighbouring countries. While there was agreement that the political process was crucial, the Council was relatively happy to let Somalis work this out themselves with the assistance of the Special Representative. Moreover, while some Council members periodically complained about the destabilizing role played by some neighbouring states (especially Eritrea, but also Ethiopia), the Council did not try to shape the regional context by enforcing its own resolutions (e.g. the arms embargo) or coercing regional spoilers. The sense of urgency that an RtoP focus might have created could have encouraged the Council to be more proactive in relation to both Somali national politics and the regional context. Overall, therefore, what is suggested here is that the lessons from the 1990s and the Security Council's engagement with the crisis in Somalia after 2005 should direct our attention to measures aimed at strengthening the implementation of Council decisions rather than finessing the decision-making process itself, which has already transformed itself informally since the 1990s.

Strengthening implementation

Building on the lessons learned from the previous section, this section identifies two ways in which RtoP can contribute to strengthening the effectiveness of enforcement measures taken to halt genocide and mass atrocities and protect the intended victims. First, through its articulation of a continuum of measures incorporating political and diplomatic strategies alongside legal, economic and military options, RtoP points towards holistic strategies of engagement that can overcome the temptation to conceive complex problems in exclusively military terms.[118] Second, by turning attention to the protection of civilians from the four crimes, RtoP provides a stimulus for new thinking about the practicalities of protection, particularly in relation to the development of doctrine and training for the protection of civilians and the commitment of the troops and resources necessary to implement protection of civilians mandates. A third area, particularly important in the Somalia case, is the engagement of regional arrangements in enforcement activities and the strengthening of cooperation between regional arrangements and the UN Security Council. This was canvassed in the previous chapter.

Complex engagement: a continuum of measures

All too often, the question of military intervention is the first port of call in international debates about how to respond to massive humanitarian emergencies, irrespective of the viability or utility of the military option. At least one commentator lays the blame for this squarely at the door of RtoP.[119] Referring to the international response to the crisis in Darfur, Alex de Waal argued that RtoP contributed to a naïve obsession with the deployment of military forces without much serious thinking about what international forces would actually do once deployed or how, exactly, they would contribute to building stable peace in the troubled Sudanese province.[120] This line of thinking created 'wildly inflated' expectations of what UN troops could do – including disarming the *Janjaweed* and providing protection to both displaced populations and those returning home.[121] According to de Waal, 'many activists and some political leaders simply assumed that an international force could succeed in the Herculean task of providing physical protection to Darfurian civilians in the middle of continuing hostilities'.[122] In the crucial period between 2004 and 2006 international actors focused on four issues relating to the deployment of peacekeepers (who would command them? How many would be deployed? What would their mandate be? Who would pay?) and ignored much more important questions about the strategic purpose of the operation. This RtoP-inspired focus on military peacekeepers drew attention away from the political process, which – de Waal argued – was a necessary precursor for the deployment of military forces.

De Waal is right to argue that in the mindset of some diplomats and commentators there remains a pervasive connection between RtoP and military intervention. A clearer example of this mindset in action was the 2008 debate about the international humanitarian response to Cyclone Nargis in Myanmar/ Burma charted in Chapter 3.[123] In that case, wherever proposals about invoking RtoP were aired, the invocation was tied to the potential use of military force. The problem highlighted by both these cases seems to be that there is something inherently militaristic about RtoP that diverts attention away from non-military solutions. On closer inspection, however, this is a problem produced by serious misunderstandings about what RtoP says (and does not say) and its potential to harness a wide range of measures – military and non-military – to the prevention of genocide and mass atrocities and protection of populations from them. As I have argued throughout this book, as agreed by states at the

World Summit, the use of military intervention is only one part of one of the three pillars that comprise RtoP. The other elements – and especially the commitments to encourage and help states to fulfil their responsibility and use a range of non-coercive measures to prevent and protect vulnerable populations – have not attracted the attention they deserve and remain under-conceptualized. Moreover, it is important to reiterate that in some cases diplomats are less sanguine about what can be achieved through the deployment of force – the European position on Somalia recounted in the previous section being a particularly good example.

A comprehensive global policy agenda based on the mandate handed down by the General Assembly in 2005 would include a whole host of measures that could be mobilized in response to episodes of genocide and mass atrocities and would involve much more than simply a military solution. This includes, better early warning of genocide and mass atrocities and briefings for the UN's decision-makers (see Chapter 6); measures to help states build the necessary capacity to prevent these crimes (see Chapter 5); measures to improve international capacity to despatch teams of peace negotiators with adequate international support; measures to enhance human rights reporting and capacity building through the UN's Human Rights Council; measures to improve the deterrence capability of the International Criminal Court; a more systematic approach to implementing the action plan for the prevention of genocide; the use of peacekeepers as preventers; and a comprehensive system for implementing and monitoring targeted sanctions.[125] If it were implemented holistically in this manner, it is not difficult to see how an RtoP lens would help mitigate against the tendency to overemphasize the military option by situating the use of force within a broader spectrum of measures that should be employed in a coordinated fashion.

Operationalizing protection: doctrine and resources

Although decision-making in the Security Council can be slow and uncertain, a somewhat more urgent problem highlighted by the Somalia case and other notable recent cases such as Darfur, is the effective *implementation* of Council mandates. In relation to Somalia, neither the IGASOM nor AMISOM mandates were implemented in full and much of the debate in the Council hinged upon divergent expectations about the capacity of regional arrangements and the UN itself to implement mandates effectively. Given that little progress is likely in relation to the decision-making process itself, it would seem sensible to focus attention on how best to implement mandates that have a protection component. The second contribution that RtoP makes to thinking about enforcement, therefore, is to foreground the need for practical thinking about how international peacekeepers should go about protecting civilians and raise the profile of shortfalls in resources and capabilities. Although questions about legality, legitimacy and political will are important, the ultimate test in the direst of situations is whether international engagement succeeds in protecting vulnerable populations. Questions about the way a peace operation is organized, configured, tasked and equipped are just as important as broader political and legal questions when it comes to protecting vulnerable populations. It should be recalled that the UN's Independent Inquiry on the Genocide in Rwanda maintained that 'a force numbering 2,500' (UNAMIR's strength at the time of the genocide) should have been able to stop or at least limit massacres at the start of the genocide.[125] Despite this, the question of how best to protect civilians from genocide and mass atrocities has received relatively little attention when compared to questions of legitimacy and legality. Indeed, there is still no military doctrine that provides guidance on how peacekeepers should go about protecting vulnerable citizens. By foregrounding the protection of potential victims, RtoP provides important impetus for developing doctrine and translating lessons learned into action.

On the question of how to improve the effectiveness of deployed peace operations, the Brahimi report identified three core requirements. First, in order to avoid repeating the mistakes made in Rwanda, Bosnia, Angola, Somalia and elsewhere, the military component of a peace operation should be robust enough to defend itself effectively, 'confront the lingering forces of war and violence' and protect civilians under its care. 'Peacekeepers who witness violence against civilians', the Report found, 'should be presumed to be authorized to stop it' within their means.[126] The Report made it clear, however, that this presumed mandate needed to be balanced against the need to match mandate and means. Second, the Report recommended that UN peacekeepers be required to have basic skills and comply with 'best practices' common to all UN missions. Finally, this demand would be supported by a renewed emphasis on training for peacekeepers and senior civilian personnel.

The development of RtoP as an international principle has been accompanied by a transformation of the place of civilian protection in peace operations. Traditionally, it was thought that peacekeepers should remain impartial and neutral and not be proactive in the protection of civilians. Although peacekeeping operations sometimes contained human rights components, only very infrequently was the protection of civilians considered a core part of the peacekeeper's mandate.[127] The Security Council has begun to take heed of RtoP in its mandating of peace operations in two ways. Today's peace operations tend to be larger and therefore better able to protect civilians than their predecessors. The UN's missions in DRC, Sudan and Darfur are all mandated to comprise in excess of 20,000 peacekeepers. Furthermore, a combination of better coordination between the Security Council and troop contributing nations, the UN's standby forces arrangements, and closer cooperation between the UN and regional organizations has seen a progressive decline in the gap between the number of troops mandated by the Security Council and the number actually deployed – the slow deployment of UNAMID in Darfur notwithstanding. Despite progress in this area, it still takes 18 months on average to deploy a peace operation fully, with significant negative consequences for endangered civilians.

Moreover, the Security Council has begun to create mandates for the protection of civilians on a more frequent basis and has gradually relaxed the early restrictions it imposed on such mandates.[128] Typically, the Council has demonstrated a preference for limiting the scope of civilian protection mandates by attaching caveats. Examples of these limits can be found in the mandates for the missions in Sudan (UNMIS), Liberia (UNMIL) and Côte d'Ivoire (UNOCI). UNMIS was mandated 'to facilitate and coordinate, within its capabilities and in its areas of deployment, the voluntary return of refugees and internally displacement persons, and humanitarian assistance, *inter alia*, by helping to establish the necessary security'.[129] The civilian protection mandates handed down to UNMIL and UNOCI were identical.[130] By contrast, however, MONUC in the DRC was originally given a narrow civilian protection mandate which was gradually extended over time. MONUC was mandated to 'ensure the protection of civilians, including humanitarian personnel, under imminent threat of physical violence' without any limiting clause.[131] The UN's mission in Burundi was also given a wide protection mandate from the outset.[132]

Thanks in large part to the Security Council's interest in the protection of civilians (into which its reaffirmations of RtoP were incorporated) and the pioneering work of analysts such as Victoria Holt, we have a relatively comprehensive understanding of what the protection of civilians by peacekeepers entails in practice, though there remains little by way of doctrinal guidance.[133] In short, it entails 'coercive protection' – the positioning of military forces between the civilian population and those that threaten them.[134] This may involve military measures to defeat and eliminate armed groups that threaten civilians. Since 2002, for instance, the UN's Standing Rules of Engagement for peace operations have authorized the use of force 'to defend any civilian person who is in need of protection.[135] Sometimes, coercive protection may involve measures short of force such as erecting military barriers around civilian populations and the gradual removal of threats through negotiated (and sometimes coerced) disarmament.[136] In the absence of military doctrine, however, we have a much less clear understanding of how these tasks should be accomplished. The UN's capstone doctrine for peace operations (rebadged 'principles and guidelines' for political reasons) limited itself to simply observing that 'most . . . peacekeeping operations are now mandated by the Security Council to protect civilians under imminent threat' and noting that this task requires coordination with the UN's civilian agencies and NGOs'.[137] This raises difficult questions about the relative importance of civilian protection and other principles of peacekeeping such as consent, impartiality and minimum force.[138] Draft UN training modules insist that these other principles do not justify inactivity in the face of atrocities but do not provide guidance on how these concerns should be reconciled.[139] But for more detailed guidance we have to make do with learning lessons from current and past missions – at least for the time being.

One of the most important examples of coercive protection was the adoption of a much more robust posture by MONUC eastern DRC. In 2005, MONUC began a process of compulsory disarmament in Ituri province around Bunia, disarming around 15,000 combatants by June. Some groups opposed forcible disarmament and in February 2005, fighters from the Nationalist and Integrationist Front (FNI) attacked and killed nine Bangladeshi peacekeepers. In response, Nepalese, Pakistani and South African peacekeepers, supported by Indian attack helicopters, pursued the FNI, killed between 50 and 60 belligerents and neutralizing their threat to civilians.[140] For its part, the Security Council further strengthened MONUC's mandate and explicitly authorized the conducting of 'cordon-and-search' operations against 'illegal armed groups' thought to the threatening the civilian population.[141]

MONUC's Pakistani contingent also adopted a robust civilian protection posture in South Kivu. Alongside Guatemalan special forces, the Pakistanis rooted out Hutu *Forces Démocratiques de Libération du Rwanda* (FDLR) militia who were associated with the 1994 Rwandan genocide and subsequent abuse of civilians in the DRC. In October 2005, MONUC issued a disarmament ultimatum to FDLR and when the rebels refused to cooperate, used helicopter gunships to destroy between 13 and 16 camps. Although the mission succeeded in weakening the FDLR and restricting its freedom of movement it neither destroyed the militia nor forced them to disarm.[142] As well as coercing the perpetrators of attacks on the civilian population, the Pakistanis also used innovative methods to protect civilians. For example, it organized a community watch in villages in Walungu territory and taught them to bang pots and blow whistles when danger was imminent. Pakistani peacekeepers were kept on high alert in the vicinity to respond to such warnings.

UN peacekeepers have therefore begun to implement RtoP by incorporating the protection of civilians into their core business. To date, while the Security Council hands down protection of civilians mandate with heightened regularity and fewer restrictions, implementation has largely relied on improvisation in the field, as the example of MONUC in Ituri province demonstrates. Despite the evident limitations of this approach, the focus on the civilian protection has contributed to the marked decline in the overall number of civilians killed in sub-Saharan African wars in the past five years.[143] RtoP can make an important contribution to the further development of civilian protection by providing the core rationale for such operations, marshalling the political will necessary to establish and equip peace operations with civilian protection mandates, and emphasizing the need for long-term and multidimensional approaches to civilian protection which incorporate the prevention of genocide, war crimes, crimes against humanity and ethnic cleansing and the rebuilding of states and societies afterwards.

This expansion in the role of peace operations gives rise to significant additional problems relating to resources, however. In the DRC, Sudan (both UNAMID and UNMIS) and Chad in particular, deployed peace operations lack the resources they need to implement their robust protection mandates.

A potential new mission in Somalia, which would need to be both large and robust, would place an additional heavy burden on the UN and it is thought unlikely that it would be able to properly staff such a mission. The root of the problem is that – despite the fact that peace operations are arguably the most important tool for exercising RtoP in the midst of a major crisis – states from the developing world that express varying levels of support for RtoP have been providing an increasingly large proportion of the UN's peacekeepers, while many of RtoP's most vocal supporters in the global north actually reduce their contribution.[144] Among the top ten contributors in the past few years are four states in Asia (Pakistan, Bangladesh, India, Nepal), four states in Africa (Nigeria, Ghana, Ethiopia and Kenya), and one each from the Middle East (Jordan) and South America (Uruguay).[145] Of these ten, the largest contributor (Pakistan) was one of the handful of states that expressed scepticism about RtoP in 2009, three others (India, Nepal, Ethiopia) had taken a somewhat sceptical line before 2009 and only three had been enthusiastic supporters of the principle (Bangladesh, Nigeria and Ghana). Over the same time period, Western governments most associated with supporting RtoP have significantly reduced the numbers of troops they contribute to UN peace operations.

According to UN figures, as of 31 December 2007, the UN was deploying 84,309 military and police personnel provided by 119 states. The main suppliers continued to be Pakistan, Bangladesh and India, each contributing over 9,000 personnel, followed by Nepal, Jordan and Ghana with about 3,500 each, and then Nigeria, Uruguay and Italy with about 2,500 each. The Permanent Five members of the Security Council were ranked 11th (France, 1,944), 13th (China, 1,824), 38th (UK, 362), 42nd (US, 316, of which only 8 were troops), and 43rd (Russia, 293). In addition, many of the most outspoken advocates of RtoP had virtually stopped contributing troops to UN operations, confining their contributions instead to police and/or military observers. For example, Canada provided only 15 troops, Norway 11, Australia 9, Sweden 3, and New Zealand just 1.

Although the West's contribution to contemporary UN peace operations is relatively small and shrinking, this does not mean it has abandoned all forms of peacekeeping. Instead, it has placed more of its personnel in so-called 'hybrid missions' involving the UN but where the Western troop contribution sits outside UN command and control structures and contributions outside the UN system altogether including unauthorized peace operations conducted with or without the consent of the host state, and financial and technical support for peace operations conducted by non-Western regional organizations such as the African Union and ECOWAS.[146] Although the West could make a significant contribution by simply increasing the number of troops and resources it provides to UN peace operations, we need to recognize that such an expanded commitment is unlikely in the short or medium term. A more profitable route therefore may be to strengthen cooperation between the UN, regional arrangements, and Western governments to allow peace operations to make more rapid use of flexible arrangements in order to generate the forces they need at the time for which they are needed. This involves recognizing that Western governments are unlikely to make large contributions of troops for protracted periods and to place those forces under UN command, but that such countries could fulfil smaller niche roles (such as air support, logistics etc.) and provide additional enforcement capacity when required (for example, around elections or to neutralize specific spoiler groups etc.). To achieve this, and to manage complex missions in a timely and efficient fashion, a more flexible command structure would need to be established that reflected the particularities of each mission.

Conclusion

There are three main reasons for thinking that the enforcement aspect of RtoP is not best advanced by focusing on decision-making in the Security Council. First, Council members are unlikely to agree to formal constraints on their room for manoeuvre (such as a code of conduct on the veto and criteria to guide decision-making) and campaigning for them to do so expends political capital that is more productively spent elsewhere. Second, even if criteria were agreed, the indeterminacy of both RtoP itself and the applicability of the criteria to a specific case make it unlikely that they would alter the positions taken by Council members, generate political will where non existed, or manufacture consensus. Third, as the detailed example of Somalia demonstrates, Council decision-making is more complex than a simple calculation of whether or not to deploy troops.

A number of critical issues emerged through examination of the lessons learned from the 1990s and the Security Council's response to the crisis in Somalia. In particular, in the case of Somalia decision-making was heavily influenced by judgments about the expected capacity of a peace operation to improve the situation on the ground, given the absence of a viable political process and an unstable security environment. European members of the Council opposed IGASOM and were reluctant to endorse a UN mission not because they were animated by sovereignty concerns, but because they judged that given the conditions, the absence of viable proposals to implement a mandate backed by a commitment from potential troop contributors made it unlikely that a deployment would have a positive effect. Given this, I suggested that efforts to strengthen the world's response to genocide and mass atrocities should focus more on the effective implementation of the Council's decisions and identified two specific areas. First, using an RtoP lens to shed light on the broad continuum of measures that the Council could use and encouraging the Council to make use of the full range of measures at its disposal. Second, more attention needs to be paid to the implementation of protection of civilians mandates in peace operations. Most especially, there is a need to develop doctrine and training on protection and to consider ways of ensuring that member states provide the necessary military capabilities. Between them, these measures would ensure that when the Council decided to act, its decisions could be properly implemented. Moreover, if the case of Somalia is anything to go by, these measures might strengthen the will to intervene to protect endangered populations because the Council is more likely to authorize protection missions if it is convinced that such missions are viable and can be used to good effect.

Conclusion

The emergence of the RtoP represents an important watershed in world politics. For the first time, in 2005, heads of state and government declared that all states have a responsibility to protect their own populations from genocide, war crimes, ethnic cleansing and crimes against humanity, that they had a duty to assist one another in this endeavour and that should an individual state manifestly fail to exercise its responsibility, the international community had a responsibility to step in. In so doing, states put a number of long-standing debates about sovereignty, human rights, and armed intervention to bed. Most notably, abusive governments can no longer claim that sovereignty shields them from opprobrium and intervention. Instead, sovereignty demands that they protect their populations from genocide and mass atrocities. Nor can bystanders any longer claim that they have no reason to assist in the prevention of mass atrocities or to step in to protect populations in peril when needed. These basic ideas, unequivocally stated in the 2005 World Summit Outcome Document, have quickly gained traction and have been unanimously reaffirmed twice by the UN Security Council and again by the General Assembly. The challenge now, governments agreed in 2009, is not to renegotiate the principle but to translate its ambitions into tangible action. RtoP's ultimate test is not the number of resolutions that endorse it, but the number of graveyards that stand empty because tragedy was averted.

With that in mind, this book has focused on RtoP in practice during its first five years. We have reviewed debates about the scope, content and implementation of the principle and its use in relation to over a dozen crises from Conakry to Colombo. We have examined claims that RtoP causes additional genocide violence, and assessed different ways of understanding its function. We have evaluated its status as a norm and considered its effectiveness in practice. And we have studied in detail four of the most pressing implementation issues raised by member states at the 2009 General Assembly debate on RtoP. Whatever one thinks of RtoP and the arguments I have presented here, one cannot claim that the principle is irrelevant or that is has not travelled a great distance in a short space of time.

By now, readers will be familiar with my argument about the nature and scope of RtoP, how it is used to best effect, and policy priorities moving forward.

I will briefly restate this here before revisiting the three explanations for the international community's dismal track record on preventing and responding to genocide and mass atrocities that I canvassed in the introduction.

RtoP is a commitment by governments to protect their populations from four crimes (genocide, war crimes, ethnic cleansing and crimes against humanity), a commitment by the international community to assist governments to exercise their responsibility, and an international commitment to take timely and decisive action, in accordance with the UN Charter, should a government manifestly fail to protect its populations. As agreed by states, RtoP relates only to the four crimes, it does not permit armed intervention without UN Security Council authorization, nor does it contain criteria to guide decision-making on the use of force, demand formal restraints on the use of the veto powers in the Security Council, or contain distinct responsibilities to prevent, react and rebuild. As agreed by states, RtoP is universal and enduring – it applies to all states, all of the time. As such, we should ask not whether RtoP applies to a given situation, but how it is best exercised. And RtoP does not limit international activism to the period immediately prior to mass atrocities, but demands a new politics that prioritizes prevention. I would challenge those who disagree to indicate where paragraphs 138–40 of the World Summit Outcome Document indicate a different vision. Of course, there are many other visions of what RtoP constitutes beyond what states have actually agreed to. Many analysts continue to refer to the ICISS report as the definitive text; others call for a wider interpretation of the principle. These positions are wholly legitimate, but it is important to distinguish what states have actually agreed and what they have not agreed, and to be open about the fact that proponents of alternative visions are, in essence, calling for RtoP's revision. My view, like that of the UN Secretary-General and most member states, is that it is far better – from the point of view of protecting people from mass atrocities – to focus on implementing what states have actually agreed, than on trying to refine and renegotiate that agreement.

With that in mind, I noted that while in practice there is no evidence to support the view that RtoP causes mass violence that would not otherwise occur, there is also little evidence to support the view that the principle acts as a *catalyst* for robust international responses, especially armed intervention, in the face of mass atrocities (see Chapter 4). But while it has failed to act as a catalyst for international action during 'loud emergencies' such as Darfur or quieter but no less significant ones such as Somalia, RtoPs has made a significant contribution in three key areas. First, it has played a useful role in diplomatic discourse, as international actors remind political leaders of their responsibilities. Second, it has served as a 'lens' to guide policy planning and decision-making, placing the focus for international engagement squarely on the protection of populations from the four crimes. In this mode, RtoP has encouraged governments and international civil servants to think holistically about protection issues. It has also brought to light a range of policy initiatives that might strengthen the capacity of states, local communities, regional arrangements and global institutions to prevent genocide and mass atrocities and better protect the victims. Third, it has generated political impetus to implement already existing legal commitments and policy agendas such as early warning, capacity building, the protection of civilians, and the prevention of armed conflict. Although perhaps not as dramatic as grandstanding (and almost always unanswered) calls for armed intervention, these three contributions have the potential to reduce the frequency of mass killing and strengthen the ability of local communities, states, and international institutions to protect people from harm when prevention fails. Perhaps the central claim of this book is that in order to realize RtoP's potential, we need to pay careful attention to its translation into practice, ensuring that value is added to current activities while preserving global consensus.

In the introduction, I suggested that the international community's poor track record when it comes to preventing mass atrocities and protecting the victims could be largely attributed to three factors: the privileging of sovereigns' rights over peoples' rights, the reluctance of governments to commit resources and people to these goals, and the inherent complexity of preventing and responding effectively to mass atrocities. It should be clear by now that I think that RtoP has already made some progress in relation to each of these (though some more than others) and that it carries the potential for further significant change.

By imbuing sovereignty with responsibilities, RtoP has recast the relationship between sovereigns' rights and peoples' rights by making the former contingent on the latter. Governments can no longer subject their populations to massive abuse without attracting international criticism, engagement and possibly coercion. Importantly, this is not an imposition on sovereignty imposed by the West on the rest, but a shared agreement among sovereigns, freely entered into. The most obvious early affect of this recalibration of sovereigns' rights and peoples' rights has been a shift in the manner of international engagement with humanitarian crises. Although some governments – most notably Sudan and Sri Lanka – have from time to time argued that domestic affairs should not be a matter of international concern, such arguments have not received much favour. Typically, where there is little doubt about the threat of mass atrocities, international engagement is framed more around the question of how best to respond rather than whether or not a response is legitimate. However, where doubts persist about the actual or impending commission of mass atrocities, as for example in the cases Georgia, Gaza and Sri Lanka, international debates do still focus on whether it is appropriate and legitimate for the international community to get involved. Of course, these debates are not easily resolved and states continue to accord different weight to sovereign rights, limiting the scope of what they understand to be legitimate international action in any given case. But if we compare contemporary debates (see Chapters 3 and 8) with those of a decade ago, which were much more concerned about the legitimacy of any form of engagement, seeing it as a potential sleight against sovereignty, it is clear to see the change in focus. In short, RtoP makes it almost impossible for states to legitimately reject international engagement when mass atrocities are occurring or are imminently apprehended. It also makes it more difficult for states to legitimize inaction by referring to sovereign rights.

RtoP has not yet significantly impacted on the willingness of governments to contribute resources and people to preventing mass atrocities and protecting the victims. As I observed in Chapter 2, there has been no palpable strengthening of international commitment in the face of atrocities in Darfur, the DRC, and Somalia. This, I suggested, was due mainly to the indeterminacy of RtoP's third pillar, which weakens its compliance-pull by making it unclear what, precisely, the principle requires of third parties (see Chapter 4). Some positive changes have been evident, though it is difficult to know RtoP's precise role in bringing them about. The most significant has come in the field of preventive diplomacy. In Guinea, Kenya, Myanmar and Sri Lanka, the perceived threat of mass atrocities prompted regional arrangements, neighbouring governments, UN officials and/or the Security Council to implore political leaders to abide by their responsibilities, refrain from committing atrocities and cooperate with the international community. Compliance with these demands was patchy, but these diplomatic efforts helped prevent the worst of what was feared. Of course, as with all preventive action, we cannot know the extent to which it was these diplomatic efforts that steered actors away from atrocities. Nor do we know whether international actors would have stepped up their engagement had diplomacy failed – indications from each of these cases were not encouraging on that score, suggesting clear limits for the time being. When evaluating RtoP's track record thus far, however, we need to bear in mind that it remains an abstract principle that is waiting to be implementing. It has not yet been translated into institutional reform, tangible capacities, habitual behaviour and new doctrines. Some of the key aspects of the implementation agenda discussed in the previous chapters should impact directly on the willingness of governments to contribute what is needed to prevent mass atrocities and protect the intended victims. Most notably, perhaps, should the UN succeed in developing an early warning capacity capable of sounding credible and timely alarms (see Chapter 6), it may be more difficult for states to refuse to provide the resources needed to save lives. Difficult, but not impossible. States will always be able to claim that prudential considerations preclude decisive action and material contributions.

This brings us to the third impediment to decisive international engagement – the difficulty of knowing what is best in any given situation. Even given the best of intentions, there is no easy way of knowing the best course of action when it comes to effectively preventing or responding to mass atrocities. As Chapter 5 made clear, we have a reasonably good idea of the factors that increase the risk of mass atrocities, but it is very difficult to predict precisely when and where they will erupt and the exact configuration of local and global factors that will propel a particular episode. Likewise, as we saw in Chapter 8 in relation to Somalia, there are often likely to be genuine disagreements about the best course of action when mass atrocities are committed. However, RtoP helps in at least three important ways. First, it adds fresh impetus to efforts to reduce the overall risk of mass atrocities (see Chapter 5), which should reduce the frequency of episodes. We do not need to know precisely when and where atrocities will happen to take steps to reduce the overall risk of atrocities – Chapter 5 identified two major areas where international efforts might reduce overall risk. Second, a system of early warning, which is a core component of RtoP, should identify potential crises before they escalate, creating an important new window of opportunity for preventive action. Third, using RtoP as a 'lens' through which to view crises, one which places the protection of populations from four specific crimes at its core, helps illuminate the sorts of activities and capacities that might be needed and drive the development of coherent protection strategies. In Chapter 7, I examined some of the capacities that regional arrangements might contribute and in Chapter 8, I looked at how strengthening protection doctrine and training, and developing innovative approaches to force generation and management issues, might improve the ability of peace operations to protect civilians from harm. This is only a small part of the protection agenda that RtoP helps bring to the fore. By developing these capacities, actors present decision-makers with a broader range of viable policy options, increasing the potential for solutions to be tailored to individual crises.

When it comes to implementing the RtoP, therefore, we are just at the very beginning of a long and winding road. To reach the destination, incremental progress is needed. The UN Secretary-General's 2009 report sets out a blueprint for implementation and identifies the important first steps. But progress needs to be cautious and measured in order to preserve the principle's greatest asset – the global consensus that underpins it. At the risk of pushing the metaphor too far, to proceed without due regard to the maintenance of this consensus would amount to accelerating too sharply, driving the RtoP principle off the road. If both consensus and forward momentum can be preserved, however, progress can be made towards a world that prevents genocide and mass atrocities and protects the intended victims habitually.

Notes

Introduction

1 Gary J. Bass, *Freedom's Battle: The Origins of Humanitarian Intervention* (London: Alfred Knopf, 2008). The Responsibility to Protect refers specifically to the crimes of genocide, war crimes, ethnic cleansing and crimes against humanity. I switch between writing them out in full and using the shorthand 'genocide and mass atrocities', 'mass atrocities' and 'mass killing'. In using each of the terms I am referring to the four RtoP crimes, unless otherwise stated.

2 Ernest R. May, *Imperial Democracy: The Emergence of America as a Great Power* (New York: Imprint Publications, 1961), p. 127.

3 The idea of an 'overlapping consensus' is based on John Rawls' insight that different ethical traditions and cultures can agree on moral principles, though arriving at those principles in different ways. See John Rawls, *Political Liberalism* (New York: Columbia University Press, 1993), pp. 33–72 and Simon Caney, *Justice Beyond Borders: A Global Political Theory* (Oxford: Oxford University Press, 2005), p. 87.

4 For instance, see Vesselin Popovski, Gregory M. Reichberg and Nicholas Turner (eds), *World Religions and Norms of War* (Tokyo: United Nations University Press, 2009).

5 E.g. Philip Cunliffe (ed.), *Critical Perspectives on the Responsibility to Protect* (London: Routledge, 2010).

6 There is a relatively large literature which holds that mass atrocities appear rational from the point of view of the perpetrator. See for example, Peter du Preez, *Genocide: The Psychology of Mass Murder* (London: Boyars/Bowedean, 1994).

7 Nicholas J. Wheeler, *Saving Strangers: Humanitarian Intervention in International Society* (Oxford: Oxford University Press, 2000), pp. 90–1.

8 Simon Chesterman, *Just War or Just Peace? Humanitarian Intervention and International Law* (Oxford: Oxford University Press, 2001), p. 80.

9 S/PV.4988, 11 June 2004, p. 4.

10 S/PV.5158, 31 March 2005. The US ultimately abstained on this issue.

11 Chesterman, *Just War or Just Peace?*, p. 231.

12 *Report of the Independent Inquiry into the Actions of the United Nations During the 1994 Genocide in Rwanda*, 12 December 1999, p. 1.

13 Alex de Waal, 'No Such Thing as Humanitarian Intervention: Why We Need to Rethink How to Realize the "Responsibility to Protect" in Wartime', *Harvard International Review*, 2007.

14 See Alex J. Bellamy, *Responsibility to Protect: The Global Effort to End Mass Atrocities* (London: Polity, 2009) and Gareth Evans, *Responsibility to Protect: Ending Mass Atrocity Crimes Once and For All* (Washington, DC: Brookings Institution, 2008).

15 I have addressed some of these issues elsewhere. See Alex J. Bellamy, *Responsibility to Protect*.

1   From idea to norm

1 RtoP relates to genocide, war crimes, ethnic cleansing and crimes against humanity. I sometimes use the labels 'genocide and mass atrocities' and 'mass atrocities' as shorthand for these crimes.

2 Conor Foley, for example, that the ICISS report's recommendations about the Security Council 'were largely ignored' when the UN came endorse RtoP. See Conor Foley, *The Thin Blue Line: How Humanitarianism Went to War* (London: Verso, 2008), p. 158. Gareth Evans disputes this view and argues that RtoP survived the process 'in tact'. Evans argues that the agreed text 'differs little from all the previous formulations in the ICISS, High Level Panel, and secretary-general's reports', seemingly ignoring the major differences between these texts and then goes on to ignore the fact that the world summit rejected the centrepiece of all these formulations, the criteria for the use of force and restraints on the veto. See Gareth Evans, *The Responsibility to Protect: Ending Mass Atrocity Crimes Once and For All* (Washington, DC: The Brookings Institution, 2008), p. 47.

3 As such, we cover similar terrain to that traversed by Ramesh Thakur and Thomas G. Weiss, 'RtoP: From Idea to Norm, and Action?', *Global Responsibility to Protect*, 1(1), 2009, pp. 22–53.

4 Annan, 'Two Concepts of Sovereignty', p. 1.

5 Lynn Hunt, *Inventing Human Rights: A History* (London: W. W. Norton and Co., 2007), p. 20.

6 Thomas G. Weiss and David A. Korn, *Internal Displacement: Conceptualization and its Consequences* (New York: Routledge, 2006), pp. 71–3.

7 Thomas G. Weiss, *Humanitarian Intervention: Ideas in Action* (Cambridge: Polity, 2007), p. 90.

8 Francis M. Deng, 'The Impact of State Failure on Migration', *Mediterranean Quarterly*, Fall 2004, p. 18.

9 Deng, 'Impact of State Failure on Migration', p. 20.

10 Francis M. Deng, 'Divided Nations: The Paradox of National Protection', *The Annals of the American Academy of Political and Social Science*, 603, January 2006, p. 218.

11 Roberta Cohen and Francis M. Deng, *Masses in Flight: The Global Crisis of Internal Displacement* (Washington, DC: The Brookings Institution, 1998), p. 275.

12 Deng, 'Impact of State Failure on Migration', p. 20.

13 Francis M. Deng, Sadikiel Kimaro, Terrence Lyons, Donald Rothchild and I. William Zartman, *Sovereignty as Responsibility: Conflict Management in Africa* (Washington, DC: The Brookings Institution, 1996), p. 1.

14 Deng *et al.*, *Sovereignty as Responsibility*, p. 28.

15 See Roberta Cohen, 'The Guiding Principles on Internal Displacement: An Innovation in International Standard Setting', *Global Governance*, 10(3), 2004 and Roberta Cohen, 'Developing an International System for Internally Displaced Persons', *International Studies Perspectives*, 7(1), 2006.

16 Principles 3 and 25 of the Guiding Principles on Internal Displacement. For a detailed explanation and commentary see Walter Kalin, 'Guiding Principles on Internal Displacement: Annotations', *American Society of International Law Studies in Transnational Legal Policy*, 32, 2000.

17 Cohen, 'Guiding Principles', p. 470.

18 Weiss and Korn, *Internal Displacement*, pp. 74–5.

19 See for instance, Bruce Jones, Carlos Pascual and Stephen John Stedman, *Power and Responsibility: Building International Order in an era of Transnational Threats* (Washington, DC: Brookings Institution, 2009).

20 Richard N. Haass, 'Defining US Foreign Policy in a Post-Post-Cold War World', the 2002 Arthur Ross Lecture, 22 April 2002.

21 Stewart Patrick, 'The Role of the US Government in Humanitarian Intervention', 5 April 2004, cited in Stuart Elden, 'Contingent Sovereignty, Territorial Integrity and the Sanctity of Borders', *SAIS Review*, 26(1), 2006, p. 15.

22 Department of Defense, *The National Defense Strategy of The United States of America*, March 2005.

23 See Bellamy, 'Responsibility to Protect or Trojan Horse?'; and Gareth Evans, 'When is it Right to Fight?', *Survival*, 46(3), 2004, pp. 59–82.

24 Tony Blair, 'Doctrine of the International Community', speech to the Economic Club of Chicago, Hilton Hotel, Chicago, 22 April 1999.

25 This is discussed in detail in Alex J. Bellamy, 'Responsibility to Protect or Trojan Horse? The Crisis in Darfur and Humanitarian Intervention after Iraq', *Ethics and International Affairs*, 19(2), 2005, pp. 31–54.

26 UN Commission on Human Rights, *Responses of Governments and Agencies to the Report of the UN Special Representative for Internally Displaced Persons*, E/CN.4/1993/SR.40, 1993.

27 E/CN.4/1993/SR.40, 1993.

28 Paul D. Williams, 'The "Responsibility to Protect", Norm Localization, and African International Society', *Global Responsibility to Protect*, 1(3), 2009, p. 397. The point about RtoP's African origins was put by Edward C. Luck, Special Adviser to the UN Secretary-General at the Arria Formula Meeting on the Responsibility to Protect, 1 December 2008, p. 1.

29 Paul D. Williams, 'From Non-Intervention to Non-Indifference: The Origins and Development of the African Union's Security Culture', *African Affairs*, 106 (423), 2007, pp. 253–79.

30 See Ben Kioko, 'The Right of Interference Under the African Union's Constitutive Act: From Non-Interference to Non-Intervention', *International Review of the Red Cross*, 85(6), 2003, p. 852.

31 Declaration of African Heads of State and Governments, 2002 – Assembly/AU. Decl. 1 (I), 10 July.

32 See Katharina P. Coleman, *International Organisations and Peace Enforcement: The Politics of International Legitimacy* (Cambridge: Cambridge University Press, 2007), pp. 73–115.

33 Coleman, *International Organisations*, pp. 116–59.

34 Kioko, 'The Right of Intervention', p. 817.

35 Kwasi Aning and Samuel Atuobi, 'Responsibility to Protect in Africa: An Analysis of the African Union's Peace and Security Architecture', *Global Responsibility to Protect*, 1(1), 2009, p. 113.

36 Williams, 'The "Responsibility to Protect"', p. 397.

37 See Greg Puley, 'The Responsibility to Protect: East, West and Southern African Perspectives on Preventing and Responding to Humanitarian Crises', Project Ploughshares working paper, no. 5, September 2005, p. 4.

38 Kofi Annan, 'Annual Report of the Secretary-General to the General Assembly', 20 September 1999.

39 Annan, 'Annual Report'.

40 Lloyd Axworthy, *Navigating a New World: Canada's Global Future* (Toronto: Alfred A. Knopf, 2003), p. 191.

41 Jennifer Bond and Laurel Sherret, *A Sight for Sore Eyes: Bringing Gender Vision to the Responsibility to Protect Framework*, United Nations International Research and Training Institute for the Advancement of Women, March 2006.

42 Kofi Annan, 'The Responsibility to Protect', address to the International Peace Academy, 15 February 2002, UN press release SG/SM/8125.

43 ICISS, *Responsibility to Protect*, p. xi.

44 ICISS, *Responsibility to Protect*, p. 21.

45 ICISS, *Responsibility to Protect*, pp. 21–2.
46 ICISS, *Responsibility to Protect*, p. 23.
47 ICISS, *Responsibility to Protect*, p. 25.
48 ICISS, *Responsibility to Protect*, p. 26.
49 ICISS, *Responsibility to Protect*, p. 32.
50 ICISS, *Responsibility to Protect*, p. 49.
51 ICISS, *Responsibility to Protect*, pp. 53–5.
52 ICISS, *Responsibility to Protect*, pp. xii–xiii.
53 ICISS, *Responsibility to Protect*, p. xii.
54 ICISS, *Responsibility to Protect*, p. 39.
55 ICISS, *Responsibility to Protect*, p. 40.
56 ICISS, *Responsibility to Protect*, p. 42.
57 Anthony Lewis, 'The Challenge of Global Justice Now', *Dædalus*, 132(1), 2003, p. 8.
58 Weiss, *Humanitarian Intervention*, p. 104.
59 Thomas Weiss, email to the author, 31 October 2007.
60 Thomas Weiss, 'The Sunset of Humanitarian Intervention? The Responsibility to Protect in a Unipolar Era', *Security Dialogue*, 35(2), 2004, pp. 135–53 and Michael Byers, 'High Ground Lost on UN's Responsibility to Protect', *Winnipeg Free Press*, 18 September 2005, p. B3.
61 Weiss, 'The Sunset of Humanitarian Intervention?', p. 139.
62 Weiss, 'The Sunset of Humanitarian Intervention?', p. 140.
63 David Chandler, '*The Responsibility to Protect:* Imposing the Liberal Peace', in Alex J. Bellamy and Paul D. Williams (eds), *Peace Operations and Global Order* (London: Routledge, 2005), pp. 59–82.
64 Chandler, 'Responsibility to Protect', p. 67.
65 Aidan Hehir offers a useful summary of these problems. Aidan Hehir, *Humanitarian Intervention: An Introduction* (Basingstoke: Palgrave, 2010), pp. 121–5.
66 On the centrality of prevention see Responsibility to Protect, p. xi and Ramesh Thakur, *The United Nations, Peace and Security: From Collective Security to the Responsibility to Protect* (Cambridge: Cambridge University Press, 2006), p. 257.
67 Nicholas J. Wheeler, 'A Victory for Common Humanity? The Responsibility to Protect after the 2005 World Summit', paper presented to a conference on 'The UN at Sixty: Celebration or Wake?', University of Toronto, 6–7 October 2005, p. 4.
68 The most detailed insiders' account of the panel's work, including its discussion of RtoP is provided by David Hannay, *New World Disorder: The UN After the Cold War – An Insider's View* (London: I. B. Tauris, 2008), pp. 211–22.
69 UN High Level Panel on Threats, Challenges and Change, *A More Secure World: Our Shared Responsibility*, A/59/565, 2 December 2004, para. 203.
70 HLP, *A More Secure World*, paras 203–7.
71 HLP, *A More Secure World*, para. 257.
72 Kofi Annan, 'In Larger Freedom: Towards Development, Security and Human Rights for all', A/59/2005, 21 March 2005.
73 Annan, 'In Larger Freedom', paras 135, 126.
74 On the initial scepticism of permanent members of the Security Council towards the RtoP see Jennifer M. Welsh, 'Conclusion: Humanitarian Intervention after 11 September', in Jennifer M. Welsh (ed.), *Humanitarian Intervention and International Relations* (Oxford: Oxford University Press, 2004), pp. 179–80.
75 The story and background to these negotiations are set out in detail in Alex J. Bellamy, *Responsibility to Protect: The Global Effort to end Mass Atrocities* (Cambridge: Polity, 2009), ch. 3.

76 E.g. see Statement by Ambassador Stafford Neil, Permanent Representative of Jamaica to the United Nations, Chairman of the Group of 77 on Cluster 1 (Freedom from Want) of the Secretary-General's Report *In Larger Freedom: Towards Development, Security and Human Rights for All*, New York, 25 April 2005.

77 Revised Draft Outcome Document (10 August 2005).

78 Pace and Deller, 'Preventing Future Genocides', p. 28.

79 Memo from Allan Rock to the author, 12 November 2007.

80 Letter from John R. Bolton.

81 Traub, *Best Intentions*, p. 373 and Stephen John Stedman, 'UN Transformation in an Era of Soft Power Balancing', *International Affairs*, 83(5), 2007, p. 940.

82 Traub, *Best Intentions*, p. 373

83 Despite having endorsed the principle two months earlier. See 'Position Paper of the People's Republic of China on the United Nations Reforms', 8 June 2005, p. 12.

84 See Yevgeny Primakov, 'UN Process, not Humanitarian Intervention, is World's Best Hope', *New Perspectives Quarterly*, 2 September 2004.

85 Statement by the Chairman of the Coordinating Bureau [Malaysia] of the Non-Aligned Movement on Behalf of the Non-Aligned Movement at the Informal Meeting of the Plenary of the General Assembly Concerning the Draft Outcome Document of the High-Level Plenary Meeting of the General Assembly Delivered by H. E. Ambassador Radzi Rahman, Charge's D'Affaires A. I. Of the Permanent Mission Malaysia to the United Nations, New York. 21 June 2005.

86 See Ifikhar Ali, 'Annan's Reform Plans Criticized by other Developing Countries', *The Nation*, 8 April 2005.

87 Memo from Allan Rock to the author, 12 November 2007.

88 Stedman, 'UN Transformation', p. 941.

89 Stedman, 'UN Transformation', p. 941 and Traub, *Best Intentions*, pp. 386–7.

90 United Nations General Assembly, '2005 Summit Outcome', A/60/L.1, 20 September 2005, paras 138–9.

91 Jutta Brunnée and Stephen J. Toope, 'The Responsibility to Protect and the Use of Force: Building Legality?', *Global Responsibility to Protect*, 2(3), 2010. Though, legally speaking, there remain important points of ambiguity. See Carlo Focarelli, 'The Responsibility to Protect Doctrine and Humanitarian Intervention: Too Many Ambiguities for a Working Doctrine', *Journal of Conflict and Security Law*, 13(2), 2008, pp. 191–213.

92 See Ekkehard Strauss, 'A Bird in the Hand is Worth Two in the Bush – On the Assumed Legal Nature of the Responsibility to Protect', *Global Responsibility to Protect*, 1(3), 2009, pp. 291–323.

93 Alistair Iain Johnston, *Social States: China in International Relations 1980–2000* (Princeton, NJ: Princeton University Press, 2008), pp. 23–6.

94 On China's position see Sarah Teitt, 'Assessing Polemics, Principles and Practices: China and the Responsibility to Protect', *Global Responsibility to Protect*, 1(2), 2009, pp. 208–36.

2 Implementing RtoP at the UN

1 The Global Centre for the Responsibility to Protect was established in 2008 by a group of prominent NGOs and activists (see www.globalRtoP.org). Its associates are: Asia-Pacific Centre for the Responsibility to Protect (www.RtoPasiapacific. org), Fundación para las Relaciones Internacionales y el Diálogo Exterior (www.fride.org), Kofi Annan International Peacekeeping Training Centre (www. kaiptc.org) and the Norwegian Institute of International Affairs (www.nupi.no). The International Coalition for the Responsibility to Protect evolved out of the

World Federalist Movement-Institute for Global Policy 'Responsibility to Protect-Civil Society' initiative which was initially established in 2003 with funding from the Canadian government to consult and promote the principle. The coalition aims to replicate the huge NGO coalition established to advocate for the international convention banning land mines (www.responsibilitytoprotect.org). The journal, *Global Responsibility to Protect*, published its first edition in 2009 and Routledge's RtoP book series is scheduled to publish its first books in 2010. For information on IRtoP and W2I see www.iRtoP.org and http://migs.concordia.ca/W2I/W2I_Project.html respectively. Ramesh Thakur also highlights the range of RtoP related activities. See Ramesh Thakur, 'The Responsibility to Protect: Yesterday, Today, Tomorrow', presentation at the Basillie School of International Affairs, Waterloo, 11 November 2009.

2 Ban Ki-moon, *Implementing the Responsibility to Protect*, report of the Secretary-General, A/63/677, 12 January 2009. The challenge of translating RtoP from words to deeds was first outlined by the Secretary-General in his 2008 speech in Berlin. See, Ban Ki-moon, 'On Responsible Sovereignty: International Cooperation for a Changed World', Berlin, SG/SM11701, 15 July 2008.

3 General Assembly Resolution 63/308, 7 October 2009.

4 Respectively, Statement by Maged Adbul Aziz, Permanent Representative of Egypt to the UN, before the tenth emergency special session (resumed) on illegal Israeli actions in occupied East Jerusalem and the rest of the Occupied Palestinian Territory, New York, 15 July 2009; Interview by Minister of Foreign Affaires of the Russian Federation Sergey Lavrov to BBC, Moscow, 9 August 2008 (available at: http://globalRtoP.org/pdf/related/GeorgiaRussia.pdf) and 'India to Sri Lanka: Killing of Tamil Civilians Must Stop', *Sindh Today*, 22 April 2009. On the opposition of these governments to RtoP in 2005 and before see Alex J. Bellamy,'Whither the Responsibility to Protect? Humanitarian Intervention and the 2005 World Summit', *Ethics and International Affairs*, 20(2), 2006.

5 Office of the President of the General Assembly, 'Concept note on responsibility to protect populations from genocide, war crimes, ethnic cleansing and crimes against humanity', July 2009 (available at: www.un.org/ga/president/63/interactive/protect/conceptnote.pdf). This line of argument was supporting by Noam Chomsky, who was invited by the PGA to address an informal interactive dialogue on RtoP.

6 For a general assessment of the Security Council's performance on the protection of civilians see Security Council Report, 'Protection of Civilians in Armed Conflict', cross-cutting report, 2009 no. 4, 30 October 2009.

7 See Nicholas J. Wheeler and Frazer Egerton, 'The Responsibility to Protect: "Precious Commitment" or a "Promise Unfulfilled"?', *Global Responsibility to Protect*, 1(1), 2009, pp. 114–32.

8 Gareth Evans, 'The Responsibility to Protect: An Idea Whose Time Has Come . . . and Gone?', Lecture to the David Davies Memorial Institute, University of Aberystwyth, 23 April 2008. The characterization of the pushback as a 'revolt' against RtoP is taken from Alex J. Bellamy, 'Realizing the Responsibility to Protect', *International Studies Perspectives*, 10(1), 2009, pp. 111–28.

9 On the effects of Iraq, see Alex J. Bellamy, *Responsibility to Protect: The Global Effort to End Mass Atrocities* (Cambridge: Polity, 2009), pp. 68–70.

10 Draft Security Council Resolution on the Protection of Civilians, third iteration, 1 December 2005. Thanks to Joanna Wenschler for providing this.

11 See S/PV.5319, 9 December 2005, pp. 10 and 19; S/PV.5319 (Resumption 1), 9 December 2005, pp. 3 and 6.

12 Security Council Report, Update Report on the 'Protection of Civilians in Armed Conflict', No. 5, 21 June 2006 and No. 1, 18 June 2007. See Security Council

Report Update, 'Protection of Civilians in Armed Conflict', No. 1, 8 March 2006.

13 Security Council Report, Update Report on the 'Protection of Civilians in Armed Conflict', No. 1, 18 June 2007.

14 See Sarah Teitt, 'Assessing Polemics, Principles and Practices: China and the Responsibility to Protect', *Global Responsibility to Protect*, 1(2), 2009, pp. 220–1.

15 S/PV.5703, 22 June 2007, p. 17.

16 Ekkehard Strauss, 'A Bird in the Hand is Worth Two in the Bush – On the Assumed Legal Nature of the Responsibility to Protect', *Global Responsibility to Protect*, 1(3), 2009, p. 307.

17 For the report, see High Level Mission of the UN Human Rights Council (2007), Report of the High Level Mission on the situation of human rights in Darfur pursuant to Human Rights Council decision S-4/101, A/HRC/4/80, 7 March. For the ensuing debate, see A/HRC/5/6, 8 June 2007.

18 HLM, Report of the High Level Mission, para. 2.

19 HLM, Report of the High Level Mission, paras 19–20.

20 HLM, Report of the High Level Mission, para. 76 emphasis in original.

21 A/HRC/5/6, 8 June 2007.

22 Naomi Kikoler, 'Responsibility to Protect', keynote paper prepared for the international conference on 'Protecting People in Conflict and Crises', Refugee Studies Centre, Oxford, September 2009, p. 8.

23 Ramesh Thakur, 'The Model of a Mediocre Secretary-General', *Ottawa Citizen*, 25 September 2009.

24 Joachim Muller and Karl B. Sauvant, 'Overview: The United Nations Year 2006/2007: A New Beginning in Difficult Times', *Annual Review of United Nations Affairs 2006/2007* (Oxford: Oxford University Press, 2007), p. xv.

25 See, for example, the Secretary-General's speeches to the Center for Strategic and International Studies in Washington, DC, 16 January 2007 (SG/SM/10842), the Royal Institute of International Affairs in London, 11 July 2007 (SG/SM/11094) and his annual address to the General Assembly, 25 September 2007 (SG/SM/11182).

26 See www.dailynews.lk/2006/09/05/fea01.asp and www.cfr.org/publication/11618/future_of_the_united_nations_rush_transcript_federal_news_service.html. Thanks to Ramesh Thakur for providing these.

27 Ramesh Thakur, 'Ban a Champion of the UN's Role to Protect', *The Daily Yuimiori*, 10 March 2009.

28 A/62/512/Add.1, 30 October 2007, para. 31.

29 A/RES/62/238, 20 February 2008. For a discussion see Strauss, 'A Bird in the Hand . . .', p. 301.

30 See Fifth Committee of the General Assembly, GA/AB/3837, 4 March 2008.

31 Thus, Luck is paid $1 a year for his services and still has neither a UN telephone or email account GA/AB/3837, 4 March 2008.

32 Edward C. Luck, 'The Responsible Sovereign and the Responsibility to Protect', *Annual Review of United Nations Affairs 2006/2007* (Oxford: Oxford University Press, 2007), pp. xxxv.

33 Ban Ki-moon, 'Responsible Sovereignty: International Cooperation for a Changed World', speech given in Berlin, 15 July 2008, SG/SM/11701.

34 Ban Ki-moon, *Implementing the Responsibility to Protect*, report of the Secretary-General, A/63/677, 12 January 2009. Its significance is spelled out by Monica Serrano, 'Implementing the Responsibility to Protect: The Power of R2P Talk', *Global Responsibility to Protect*, 2 (1/2), 2010, p. 2.

35 *Implementing the Responsibility to Protect*, para. 2.

36 *Implementing the Responsibility to Protect*, para. 3.

37   *Implementing the Responsibility to Protect*, para. 12.
38   World Summit Outcome Document, para. 138.
39   *Implementing the Responsibility to Protect*, para. 11(a).
40   World Summit Outcome Document, para. 139.
41   A/60/L.1, 20 September 2005, paras 138–40. See *Report of the Secretary-General on Implementing the Responsibility to Protect A/63/677*, 12 January 2009 (hereafter *Implementing the Responsibility to Protect*).
42   *Implementing the Responsibility to Protect*, para. 10(a).
43   *Implementing the Responsibility to Protect*, para. 10 (b-d).
44   *Implementing the Responsibility to Protect*, paras 15 and 22.
45   *Implementing the Responsibility to Protect*, para. 16.
46   *Implementing the Responsibility to Protect*, para. 17.
47   *Implementing the Responsibility to Protect*, para. 19.
48   *Implementing the Responsibility to Protect*, para. 20.
49   *Implementing the Responsibility to Protect*, para. 21.
50   *Implementing the Responsibility to Protect*, para. 28
51   *Implementing the Responsibility to Protect*, para. 29.
52   *Implementing the Responsibility to Protect*, para. 32.
53   *Implementing the Responsibility to Protect*, para. 32
54   *Implementing the Responsibility to Protect* para. 46.
55   *Implementing the Responsibility to Protect*, para. 43.
56   *Implementing the Responsibility to Protect*, para. 44.
57   *Implementing the Responsibility to Protect*, paras 38 and 39.
58   *Implementing the Responsibility to Protect*, para. 40.
59   *Implementing the Responsibility to Protect*, para. 49.
60   *Implementing the Responsibility to Protect*, para. 57.
61   *Implementing the Responsibility to Protect*, para. 61.
62   *Implementing the Responsibility to Protect*, para. 62.
63   *Implementing the Responsibility to Protect*, para. 64.
64   *Implementing the Responsibility to Protect*, para. 65.
65   *Implementing the Responsibility to Protect*, annex.
66   Participants at a workshop mainly comprising UN officials and diplomats preferred 'normalising' to 'mainstreaming' to emphasise the fact that RtoP is embedded in existing law. See Stanley Foundation, *Implementing the Responsibility to Protect* conference report, New York, 15–17 January 2010, p. 22.
67   Jennifer Welsh, 'Turning Words into Deeds? The Implementation of 'The Responsibility to Protect', *Global Responsibility to Protect*, 2(1/2), 2010, p. 155.
68   Welsh, 'Turning Words into Deeds', p. 156.
69   On this see Barnett R. Rubin and Bruce D. Jones, 'Prevention of Violent Conflict: Tasks and Challenges for the United Nations', *Global Governance*, 13, 2007, pp. 391–408.
70   Ramesh Thakur, 'Ban a Champion of UN's Role to Protect', *Daily Yomiuri*, 10 March 2009
71   Edward Luck has also responded to some of these criticisms. See Edward C. Luck, 'A Response', *Global Responsibility to Protect*, 2(1/2) 2010.
72   See, Alex J. Bellamy and Paul D. Williams, *Understanding Peacekeeping*, 2nd edition (Cambridge: Polity, 2010), ch. 14.
73   ICISS, *Responsibility to Protect* (Ottawa: IDRC, 2001), p. xi and Ramesh Thakur, *The United Nations, Peace and Security: From Collective Security to Responsibility to Protect* (Cambridge: Cambridge University Press, 2006), p. 257.
74   International Coalition for the Responsibility to Protect (ICRtoP), 'Report on the General Assembly Plenary Debate on the Responsibility to Protect', 15 September 2009, p. 3. On the position of Asian governments see Alex J. Bellamy

and Sara E. Davies, 'The Responsibility to Protect in Southeast Asia: Progress and Problems', *Security Dialogue*, 40(6), 2009.

75 International Coalition for the Responsibility to Protect, 'Report on the General Assembly Plenary Debate on the Responsibility to Protect', 15 September 2009, p. 3.

76 See Global Centre for the Responsibility to Protect, 'Implementing the responsibility to protect Responding to the UN Secretary-General's report on the responsibility to protect populations from genocide, war crimes, ethnic cleansing and crimes against humanity', June 2009, p. 3.

77 See Office of the President of the General Assembly, 'Concept Note on Responsibility to Protect Populations from Genocide, War Crimes, Ethnic Cleansing and Crimes Against Humanity', undated (July 2009); ICRtoP, 'Report on the General Assembly Plenary Debate', p. 3; and Global Centre for the Responsibility to Protect, 'Implementing the Responsibility to Protect: The 2009 General Assembly Debate: An Assessment', August 2009, p. 3.

78 Including 51 statements from sub-Saharan Africa, the Asia-Pacific, Latin America and the Carribbean. Global Centre, 'Implementing', p 1.

79 The statement of the Non-Aligned Movement (NAM) is particularly instructive here. See Statement by Maged A. Abdelaziz, Permanent Representative of Egpyt, on Behalf of the Non-Aligned Movement on Agenda Item 44 and 107: 'Integrated and coordinated implementation of and follow-up to the outcomes of the major United Nations conferences and summits in the economic, social and related fields; follow-up to the outcome of the Millennium Summit: report of the Secretary-General', New York, 23 July 2009. According to the Global Centre, 40 states explicitly welcomed the Secretary-General's report and over 50 endorsed his interpretation of RtoP as involving three pillars. Global Centre, 'Implementing', p. 2. It is worth stressing that the NAM conveyed 'its appreciation' to the Secretary-General for his report.

80 See Statement of Hilario G. Davide Jr., Permanent Representation of the Philippines to the United Nations to the Thematic Debate on the Report of the Secretary-General on Implementing the Responsibility to Protect (A/63/677), New York, 23 July 2009 and Statement by Jim McLay, Permanent Representative of New Zealand to the United Nations to the United Nations, 17 July 2009.

81 E.g. see statement by Leslie K. Christian, Ambassador and Permanent Representative of Ghana to the United Nations on Agenda Items 44 and 107: 'Integrated and coordinated implementation of and follow-up to the outcomes of the major United Nations conferences and summits in the economic, social and related fields; follow-up to the outcome of the Millennium Summit: report of the Secretary-General', 23 July 2009 and Statement by Claudia Blum, Permanent Representative of Colombia to the United Nations, 23 July 2009.

82 Statement by Maged A. Abdelaziz, Permanent Representative of Egypt, on Behalf of the Non-Aligned Movement on Agenda Items 44 and 107: 'Integrated and coordinated implementation of and follow-up to the outcomes of the major United Nations conferences and summits in the economic, social and related fields; follow-up to the outcome of the Millennium Summit: report of the Secretary-General', New York, 23 July 2009.

83 See Global Centre, 'Implementing', p. 6.

84 Statement of Hilario G. Davide Jr., Permanent Representation of the Philippines to the United Nations to the Thematic Debate on the Report of the Secretary-General on Implementing the Responsibility to Protect (A/63/677), New York, 23 July 2009

85 ICRtoP, 'Report on the General Assembly Plenary Debate', pp. 7–8.

86   Global Centre for the Responsibility to Protect, Reflections on the UN General Assembly Debate on the Responsibility to Protect', meeting summary, 26 October 2009, p. 2.

87   A/RES/63/308, 7 October 2009.

88   See Global Centre, 'Implementing', pp. 6–7 and Asia-Pacific Centre for the Responsibility to Protect, 'Implementing the Responsibility to Protect: Asia-Pacific in the 2009 General Assembly Dialogue', October 2009, pp. 12–17.

3   Humanitarian crises since 2005

1   For an account of the war in Congo see Gerard Prunier, *Africa's World War: Congo, the Rwandan Genocide and the Making of a Continental Catastrophe* (Oxford: Oxford University Press, 2008). Some put the total casualty figure at over 5 million. See Roberta Cohen and Francis M. Deng, 'Mass Displacement Caused by Conflicts and One-Sided Violence: National and International Responses, *SIPRI Yearbook 2009: Armaments, Disarmament and International Security*, p. 23.

2   Alan Doss, Briefing to the UN Security Council, 26 November 2008, p. 2.

3   For an account see Victoria K. Holt and Tobias C. Berkman, *The Impossible Mandate? Military Preparedness, the Responsibility to Protect and Modern Peace Operations* (Washington, DC: Henry L. Stimson Center, 2006), pp. 165–6.

4   See Alex J. Bellamy, 'A Responsibility to Protect or a Trojan Horse? The Crisis in Darfur and Humanitarian Intervention after Iraq', *Ethics and International Affairs*, 19(2), 2005.

5   House of Commons [UK] International Development Committee, *Darfur, Sudan, the Responsibility to Protect*, Fifth Report of Session 2004–5 ,Volume 1, 16 March 2005, p. 19

6   See, *inter alia*, David Mepham, *Darfur: The Responsibility to Protect* (London: Institute of Public Policy Research, 2007), Cristina Badescu and Linnea Bergholm, 'Responsibility to Protect and the Conflict in Darfur: The Big Let Down', *Security Dialogue*, 40(3), 2009, pp. 287–309 and Lee Feinstein, *Darfur and Beyond: What is Needed to Prevent Mass Atrocities* (Washington, DC: Council on Foreign Relations, 2007).

7   Alex de Waal, 'Darfur and the Failure of the Responsibility to Protect', *International Affairs*, 83(6), 2007, pp. 1039–54.

8   Roberto Belloni, 'The Tragedy of Darfur and the Limits of the Responsibility to Protect', *Ethnopolitics*, 5(4), 2006, pp. 327–46.

9   Alan J. Kuperman, 'Darfur: Strategic Victimhood Strike Again?', *Genocide Studies and Prevention*, 4(3), 2009, pp. 281–303.

10   See Edward C. Luck, 'Implementing the Responsibility to Protect at the United Nations', lecture at The University of Queensland, 3 August 2009 and the International Crisis Group, 'Getting the UN into Darfur', Africa Briefing No. 43, 12 October 2006.

11   This is a point we will return to in Chapter 4. Luck recognises that RtoP will only deliver these effects once it starts to affect the way that states calculate their interests. See Edward C. Luck, 'Sovereignty, Choice and the Responsibility to Protect', *Global Responsibility to Protect*, 1(1), 2009, pp. 10–21. On botched peacemaking see Julie Flint and Alex de Waal, *Darfur: Short History of the Long War*, 2nd edition (London: Zed, 2008) and on the limits of the world's support for AMIS see Paul D. Williams, 'Military Responses to Mass Killing: The African Union Mission in Sudan', *International Peacekeeping*, 13(2), 2006, pp. 168–83.

12   E.g. Evans, *Responsibility to Protect*, p. 106; Desmond Tutu, 'Taking the Responsibility to Protect', *New York Times*, 9 November 2008; Donald Steinberg, 'Responsibility to Protect: Coming of Age?', *Global Responsibility to Protect*, 1(4),

2009, pp. 432–41. For the most comprehensive account to date see Elizabeth Lindenmayer and Josie Lianna Kaye, 'A Choice for Peace? The Story of Forty-One Days of Mediation in Kenya', International Peace Institute, August 2009.

13 Cited in Roger Cohen, 'How Kofi Annan Rescued Kenya', *New York Review of Books*, 55(13), 14 August 2008.

14 Statement attributable to the Spokesperson for the Secretary-General on the situation in Kenya, New York, 2 January 2008.

15 Ban Ki-moon, Address to the Summit of the African Union, Addis Ababa, 31 January 2008. See International Crisis Group, 'Kenya in Crisis', *Africa Report*, no. 137, 21 February 2008. Public Radio International, 'The Responsibility to Protect', 7 March 2009.

16 S/PRST/2008/4, 6 February 2008

17 International Crisis Group, 'Kenya in Crisis', *Africa Report*, no. 137, 21 February 2008. Public Radio International, 'The Responsibility to Protect', 7 March 2009.

18 These views are expressed in Sean Harder, 'How they Stopped the Killing', The Stanley Foundation, June 2009.

19 Keynote Address by Jean Ping, Chairperson of the AU Commission, at the Roundtable High-Level Meeting of Experts on 'The Responsibility to Protect in Africa', Addis Ababa, 23 October 2008.

20 For a detailed account of the conflict see the Report of the Independent International Fact-Finding Mission on the Conflict in Georgia, September 2009.

21 This is extensively cited in International Crisis Group, 'Russia vs. Georgia: The Fallout', Europe Report no. 195, 22 August 2008, esp. pp. 2–3.

22 Interview by Minister of Foreign Affairs of the Russian Federation Sergey Lavrov to the BBC', Moscow, 9 August 2008.

23 GA/10850, 28 July 2009, p. 14.

24 Lloyd Axworthy and Alan Rock, 'R2P: A New and Unfinished Agenda', *Global Responsibility to Protect*, 1(1), 2009, p. 59 and Global Centre for the Responsibility to Protect, 'The Georgia-Russia Crisis and the Responsibility to Protect: Background Note', 19 August 2008.

25 Gareth Evans, 'Russia, Georgia and the Responsibility to Protect', *Amsterdam Law Forum*, 1(2), 2009.

26 Elena Jurado, 'A Responsibility to Protect?', *New Statesman*, 15 August 2008.

27 Jurgen Haacke, 'Myanmar, the Responsibility to Protect and the Need for Practical Assistance', *Global Responsibility to Protect*, 1(2), 2009, p. 156.

28 'World Fears for Plight of Myanmar Cyclone Victims', *New York Times*, 13 May 2008.

29 Reports also began to emerge of military officers hoarding aid for themselves and selling it on the black markets. 'World Fears for Plight of Myanmar Cyclone Victims', *New York Times*, 13 May 2008.

30 'World Fears for Plight of Myanmar Cyclone Victims', *New York Times*, 13 May 2008.

31 Andrew O'Neil, 'Kosovo Aid the Model', *The Australian*, 14 May 2008.

32 For a detailed examination of this question, coming ultimately to the same view as that of Southeast Asian governments, see Rebecca Barber, 'The Responsibility to Protect the Survivors of Natural Disaster: Cyclone Nargis, a Case Study', *Journal of Conflict and Security Law*, 2009, pp. 1–32.

33 Edward Luck, briefing on 'International Disaster Assistance: Policy Options', to the US Senate Committee on Foreign Relations, 17 June 2008. On Holmes see Julian Borger and Ian MacKinnon, 'Bypass Junta's Permission for Aid, US and France Urge', *The Guardian*, 9 May 2008. See, 'World Fears for Plight of Myanmar Cyclone Victims', *New York Times*, 13 May 2008. On the potential

negative impact on aid delivery see Hannah Ruth Chia, 'Crisis in Myanmar and the Responsibility to Protect', *RSIS Commentaries (S. Rajaratnam School of International Studies, Nanyang Technical University Singapore)*, 14 May 2008, p. 2.

34 Julian Borger and Ian MacKinnon, 'Bypass Junta's Permission for Aid, US and France Urge', *The Guardian*, 9 May 2008. Britain later backtracked somewhat, indicating that it would welcome 'discussion' of the Responsibility to Protect. See, 'World Fears for Plight of Myanmar Cyclone Victims', *New York Times*, 13 May 2008.

35 'World Fears for Plight of Myanmar Cyclone Victims', *New York Times*, 13 May 2008.

36 This account has been repeated to the authors by several people.

37 On the anecdotal evidence see Evans, *Responsibility to Protect*, Haacke, 'Myanmar', and Ramesh Thakur and Thomas G. Weiss, 'R2P: From Idea to Norm, and Action?', *Global Responsibility to Protect*, 1(1), 2009, pp. 48–9.

38 See International Human Rights Clinic at Harvard Law School, *Crimes in Burma*, May 2009. On the regime's very real, but very paranoid, fear of Western invasion see Andrew Selth, 'Even Paranoids Have Enemies: Cyclone Nargis and Myanmar's Fears of Invasion', *Contemporary Southeast Asia*, 30(3), 2008, pp. 379–402.

39 See, especially, Report of the United Nations Fact Finding Mission on the Gaza Conflict, 'Human Rights in Palestine and Other Occupied Arab Territories', UN Human Rights Council, A/HRC/12/48, 15 September 2009. The Fact Finding Mission was led by the highly respected judge, Richard Goldstone and although unsurprisingly criticised as biased by Israel represents the most detailed account of war, supported by a significant amount of evidence. Also see International Crisis Group, 'Ending the War in Gaza', Middle East Briefing no. 26, 5 January 2009.

40 Report of the UN Fact Finding Mission, para. 1691. See GA/10882 and GA/10883, 5 November 2009.

41 Executive Committee of the World Council of Churches, Statement on the Gaza War, 17–20 February 2009 and Oxfam International, 'Oxfam Calls for an End to Gaza Fighting', 21 January 2008.

42 See Gareth Evans, 'The Responsibility to Protect and the Situation in Gaza, December 2008/January 2009', 16 January 2009.

43 Statement by Ambassador Eshagh Al-Habib, Deputy Permanent Representative of the Islamic Republic of Iran to the United Nations, on Agenda item 44 and 107, New York, 28 July 2009. A view shared by Cuba, see Statement by Anet Pivo Rivero, Representative of Cuba, at the Plenary Meeting of the General Assembly 63rd Session, Regarding the Report of the Secretary-General, 'Implementing the Responsibility to Protect', New York, 23 July 2009, p. 3.

44 Statement by Ms. Feda Abdelhady Nasser, Charge' d'Affaires, Permanent Observer Mission of Palestine to the United Nations, General Assembly Debate on 'The Responsibility to Protect', 24 July 2009, p. 2.

45 On general conditions see Gethin Chamberlain, 'Civilians held in Sri Lanka camps face disease threat', *The Guardian*, 20 April 2009.

46 Rhys Blakely, 'UNICEF Worker James Elder Expelled from Sri Lanka over Media Comments', *The Times*, 7 September 2009.

47 James Traub, 'At Risk in Sri Lanka's War', *Washington Post*, 22 April 2009.

48 Open Letter from the Global Centre for the Responsibility to Protect to the UN Security Council, signed by Jan Egeland, Gareth Evans, Juan Mendez, Mohammed Sahnoun, Monica Serrano, Ramesh Thakur and Thomas G. Weiss, 15 April 2009.

49 Mary Ellen O'Connell, 'Sri Lanka Needs Peace, Not R2P', e-IR, 28 April 2009.

50 Ramesh Thakur, 'West Shouldn't Fault Sri Lankan Government Tactics', *Daily Yomiuri*, 12 June 2009. A similar line was taken by Jorge Heine, a colleague of

Thakur's at the University of Ottawa. See Jorge Heine, 'Misapplying the R2P in Sri Lanka', *The Hindu*, 27 June 2009.

51 'On Sri Lanka, Mexico Invokes Responsibility to Protect', *Inner City Press*, 13 April 2009

52 Security Council Report, *Protection of Civilians in Armed Conflict*, cross-cutting report, no. 4, 30 October 2009, pp. 16–19.

53 'India to Sri Lanka: Killings of Tamil Civilians Must Stop', *Sindh Today*, 22 April 2009.

54 The report was not released to the public but its contents were widely leaked. See Neil MacFarquhar, 'UN Panel Calls for Court in Guinea Massacre', *New York Times*, 21 December 2009.

55 Reported by Global Centre for the Responsibility to Protect, 'The International Response to 28 September 2009 Massacre in Guinea and the Responsibility to Protect', Policy Brief, January 2010, p. 3.

56 Global Centre, 'International Response', p. 3.

57 Statement Attributable to the Spokesperson for the UN Secretary-General, 28 September 2009.

58 Statement Attributable to the Spokesperson for the UN Secretary-General, 18 November 2009.

59 Security Council Report, 'Peace Consolidation in West Africa: Guinea', no. 3, 11 January 2010, pp. 3–4.

60 Security Council Report, 'Peace Consolidation in West Africa: Guinea', no. 3, 11 January 2010, p. 2.

61 Security Council Report, 'Peace Consolidation', pp. 5–6.

62 S/PRST/2010/3, 16 February 2010.

63 'Guineans Laud Deal on Military Leader, Election Plans', *The Guardian*, 18 January 2010, and Statement Attributable to the Spokesperson for the UN Secretary-General, 18 January 2010.

64 'Guineans Laud Deal on Military Leader, Election Plans', *The Guardian*, 18 January 2010.

65 Global Centre, 'International Response', p. 4.

66 See www.iraqbodycount.org

67 See Campaign for Innocent Victims in Conflict (CIVIC), *Losing the People: The Costs and Consequences of Civilian Suffering in Afghanistan*, 2009, p. 25.

68 Both Amnesty International and Human Rights Watch have found that war crimes have been committed against the civilian population, including by Ethiopia.

69 See 'Somalia Conflict Kills More than 2,100 this year', *Reuters*, 26 June 2008.

70 'Re-branding Responsibility to Protect, Gareth Evans says Somalia's not covered', *Inner City Press*, 17 September 2009 and Evans, *Responsibility to Protect*, p. 76.

71 On African solutions see Paul D. Williams, 'Keeping the Peace in Africa: Why "African Solutions" Are Not Enough', *Ethics and International Affairs*, 22(3), 2008. On AMISOM, see Paul D. Williams, 'Into the Mogadishu Maelstrom: The African Union Mission in Somalia', *International Peacekeeping*, 16(4), 2009, pp. 514–30.

72 Interviews conducted with UN officials, 2009.

73 This claim was made by Ashraf Qazi, the UNMIS SRSG. See 'Sudan: Violence Hurting Aid Efforts in the South', IRIN, 16 June 2009.

74 See http://protection.unsudanig.org/.

75 The view that the parties do not believe their interests to be served by resorting to force is set out by International Crisis Group, *Sudan's Comprehensive Peace Agreement: Beyond the Crisis*, Africa Briefing No. 50, 13 March 2008.

76 One that has is the Aegis Trust.

77 Vaclav Havel, Kjell Bondevik and Elie Wiese, 'Foreword', to *Failure to Protect: The Ongoing Challenge of North Korea*, DLA Piper/Committee for Human Rights in North Korea/The Oslo Centre, 2008.

78 Edward C. Luck, 'Implementing the Responsibility to Protect at the United Nations', lecture to the University of Queensland, Australia, 3 August 2009, pp. 10–11.

79 Human Rights Watch, 'Burma: Landmines Kill, Maim and Starve Civilians', Human Rights Watch, 20 December 2006 and Human Rights Documentation Unit, *Burma Human Rights Yearbook 2006*, pp. 420–60.

80 For example, see Kavita Shukla, 'The International Community's Responsibility to Protect', *Forced Migration Review*, 30, 2009, pp. 7–9. In 2009, the Oslo Peace Research Institute (PRIO) held a workshop on the question of whether there was a responsibility to protect civilians from crimes against humanity in Eastern Burma, Oslo, 23 April 2009

81 Global Centre for the Responsibility to Protect, 'Applying the Responsibility to Protect to Burma/Myanmar', March 2010.

4   An assessment after five years

1   This section is based on Alex J. Bellamy and Paul D. Williams, 'On the Limits of Moral Hazard: The Responsibility to Protect, Armed Conflict and Mass Atrocities', unpublished paper.

2   Alan J. Kuperman, 'Rethinking the Responsibility to Protect', *Whitehead Journal of Diplomacy and International Relations*, Winter/Spring, 2009, p. 36 and Alan J. Kuperman, 'Review of Gareth Evans, *The Responsibility to Protect*', *Political Science Quarterly*, 124(3), pp. 590–1.

3   Kuperman, 'Rethinking the Responsibility to Protect', pp. 33, 36, 40.

4   Kuperman, 'Rethinking the Responsibility to Protect', p. 37 emphasis added.

5   Edward N. Luttwak, 'Give War a Chance', *Foreign Affairs*, 78(4), 1999, pp. 36–44.

6   Charles Wolff, 'Financial Crises and the Challenge of Moral Hazard', *Society*, 36 (July-August), 1999, p. 60.

7   Timothy W. Crawford and Alan J. Kuperman, 'Introduction: Debating the Hazards of Intervention', *Ethnopolitics*, 4(2), 2005, p. 143.

8   Timothy W. Crawford, 'Moral Hazard, Intervention and Internal War: A Conceptual Analysis', *Ethnopolitics*, 4(2), 2005, p. 179

9   Arman Grigorian, 'Third–Party Intervention and Escalation in Kosovo: Does Moral Hazard Explain it?', *Ethnopolitics*, 4(2), 2005, p. 197.

10 Alan J. Kuperman, 'The Moral Hazard of Humanitarian Intervention: Lessons from the Balkans', *International Studies Quarterly*, 52(1), 2008, p. 51.

11 Alan J. Kuperman, 'Suicidal rebellions and the moral hazard of humanitarian intervention', *Ethnopolitics*, 4(2), 2005, p. 150,

12 Kuperman, 'Suicidal Rebellions', pp. 156–7 and Kuperman, 'Moral Hazard of Humanitarian Intervention', pp. 50–1.

13 Kuperman, 'Rethinking the Responsibility to Protect', p. 34.

14 Alan J. Kuperman, 'Transnational Causes of Genocide, or how the West exacerbates ethnic conflict', in R. G. C. Thomas (ed.), *Yugoslavia Unraveled* (Lanham, MD: Lexington Books, 2003), p. 57; Alan J. Kuperman, 'Humanitarian Hazard: Revisiting Doctrines of Intervention', *Harvard International Review*, 26(1), 2004, p. 64 and Crawford, 'Moral Hazard', p. 187.

15 Jon Western, 'The Illusions of Moral Hazard: A Conceptual and Empirical Critique', *Ethnopolitics*, 4(2), 2005, pp. 225–36.

16 Lotta Harbom and Peter Wallensteen, 'Armed Conflict, 1989–2006', *Journal of Peace Research*, 44(5), 2007, p. 625. Thanks to Paul D. Williams for identifying this piece of research.

17 There is now a large degree of consensus that the overall number of armed conflicts has declined significantly since a peak in the early 1990s. See for example the

data produced by the Political Instability Task Force at http://globalpolicy. gmu.edu/pitf; the Uppsala Conflict Data Program at www.pcr.uu.se/research/ UCDP; the Centre for Systemic Peace at www.systemicpeace.org/conflict.htm; and the Heidelberg Conflict Barometer at http://hijk.de/en/konflictbarometer/ index.html. There is also a broad consensus that the number of major intrastate armed conflicts has declined over the same period. See Edward Newman, 'Conflict Research and the "Decline" of Civil War', *Civil Wars*, 11(3), 2009, pp. 255–78. There is also data which confirms that the number of fatalities caused by 'one-sided' violence has also declined as RtoP has become more prominent. (The UCDP define 'one-sided violence' as 'the use of armed force by the government of a state or a formally organized group against civilians which results in at least 25 deaths in a year. Extrajudicial deaths in custody are excluded.') See www.prc.uu.se/research/UCDP/graphs/one-sidedfatalities2007.gif.

18 Although Croatia initially indicated its intention to declare independence in June, it agreed to defer its declaration by three months. As such, independence was not formally declared until early October 1991, *after* the launch of the JNA's offensive which began on 19 September.

19 Kuperman, 'Transnational Causes of Genocide' and Kuperman, 'Moral Hazard of Humanitarian Intervention'.

20 Some of these were identified by Jon Western, 'Illusions of Moral Hazard'.

21 See Bellamy and Williams, 'On the Limits of Moral Hazard'.

22 Kuperman, 'Suicidal Rebellions' and Kuperman, 'Moral Hazard of Humanitarian Interventions'.

23 Kuperman, 'Transnational Causes of Genocide', p. 62.

24 Kuperman, 'Suicidal Rebellions', p. 159).

25 Cited in Steven L. Burg and Paul S. Shoup, *The War in Bosnia-Herzegovina* (Armonk, NY: M.E. Sharpe, 1999), p. 47.

26 This policy was revised in favor of supporting arrangements brought about by peaceful change only in July 1991. See Wayne Bert, *The Reluctant Superpower: United States' Policy in Bosnia 1991–1995* (Basingstoke: Macmillan, 1997), pp. 137–9.

27 For instance, Martha Finnemore, *The Purposes of Intervention* (Ithaca, NY: Cornell University Press, 2003) and Nicholas J. Wheeler, *Saving Strangers: Humanitarian Intervention in World Politics* (Oxford: Oxford University Press, 2000).

28 It is this logic that allowed the Secretary-General's Special Adviser, Edward Luck, to argue that Darfur is not a good test case for RtoP. See Edward Luck, 'The United Nations and the Responsibility to Protect at the United Nations', *Stanley Foundation Policy Brief*, August 2008, p. 6.

29 For instance, Barbara Harff, 'No Lessons Learnt from the Holocaust? Assessing Risks of Genocide and Political Mass Murder since 1955', *American Political Science Review*, 97(1), 2003. Barbara Harff, 'The Etiology of Genocides', in Isidor Wallimann and Michael N. Dobkowski (eds), *Genocide and the Modern Age: Etiology and Case Studies of Modern Death* (Syracuse: Syracuse University Press), p. 54, Stanton, 'The Eight Stages of Genocide', Hilberg, *The Destruction of the European Jews*, Kuper, *Genocide*, Harff, 'No Lessons Learnt from the Holocaust?', Harff, 'The Etiology of Genocides', Helen Fein, *Accounting for Genocide: National Responses and Jewish Victimisation During the Holocaust* (New York: Collier Macmillan, 1979), Barbara Harff and Ted Robert Gurr, 'Systematic Early Warning of Humanitarian Emergencies', *Journal of Peace Research*, 35(5), 1998, Manus Midlarksy, *The Killing Trap: Genocide in the Twentieth Century* (Cambridge: Cambridge University Press, 2005), and Stuart J. Kaufman, *Modern Hatreds: The Symbolic Politics of Ethnic War* (Ithaca, NY: Cornell University Press, 2001).

30 E.g. Victoria K. Holt and Glyn Taylor, *Protecting Civilians in the Context of UN Peacekeeping Operations: Successes, Setbacks and Remaining Challenges*, study

commissioned by the UN DPKO, November 2009 and Alex J. Bellamy and Paul D. Williams, 'Protecting Civilians in Uncivil Wars' in Sara E. Davies and Luke Glanville (eds), *Protecting the Displaced* (The Hague: Brill, 2010).

31 Gareth Evans, 'The Responsibility to Protect in International Affairs: Where to From Here?', keynote lecture at the Australian Catholic University, Melbourne, 27 November 2009. This view has also been expressed to the author by Ramesh Thakur and Don Hubert.

32 Gareth Evans, 'The Responsibility to Protect: An Idea Whose Time Has Come . . . and Gone?', *International Relations*, 22(3), 2008, pp. 294–5.

33 See Marc Saxer, 'The Politics of Responsibility to Protect', FES Briefing Paper No. 2, Berlin, April 2008, p. 4.

34 Eli Stamnes, ' "Speaking RtoP" and the Prevention of Mass Atrocities', *Global Responsibility to Protect*, 1(1), 2009, p. 77.

35 Evans, 'The Responsibility to Protect', p. 294.

36 A case Stamnes makes persuasively throughout her article. Stamnes, 'Speaking RtoP', pp. 70–89.

37 Martha Finnemore and Kathryn Sikkink, 'International Norm Dynamics and Political Change', *International Organization*, 52(4), 1998, p. 891.

38 E.g. on RtoP as a norm see Evans, *Responsibility to Protect*, p. 55; Ramesh Thakur, 'Goals and Action', *Ottawa Citizen*, 15 February 2008, at www.canada.com/ottawacitizen/news/opinion/story.html?id=83ab727c-430b-4507-b2b0-ffcf96d 93a19 and Teresa Chataway, 'Towards Normative Consensus on Responsibility to Protect', *Griffith Law Review*, 16(1), 2007.

39 As the Secretary-General noted. Ban, *Implementing the Responsibility to Protect*, para. 13. See William Schabas, *Genocide in International Law: The Crimes of Crimes* (Cambridge: Cambridge University Press, 2000), and Yoram Dinstein, *The Conduct of Hostilities under the Law of International Armed Conflict* (Cambridge: Cambridge University Press, 2004).

40 See Ward Thomas, *Ethics of Destruction: Norms and Force in International Relations* (Ithaca, NY: Cornell University Press, 2001) and Hugo Slim, *Killing Civilians: Method, Madness and Morality in War* (New York: Columbia University Press, 2008).

41 A view put forth by Edward Luck.

42 Discussed in more detail below. According to Thomas Franck, the compliance-pull of a norm or rule has four properties: determinacy, symbolic validation, coherence and adherence. See Thomas Franck, *The Power of Legitimacy Among Nations* (New York: Oxford University Press, 1990), p. 49.

43 See Luck, 'The United Nations and the Responsibility to Protect', p. 5; ILC, Draft Articles on the Responsibility of States for Internationally Wrongful Acts, 2001, available at http://untreaty.un.org/ilc/texts/instruments/english/commentaries/9_6_2001.pdf; Louise Arbour, 'The Responsibility to Protect as a Duty of Care in International Law and Practice', *Review of International Studies*, 34(3), 2008, pp. 445–58; and A/CN.4/553, para. 10

44 Jose E. Alvarez, 'The Schizophrenias of RtoP', Panel Presentation at the 2007 Hague Joint Conference on Contemporary Issues of International Law: Criminal Jurisdiction 100 Years After the 1907 Hague Peace Conference, The Hague, The Netherlands, June 30, 2007 p. 12 (available at: www.asil.org/pdfs/RtoPPanel.pdf) and Jerry Fowler, 'A New Chapter of Irony: The Legal Definition of Genocide and the Implications of Powell's Determination', in Samuel Totten and Eric Markusen (eds), *Genocide in Darfur: Investigating the Atrocities in the Sudan* (London: Routledge, 2006), p. 131.

45 This idea, and way of formulating it, is borrowed from Nicholas J. Wheeler, *Saving Strangers: Humanitarian Intervention in World Politics* (Oxford: Oxford University Press, 2000). It is based on Quentin Skinner, 'Analysis of Political Thought and

Action', in James Tully (ed.), *Meaning and Context: Quentin Skinner and His Critics* (Cambridge: Polity, 1988), p. 117.

46 Franck, *Power of Legitimacy*, p. 52.
47 Franck, *Power of Legitimacy*, p .52.
48 Skinner, 'Analysis of Political Thought and Action', p. 117.
49 A problem identified by Alex de Waal in relation to Darfur. See Alex de Waal, 'Darfur and the Failure of the Responsibility to Protect', *International Affairs*, 83(6), 2007, pp. 1039–54.
50 This argument is a particular feature of debates about RtoP in Darfur. See Mepham, *Darfur*, Badescu and Bergholm, 'Responsibility to Protect', and Feinstein, *Darfur and Beyond*.
51 See www.pcr.uu.se/research/UCDP/graphs/non_state_region_2007.gif and Alex J. Bellamy, *Massacres and Morality: Atrocities in an Age of Non-Combatant Immunity* (Oxford: Oxford University Press, forthcoming).
52 See www.pcr.uu.se/research/UCDP/graphs/conflict_region_2008.gif.
53 This is not to say, however, that the principle's advocates do not try. See Evans, *Responsibility to Protect*, pp. 67–8.
54 A finding consistent with the argument presenting by Rajan Menon, 'Pious Words, Puny Deeds: The "International Community" and Mass Atrocities', *Ethics and International Affairs*, 23(3), 2009, pp. 225–34.
55 Sri Lanka's civilian toll stands at around 3,000 but many of these were unintentionally killed.
56 Alex J. Bellamy and Paul D. Williams, 'The West and Contemporary Peace Operations', *Journal of Peace Research*, 46(1), 2009, pp. 39–57 and Brian Barbour and Brian Gorlick, 'Embracing the Responsibility to Protect: A Repertoire of Measures Including Asylum for Potential Victims', *International Journal of Refugee Law*, 20(4), 2008, pp. 533–66.
57 These helpful distinctions are drawn by Jonathan Symons, *International Legitimacy: Contesting the Domestic Analogy*, Ph.D. thesis, University of Melbourne, 2007, p. 121. The mimicry label is taken from Alistair Iain Johnston, *Social States: China in International Institutions, 1980–2000* (Princeton, NJ: Princeton University Press, 2008).
58 The centrality of transforming national interests is recognized by Edward Luck, 'Sovereignty, Choice and the Responsibility to Protect', pp. 20–1.

5   Economic development and democratization

1 ICISS, *The Responsibility to Protect*, p. 23.
2 Evans, *The Responsibility to Protect*, p. 87 ff.
3 International Coalition for the RtoP, *Report on the General Assembly Debate*, pp. 6–8.
4 Gareth Evans, 'The Responsibility to Protect in International Affairs', Australian Catholic University, Melbourne, 27 November 2009.
5 See Thomas Pogge, *Politics as Usual* (Cambridge: Polity, 2010).
6 See Asia-Pacific Centre for the Responsibility to Protect, *Implementing the Responsibility to Protect: Asia-Pacific in the 2009 General Assembly Dialogue*, October 2009, p. 15.
7 Michael Newman, *Humanitarian Intervention: Confronting the Contradictions* (London: Hurst, 2009).
8 Conor Cruise O'Brien, *United Nations: Sacred Drama* (London: Hutchinson and Co., 1968).
9 And is also based on a fiction conjured up by New York based diplomats. The result is that the north-south schism is more pronounced at the UN in New York

than in national capitals. See Thomas G. Weiss, *What's Wrong with the United Nations and How to Fix It* (Cambridge: Polity, 209), p. 50 ff.

10   This was made clear in the work of the High Level Panel, see David Hannay, *New World Disorder* (London: I.B. Tauris, 2008).

11   Ban Ki-moon, *Implementing the Responsibility to Protect*, para. 43.

12   Ban Ki-moon, *Implementing the Responsibility to Protect*, paras 43 and 44.

13   Ted Robert Gurr, *Peoples Versus States: Minorities at Risk in the New Century* (Washington, DC: United States Institute of Peace, 2000).

14   According to Semelin, mainly weak states. See Jacques Semelin, 'Toward a Vocabulary of Massacre and Genocide', *Journal of Genocide Research*, 5(2), 2003, pp. 193–210. Also see Kal Holsti, 'The Political Sources of Humanitarian Disasters' in E. W. Nafziger, F. Stewart and R. Vayrynen (eds), *The Origins of Humanitarian Emergencies: War and Displacement in Developing Countries* (Oxford: Oxford University Press, 2000).

15   The exception being rioting and mass violence that accompanied Indian partition in 1947.

16   Of those, East Germany, South Vietnam, Yugoslavia and Zanzibar cease to exist.

17   Though at least one recent account of RtoP disputed that there was any major connection between war and atrocities. See Serena K. Sharma, 'Towards a Global Responsibility to Protect: Setbacks on the Path to Implementation', *Global Governance*, 16(1), 2010, pp. 121–38.

18   Bartrop, 'Relationship Between War and Genocide', p. 525; Barbara Harff and Ted Robert Gurr, 'Victims of the State: Politicides and Group Repression from 1945–1995', in Albert Jongman (ed.), *Contemporary Genocide: Causes, Cases, Consequences* (Leiden: Den Haag, 1996), pp. 49–51; and Barbara Harff, 'No Lessons Learned from the Holocaust? Assessing the Risks of Genocide and Political Mass Murder since 1955', *American Political Science Review*, 97(1), 2003, pp. 57–73.

19   Jeffrey Dixon, 'What Causes Civil Wars? Integrating Quantitative Research Findings', *International Studies Review*, 11(4), 2009, p. 708.

20   These, and other, pitfalls with the quantitative approach have been identified by Christopher Cramer, *Civil War is Not a Stupid Thing: Accounting for Violence in Developing Countries* (London: Hurst and Co., 2006).

21   Dixon, 'What Causes Civil Wars?', p. 720. Dixon identifies these as areas of 'high confidence' in the findings.

22   Macartan Humphreys, 'Economics and Violent Conflict', working paper, Harvard University 2003.

23   James D. Fearon and David D. Laitin, 'Ethnicity, Insurgency and Civil War', *American Political Science Review*, 97(1), 2003, pp. 75–90.

24   Nicholas Sambanis, 'What is Civil War? Conceptual and Empirical Complexities of an Operational Definition', *Journal of Conflict Resolution*, 48(6), 2004, pp. 814–58.

25   For an excellent review of the relevant literature see Susan E. Rice, Corinne Graff and Janet Lewis, 'Poverty and Civil War: What Policymakers Need to Know', The Brookings Institution, 2006, pp. 6–8.

26   See Gudrun Østby, Ragnhild Nordås and Jan K. Rød, 'Regional Inequalities and Civil Conflict in Sub-Saharan Africa', *International Studies Quarterly*, 53(2), 2009, pp. 301–24.

27   Cramer, *Civil War is Not a Stupid Thing*.

28   It was not ever thus, of course, and some inter-state wars in particular were associated with economic growth as a result of state led spending. But there is little evidence to support the view that contemporary economies grow as a result of civil war.

29 See Paul Collier, *The Bottom Billion: Why the Poorest Countries are Failing and What Can be Done About It* (Oxford: Oxford University Press, 2007), p. 19.
30 This is the main thesis advanced by Collier in *The Bottom Billion*.
31 Dixon, 'What Causes Civil War?', p. 720.
32 'Instability' is a much broader category than civil war. See Jack A. Goldstone, Robert H. Bates, David L. Epstein, Ted Robert Gurr, Michael B. Lustick, Monty G. Marshall, Jay Ulfelder and Mark Woodward, 'A Global Model for Forecasting Political Instability', *American Journal of Political Science*, 54(1), 2010, pp. 190–208.
33 S. Brock Bloomberg and Gregory D. Hess, 'The Temporal Links Between Conflict and Economic Activity', *Journal of Conflict Resolution*, 46(1), 2002, p. 74; Paul Collier and Anke Hoeffler, 'Greed and Grievance in Civil War', Oxford Economic Papers, 56, 2004, pp. 563–95; and Ted Robert Gurr, *Why Men Rebel* (Princeton, NJ: Princeton University Press, 1970).
34 Harff, 'No Lessons Learnt', p. 65.
35 Hilberg, *The Destruction of the European Jews*, p. 83.
36 Rounaq Jahan, 'Genocide in Bangladesh', in Samuel Totten, William S. Parsons, Israel W. Charny (eds), *Century of Genocide: Eyewitness Accounts and Critical Views* (New York and London: Garland Publishing, 1997), p. 293.
37 See Ted Robert Gurr, *Minorities at Risk: A Global View of Ethnopolitical Conflict* (Washington, DC: United States Institute of Peace, 1993), E. W. Nafziger, F. Stewart and R. Vayrynen (eds), *The Origins of Humanitarian Emergencies: War and Displacement in Developing Countries* (Oxford: Oxford University Press, 2000) and E. W. Nafziger, F. Stewart and R. Vayrynen (eds), *Weak States and Vulnerable Economies: Humanitarian Emergencies in the Third World* (Oxford: Oxford University Press, 2000).
38 On data problems with inequality measures see Christopher Cramer, 'Does Inequality Cause Conflict?', *Journal of International Development*, 15(4), 2003, pp. 397–412, on the selection bias problem see Dixon, 'What Causes Civil War?', p. 725 and on the problems associated with identifying 'groups' see Christopher Cramer, 'Homo Economicus Goes to War: Methodological Individualism, Rational Choice, and the Political Economy of War', *World Development*, 30(11), 2002, pp. 1845–64.
39 Cramer, *Civil War is Not a Stupid Thing*, p. 10. Although Cramer is deeply critical of the econometric approach to identifying the causes of civil war and especially critical of the putative link between income inequality and war, he does accept a link between overall income and war and suggests a focus on growth and employment rather than asset redistribution.
40 This idea, that fragile economies constitute a 'root cause' – a necessary but not sufficient cause of armed conflict, unites several theories that otherwise disagree profoundly. See Paul Collier et al., *Breaking the Conflict Trap: Civil War and Development Policy* (New York: Oxford University Press for the World Bank, 2003) and Ted Robert Gurr, *Why Men Rebel* (Princeton, NJ: Princeton University Press, 1970).
41 An argument put forth in relation to Sierra Leone by Jimmy D. Kandeh, 'The Criminalization of the RUF Insurgency in Sierra Leone', in Cynthia J. Arnson and I. William Zartman (eds), *Rethinking the Economics of War: The Intersection of Need, Creed and Greed* (Baltimore: Johns Hopkins University Press, 2005), pp. 84–106.
42 Frances Stewart, 'Horizontal Inequalities as a Source of Conflict', in Fen Osler Hampson and David Malone (eds), *From Reaction to Conflict Prevention: Opportunities for the UN System* (Boulder, CO: Lynne Rienner 2002), p. 116.
43 Collier, *Bottom Billion*, p. 20.

44 Respectively, R. J. Rummel, *Death by Government* (New Brunswick: Transaction Publishers, 1994), Alexander B. Downes, *Targeting Civilians in War* (Ithaca, NY: Cornell University Press, 2008), and Jack Goldstone *et al.*, 'A Forecasting Model of Political Instability', American Political Science Association Annual Meeting, September 2005.

45 See the graph at www.systemicpeace.org/polity/polity4.htm.

46 Goldstone *et al.*, 'A Global Model', pp. 200–1.

47 Paul Collier, *Wars, Guns and Votes: Democracy in Dangerous Places* (London: The Bodley Head, 2009), pp. 15–50.

48 This analysis omits the slaughter of tens of millions of people by Stalin's Soviet Union because it predates 1945.

49 Benjamin A. Valentino, *Final Solutions: Mass Killing and Genocide in the 20th Century* (Ithaca, NY: Cornell University Press, 2004), p. 73.

50 These ideologies are examined in Alex J. Bellamy, *Massacres and Morality: Mass Killing in an Age of Non-Combatant Immunity* (Oxford: Oxford University Press, forthcoming).

51 Of course, there are other cases of rightist governments responding the leftist insurgencies with campaigns of mass killing (e.g. Guatemala, Peru, South Vietnam).

52 See Tim Besley, *Principled Agents? The Political Economy of Good Governance* (Oxford: Oxford University Press, 2006).

53 David Lake and Matthew Baum, 'The Invisible Hand of Democracy: Political Control and the Provision of Public Services', *Comparative Political Studies*, 34(6), 2001, pp. 587–621.

54 J. M. Owen, 'How Liberalism Produces Democratic Peace', *International Security*, 19(2), 1994, p. 90.

55 Owen, 'How Liberalism Produces Democratic Peace', p. 90.

56 According to Stuart Kaufman, motives and opportunities are two of three necessary *and sufficient* causes of war, the third being a specific trigger such as an event or crisis. See Stuart Kaufman, *Modern Hatreds: The Symbolic Politics of Ethnic War* (Ithaca, NY: Cornell University Press, 2001).

57 Paul Collier, 'Doing Well out of War: An Economic Perspective', in Mats Berdal and David M. Malone (eds), *Greed and Grievance: Economic Agendas in Civil Wars* (Boulder, CO: Lynne Rienner, 2000), pp. 91–112.

58 See David Keen, *Complex Emergencies* (Cambridge: Polity, 2008), p. 29.

59 Keen, *Complex Emergencies*, p. 30.

60 See Ted Robert Gurr, *Why Men Rebel* (Princeton, NJ: Princeton University Press, 1970) and David A. Welch, *Justice and the Genesis of War* (Cambridge: Cambridge University Press, 1993).

61 Frances Stewart, 'Horizontal Inequalities as a Source of Conflict', p. 109.

62 On the heightened competition for land and resources see Gerard Prunier, *Darfur: The Ambiguous Genocide* (London: Hurst, 2005), pp. 3–4.

63 This is given as a reason why Kenya avoided tribal conflicts in the 1960s and 1970s. See J. Klugman, 'Kenya: Economic Decline and Ethnic Politics', in Nafziger, Stewart and Vayrnen (eds), *Weak States and Vulnerable Economies*.

64 Barbara F. Walter, 'Does Conflict Beget Conflict? Explaining Recurrent Civil War', *Journal of Peace Research*, 41(3), 2004, p. 371.

65 Keen, *Complex Emergencies*, p. 52.

66 Cited by Keen, *Complex Emergencies*, p. 54.

67 E.g. see UN Population Fund, *Population and Poverty: Achieving Equity, Equality and Sustainability*, Population and Development Strategies Series, No. 8, 2003 and Sara E. Davies, *The Politics of Global Health* (Cambridge: Polity, 2010).

68 See Lael Brainard and Derek Choller, *The Tangled Web: The Poverty-Insecurity Nexus*, Brookings–Blum Roundtable, August 2006.

69 Marcatan Humphrys and Ashutosh Varshney, 'Violent Conflict and the Millennium Development Goals: Diagnosis and Recommendations', paper presented to the Millennium Development Goals Poverty Task Force Workshop, Bangkok, June 2004.

70 This link is well established. On Bosnia see Susan L. Woodward, *Balkan Tragedy: Chaos and Dissolution After the Cold War* (Washington, DC: The Brookings Institution, 1995). On Rwanda and Sierra Leone see Paul D. Williams, 'Peace Operations and the International Financial Institutions: Insights from Rwanda and Sierra Leone', *International Peacekeeping*, 11(1), 2004, pp. 103–23.

71 See William Reno, 'Shadow States and the Political Economy of Civil Wars', in Mats Berdal and David M. Malone (eds), *Greed and Grievance: Economic Agendas in Civil Wars* (Boulder, CO: Lynne Rienner, 2000), pp. 43–68.

72 Karen Ballentine, 'Introduction' in Ballentine and Sherman (eds), *Political Economy of Civil War*, p. 9.

73 Stewart, 'Horizontal Inequalities', p. 115.

74 Fearon and Laitin, 'Ethnicity, Insurgency and Civil War', pp. 75–90.

75 This phenomenon has been widely discussed and demonstrated. See, for example, Paivi Lujala, Nils Petter Gleditsch and Elisabeth Gilmore, 'A Diamond Curse? Civil War and a Lootable Resource', *Journal of Conflict Resolution*, 49(4), 2005, pp. 538–62, Collier, *Bottom Billion*, ch. 3, and David Keen, *The Economic Functions of Violence in Civil War*, Adelphi Paper No. 320 (Oxford: Oxford University Press for the IISS, 1998).

76 Jack Goldstone *et al.*, *State Failure Task Force: Phase III Findings*, 2000, p. 39, and Collier and Hoeffler, 'Greed and Grievance in Civil War', pp. 563–95. Barbara Walter reaches a similar conclusion but argues that the impact of enrolments is relatively small. Walter, 'Does Conflict Beget Conflict?', pp. 371–88.

77 See Rice, Graff and Lewis, 'Poverty and Civil War', p. 11.

78 Williams, 'Peace Operations and International Financial Institutions'.

79 See Williams, 'Peace Operations and International Financial Institutions', Collier, *Bottom Billion*

80 Collier, *Bottom Billion*, pp. 65–6.

81 Collier, *Bottom Billion*, p. 103.

82 For instance, Raila Odinga employed ethnic vilification and violence and succeeded in securing over 95 per cent of the vote from his own ethnic group.

83 Coming at the problem from different perspectives, all agree that aid effectiveness is determined in large part by local political conditions and that aid given in a context of corrupt and authoritarian government does little, if any, good. See Collier, *Bottom Billion;* Dambisa Moya, *Dead Aid: Why Aid is not Working and How There is Another Way for Africa* (London: Penguin, 2009) and Fiona Terry, *Condemned to Repeat: The Paradox of Humanitarian Action* (Ithaca, NY: Cornell University Press, 2002).

84 General Assembly Resolution 60/180, 30 December 2005, para. 15

85 Chairman's Summary of the Country-Specific Meeting of the Peacebuilding Commission, 13 December 2006, para. 14.

86 'PBC Update: First Lessons Learned on Sierra Leone', Center for UN Reform Education, 20 February 2007.

87 'Presidential Runoff in Sierra Leone Went Smoothly, Observers Say', *International Herald Tribune*, 9 September 2007 and Statement Attributable to the Spokesman of the UN Secretary-General, 10 September 2007.

88 HLP, *A More Secure World*, p. 83.

89 HLP, *A More Secure World*, p. 83.

90 Ponzio, 'Peacebuilding Commission', p. 8 and Susan C. Breau, 'The Impact of Responsibility to Protect on Peacekeeping', *Journal of Conflict and Security Law*, 11(3), 2007, p. 455.

91 Kofi Annan, 'In Larger Freedom: Towards Development, Security and Human Rights for All', addendum, A/59/2005/Add.2, 23 May 2005, para. 17.
92 Almqvist, 'Peacebuilding Commission', p. 7.
93 A/59/2005/Add.2, paras 31–4
94 World Summit Outcome Document, para. 98.
95 Ponzio, 'Peacebuilding Commission', p. 8.
96 A/59/2005/Add.2, para. 21.
97 General Assembly Resolution 60/180, 30 December 2005, para. 23.
98 Among the most strident of critics is Moyo, *Dead Aid*. Paul Collier estimates that foreign aid to the world's poorest countries may have added around 1 per cent to economic growth over the past thirty years, in many cases constituting the difference between stagnation and decline. Collier, *Bottom Billion*, p. 100.
99 Collier, *Bottom Billion*, p. 100.
100 Stewart, 'Horizontal Inequalities', p. 131.
101 The seminal study of the relationship between aid and democratic governance is Jakob Svensson, 'Aid, Growth and Democracy', *Economics and Politics*, 11(3), 1999, pp. 275–97.
102 See Steven Radelet, *Challenging Foreign Aid: A Policymaker's Guide to the Millennium Challenge Account* (Washington, DC: Center for Global Development, 2003).
103 See Alex de Waal, *Famine Crimes: Politics and the Disaster Relief Industry in Africa* (Oxford: James Currey, 1997).
104 Collier, *Wars, Guns and Votes*, p. 214.
105 Collier, *Wars, Guns and Votes*, p. 221.
106 The centrality of government accountability has been widely recognised in a variety of contexts. Alex de Waal, for instance, has noted its importance for avoiding famine. See de Waal, *Famine Crimes*.
107 Mark Duffield, 'The Political Economy of Internal War', in Joanna Macrae and Anthony Zwi (eds), *War and Hunger: Rethinking International Responses to Complex Emergencies* (London: Zed Books for Save the Children, 1994), pp. 57–64.
108 See Deborah Brautigam, Mick Moore and Odd-Helge Fieldstad (eds), *Taxation and Statebuilding in Developing Countries: Capacity and Consent* (Cambridge: Cambridge University Press, 2008).
109 Collier, *Bottom Billion*, p. 119.
110 Based on recommendations offered by Collier, *Bottom Billion* and Stewart, 'Horizontal Inequalities'.
111 Collier, *Bottom Billion*, p. 160.
112 On the former see Kapstein and Converse, *The Fate of Young Democracies* and on the latter see Ethan B. Kapstein, *Economic Justice in an Unfair World: Toward a Level Playing Field* (Princeton, NJ: Princeton University Press, 2006).
113 David M. Malone and Jake Sherman, 'Economic Factors in Civil Wars: Policy Considerations', in Arnson and Zartman (eds), *Rethinking the Economics of War*, pp. 234–55.
114 Kapstein and Converse, *Fate of Young Democracies*, pp. 40–1.
115 This is the main thesis presented by Kapstein and Converse, *Fate of Young Democracies*.
116 See Philip Keefer, 'Clientalism, Credibility and the Policy Choices of Young Democracies', *American Journal of Political Science*, 51(4), pp. 804–21.
117 Collier, *Wars, Guns and Votes*, p. 32.
118 Collier, *Wars, Guns and Votes*, pp. 198–212.
119 See Kapstein and Converse, *Fate of Young Democracies*, pp. 144–5.
120 Kapstein and Converse, *Fate of Young Democracies*, p. 146.
121 Michael Barnett, 'On Gareth Evans, *The Responsibility to Protect . . .*', *Global Responsibility to Protect*, 2(1/2), 2010.

6   Early warning

1   This chapter is based on research funded by the Australian Research Council and conducted by Alex J. Bellamy, Sara E. Davies and Stephen McLoughlin.

2   Clingendael, *Conflict Prevention and Early Warning in the Political Practice of International Organizations*, 1996, p. 1 and Michael Lund, *Preventing Violent Conflict: A Strategy for Preventative Diplomacy* (Washington, DC: US Institute of Peace, 1996).

3   OECD, *Preventing Violence and State Collapse: The Future of Conflict Early Warning and Response*, 2009, p. 54.

4   James S. Sutterlin, 'Early Warning and Conflict Prevention: The Role of the United Nations', in Klaas van Walraven (ed.), *Early Warning and Conflict Prevention* (The Hague: Kluwer, 1998), p. 125.

5   On the CIA warning about Bosnia see Stephen Rosenfeld, 'A Timely Warning: The CIA Predicts a Blowup in Yugoslavia', *Washington Post*, 30 November 1990. On General Dallaire's warning about the Rwandan genocide see Michael Barnett, *Eyewitness to a Genocide: The United Nations and Rwanda* (Ithaca, NY: Cornell University Press, 2002), pp. 77–88.

6   A problem identified by Barnett R. Rubin and Bruce D. Jones, 'Prevention of Violent Conflict: Tasks and Challenges for the United Nations', *Global Governance*, 13, 2007, pp. 391–408.

7   On the rapid escalation of violent conflict in general see Peter Wallersteen and Margareta Sollenberg, 'Armed Conflict, 1989–1999', *Journal of Peace Research*, 37(5), 2000, p. 640.

8   Stephen Stedman, 'Alchemy for a New World Order: Overselling "Preventive Diplomacy"', *Foreign Affairs*, 74, May/June 1995, p. 16.

9   The phrase 'culture of prevention' was first developed in the 1990s by Michael Lund as a way of elevating structural prevention. Michael Lund, *Preventing Violent Conflict: A Strategy for Preventative Diplomacy* (Washington, DC: US Institute of Peace, 1996). It was subsequently adopted by UN Secretary-General, Kofi Annan. Kofi Annan, *Prevention of Armed Conflict: Report of the Secretary-General*, A/55/985–S/2001/574, 7 June 2001, paras 161–2.

10   Ken Menkhaus, 'Conflict Prevention and Human Security: Issues and Challenges', *Conflict, Security and Development*, 4(3), 2004, p. 430.

11   57th General Assembly, 2003, Resolution 337. See Kanninen and Kumar, 'Evolution of the Doctrine and Practice', p. 60.

12   Peter Wallensteen, *Understanding Conflict Resolution: War, Peace and the Global System* (London: Sage, 2002).

13   For an outline of the debate see OECD, *Preventing Violence*, pp. 58–60.

14   Alex Austin, 'Early Warning and the Field: A Cargo Cult Science?', in Martina Fischer, Hans J. Gießmann and Beatrix Schmelzle (eds), *Berghof Handbook for Conflict Transformation* (Berghof Research Centre for Constructive Conflict Management, 2004), p. 5.

15   Austin, 'Early Warning and the Field', p. 5.

16   OECD, *Preventing Violence*, p. 47.

17   Henrik Lundin, 'Crisis and Conflict Prevention, with an Internet Based Early Warning System', August 2004, www.sipri.org/databases/first/early_warning/hl_report, accessed 4 March 2009.

18   Lundin, 'Crisis and Conflict', p. 10.

19   Lundin, 'Crisis and Conflict', p. 10.

20   Austin, 'Early Warning and the Field', p. 9.

21   Jack Goldstone, Robert H. Bates, David L. Epstein, Ted Robert Gurr, Michael B. Lustik, Monty G. Marshall, Jay Ulfelder, Mark Woodward, 'A Global Model

for Forecasting Political Instability', *American Journal of Political Science*, 54(1), 2010, pp. 190–208.

22   OECD, *Preventing Violence*, p. 47.

23   Jack A. Goldstone, 'Using Quantitative and Qualitative Models to Forecast Instability', US Institute of Peace, Special Report No. 204, March.

24   Lawrence Woocher, 'Early Warning for the Prevention of Genocide and Mass Atrocities', paper presented to the International Studies Association, 2007 and OECD, *Preventing Violence*, p. 43.

25   On data problems see Christopher Cramer, *Civil War is Not a Stupid Thing: Accounting for Violence in Developing Countries* (London: Hurst and Co., 2006), esp. pp. 61–74.

26   Austin, 'Early Warning', p. 10.

27   Woocher, 'Early Warning and the Prevention of Genocide'.

28   Austin, 'Early Warning', p. 10.

29   Barbara Harff, 'No Lessons Learned from the Holocaust? Assessing Risks of Genocide and Political Mass Murder since 1955', *American Political Science Review*, 97(1), 2003.

30   See Severine Autusserre, *The Trouble with the Congo: Local Violence and the Failure of International Peacebuilding* (Cambridge: Cambridge University Press, 2010).

31   Quincy Wright, 'Project for a World Intelligence Center', *Journal of Conflict Resolution*, 93–7(1/4), 1957, p. 94. On Eisenhower see Walter A. Dorn, 'Early Warning and Late Warning by the UN Secretary-General of Threats to the Peace: Article 99 Revisited', in Albrecht Schnabel and David Carment (eds), *Conflict Prevention: from Rhetoric to Reality (Vol 1)* (Lanham, MD: Lexington Books, 2004), p. 324.

32   Oliver Ramsbotham, Tom Woodhouse and Hugh Miall, *Contemporary Conflict Resolution* (Cambridge: Polity Press, 2005), p. 112.

33   Mark W. Zacher, *Dag Hammarskjöld's United Nations* (New York: Columbia University Press, 1970), pp. 67–8

34   David Carment, 'Conflict Prevention – Taking Stock', in David Carment and Albrecht Schnabel (eds), *Conflict Prevention: Path to Peace or Grand Illusion?* (Tokyo: United Nations University Press, 2003), p. 13.

35   Carment, 'Conflict Prevention', p. 13.

36   K. Rupesinghe, 'Early Warning: Some Conceptual Problems', *Bulletin of Peace Proposals*, 20(2), 1989 and Howard Adelman, 'Humanitarian and Conflict-oriented Early Warning: A Historical Background Sketch', in Klaas van Walraven, *Early Warning and Conflict Prevention*, p. 45.

37   Perez de Cuellar, quoted in Carment, 'Conflict Prevention', p. 15.

38   Connie Peck, *Sustainable Peace: The Role of the UN and Regional Organisations in Preventing Conflict* (Lanham, MD: Rowman and Littlefield Publishers, 1998), p. 72.

39   Dorn, 'Early Warning and Late Warning', p. 323.

40   Juergen Dedring, 'The Security Council in Preventive Action', in Peter Wallensteen (ed.), *Preventing Violent Conflicts: Past Record and Future Challenges* (Stockholm: Department of Peace and Conflict Research, Uppsala University, 1998), p. 49.

41   B. G. Ramcharan, *The International Law and Practice of Early Warning and Preventive Diplomacy* (The Hague: Kluwer, 1991), p. 67.

42   Ramcharan, *International Law*, p. 45.

43   Boothby and D'Angelo, 'Building Capacity', p. 252.

44   Kanninen and Kumar, 'Evolution of the Doctrine and Practice', p. 50.

45   Peck, 'Sustainable Peace', p. 73.

46 Andrew Mack and Kathryn Furlong, 'When Aspiration Exceeds Capability: The UN and Conflict Prevention', unpublished paper, p. 6.

47 Sutterlin, 'Early Warning and Conflict Prevention', p. 124.

48 Kanninen and Kumar, 'Evolution of the Doctrine and Practice', p. 52.

49 Boothby and D'Angelo, 'Building Capacity', p. 252.

50 Simon Chesterman, 'Shared Secrets: Intelligence and Collective Security', 2006, www.longmedia.com.au, accessed 4 May 2008, p. 24.

51 Peck, 'Sustainable Peace', p. 69.

52 Ramcharan, 'The International Law', p. 47.

53 James S. Sutterlin, *The United Nations and the Maintenance of International Security: A Challenge to be Met* (Westport, CT: Praeger, 2003), p. 133.

54 Boutros Boutros-Ghali, *An Agenda for Peace: Preventive Diplomacy, Peace-Making and Peace-Keeping*, A/47/277 and S/24111, 17 June 1992.

55 Independent Working Group on the Future of the United Nations, *The United Nations in its Second Half Century* (New York: Ford Foundation, 1995).

56 Annex A, A/50/853, 22 December 1995, paras 113, 120–1. Cited in John G. Cockell, 'Early Warning Analysis and Policy Planning in UN Preventive Action', in David Carment and Albrecht Schnabel (eds), *Conflict Prevention: Path to Peace or Grand Illusion?* (Tokyo: UN University Press, 2003), p. 186.

57 Report of the Secretary-General on the Work of the Organization Joint Inspection Unit: Strengthening the United Nations Capacity for Conflict Prevention, 1997, paras 19 and 26. Analysis from Mack and Furlong, 'When Aspiration Exceeds Capability', pp. 6–7.

58 Howard Adelman and Astri Suhrke, *The International Response to Conflict and Genocide: Lessons From the Rwanda Experience. Volume 2: Early Warning and Conflict Management*, Joint Evaluation of Emergency Assistance to Rwanda, Michelson Institute, Copenhagen, 1996, p. 80.

59 Cockell, 'Early Warning', p. 187.

60 Report of the Panel on United Nations Peace Operations, A/55/305 – S/2000/809, 21 August 2000, Section G.

61 Howard Adelman, 'Humanitarian and Conflict-Oriented Early Warning', in Klaas van Walraven (ed.), *Early Warning and Conflict Prevention: Limitations and Possibilities* (The Hague: Kluwer Law International, 1998), p. 47.

62 Tapio Kanninen, 'Recent Initiatives by the Secretary-General and the UN System in Strengthening Conflict Prevention Activities', *International Journal on Minority and Group Rights*, 39–43(8/1), p. 40.

63 This discussion is based on Boothby and D'Angelo, 'Building Capacity', p. 260.

64 Derek Boothby and George D'Angelo, 'Building Capacity Within the United Nations: Cooperation on the Prevention of Violent Conflicts', in David Carment and Albrecht Schnabel (eds), *Conflict Prevention: From Rhetoric to Reality (Vol 2)* (Lanham, MD: Lexington Books, 2004), pp. 255–6.

65 Boothby and D'Angelo, 'Building Capacity Within the United Nations', p. 257.

66 Barnett R. Rubin and Bruce Jones, 'Prevention of Violent Conflict: Tasks and Challenges for the United Nations', *Global Governance*, 391–408(13/3), 2007, p. 404.

67 Kofi Annan, 'Prevention of Armed Conflict: Report of the Secretary-General', A/55/985-S/2001/574, 7 June 2001, p. 19

68 Annan, 'Prevention of Armed Conflict', p. 20.

69 A/RES/57/337, 18 July 2003.

70 Kofi Annan, 'Progress Report on the Prevention of Armed Conflict: Report of the Secretary-General', A/60/891, 18 July 2006, p. 27.

71 Rubin and Jones, 'Prevention of Violent Conflict', p. 405.

72   Boothby and D'Angelo, 'Building Capacity Within the UN', p. 259.
73   Boothby and D'Angelo, 'Building Capacity Within the UN', p. 261.
74   Boothby and D'Angelo, 'Building Capacity Within the UN', p. 261.
75   Juan Méndez, press conference, New York, 9 April 2006.
76   'Guidance Note: Genocide Prevention', results of the 26 July 2005 meeting between the UNA-USA and the Special Adviser on the Prevention of Genocide.
77   Juan Méndez, interview with Jerry Fowler, Holocaust Memorial Museum, 16 February 2006.
78   'Groups Protest Weakening of UN Position Against Genocide', UN DPA, 14 February 2007.
79   Reported by Inner City Press, 15 February 2007.
80   Office of the Special Adviser for the Prevention of Genocide 'Analysis Framework', 2009, www.un.org/preventgenocide/adviser/pdf/OSAPG%20Analysis FrameworkExternalVersion.pdf, accessed 18 March 2010.
81   A/62/512/Add.1, 30 October 2007, para. 31.
82   *Implementing the Responsibility to Protect*, annex.
83   'Implementing the Responsibility to Protect', Stanley Foundation workshop report, New York, 15–17 January 2010, p. 12.
84   This basic approach was proposed by Woocher, 'Early Warning for the Prevention of Genocide'.
85   'Implementing the Responsibility to Protect', Stanley Foundation, p. 15.
86   'Implementing the Responsibility to Protect', Stanley Foundation, p. 14.

7   Regional arrangements

1   Edward Luck, 'The United Nations and the Responsibility to Protect', The Stanley Foundation Policy Analysis Brief, August 2008, pp. 6 and 8.
2   Set out in Co-Chairs, 'Concept Paper', Council for Security Cooperation in the Asia-Pacific Study Group for the Responsibility to Protect, Jakarta, November 2009.
3   H.E. Dr. N. Hassan Wirajuda Minister for Foreign Affairs Republic of Indonesia, Keynote Speech, At the 2nd Roundtable Discussion on Human Rights in ASEAN: Challenges and Opportunities for Human Rights in a Caring and Sharing Community, 18 December 2006. Available at: www.indonesia-ottawa.org/information/details.php?type=speech&id=130; S/PR.5649, 28 March 2007, pp. 12–13; Katherine N. Andrews and Victoria K. Holt, 'United Nations-African Union Coordination on Peace and Security in Africa', *Future of Peace Operations Program: A Better Partnership for African Peace Operations*, The Henry L. Stimson Center, Issue Brief, August 2007, p. 1. www.stimson.org/fopo/pdf/Stimson_AU-UNBrief_Aug07.pdf
4   Edward Luck, 'Sovereignty, Choice, and the Responsibility to Protect', *Global Responsibility to Protect*, 1(1), 2009, pp. 1–12; David Carment and Martin Fischer, 'R2P and the Role of Regional Organisations in Ethnic Conflict Management, Prevention and Resolution: The Unfinished Agenda', *Global Responsibility to Protect*, 1(3), 2009, pp. 261–89.
5   Justin Morris and Hilaire McCoubrey, 'Regional Peacekeeping and the Post-Cold War Era', *International Peacekeeping*, 6(2), 1999, p. 133. Some parts of the following discussion draw on Alex J. Bellamy and Paul D. Williams, *Understanding Peacekeeping*, 2nd edition (Cambridge: Polity, 2010), esp. pp. 300–10.
6   See F. O. Wilcox, 'Regionalism and the United Nations', *International Organization*, 19(3), 1965, pp. 789–811.

7 Alex J. Bellamy and Paul D. Williams, 'Who's Keeping the Peace? Regionalization and Contemporary Peace Operations', *International Security*, 29(4), 2005, pp. 161–4.

8 Asbjorn Eide, 'Peace-Keeping and Enforcement by Regional Organizations: Its Place in the United Nations System', *Journal of Peace Research*, 3(2), 1966, p. 129.

9 Christine Gray, *International Law and the Use of Force* (Oxford: Oxford University Press, 2000), p. 202.

10 For an excellent outline and critique of this stance see Paul D. Williams, 'Keeping the Peace in Africa: Why "African" Solutions Are Not Enough', *Ethics & International Affairs*, 22(3), 2008.

11 Paul F. Diehl and Y-I Cho, 'Passing the Buck in Conflict Management: The Role of Regional Organizations in the Post-Cold War Era', *Brown Journal of World Affairs*, 12(2), 2006, p. 193.

12 ICISS, *The Responsibility to Protect: Research, Bibliography, Background* (Ottawa: International Development Research Centre, 2001), p. 168; Birger Heldt, 'Trends from 1948 to 2005: How to View the Relation between the United Nations and Non-UN Entities', in Donald C. F. Daniel, Patricia Taft and Sharon Wiharta (eds), *Peace Operations: Trends, Progress and Prospects* (Washington, DC: Georgetown University Press, 2008).

13 The list draws on Bellamy and Williams, *Understanding Peacekeeping*, table 13.2, p. 308. On the Solomon Islands see Asia-Pacific Centre for the Responsibility to Protect, *RAMSI and Pillar Two of the Responsibility to Protect*, 2009.

14 Boutros Boutros-Ghali, *An Agenda for Peace* (New York: UN Department of Public Information, 1992), paras 63–5.

15 Bellamy and Williams, *Understanding Peacekeeping*, p. 306.

16 A/RES/60/1 (2005), paras 93, 138, 139.

17 Mark Malan, 'Africa: Building Institutions on the Run', in Donald C. F. Daniel, Patricia Taft and Sharon Wiharta (eds), *Peace Operations: Trends, Progress and Prospects* (Washington, DC: Georgetown University Press, 2008), pp. 90–106.

18 See the chapter on ECOMOG in Katharina Coleman, *Regional Organisations and Peace Enforcement: The Politics of International Legitimacy* (Cambridge: Cambridge University Press, 2007).

19 S/PV.3868, 31 March 1999.

20 See Nicholas J. Wheeler, *Saving Strangers: Humanitarian Intervention in International Society* (Oxford: Oxford University Press, 2000), p. 259.

21 S/PV.3930, 23 September 1999.

22 S/PV.3930, 23 September 1999.

23 S/PV.3988, 24 March 1999.

24 S/PV.3988, 24 March 1999; S/PV.3989, 26 March 1999.

25 S/PV.3988, 24 March 1999; S/PV.3989, 26 March 1999.

26 Mark Devenport, 'Kofi Annan's delicate balance', *BBC News*, 13 April 1999. http://news.bbc.co.uk/2/hi/special_report/1999/03/99/kosovo_strikes/318104.stm.

27 ICISS, *The Responsibility to Protect: Research, Bibliography, Background*, pp. 169–70.

28 Bellamy and Williams, *Understanding Peacekeeping*, pp. 307–8.

29 Permanent Mission of the People's Republic of China to the UN, 'Concept Paper: Cooperation Between the United Nations and Regional and Sub-Regional Organizations in Maintaining International Peace and Security', 8 January 2010.

30 Ban, *Implementing the Responsibility to Protect*, p. 13.

31 Ban, *Implementing the Responsibility to Protect*, paras 37 and 38.

32 United Nations Secretary-General, 'A regional-global partnership: challenges and opportunities', Report of the Secretary-General, A/61/204-S/2006/590, 28 July

2006, p. 6; United Nations Secretary-General, 'Report of the Secretary-General on the relationship between the United Nations and regional organisations, in particular the African Union, in the maintenance of international peace and security', S/2008/186, 7 April 2008, p. 14.

33 A/63/677, paragraph 40; A/61/204-S/2006/590, pp. 11–13.
34 A/63/677, paragraph 51.
35 A/63/677, paragraph 50.
36 Though the African Union allows for its Peace and Security Council to authorise an intervention to restore peace and security, and that this intervention may be legitimate and legal under the AU charter if not under the UN.
37 A/63/677, paragraph 57.
38 A/63/677, paragraph 58.
39 Small Arms Survey, *Small Arms Survey 2009: Shadows of War* (Cambridge: Cambridge University Press, 2009), Chapter 2; Small Arms Survey, *Small Arms Survey 2008: Risk and Resilience* (Cambridge: Cambridge University Press, 2008), Chapter 4.
40 A/63/677, paragraph 58.
41 Global Centre for the Responsibility to Protect, 'Implementing the Responsibility to Protect. The 2009 General Assembly Debate: An Assessment', August 2009, p. 2.
42 Global Centre, 'Implementing', p. 9.
43 Global Centre, 'Implementing', p. 9.
44 Global Centre, 'Implementing', p. 9.
45 Important exceptions are David Carment and Martin Fischer, 'R2P and the Role of Regional Organisations in Ethnic Conflict Management, Prevention and Resolution: The Unfinished Agenda', *Global Responsibility to Protect*, 1(3), 2009, pp. 261–90; Kristin M. Haugevik, 'Regionalising the Responsibility to Protect: Possibilities, Capabilities and Actualities', *Global Responsibility to Protect*, 1(2), 2009, pp. 346–63.
46 Carment and Fischer, 'R2P and the Role of Regional Organisations', pp. 284, 288.
47 Amitav Acharya, 'How Ideas Spread: Norm Localization and Institutional Change in Asian Regionalism', *International Organization* 58, 2004, pp. 239–75.
48 Carment and Fischer, 'R2P and the Role of Regional Organizations'.
49 Global Centre, 'Implementing', pp. 4, 9, and Asia-Pacific Centre for the Responsibility to Protect, 'Asia-Pacific in the 2009 General Assembly Dialogue', July 2009, pp. 19–20, 23–4.
50 Which are: Agriculture and Rural Development; Health and Population Activities; Women, Youth and Children; Environment and Forestry; Science and Technology and Meteorology; Human Resources Development; and Transport.
51 Haugevik, 'Regionalising the Responsibility to Protect', pp. 360–1.
52 Haugevik, 'Regionalising the Responsibility to Protect', p. 362.
53 Bob McMullan and Dave Peebles, 'The Responsibility to Protect: Lessons from RAMSI', unpublished paper, 2006, p. 5.
54 Ellie Wainwright, 'Our Failing Neighbour – Australia and the future of Solomon Islands', Australian Strategic Policy Institute, 10 June 2003.
55 John Howard, Statement to Parliament on the Regional Assistance Mission to the Solomon Islands, 12 August 2003.
56 Ellie Wainwright, 'Responding to State Failure – the Case of Australia and the Solomon Islands', *Australian Journal of International Affairs*, 57(3), 2003, p. 49.
57 McMullan and Peebles, 'The Responsibility to Protect', p. 6.
58 Australian Federal Police, *Annual Report 2005–6* (Canberra: Commonwealth of Australia, 2006), p. 58.

59 Australian Federal Police, *Annual Report*, p. 59.
60 McMullan and Peebles, 'The Responsibility to Protect', p. 6.

8 The UN Security Council and the use of force

1 Kofi Annan, 'Two Concepts of Sovereignty', *The Economist*, 18 September 1999.
2 Nicholas J. Wheeler, 'A Victory for Common Humanity? The Responsibility to Protect after the 2005 World Summit', paper presented to a conference on 'The UN at Sixty: Celebration or Wake?', Faculty of Law, University of Toronto, 6–7 October 2005, p. 1.
3 See Edward C. Luck, 'The Responsible Sovereign and the Responsibility to Protect', *Annual Review of United Nations Affairs 2006/2007* (New York: Oxford University Press, 2008), vol. 1, pp. xxxiii–xliv.
4 ICISS, *Responsibility to Protect*, p. 50.
5 Alicia L. Bannon, 'The Responsibility to Protect: The UN World Summit and the Question of Unilateralism', *The Yale Law Journal*, 115, 2006, p. 1158.
6 Stephen John Stedman, 'UN Transformation in an Era of Soft Balancing', *International Affairs*, 83(5), 2007, pp. 933, 938.
7 Robert Jackson, 'War Perils in the Responsibility to Protect', *Global Responsibility to Protect*, 2(1/2), 2010.
8 The quote is from Marc Saxer, 'The Politics of Responsibility to Protect', p. 6.
9 Nicholas J. Wheeler, 'Legitimating Humanitarian Intervention: Principles and Procedures', *Melbourne Journal of International Law*, 2(2), 2001, p. 566.
10 See, for instance, Independent International Commission on Kosovo, *Kosovo Report: Conflict, International Response, Lessons Learned* (Oxford: Oxford University Press, 2000), opening summary. This line of reasoning is also developed later in the report.
11 Thakur, *The United Nations, Peace and Security*, p. 260.
12 Ramesh Thakur, 'A Shared Responsibility for a More Secure World', *Global Governance*, 11(3), 2005, p. 284.
13 Ramesh Thakur, 'Iraq and the Responsibility to Protect', *Behind the Headlines*, 62(1), 2004, pp. 1–16.
14 Jennifer M. Welsh, 'Conclusion: Humanitarian Intervention after 11 September', in Jennifer M. Welsh (ed.), *Humanitarian Intervention and International Relations* (Oxford: Oxford University Press, 2004), p. 180. This led prominent observers to write in 2004 that, 'the Bush administration does not and will not accept the substance of the report or support any formal declaration or resolution about it', S. Neil Macfarlane, Carolin J. Thiekling and Thomas G. Weiss, '*The Responsibility to Protect: Is Anyone Interested in Humanitarian Intervention?*', *Third World Quarterly*, 25(5), 2004, p. 983. The US did not change its position on criteria. See Sir Adam Roberts, 'The United Nations and Humanitarian Intervention', in Welsh (ed.), *Humanitarian Intervention*, p. 90.
15 Yevgeny Primakov, 'UN Process, not Humanitarian Intervention, is World's Best Hope', *New Perspectives Quarterly*, 2 September 2004.
16 Welsh, 'Conclusion', p. 204, n. 4.
17 See 'British PM Urges Tougher Stance Against Brutal Regimes', *Agence-France Press*, 14 July 2003 and Kevin Ward, 'Process Needed so Countries Know When to Intervene to Protect Human Rights', *CBS (Canada)*, 13 July 2003.
18 'Civil Society Meeting on the Responsibility to Protect', Final Report, Ottawa, 8 April 2003, p. 9.
19 UN High Level Panel on Threats, Challenges and Change, *A More Secure World: Our Shared Responsibility*, A/59/565, 2 December 2004, para. 203, and Kofi Annan,

'In Larger Freedom: Towards Development, Security and Human Rights for All', A/59/2005, 21 March 2005, para. 126.

20 William R. Pace and Nicole Deller, 'Preventing Future Genocides: An International Responsibility to Protect', *World Order*, 36(4), 2005, p. 25.

21 African Union Executive Council, 'The Common African Position on the Proposed Reform of the United Nations', ext/EX.CL/2(VII), Addis Ababa, 7–8 March 2005, section B (i).

22 Pace and Deller, 'Preventing Future Genocides', p. 28.

23 Memo from Allan Rock to the author, 12 November 2007.

24 This is a good example of a 'moral limit' in international politics. For a thorough investigation of moral limits see Richard M. Price (ed.), *Moral Limit and Possibility in World Politics* (Cambridge: Cambridge University Press, 2008).

25 Ban Ki-moon, *Implementing the Responsibility to Protect*.

26 'Position Paper of the People's Republic of China on the United Nations Reforms', 8 June 2005.

27 See Jeffrey Boutwell, 'Report on the Pugwash Study Group on Intervention, Sovereignty and International Security meeting', Venice, Italy, 10–11 December 1999; Weiss and Hubert, *The Responsibility to Protect, Supplementary Volume*, pp. 351–2; Welsh, 'Conclusion'; and Wheeler, 'Legitimating Humanitarian Intervention'.

28 On Kosovo see Simon Chesterman, *Just War or Just Peace? Humanitarian Intervention and International Law* (Oxford: Oxford University Press, 2001), p. 221. See Chapter 3 on Georgia.

29 On Darfur: Gareth Evans' International Crisis Group argued not. See International Crisis Group, 'Getting the UN Into Darfur', Africa Briefing No. 43, 12 October 2006, pp. 15–17. Others such as Eric Reeves and Samantha Power disagree with this perspective. On Sri Lanka, contrast the views of Ramesh Thakur (arguing against international engagement and criticism of the government) and those of Jan Egeland (former UN Humanitarian Coordinator) and James Traub (Policy Director, Global Centre). The lines of the debate on Myanmar/Cyclone Nargis are set out in Chapter 3.

30 Susan C. Breau, 'The Impact of Responsibility to Protect on Peacekeeping', *Journal of Conflict and Security Law*, 11(3), 2007, pp. 450–2 and Victoria K. Holt and Tobias C. Berkman, *The Impossible Mandate? Military Preparedness, The Responsibility to Protect and Modern Peace Operations* (Washington, DC: The Henry L. Stimson Center, 2006), pp. 201–24.

31 Nicholas J. Wheeler and Justin Morris, 'Justifying the Iraq War as a Humanitarian Intervention: The Cure is Worse than the Disease', in Ramesh Thakur and Waheguru Pal Singh Sidhu (eds), *The Iraq Crisis and World Order* (Tokyo: UN University Press, 2006), p. 460.

32 Bellamy, 'Responsibility to Protect or Trojan Horse?', Paul D. Williams and Alex J. Bellamy, 'The Responsibility to Protect and the Crisis in Darfur', *Security Dialogue*, 36(1), 2005, pp. 27–47.

33 See for example Richard B. Lillich (ed.), *Humanitarian Intervention and the United Nations* (Charlottesville, VG: University Press of Virginia, 1973).

34 Tony Blair, 'Doctrine of the International Community', speech to the Economic Club of Chicago, Hilton Hotel, Chicago, 22 April 1999. See John Kampfner, *Blair's Wars* (London: The Free Press, 2003), pp. 50–3 and Wheeler, 'Legitimating Humanitarian Intervention', p. 564 n. 51.

35 Independent International Commission on Kosovo, *Kosovo Report: Conflict, International Response, Lessons Learned* (Oxford: Oxford University Press, 2000), opening summary.

36 Nicholas J. Wheeler, *Saving Strangers: Humanitarian Intervention in International Society* (Oxford: Oxford University Press, 2000), p. 279 and Michael Byers, *War Law: International Law and Armed Conflict* (London: Atlantic Books, 2005), p. 101.

37 For the full range of views on Kosovo, see Albrecht Schnabel and Ramesh Thakur (eds), *Kosovo and the Challenge of Humanitarian Intervention: Selective Indignation, Collective Action and International Citizenship* (Tokyo: UN University Press, 2000).

38 For a discussion of borderline legitimacy judgments in relation to intervention see Ian Clark, *Legitimacy in International Society* (Oxford: Oxford University Press, 2005), pp. 199–205. The case for maintaining an ad hoc approach to intervention has been set out by Chris Brown. See Chris Brown, 'Selective Humanitarianism: In Defence of Inconsistency', in Deen K. Chatterjee and Don E. Scheid (eds), *Ethics and Foreign Intervention* (Cambridge: Cambridge University Press, 2003). Brown rearticulated this message in relation to RtoP in Chris Brown, 'Review of Gareth Evans, *Responsibility to Protect*', *Global Responsibility to Protect*, 2(1/2), 2010.

39 Thakur, *The United Nations, Peace and Security*, p. 260.

40 Wheeler, *Saving Strangers*, pp. 208–41.

41 Security Council Report, 'Reduced Security Council Decision Making in 2009: A Year of Decline or are the Statistics Misleading?', 22 January 2010, p. 1.

42 It has been observed that the council generates a sense of identity and belonging among its members which assists this cooperative approach. See David L. Bosco, *Five to Rule them All: The UN Security Council and the Making of the Modern World* (Oxford: Oxford University Press, 2009), p. 6.

43 Alex J. Bellamy and Paul D. Williams, *Understanding Peacekeeping*, 2nd edition (Cambridge: Polity, 2010), p. 93.

44 Independent Commission, Report of the Independent Inquiry into the Actions of the United Nations During the 1994 Genocide in Rwanda, 12 December 1999, p. 2.

45 Independent Commission, p. 2.

46 Kofi Annan, *Report of the Secretary-General Pursuant to General Assembly Resolution 53/35: The Fall of Srebrenica*, A/54/549, 15 November 1999, para. 488.

47 Annan, *Report of the Secretary-General*, paras 496–7.

48 Marack Goulding, 'The Use of Force by the United Nations', *International Peacekeeping*, 3(1), 1996, pp. 15–17.

49 Annan, *Report of the Secretary-General*, para. 498.

50 Annan, *Report of the Secretary-General*, para. 502.

51 *Report of the Panel on Peacekeeping Operations*, A/55/305, S/2000/809, 2000, para. 64.

52 Christine Gray, 'Peacekeeping After the Brahimi Report: Is There a Crisis of Credibility for the UN?', *Journal of Conflict and Security Law*, 6(2), 2001, p. 268.

53 This assessment was offered by Human Rights Watch in 2007, further documented in 2008 and confirmed by the UN High Commissioner for Human Rights in 2009. See Human Rights Watch, *So Much to Fear: War Crimes and the Devastation of Somalia*, 8 December 2008 and UN News, 'Reports from Somalia Suggest Possible War Crimes', 10 July 2009.

54 See Chapter 2. The notion that RtoP might not apply was aired by staff from the Global Center for the Responsibility to Protect at the 2010 annual conference of the International Studies Association, New Orleans.

55 IGAD comprises Djibouti, Ethiopia, Eritrea, Kenya, Somalia and Sudan.

56 International Crisis Group, *Somalia: Continuation of War by Other Means?* Africa Report No. 88, 21 December 2004, p. 2.

57 E.g. see Cedric Barnes and Harun Hassan, 'The Rise and Fall of Mogadishu's Islamic Courts', *Journal of Eastern African Studies*, 1(2), 2007, pp. 151–60.

58 Security Council Report, 'Update – Somalia', May 2006.
59 See the Council's Presidential Statement, S/PRST/2006/11, 15 March 2006.
60 'Jowhar Calm but Residents Scared', *BBC News*, 14 June 2006. In 2009, the US confirmed that supplied arms to the TFG. See, 'US Says Weapons Sent to Somalia', *BBC News*, 26 June 2009.
61 'Somali Islamists Declare Jihad on Warlords', *Agence France-Presse*, 22 April 2006.
62 Security Council Report, 'Somalia Update', July 2006 and September 2006.
63 Security Council Report, 'Somalia Update', September 2006.
64 Michael Weinstein, 'An Interim Agreement Gives Islamists Edge in Somalia', Institute for Security Studies (Pretoria), 13 September 2006.
65 Security Council Report, 'Somalia Update', October 2006.
66 Kofi Annan, *Report of the Secretary-General on the Situation in Somalia*, S/2006/418, 20 June 2006, para. 22.
67 Mike Pflanz, 'Somalia bows to Islamic Militia with Power-Sharing Deal', *Daily Telegraph*, 5 September 2006.
68 Security Council Report, 'Somalia – update', December 2006.
69 In informal briefings to the Council. Security Council Report, 'Somalia – update', December 2006.
70 On the initial strikes see International Crisis Group, 'Somalia: The Tough Part is Ahead', Africa Brief No. 45, 26 January 2007.
71 On the perception that AMISOM was connected to Ethiopia see Paul D. Williams, 'Into the Mogadishu Maelstrom: The African Union Mission in Somalia', *International Peacekeeping*, 16(4), 2009, p. 517. This problem was not helped by the indiscriminate use of force by Ethiopia and its allies. See Human Rights Watch, *Shell-Shocked: Civilians Under Siege in Mogadishu*, 12 August 2007.
72 African Union Peace and Security Council communiqué, 17 January 2007. The reference to the transfer to a UN mission is contained in paragraph 9. In a 2007 report for the Stimson Center, Katherine Andrews and Victoria Holt described the assumption that AMISOM would hand over to the UN as 'tenuous', given the conditions inside Somalia. Katherine Andrews and Victoria Holt, 'United Nations-African Union Coordination on Peace and Security in Africa', Stimson Center Issue Brief, August 2007, p. 8.
73 Security Council Report, 'Somalia – Update', March 2007.
74 UNAMID was eventually mandated by Resolution 1769 (31 July 2007), but the Council first mandated a UN presence in Darfur in Resolution 1706 (2006) and the deployment of a larger contingent to Darfur was under active consideration.
75 Resolution 1744 (2007), para. 9.
76 Security Council Report, 'Somalia – Update', February 2007.
77 'Ghana's Leader Calls on UN to Prepare to Step up its Role in Somalia', UN News, 25 September 2007.
78 See e.g. Wairagala Wakabi, 'Health and the Humanitarian Situation in Somalia', *The Lancet*, 370(9594), 2007, pp. 1201–2 and 'Violence in Somalia Furthers Humanitarian Crisis', *PBS News Hour*, 26 January 2007. On 30 October 2007, 39 aid agencies including Care, Concern, Oxfam, Save the Children and World Vision issued a statement on the deteriorating humanitarian conditions in Somalia, pointing to 360,000 newly displaced people.
79 Security Council Report, 'Somalia', June 2007 update.
80 'Somali Opposition Alliance Begins Fight Against Ethiopia', *Agence-France Presse*, 20 September 2007.
81 The precise roots of al-Shabaab remains veiled in mystery. See Barnes and Hassan, 'The Rise and Fall of Mogadishu's Islamic Courts' and International Crisis Group, 'Somalia: To Move Beyond the Failed State', Africa Report No. 147, 23 December 2008, p. 11.

82 Richard Cornwell, 'Somalia Collapsing Inwards', Institute for Security Studies (Pretoria), 25 October 2007.
83 Security Council Report, 'Somalia Update', June 2007. The TFG detained the head of the World Food Programme for five days in mid-October, halting distribution of food. Security Council Report, 'Somalia Update', November 2007.
84 Williams, 'Mogadishu Maelstrom', p. 519.
85 Security Council Report, 'Somalia Update', July 2007.
86 Eritrea suspended its membership on IGAD in April 2007.
87 On Ethiopian withdrawal see Williams, 'Mogadishu Maelstrom', p. 519.
88 Quoted in Security Council Report, 'Somalia Update', April 2007.
89 In June 2007, OCHA estimated that 365,000 had been newly displaced, but the TFG put the figure at around 10 per cent of this, between 30,000 and 40,000. Security Council Report, 'Somalia Update', June 2007.
90 'Somali Clan Unity Deal Rejected', *BBC News*, 17 September 2007.
91 Ban Ki-moon, *Report of the Secretary-General on the Situation in Somalia*, S/2007/204, 13 April 2007, para. 60.
92 On the French offer see Security Council Report, 'Somalia Update', October 2007.
93 Statement by the President of the Security Council, S/PRST/2007/13, 30 April 2007.
94 Ban Ki-moon, *Report of the Secretary-General on the Situation in Somalia*, S/2007/381, 25 June 2007, paras 33–47.
95 Ban Ki-moon, *Report of the Secretary-General on the Situation in Somalia*, S/2007/658, 7 November 2007, paras 33–4.
96 On Ould-Abdallah's statement see Security Council press statement, SC/9203, 17 November 2007.
97 'UN Envoy Says Somali War Crimes Suspects Should Face ICC', *Agence-France Presse*, 13 November 2007.
98 S/PV.5837, 15 February 2007.
99 Security Council Report, 'Somalia Update', March 2008.
100 Ban Ki-moon, *Report of the Secretary-General on the Situation in Somalia*, S/2008/178, 14 March 2008, paras 37–40.
101 Security Council Watch, 'Somalia – Update', April 2008.
102 S/PV.5942, 23 July 2008.
103 Security Council Report, 'Somalia Update', April 2008.
104 Security Council Report, 'Somalia Update', April 2008.
105 Security Council Report, 'Update Somalia', September 2008.
106 Security Council Report, 'Update Somalia', September 2008.
107 Security Council Report, 'Somalia Update', October 2008. See Presidential Statement, S/PRST/2008/33.
108 Security Council Report, 'Somalia Update', November 2008.
109 Council members were reportedly 'bewildered' by the different positions. Security Council Report, 'Somalia Update', October 2008.
110 Security Council Report, 'Somalia Update', December 2008.
111 S/PV.6046, 16 December 2006.
112 Nonetheless, the trust fund was able to generate sufficient donations to cover much of the shortfall for AMISOM. See Cedric de Coning, 'The Evolution of Peace Operations in Africa: Trajectories and Trends', *Journal of International Peacekeeping*, 14(1–2), 2010, p. 20.
113 Ban Ki-moon, 'Report of the Secretary-General on the Situation in Somalia', S/2009/132, 9 March 2009.
114 Security Council Report, 'Update Somalia', June 2009.

115 Security Council Report, 'Update Somalia', June 2009.
116 Security Council Watch, 'Update Report Somalia', September 2009.
117 On the central role of protection in the legitimation of peace operations see Siobhan Wills, *Protecting Civilians* (Oxford: Oxford University Press, 2009).
118 A problem identified by Alex de Waal, 'Darfur and the Failure of the Responsibility to Protect', *International Affairs*, 83(6), 2007, pp. 1039–54.
119 Alex de Waal, 'Darfur and the Failure of the Responsibility to Protect', *International Affairs*, 83(6), 2007, pp. 1039–54.
120 The principal example pointed to by de Waal was a report by the International Crisis Group. International Crisis Group, *To Save Darfur*, ICG Report 105, 17 March 2006.
121 De Waal, 'Darfur and the Failure of Responsibility to Protect', p. 1043.
122 De Waal, 'Darfur and the Failure of Responsiblity to Protect', p. 1044. In 2004, de Waal argued that foreign troops could make a 'formidable difference' to the lives of Darfuri civilians, writing that,

> The immediate life and death needs of Darfur's people cannot wait for these negotiations to mature. A British brigade could make a formidable difference to the situation. It could escort aid supplies into rebel-held areas, and provide aerial surveillance, logistics and back-up to ceasefire monitoring, helping to give Darfurian villagers the confidence to return to their homes and pick up their lives.

(Alex de Waal, 'Darfur's Deep Grievances Defy all Hopes for an Easy Solution', *The Observer*, 25 July 2004.)
123 The following passage draws on Asia-Pacific Centre for the Responsibility to Protect, *Myanmar/Burma Brief No. 2: Cyclone Nargis and the Responsibility to Protect*, 16 May 2008.
124 These, and other, measures are discussed in detail in Alex J. Bellamy, *Responsibility to Protect: The Global Effort to End Mass Atrocities* (Cambridge: Polity, 2009).
125 Independent Commission, *Report of the Independent Inquiry into the Actions of the United Nations During the 1994 Genocide in Rwanda*, 12 December 1999, p. 2.
126 *Report of the Panel on Peacekeeping Operations*, para. 62.
127 See K. Månsson, 'Integration of Human Rights in Peace Operations: Is There an Ideal Model?', *International Peacekeeping*, 13(4), 2006, pp. 547–63.
128 On the links between this mandating practice and RtoP see Susan C. Breau, 'The Impact of Responsibility to Protect on Peacekeeping', *Journal of Conflict and Security Law*, 11(3), 2007, esp. pp. 450–2.
129 UN Security Council Resolution 1590, 24 March 2005.
130 UN Security Council Resolutions 1509, 19 September 2003 and Resolution 1528, 27 February 2004 respectively.
131 UN Security Council Resolution 1565, 1 October 2004. For a discussion see K. Månsson, 'Use of Force and Civilian Protection: Peace Operations in the Congo', *International Peacekeeping*, 12(4), 2005, pp. 503–19.
132 Victoria K. Holt and Tobias C. Berkman, *The Impossible Mandate? Military Preparedness, The Responsibility to Protect and Modern Peace Operations* (Washington, DC: The Henry L. Stimson Centre, 2006), pp. 201–24.
133 See Victoria K. Holt, *The Responsibility to Protect: Considering the Operational Capacity for Civilian Protection* (Washington, DC: Henry L. Stimson Centre, 2005) and Holt and Berkman, *The Impossible Mandate?*
134 Thomas G. Weiss, 'The Humanitarian Impulse', David M. Malone (ed.), *The UN Security Council: From the Cold War to the 21st Century* (Boulder, CO: Lynne Rienner, 2004), p. 48.

135 D. S. Blocq, 'The Fog of UN Peacekeeping: Ethical Issues Regarding the Use of Force to Protect Civilians in UN Operations', *Journal of Military Ethics*, 5(3), 2006, p. 205.

136 Holt and Berkman, *The Impossible Mandate?*, p. 52.

137 UN Department of Peacekeeping Operations, *United Nations Peacekeeping Operations: Principles and Guidelines*, 18 January 2008, para. 42.

138 The so-called holy trinity. See Alex J. Bellamy, Paul D. Williams and Stuart Griffin, *Understanding Peacekeeping* (Cambridge: Polity, 2004).

139 Holt and Berkman, *The Impossible Mandate?*, p. 190.

140 Holt and Berkman, *The Impossible Mandate?*, p. 165.

141 UN Security Council Resolution 1592, March 2005.

142 Holt and Berkman, *The Impossible Mandate?*, pp. 166–7.

143 Human Security Report Project, *Human Security Brief 2007*, pp. 22–30.

144 The proceeding discussion draws on Alex J. Bellamy and Paul D. Williams, *Understanding Peacekeeping*, 2nd edition (Cambridge: Polity, 2010), pp. 60–1.

145 Based on data provided in Edward C. Luck, *UN Security Council: Practice and Promise* (London: Routledge, 2006), p. 39.

146 Alex J. Bellamy and Paul D. Williams, 'The West and Contemporary Peace Operations', *Journal of Peace Research*, 46(1), 2009, pp. 39–57.

Select bibliography

Aning, K. and S. Atuobi (2009), 'Responsibility to Protect in Africa: An Analysis of the African Union's Peace and Security Architecture', *Global Responsibility to Protect*, 1(1).

Annan, K. (1999), 'Two Concepts of Sovereignty', *The Economist*, 18 September.

Axworthy, L. (2003) *Navigating a New World: Canada's Global Future* (Toronto: Alfred A. Knopf).

Axworthy, L. and A. Rock (2009), 'R2P: A New and Unfinished Agenda', *Global Responsibility to Protect*, 1(1).

Badescu, C. and L. Bergholm (2009), 'Responsibility to Protect and the Conflict in Darfur: The Big Let Down', *Security Dialogue*, 40(3).

Bannon, A. L. (2006), 'The Responsibility to Protect: The UN World Summit and the Question of Unilateralism', *The Yale Law Journal*, 115.

Barber, R. (2009), 'The Responsibility to Protect the Survivors of Natural Disaster: Cyclone Nargis, a Case Study', *Journal of Conflict and Security Law*.

Barbour, B. and B. Gorlick (2008), 'Embracing the Responsibility to Protect: A Repertoire of Measures Including Asylum for Potential Victims', *International Journal of Refugee Law*, 20(4).

Bass, G. J. (2008), *Freedom's Battle: The Origins of Humanitarian Intervention* (London: Alfred Knopf).

Bellamy, A. J. (2005), 'Responsibility to Protect or Trojan Horse? The Crisis in Darfur and Humanitarian Intervention after Iraq', *Ethics and International Affairs*, 19(2).

Bellamy, A. J. (2006), 'Whither the Responsibility to Protect? Humanitarian Intervention and the 2005 World Summit', *Ethics and International Affairs*, 20(2).

Bellamy, A. J. (2009), *Responsibility to Protect: The Global Effort to End Mass Atrocities* (London: Polity).

Bellamy, A. J. (2009), 'Realizing the Responsibility to Protect', *International Studies Perspectives*, 10(1).

Bellamy, A. J. and P. D. Williams (eds) (2005), *Peace Operations and Global Order* (London: Routledge).

Bellamy, A. J. and P. D. Williams (2009), 'The West and Contemporary Peace Operations', *Journal of Peace Research*, 46(1).

Bellamy, A. J. and S. E. Davies (2009), 'The Responsibility to Protect in Southeast Asia: Progress and Problems', *Security Dialogue*, 40(6).

Belloni, R. (2006), 'The Tragedy of Darfur and the Limits of the Responsibility to Protect', *Ethnopolitics*, 5(4).

Bosco, D. L. (2009), *Five to Rule them All: The UN Security Council and the Making of the Modern World* (Oxford: Oxford University Press).

Breau, S. C. (2007), 'The Impact of Responsibility to Protect on Peacekeeping', *Journal of Conflict and Security Law*, 11(3).

Brunnée, J. and S. J. Toope (2010), 'The Responsibility to Protect and the Use of Force: Building Legality?', *Global Responsibility to Protect*, 2(3).

Carment, D. and A. Schnabel (eds) (2003), *Conflict Prevention: Path to Peace or Grand Illusion?* (Tokyo: United Nations University Press).

Chatterjee, K. and D. E. Scheid (eds) (2003), *Ethics and Foreign Intervention* (Cambridge: Cambridge University Press).

Chesterman, S. (2001), *Just War or Just Peace? Humanitarian Intervention and International Law* (Oxford: Oxford University Press).

Coleman, K. P. (2007), *International Organisations and Peace Enforcement: The Politics of International Legitimacy* (Cambridge: Cambridge University Press).

Cohen, R. (2004), 'The Guiding Principles on Internal Displacement: An Innovation in International Standard Setting', *Global Governance*, 10(3).

Cohen, R. (2006), 'Developing an International System for Internally Displaced Persons', *International Studies Perspectives*, 7(1).

Cohen, R. and F. M. Deng (1998), *Masses in Flight: The Global Crisis of Internal Displacement* (Washington, DC: The Brookings Institution).

Collier, P. (2007), *The Bottom Billion: Why the Poorest Countries are Failing and What Can be Done About It* (Oxford: Oxford University Press).

Collier, P. (2009), *Wars, Guns and Votes: Democracy in Dangerous Places* (London: The Bodley Head).

Collier, P., V. L. Elliot, H. Hegre, A. Hoeffler, M. Reynal-Querol and N. Sambanis (2003), *Breaking the Conflict Trap: Civil War and Development Policy* (New York: Oxford University Press for the World Bank).

Carment, D. and M. Fischer (2009), 'R2P and the Role of Regional Organisations in Ethnic Conflict Management, Prevention and Resolution: The Unfinished Agenda', *Global Responsibility to Protect*, 1(3).

Cramer, C. (2006), *Civil War is Not a Stupid Thing: Accounting for Violence in Developing Countries* (London: Hurst and Co., 2006).

Cunliffe, P. (ed.) (2010), *Critical Perspectives on the Responsibility to Protect* (London: Routledge).

Deng, F. M. (2004), 'The Impact of State Failure on Migration', *Mediterranean Quarterly*, Fall.

Deng, F. M. (2006), 'Divided Nations: The Paradox of National Protection', *The Annals of the American Academy of Political and Social Science*, 603, January.

Deng, F. M., S. Kimaro, T. Lyons, D. Rothchild and I. W. Zartman (1996), *Sovereignty as Responsibility: Conflict Management in Africa* (Washington, DC: The Brookings Institution).

de Waal, A. (2007) 'Darfur and the Failure of the Responsibility to Protect', *International Affairs*, 83(6).

Downes, A. B. (2008), *Targeting Civilians in War* (Ithaca, NY: Cornell University Press).

Elden, S. (2006), 'Contingent Sovereignty, Territorial Integrity and the Sanctity of Borders', *SAIS Review*, 26(1).

Evans, G. (2004), 'When is it Right to Fight?', *Survival*, 46(3).

Evans, G. (2008), 'The Responsibility to Protect: An Idea Whose Time Has Come . . . and Gone?', *International Relations*, 22(3).

Evans, G. (2008), *Responsibility to Protect: Ending Mass Atrocity Crimes Once and For All* (Washington, DC: Brookings Institution).

Evans, G. (2009), 'Russia, Georgia and the Responsibility to Protect', *Amsterdam Law Forum*, 1(2).

Goldstone, J. A., R. H. Bates, D. L. Epstein, T. R. Gurr, M. B. Lustick, M. G. Marshall, J. Ulfelder and M. Woodward (2010), 'A Global Model for Forecasting Political Instability', *American Journal of Political Science*, 54(1).

Feinstein, L. (2007), *Darfur and Beyond: What is Needed to Prevent Mass Atrocities* (Washington, DC: Council on Foreign Relations).

Finnemore, M. (2003), *The Purposes of Intervention* (Ithaca, NY: Cornell University Press).

Focarelli, C. (2008), 'The Responsibility to Protect Doctrine and Humanitarian Intervention: Too Many Ambiguities for a Working Doctrine', *Journal of Conflict and Security Law*, 13(2).

Franck, T. (1990), *The Power of Legitimacy Among Nations* (New York: Oxford University Press).

Foley, C. (2008), *The Thin Blue Line: How Humanitarianism Went to War* (London: Verso).

Haacke, J. (2009) 'Myanmar, the Responsibility to Protect and the Need for Practical Assistance', *Global Responsibility to Protect*, 1(2).

Hannay, D. (2008), *New World Disorder: The UN After the Cold War – An Insider's View* (London: I. B. Tauris).

Harff, B. (2003), 'No Lessons Learned from the Holocaust? Assessing the Risks of Genocide and Political Mass Murder since 1955', *American Political Science Review*, 97(1).

Haugevik, K. M. (2009), 'Regionalising the Responsibility to Protect: Possibilities, Capabilities and Actualities', *Global Responsibility to Protect*, 1(2).

Hehir, A. (2010), *Humanitarian Intervention: An Introduction* (Basingstoke: Palgrave).

Holt, V. K. and T. C. Berkman (2006), *The Impossible Mandate? Military Preparedness, the Responsibility to Protect and Modern Peace Operations* (Washington, DC: Henry L. Stimson Center).

International Commission on Intervention and State Sovereignty (2001), *The Responsibility to Protect* (Ottawa: IDRC).

Jackson, R. (2010), 'War Perils in the Responsibility to Protect', *Global Responsibility to Protect*, 2(1/2).

Jones, B., C. Pascual and S. J. Stedman (2009), *Power and Responsibility: Building International Order in an era of Transnational Threats* (Washington, DC: Brookings Institution).

Kapstein, E. B. and N. Converse (2008), *The Fate of Young Democracies* (Cambridge: Cambridge University Press).

Kaufman, S. (2001) *Modern Hatreds: The Symbolic Politics of Ethnic War* (Ithaca, NY: Cornell University Press, 2001).

Keen, D. (2008), *Complex Emergencies* (Cambridge: Polity)

Kuperman, A. J. (2009), 'Darfur: Strategic Victimhood Strike Again?', *Genocide Studies and Prevention*, 4(3).

Kuperman, A. J. (2009), 'Rethinking the Responsibility to Protect', *Whitehead Journal of Diplomacy and International Relations*, Winter/Spring.

Lillich, R. B. (ed.) (1973), *Humanitarian Intervention and the United Nations* (Charlottesville, VG: University Press of Virginia).

Luck, E. C. (2006), *UN Security Council: Practice and Promise* (London: Routledge).

Luck, E. C. (2007), 'The Responsible Sovereign and the Responsibility to Protect', *Annual Review of United Nations Affairs 2006/2007* (Oxford: Oxford University Press).

Luck, E. C. (2009), 'Sovereignty, Choice and the Responsibility to Protect', *Global Responsibility to Protect*, 1(1).

Luck, E. C. (2010), 'A Response', *Global Responsibility to Protect*, 2(1/2).

Macfarlane, S. N., C. J. Thiekling and T. G. Weiss (2004), 'The Responsibility to Protect: Is Anyone Interested in Humanitarian Intervention?', *Third World Quarterly*, 25(5).

Malone, D. M. (ed.) (2004), *The UN Security Council: From the Cold War to the 21st Century* (Boulder, CO: Lynne Rienner).

Menon, R. (2009), 'Pious Words, Puny Deeds: The "International Community" and Mass Atrocities', *Ethics and International Affairs*, 23(3).

Mepham, D. (2007), *Darfur: The Responsibility to Protect* (London: Institute of Public Policy Research).

Moya, D. (2009), *Dead Aid: Why Aid is not Working and How There is Another Way for Africa* (London: Penguin).

Nafziger, E. W., F. Stewart and R. Vayrynen (eds) (2000), *The Origins of Humanitarian Emergencies: War and Displacement in Developing Countries* (Oxford: Oxford University Press).

Newman, M. (2009), *Humanitarian Intervention: Confronting the Contradictions* (London: Hurst).

Rubin, B. R. and B. D. Jones (2007), 'Prevention of Violent Conflict: Tasks and Challenges for the United Nations', *Global Governance*, 13.

Schnabel, A. and R. Thakur (eds) (2000), *Kosovo and the Challenge of Humanitarian Intervention: Selective Indignation, Collective Action and International Citizenship* (Tokyo: UN University Press).

Serrano, M. (2010), 'Implementing the Responsibility to Protect: The Power of R2P Talk', *Global Responsibility to Protect*, 2(1/2).

Sharma, S. K. (2010), 'Towards a Global Responsibility to Protect: Setbacks on the Path to Implementation', *Global Governance*, 16(1).

Slim, H. (2008), *Killing Civilians: Method, Madness and Morality in War* (New York: Columbia University Press).

Stamnes, E. (2009), ' "Speaking RtoP" and the Prevention of Mass Atrocities', *Global Responsibility to Protect*, 1(1).

Stedman, S. J. (2007), 'UN Transformation in an Era of Soft Power Balancing', *International Affairs*, 83(5).

Steinberg, D. (2009), 'Responsibility to Protect: Coming of Age?', *Global Responsibility to Protect*, 1(4).

Strauss, E. (2009), 'A Bird in the Hand is Worth Two in the Bush – On the Assumed Legal Nature of the Responsibility to Protect', *Global Responsibility to Protect*, 1(3).

Sutterlin, J. S. (2003) *The United Nations and the Maintenance of International Security: A Challenge to be Met* (Westport, CT: Praeger).

Teitt, S. (2009), 'Assessing Polemics, Principles and Practices: China and the Responsibility to Protect', *Global Responsibility to Protect*, 1(2).

Terry, F. (2002), *Condemned to Repeat: The Paradox of Humanitarian Action* (Ithaca, NY: Cornell University Press).

Thakur, R. (2005), 'A Shared Responsibility for a More Secure World', *Global Governance*, 11(3).

Thakur, R. (2006), *The United Nations, Peace and Security: From Collective Security to the Responsibility to Protect* (Cambridge: Cambridge University Press).

Thakur, R. and T. G. Weiss (2009), 'RtoP: From Idea to Norm, and Action?', *Global Responsibility to Protect*, 1(1).

Traub, J. (2007), *Best Intentions: Kofi Annan and the UN in the Era of American World Power* (New York: Picador).

Valentino, B. A. (2004), *Final Solutions: Mass Killing and Genocide in the 20th Century* (Ithaca, NY: Cornell University Press).

Weiss, T. G. (2004), 'The Sunset of Humanitarian Intervention? The Responsibility to Protect in a Unipolar Era', *Security Dialogue*, 35(2).

Weiss, T. G. (2007), *Humanitarian Intervention: Ideas in Action* (Cambridge: Polity).

Weiss, T. G. (2009), *What's Wrong with the United Nations and How to Fix It* (Cambridge: Polity).

Weiss, T. G. and D. A. Korn (2006), *Internal Displacement: Conceptualization and its Consequences* (New York: Routledge).

Welsh, J. M. (ed.) (2004), *Humanitarian Intervention and International Relations* (Oxford: Oxford University Press).

Welsh, J. M. (2010), 'Turning Words into Deeds? The Implementation of "The Responsibility to Protect" ', *Global Responsibility to Protect*, 2(1/2).

Western, J. (2005), 'The Illusions of Moral Hazard: A Conceptual and Empirical Critique', *Ethnopolitics*, 4(2).

Wheeler, N. J. (2000), *Saving Strangers: Humanitarian Intervention in International Society* (Oxford: Oxford University Press).

Wheeler, N. J. (2001), 'Legitimating Humanitarian Intervention: Principles and Procedures', *Melbourne Journal of International Law*, 2(2).

Wheeler, N. J. and F. Egerton (2009), 'The Responsibility to Protect: "Precious Commitment" or a "Promise Unfulfilled"?', *Global Responsibility to Protect*, 1(1).

Williams, P. D. (2007), 'From Non-Intervention to Non-Indifference: The Origins and Development of the African Union's Security Culture', *African Affairs*, 106(423).

Williams, P. D. (2009), 'The "Responsibility to Protect", Norm Localization, and African International Society', *Global Responsibility to Protect*, 1(3).

Williams, P. D. and A. J. Bellamy, 'The Responsibility to Protect and the Crisis in Darfur', *Security Dialogue*, 36(1).

Wills, S. (2009), *Protecting Civilians* (Oxford: Oxford University Press).

Index

#0210 - 270417 - C0 - 234/156/14 - PB - 9780415567367